Richard S. Hodgson

Successful Catalog Marketing

How to plan, create, merchandise, and market to sell more products

DARTNELL Chicago / Boston / London / Sydney

DARTNELL is a publisher serving the world of business with books, manuals, newsletters, bulletins, and training materials for executives, managers, supervisors, salespeople, financial officials, human resources professionals, and office employees. In addition, Dartnell produces management ans sales training films and audiocassettes, publishes many useful business forms and offers many of its materials in languages other than English. Established in 1917, Dartnell serves the world's complete business community. For catalogs and product information write. THE DARTNELL CORPORATION, 4660 Ravenswood Avenue, Chicago, Illinois 60640-4595 USA. Phone: 800-621-5463. In Illinois: (312) 561-4000.

This publication may not be reproduced, stored in a retrieval system, or transmitted in whole or in part, in any form or by any means, electronic, mechanical, photocopying, recording, or otherwise, without the prior written permission of THE DARTNELL CORPORATION, 4660 Ravenswood Avenue, Chicago, IL 60640-4595.

This publication is designed to provide accurate and authoritative information in regard to the subject matter covered. It is sold with the understanding that the publisher is not engaged in rendering legal, accounting, or other professional service. If legal advice or other expert assistance required, the services of a competent professional person should be sought.

From a Declaration of Principles jointly adopted by a Committee of the American Bar Association and Committee of Publishers.

Published by

The Dartnell Corporation
4660 Ravenswood Avenue
Chicago, IL 60640

Chicago/Boston/London/Sydney

© 1991 The Dartnell Corporation

Printed in the U.S.A. by The Dartnell Press
ISBN 0-85013-177-4

Contents

List of Illustrations **ix**
Foreword by Bob Stone **xi**

1 The Great American Catalog Boom — 1

How Many Catalogs? **2**
The Age of Specialization **3**
The Catalog Age **4**
Catalogs in the Age of Electronics **13**
Catalogs Throughout the World **14**

2 The Key Ingredients of Catalog Marketing — 15

How Catalog Marketing Is Different **15**
The Four Key Words **19**
What It Takes to Start a Mail Order Catalog **27**

3 Ten Ways to Win...or Lose...in Today's Highly Competitive Catalog World — 33

The Right Thinking **34**
A Unique Selling Position **34**
Involvement of Management **40**
Long-Range Strategy **42**
A Willingness to Gamble **43**
The Right Product Selection **43**
The Importance of Mailing Lists **45**
An Open-Door Organization **46**
Catalog-Oriented Personnel and Facilities **47**
Emphasis on the Back End **49**

4   Investing for Customers: Building and Maintaining a Database for Your Catalog   51

Database vs. Mailing List   **51**
Basic Mailing List Information   **52**
Business, Professional & Industrial Lists   **53**
Creating a Customer Profile   **56**
RFMR Profile   **57**
Lifestyle Indicators   **59**
Screening Codes   **60**
Overlays   **61**
How to Build a Mailing List   **63**
The Relative Value of Outside Lists   **66**
Eliminating Duplication   **68**
Mailing List Security   **69**
Sources of List Information   **69**
List Service Organizations   **70**
Friend-Get-a-Friend   **74**
Mailing Lists—The Cornerstone of Catalog Marketing Programs   **75**
Eight "Usually Reliable Truths" about Mailing Lists   **77**
Circles of Convenience   **78**

5   Selecting Products for Your Catalog   81

Buyers, Rebuyers, and Merchandisers   **82**
Where to Find Products   **83**
The Importance of Unique and Exclusive Products   **87**
Product Innovation   **90**
How to Select Good Mail Order Products   **98**
The 10 Key Factors in Selecting Catalog Merchandise   **100**
The Ultimate Authority—Your Customer   **103**

6   Organizing Your Catalog   105

Indexes and Tables of Contents   **106**
How Many Pages Should Your Catalog Have?   **107**
The Importance of Spreads   **109**
Creating Eye-Flow   **109**
Establishing Starting Points   **113**
Developing Catalog Continuity   **114**
Developing Change of Pace   **117**
Magalogs and Catazines   **118**

7   Effective Catalog Design   123

Beware of Art Directors **123**
Selection of Typefaces **124**
Tips for More Effective Catalog Design **138**
Grid Layouts **141**

8   Writing Catalog Copy   143

Kaleidoscope Copy Guidelines **143**
Features vs. Benefits **147**
Adding the Personal Touch **159**
Before the Writing Starts **165**
Editing Copy **168**
COIK **169**
The Copywriter's Packet **169**
Tom Collins's Checklist: What Good Catalog Copy Should Provide **173**
Twenty Questions to Ask about Your Catalog Copy **174**

9   Catalog Hot Spots, Covers, and Wraps   175

Covers and Other Hot Spots **175**
Catalog Wraps **189**
Checklists for Selecting Merchandise for Cover Presentation **203**

10   Making It Easy to Order   205

Don't Reinvent the Wheel **205**
Make Your Order Form Look Inviting **206**
Ask for Information "as Given" **208**
Avoid Confusion **209**
Don't Expect Your Customer to Be an Accountant **210**
Keep Shipping and Handling Uncomplicated **210**
Sell Something **215**
Handling Supplemental Information **217**
A Well-Organized Gift Shipment Order Form **217**
Response Envelopes **224**
Order Forms in Business-to-Business Catalogs **228**
Testing Order Forms **229**

The Order Form Portfolio   231

11 Producing the Catalog — 261

- The Production Team **263**
- Selecting a Printing Process **264**
- Selecting Paper for Your Catalog **267**
- Selecting a Printer **269**
- Selecting a Color Separator **272**
- Selecting a Photographer **274**
- Art vs. Photography **279**
- Other Production Considerations **282**

12 Evaluating Catalog Results — 283

- Efficiency per Square Inch **283**
- Presentation Factors **286**
- Catalog Projections **287**
- Establishing Catalog Costs **289**
- Production Cost Analysis **290**
- Flow Chart Analysis **290**

13 Don't Stop Marketing When the Catalogs Go to the Post Office — 293

- Order Acknowledgments **294**
- Instant Response **297**
- Better Packaging **298**
- Better Packaging Material **299**
- Ship Letters **300**
- Customer Service Enclosures **304**
- Adding a Little Extra **316**
- Other Package Enclosures **317**
- Follow-ups **320**
- The Personal Touch **325**
- In Summary **331**

14 Developing a Customer Service Program — 331

- Creating a Customer Service Plan **335**
- Measuring Customer Service Effectiveness **339**

15   How to Expand An Existing Catalog Business   345

Mailing Multiple Catalogs **345**
Special Catalog Editions **349**
Developing Spin-off Catalogs **352**
Moving off a Plateau **352**
Balancing Seasonality **353**
Using Alternate Direct Mail Media **353**
Telephone Marketing **361**

Appendix A: The Mail Order Rule **363**
Appendix B: Ethical Business Practice **381**
Appendix C: Mailing List Practices **387**
Appendix D: Personal Information Protection **391**
Bibliography **393**
About the Author **395**
Index **397**

Illustrations

FIGURE		PAGE
2–1	Catalog Response Curves	17
2–2	Perceived Availability	19
2–3	Offering "Exclusive" Products	20
2–4	Perceived Authority	21
2–5	Perceived Value	22
2–6	Specials of the Month	23
2–7	Perceived Satisfaction	25
2–8	The Ultimate Guarantee	26
3–1	Creating a Unique Selling Position	35
3–2	No Frills	37
3–3	Maintaining a Consistent Image	38
3–4	Maintaining a Reputation	41
3–5	Exclusive Products	44
5–1	Unique Guarantee	88
5–2	An Effective Combination Offer	88
5–3	Exclusive Designs	89
5–4	Office Products for the Home	90
5–5	Change Product Form	92
5–6	Add a Service	93
5–7	Combine	94
5–8	Reintroduce	95
5–9	Personalize	95
5–10	Add Fun	96
5–11	Change Countries	97
5–12	Add a Celebrity	97
6–1	Pictorial Indexes	108
6–2	Catalog Eye-Flow	110
6–3	Using Gaze Motion Effectively	111
6–4	Focal Point	111
6–5	Gaze Motion	112
6–6	Structural Motion	113
6–7	Giving the Reader a Starting Point	114
6–8	How to Lose Customers and Get Them Back	116
6–9	Long Copy Classic	119
6–10	Refreshing a Catalog	120
7–1	Roman vs. Sans Serif Typefaces	125
7–2	Ragged Typesetting Reduces Comprehension	126
7–3	Reverse Type Reduces Sales	128
7–4	Avoid Type Surprinted on Illustrations	133
7–5	Placement of Captions	134
7–6	The "Continuous Circle"	136
7–7	Breaking Up Copy	137
7–8	Breaking Up Copy	137
7–9	Basic Eye-Flow	139
7–10	The Power of a Single Element	140
7–11	The Grid Layout	141
8–1	Strong on Benefits	146
8–2	Integrating Features and Benefits	149
8–3	Benefits-Oriented Copy	151
8–4	The "Which Means" Technique	152
8–5	Stressing Benefits in Headings	153
8–6	Matching Benefits and Features in Long Copy	154
8–7	Weaving Benefits into Long Copy	156
8–8	Making a Common Product Unique	158
8–9	Humor in Copy	162
8–10	Philosophy	163
8–11	The Right Stuff	163
8–12	Rocking the Boat	163
9–1	Using Covers to Lead into Editorial-Style Presentations	177
9–2	Jet-Ink Personalization	181
9–3	Catalog Letters	184
9–4	Typical Catalog Letter	185
9–5	Creating Additional Hot Spots	187
9–6	Stopper Pages	188
9–7	Divider Pages	190
9–8	Personalized Catalog Wrap	192

FIGURE		PAGE
9–9	Extra Personalization Opportunities	194
9–10	The Personalized Message	198
10–1	Making It Easy to Order	207
10–2	Promoting Impulse Sales	216
10–3	Gift Shipment Order Form	220
10–4	Providing Detailed Ordering Information	222
10–5	Placement of Impulse Items	223
10–6	Reply Envelopes	224
10–7	Catalog Order Cards	225
10–8	Action Devices	227
10–9	Bonus Seal	228
11–1	Location Photography	276
11–2	Drawings for Detail	280
11–3	Unique Art Style	281
12–1	Profitability Formula	284
12–2	Marked-up Catalog Spread	285
13–1	Back Order Notices	295
13–2	Order Acknowledgments	296
13–3	Welcoming a New Customer	297
13–4	Ship Letters	301
13–5	Creating a Personal Bond with Customers	303
13–6	Customer Service Enclosures	305
13–7	Making Returns Easy	306
13–8	The Informal Touch	306
13–9	A Unique Solution	309
13–10	Emphasizing Product Benefits	313
13–11	A Little Extra	317
13–12	Package Enclosures	318
13–13	Follow-Ups	321
13–14	Another Reason to Buy	322
13–15	Catalog Bind-In	324
13–16	Apologizing for Mistakes	326
13–17	Reactivating Customers	328
14–1	Quill's Bill of Rights	340
14–2	Lands' End Principles of Doing Business	341
14–3	The Golden Rule of L.L. Bean	342
14–4	The Sears Guarantee	343
15–1	Catalogs for Prospecting	350
15–2	Adding Products for Special Customers	351
15–3	Solo Mailings	355
15–4	Card Decks	356
15–5	Mini Catalogs	357
15–6	Self-Mailers	359
15–7	Newsletters	360
15–8	Monthly Newsletters	361

TABLE		PAGE
7–1	Typeface Selection and Headline Comprehension	127
7–2	How Reverse Type Affects Comprehension	129
7–3	How Color Affects Comprehension	130
7–4	Relationship of Headline and Body Copy	130
7–5	How Color Background Affects Comprehension	131
7–6	Comprehension: Black on Gray vs. Black on White	132

© COPYRIGHT 1991 DARTNELL CORPORATION

Foreword

by Bob Stone

You won't find it in the *Guinness Book of World Records,* but America's longest running love affair is, without doubt, with the catalog.

In this great book Dick Hodgson chronicles the growth of the catalog from inception to modern day. When Wards and Sears launched their first catalogs, rural America had unfulfilled wishes, wishes that they too would have access to goods readily available to "city folks." Thus, the great "Wish Book" grew and prospered.

But as America grew from an agricultural nation into an industrial nation the wishes grew and expanded from farm to small town to big city. The proliferation of shopping centers notwithstanding, all of America continues with its catalog love affair.

The suitors have changed—*dramatically.* The reasons for shopping by catalog have changed—*dramatically.* Two-income families have little time or desire to store-shop. They love the convenience, the time they save, the assortments they are offered.

Businesspeople no longer have time to see an endless parade of salespeople: the trend is to limit sales calls to capital goods purchasers. The catalog serves their needs for most supply items and services.

Successful Catalog Marketing traces the history of catalogs for but one purpose: to put the opportunities in catalog marketing in proper perspective in today's environment. I regard this book as the definitive work. Nothing before it has been so complete, so instructive, so fascinating.

There isn't a chapter in this book that should be skimmed over. But if I were to single out just two chapters that are *musts,* they would be Chapter 4—"Investing for Customers" and Chapter 5—"Selecting Products for Your Catalog."

In Chapter 4, Dick Hodgson teaches a lesson you should ignore only at your own peril: If you don't have sufficient capital to invest in a large and responsive customer base, stay out of the catalog business.

In Chapter 5, Hodgson deals with the heart of every successful catalog—product selection. To capsulize what Dick is saying here: If you aren't an intuitive merchandiser, or if you don't have one on board, stay out of the catalog business . . . even if you have lots of capital!

What I am saying in this Foreword is based not only upon having read the text. It is based as well upon having known Dick Hodgson for the better part of his star-studded career.

I've known Dick as editor, entrepreneur, author, lecturer, and business consultant. If I were limited to a discussion of just one of his talents, I would select *superb teacher.*

Over the years I've been privileged, on occasion, to share the same speakers' platform with Dick. I've observed that, at the conclusion of every Hodgson presentation, people gather around him because they want to learn more. *Successful Catalog Marketing* is the *more.*

You'll be learning more—neophyte or seasoned catalog marketer—not for a fleeting moment, but for the rest of your career. Make the most of it!

The Great American Catalog Boom

1

If Richard Warren Sears were suddenly to reappear on the scene and look inside his mailbox, he would likely be amazed at its contents. At the turn of the century, his 13-year-old catalog had surpassed the somewhat older Montgomery Ward catalog, making Sears America's leading mail order firm—a position which it has maintained ever since.

Until the 1960s, the mail order catalog field was dominated by the "Big Five"—Sears, Montgomery Ward, Spiegel, Aldens, and National Bellas-Hess. While many Americans had a favorite specialty catalog—perhaps a seed or nursery catalog—or maybe were early customers of the legendary L.L.Bean, the average household did relatively little mail order shopping from anything other than "the big books."

But take a look inside the mailboxes of today. What a change! For the 10 to 15 percent of American households with frequent mail order buyers, few days go by without at least one new catalog making its appearance. And it isn't just the home mailboxes of America that are seeing an increased quantity of catalogs each year. Even more mail order catalogs are arriving annually at the mailrooms of offices throughout the United States.

How Many Catalogs?

Unfortunately, there are no reliable statistics to measure catalog growth—statistics are kept by "industry," and catalogs are not an industry. They're a "marketing method" used by lots of different industries. On top of that, there is no widely accepted definition of a "catalog." Is a single sheet with a dozen items listed for sale a catalog? Or does a catalog have to have 24 pages, as the post office used to require to qualify for a special catalog rate? Nobody yet has come up with an acceptable answer.

For purposes of this book, I find it necessary to coin some kind of working guidelines. So, for this purpose alone, I suggest a "catalog" should meet these qualifications:

- It is a printed presentation with a minimum of 20 products and includes the prices at which these products can be purchased.
- It is in booklet format and has sufficient bound pages to indicate it has been designed for retention.
- It contains sufficient information about each product so purchasing the products can be done by mail or phone (although this doesn't exclude the possibility that the actual purchasing may be done in a store or as the result of a salesperson's call).

By that definition, there are at least 100,000 different American businesses issuing catalogs regularly—and many of these businesses issue two or more different catalogs each year. The majority are specialized catalogs aimed at businesses and professions. In addition, there are thousands of catalogs used by retailers to create traffic for their stores. And there are well over 10,000 different consumer mail order catalogs.

At first glance, those figures might seem extremely high. But we studied 15 different published directories of consumer and business-to-business mail order catalogs and found 6,180 unduplicated listings. We then compared those listings with catalogs we had personally received during a 12-month period and discovered 418 "new" catalogs which weren't included in any of the directory listings. And those 418 additional catalogs we found in our files represent only a small portion of the regularly published mail order catalogs we know to exist, even though they weren't listed in any of the directories.

Consumer and business-to-business mail order catalogs, of course, account for only a small percentage of American catalogs. There are, for example, 7,798 colleges, universities, and trade and technical schools, each of which publishes catalogs. Thousands of retailers have added catalogs to their arsenal of promotional weapons. For example, few, if any, of the 1,685 major department stores in America don't have their own catalogs.

Then consider the distribution field, where catalogs are a way of life. There are 15,190 industrial distributors in America, 5,020 building material distributors, 3,369 automotive wholesalers, and 3,166 audiovisual wholesalers. That's 26,745 distributors in those four fields alone, and if just half of them have catalogs, another 13,373 catalogs have to be added to the total.

But without question, the largest group in catalog publishing is represented by American manufacturers. Take a look at some of the numbers:

- 10,783 furniture manufacturers
- 5,849 electronics manufacturers
- 3,774 jewelry manufacturers
- 2,514 ladies' dresses manufacturers
- 2,148 auto accessory manufacturers
- 1,979 sporting goods manufacturers
- 1,630 paint and varnish manufacturers
- 1,547 curtain and drapery manufacturers
- 1,120 computer manufacturers
- 1,069 men's clothing manufacturers

Just those 10 fields add up to 32,413 American manufacturers. If you consider that any of these manufacturers with multiple products *must* have a catalog (and probably at least half of those on the list above do have multiple products), at least 16,207 additional catalogs must be added to the total.

When you consider that these lists are just "starters," there is every indication that there are far more catalogs today than almost everyone has assumed. And the number keeps growing every year.

The Age of Specialization

The catalog field has followed in the path of American magazines. Remember when *Life, Look,* and *The Saturday Evening Post*—and few other magazines—were to be found in the average American home? But today these weekly magazines have disappeared or taken on a different look, and American homes are filled with dozens of specialty magazines.

This is what has been happening to catalogs. The field so long dominated by "the big books" is now filled with thousands of specialty catalogs, each tailored to the specific tastes and interests of a relatively small portion of the American population.

Today there are specialized catalogs for left-handers, owners of pampered poodles, jigsaw puzzle addicts, and caviar fanciers . . . for soldiers of fortune, bow and arrow hunters, fly fishermen, and avid backpackers . . . for pregnant business executives, world travelers, lovers of popcorn, and former Philadelphians who miss the taste of a good old-fashioned hoagie . . . for teenagers, mothers-to-be, senior citizens, and gentlemen farmers . . . for clockmakers, rug hookers, woodworkers, and candlemakers . . . even the very successful catalog of the San Francisco Music Box Company, with page after page of nothing but music boxes.

Catalogs generally fall into three basic categories:

- *Mail Order Catalogs*—both consumer and business-to-business—which represent "stores in print." All of the selling is done without any direct contact between the seller and the buyer.
- *Retail Traffic-Building Catalogs*—used to entice buyers to come into a store to complete the marketing transaction.
- *Reference Catalogs*—most frequently used in business and industry to facilitate various types of sales contacts. These catalogs usually contain detailed product descriptions but may or may not include pricing information bound into the catalog.

While there are some major differences most of the "basics" fit all three catalog types. Similarly, the basics have universal application in all countries.

The Catalog Age

There are many factors behind America's new love affair with its catalogs. But eight principal trends have spurred the growth of catalogs:

The Information Society

In his 1982 book, *Megatrends* (must reading for anyone in the direct marketing field), John Naisbitt points out the dramatic change from an Industrial Society to an Information Society—the change of America from a predominantly blue-collar to a white-collar market. In the 1950s, 60 percent of American households received their primary income from agricultural and manufacturing jobs, with only 17 percent coming from information jobs (programmers, teachers, clerks, managers, professionals, bankers, etc.). Today it's just the other way around. Now only 16 percent of American households get their primary income from blue-collar occupations, while over 60 percent of the households get primary income from white-collar occupations.

Interestingly, although many believe we've moved from an industrial to a service society, the number of Americans in "service" jobs has remained a consistent 11 or 12 percent since 1950.

David Burch of MIT notes: "We are working ourselves out of the manufacturing business and into the thinking business." That's what the so-called Information Society is all about.

One of the key factors involved is the impact of computers. Naisbitt notes that 75 percent of all jobs today involve computers in some way. This leads to a reduction in the "Information Float"—the time it takes for a piece of information to move from one point to another. Communications technology keeps improving . . . and with that comes a constant reduction in the Information Float.

The significance of this for catalogers is that the nature of markets has changed significantly. Consider the fact that the "Big Five"—the big general mail order catalogs of the past—once dominated direct marketing, capturing over 80 percent of mail order sales. The market for the original Big Five (Sears, Ward's, Spiegel, Aldens, and National Bellas-Hess) was the blue-collar households. Today the Big Five has become the "Big Book Two" (just Sears and Penney's, which entered mail order in the 1960s), and their total percentage of mail order sales in the United States is well under 20 percent and declining.

Spiegel is a good example of how much things have changed. It no longer has a general catalog business. Instead, it chose to get away from the blue-collar market and concentrate on working women in the white-collar market. It took many years of transition, but today Spiegel's sales volume is larger than it was back in its general catalog days.

The white-collar market tends to be better educated and more demanding. It is also "time short" and doesn't want to spend nonworking hours shopping. Thus catalogs and other direct response mailings offer a way to free up nonworking hours for leisure activities more pleasurable than shopping. But to reach this ever-expanding market you have to be more sophisticated.

Mobility and Changing Loyalties

Until the years immediately following World War II, the majority of Americans did the bulk of their shopping in locally owned and operated stores. They seldom ventured very far from their neighborhoods to do their shopping and bought whatever their local storekeepers carried in stock. For many, it somehow seemed to be an injustice to their friendly neighborhood "Mom and Pop" merchants to place orders with someone they didn't know, located outside the area where they lived or worked.

Then, as people became more mobile, shopping horizons expanded. Shopping centers and shopping malls attracted a nation on wheels—and Americans became exposed to a wide variety of merchandise from which to choose. And they began doing the bulk of their shopping in stores owned and operated by people who weren't their neighbors and friends. Once the close bond between storekeeper and customer was broken, it was just a small step to begin considering the even wider array of products that could be found in mail order catalogs.

Another form of mobility is the movement of families away from the cities. Former city dwellers in vast numbers have moved away from the cities into suburbs, small towns, and rural areas—areas where availability of many types of products is less common.

For catalog marketers, this trend is highly important. The former city dwellers bring along the tastes of the city, which often can't be filled by easily reached retail establishments . . . and mail order becomes the way to acquire what they want. And these city-born tastes often rub off on their rural neighbors, further adding to the market potential for catalog marketers.

Along with all of the mobility came a change in the nature of the typical retail store—particularly in the character of sales personnel. Until a couple of decades ago, young men and women took a sales job in a store with the idea they were embarking on a career. They dedicated themselves to retail selling. Now salesclerking is simply an entry-level job—something to do until "something better" comes along. As a result, retail sales personnel often know little about the products they sell and don't make any real effort to develop long-term relationships with the people to whom they sell these products.

There's also been an explosion in technology. Some years back, if clerks in a dry goods store knew the difference between cotton, wool, and silk, they could handle questions about 90 percent of the merchandise in stock. Today, with all of the synthetics, special weaves, and blends, a clerk in a similar store almost has to be an engineer to be fully informed about all the fabrics in stock. Or think of the clerk in a camera store. It wasn't so long ago that all you had to know was the difference between a folding camera and a box camera and you could handle most everything you sold. Today you *do* have to be an engineer to fully understand all of the differences in the merchandise in a camera store.

"It's gotten so bad," Stanley Marcus of Neiman-Marcus in Dallas quipped, "that when salespeople take a break for lunch, we have to retrain them when they get back."

The net result of these changes has been that consumers today usually don't expect to receive comprehensive product information from most retail sales personnel. Often they can find more complete, reliable, and understandable information for making buying decisions in printed catalogs.

Today's catalogs, with warm and friendly—and informative—copy, have taken over the role of yesterday's Mom and Pop retailers and the dedicated salespeople who used to work for them.

Working Women

Back in 1947, only 17 million American women were in the labor force. By 1982, their numbers had increased to 49 million . . . and the number keeps increasing every year.

While many of these employed females are single, a substantial portion represent an additional source of income for their families. In 1985, 42 percent of U.S. families had two earners and 14 percent had three or more. That adds up to 56 percent of all American families with multiple incomes.

In addition to the fact that multiple incomes for a family means more money to spend, there is special significance for catalogers to the constantly increasing number of wage-earning married females. In the typical dual income family, the male wage earner is still primarily responsible for the basic family necessities—food, housing, transportation, etc. As a result, the female wage earner's income becomes the discretionary funds for the family. And since she earns that money, she has primary control over how it will be spent.

Most mail order buying, of course, is discretionary. And with increasing control of discretionary funds in the hands of women, there has been a "feminizing" of direct marketing. You need only take a look at the male-female split on mail order buying lists. It wasn't that long ago that the typical mail order catalog list was 50 percent male, 50 percent female. Take a look today. In general, you find catalog buyers' lists are now 80 percent female and only 20 percent male.

And it isn't just consumer mail order catalogs that have felt this impact. For many years, business-to-business catalogs were strictly "masculine" in design and copy style. But as the percentage of females in business buying positions has increased, there has been a feminizing of business catalogs, too. In many fields, such as office and computer supplies, it is estimated that over 50 percent of the buying is being done today by women.

Changing Population Patterns

While you weren't looking, the Baby Boomers—the generation born between 1946 and 1960—began celebrating their 40th birthdays in 1986. This "coming of age" of the Baby Boomers represents a significant change in catalog marketing opportunities.

Between 1970 and 1985, there was only a 15 percent increase in total U.S. population—from 203 million in 1970 to 239 million in 1985. But:

- Ages 25-29 showed a 38 percent increase.
- Ages 30-34 showed a 44 percent increase.
- Ages 35-39 showed a 35 percent increase.

Why is this so important? When you describe the typical Baby Boomer household, you find an interesting parallel with the description of the typical mail order buyer. Consider, for example, this definition from Mediamark Research, Inc.:

> The typical mail order customer is between the ages of 35 and 44, earns more than $30,000 a year, lives outside a metropolitan area, is a college graduate, is married, and has at least one child living at home.

That's your typical Baby Boomer!

There are at least two important reasons why the growth in Baby Boomer households is likely to play an important role in catalog marketing in the future.

1. The Baby Boomers are the first generation entering their prime catalog buying years with substantial previous experience in mail order buying. Even as teenagers, these Baby Boomers began responding to mail order offers—record clubs, specialized teen and young adult clothing, cosmetics, etc. Thus they're entering their prime mail order buying years already accepting mail order buying as a way to spend their money. (And this doesn't just affect consumer purchases. Increases in consumer mail order buying carry over into the business sector. Having developed mail order buying patterns at home makes it easy to accept such patterns on the job.)
2. A substantial number of Baby Boomer households fall into the dual income category with more discretionary income to spend.

There's a companion age-related trend which is also of importance to catalog marketers—the Affluent Maturity Market. For every ten Baby Boomers, there are about nine consumers aged 50 and over. In their book, *Why They Buy,* Robert B. Settle and Pamela L. Alreck tell about this growing market:

> This group is extremely affluent, with about half the discretionary buying power of the nation and over three-quarters of the personal financial assets. So you would think that consumer marketers would have descended on this greying group with a vengeance—but, in fact,

they've often been ignored in favor of everybody's fascination, the Baby Boom generation. Actually, there are a couple of legitimate reasons why marketers don't approach the 50 and over consumer market boldly and directly: First, they're a pretty diverse group, and second, it's difficult to address them by age without offending them.

For catalogers, this older generation represents a very important market—not just because they have money, but because the majority have already discovered mail order buying and are likely to shy away from traditional retail shopping areas dominated by the Baby Boomers and their offspring.

Computerized Mailing Lists

The computer was late in coming to the catalog field—but when it finally began to be utilized extensively in the 1970s, the whole nature of direct marketing changed rapidly.

The biggest impact was on mailing lists. (Today everyone seems to be talking about "data bases" . . . but for the majority of catalogers, "data base" is simply a synonym for "mailing list." Of course, when you say you're working on a data base, you usually get a better salary than when you simply work on a mailing list.)

Without the application of computer technology, catalogs had to be mailed primarily to "suspects." About the only kind of segmentation practical was identifying those who had already bought something and those who hadn't, plus a limited amount of geographic segmentation. We knew there were differences between the people who lived in Portland, Oregon, and those in Portland, Maine, or between those who lived in the North and those who lived in the South.

For customers, we applied the RFM formula—separating customers by Recency (how recently they had bought), Frequency (how often they bought), and Monetary Value (how much money they spent with us). But for the suspects, about all we could do was to select by geographical area—and then primarily state by state.

But computer sophistication made it possible to separate "prospects" from "suspects" and introduce more sophisticated forms of segmentation. The science of demographics suddenly became important. With the then-new ZIP Code program of the post office, catalogers began using Census Bureau data to create demographic profiles of each five-digit ZIP Code and using those profiles to eliminate groups of people who were less likely to buy.

Demographics are described as the "externals" of people, and almost always these identifiers are applied to groups of people, rather than individuals—such things as average income of a group, average level of education, percentage of homeowners versus renters, etc.

Today, however, the trend is toward psychographics—the "internals" of individuals, their "lifestyles." Not how much money they make, but how they use their money. Not how much education they have, but how they are applying that education.

The real importance of psychographics lies in the change from dealing with relatively large groups to dealing with people one at a time. Most of the lifestyle indicators come from the differences in products customers purchase and use. With today's computer technology, catalogers are using multiple overlays. They combine such things as the type of car owned with kinds of magazines and books read. Then they add the organization to which someone belongs and the categories of products purchased. By comparing such information as it relates to prospects with the profiles catalogers create of their own mail order customers, it's possible not only to key in on the best prospects but, perhaps more important, to save a lot of money by deleting nonprospects when mailing to outside lists.

Catalog marketers are really just beginning to understand how to meaningfully apply psychographic overlays, but they've come a long way from the precomputer days when there was little, if any, list segmentation.

Another significant change has been in the number of lists available for rental or exchange. These lists differ from the "compiled lists," which were often the only ones available some years ago. "Rental lists" are lists of people who *have done something*—buying a product, requesting a specific catalog, etc.; compiled lists are made up of people who simply *are something*. Since there is a significant difference in the level of response from lists of people who have already taken the kind of action you are asking them to take (buying from a catalog) and those who just "are something," the increased availability of rental lists makes it economical to do prospecting mailings to build a catalog buyers list.

Equally important is the growing practice of exchanging lists. Often list owners will not rent their lists to those they consider competitors—but they will exchange lists. ("I'll let you mail to 10,000 of my last year's buyers if you let me mail to 10,000 of your last year's buyers.")

Today the greatest amount of catalog prospecting is done by mailing actual catalogs to lists of known catalog buyers. This has generally proved far more economical than running newspaper and magazine advertisements to solicit catalog requests and then trying to convert those requestees into customers.

Telephones and Credit Cards

A big change in catalog marketing that really began in a meaningful way in the 1970s resulted from the availability of national credit cards . . . and the use of WATS telephone service—800 numbers for placing orders.

Until travel and entertainment and bank cards came along, most catalog marketers had no easy way to offer credit to their customers. Those who had in-house credit plans had already discovered that credit orders were generally 30 to 35 percent larger than cash orders. But the majority of catalogs were too small to develop their own in-house credit programs—and the COD service of the post office didn't produce the increase in order size that credit programs provided.

Today the average American carries seven different credit cards—and doesn't hesitate to use them when placing mail orders.

And when combined with toll-free telephone order placing (and every phone order by its very nature has to be a credit order), the average order size can be increased by an additional 20 to 40 percent through simple no-pressure suggestive selling.

Today it is estimated that well over 50 percent of the "mail orders" which previously were sent via the postal service now come in by phone—and some companies report getting 80 percent or more of their catalog orders by phone.

Unfortunately, most catalog marketers have not yet developed the skills needed to create and maintain suggestive selling programs among their telephone order-taking personnel. But there are companies that have developed special telephone selling programs—both inbound and outbound—and have registered sales increases of as much as 100 percent.

Multiple Options

John Naisbitt points out that personal choices for Americans remained rather narrow and limited from the postwar period through much of the 1960s. Many of us lived the simple lives portrayed in such television series as "Leave It To Beaver" and "Father Knows Best"—Father went to work, Mother kept house and raised 2.4 children. There were few decisions to make—it was an either/or world.

Not anymore. The social upheavals of the late 1960s precipitated a wave of change that has fractured society into a multitude of diverse groups with an amazingly wide range of tastes and values. Everyone, it seems, now wants to do his or her own thing . . . and for each whim and fancy, there's a specialized mail order catalog to provide exactly what's wanted at the moment.

The conformity of a Mass Society is a thing of the past. No longer are the general merchandise catalogs capable of providing "what everybody wants." The demand for multiple options has spawned a host of specialty catalogs. This frequently leads to a question concerning the so-called "catalog glut." With so many catalogs around, how can the American consumer keep up with the deluge arriving in his or her mailbox?

It's not unusual for a mail order "multi-buyer" (one whose name appears on multiple lists of mail order buyers) to receive between 300 and 1,000 different mail order catalogs a year. Few, if any, read each of these catalogs. But catalog marketers deal in averages. Every effort is made to reduce the number of catalogs sent to those who have no interest in the products being offered . . . and then you cross your fingers, hoping that a profitable percentage of those catalogs mailed result in orders received.

There is a problem in overuse of multi-buyer lists. American catalog companies concentrate heavily on mailing to those who have given evidence of already being regular mail order buyers. Thus, most catalogs are mailed to a narrow percentage of households. It's been estimated that 15 percent of American households receive 85 to 90 percent of all mail order catalogs.

The other side of this picture—and the big opportunity for catalog marketers in the future—is the other 85 percent of U.S. households—those not yet receiving many mail order catalogs because they haven't yet been introduced to buying by mail.

In the U.S., you can do very well by concentrating on a small percentage of the households. If you can attract just 10 percent as buyers, you end up with a customer base of over 8.5 million buyers! There's no such luxury for mail order catalogers in other parts of the world. In most countries, you need to penetrate the market in depth to succeed—and many mail order companies in other parts of the world have learned to do just that (a lesson American catalog marketers need to learn from their counterparts elsewhere).

The High Cost of Selling

Another significant trend—and one that has been particularly important for business-to-business selling—has been the increasing costs of selling by traditional methods.

The cost of a typical industrial sales call, for example, has increased from about $50 in 1950 to well over $250 today. It's estimated that it takes over five sales calls to get the first order . . . and there are few marketing situations which permit expenses of over $1,000 to obtain a new customer.

One estimate says that, in days past, a distributor had one marketing person in the office to back up 20 salespeople "on the road." Today, with a combination of catalogs and telephone selling, it's more common to have 20 in the office to back up one on the road.

This has brought about a dramatic change in the nature of many catalogs. In the past, it was assumed that there would be someone "on the spot" to amplify what was presented in a catalog and to answer any questions a potential buyer might have. Today the catalog frequently has to do the entire selling job.

Catalogs in the Age of Electronics

For many years, a host of futurists regularly predicted that the printed catalog would soon go the way of the dinosaur and be replaced by electronic shopping. Billions of dollars were spent trying to introduce interactive electronic shopping to consumers and businesses around the world. What these futurists overlooked, however, was that, although the technology had arrived, buyers didn't feel any need to change the ways in which they were doing their shopping. As a result, one by one, each of the interactive electronics shopping programs failed.

Initially, there was optimism as new interactive systems were introduced. They were installed in homes and businesses of those eager to be part of something new and, like a new toy, they got a lot of use. Not only did the people who had them love to experiment with their use, but they were happy to show off their new "toy" to neighbors and friends, and the initial usage seemed to indicate instant success. But after the novelty wore off, and efforts were made to introduce these new systems to a wider audience, it quickly became obvious there was no vast market demand for interactive electronic shopping.

The only exception has been noninteractive electronic shopping—the home video shopping networks, which don't require buyers to learn anything they don't already know. It's simply a matter of being able to turn on a television set and dial a telephone—something both simple and common for everyone. In just two years, the three major home video shopping networks were able to post annual sales of over $1.5 billion. Research indicates, however, that this vast volume of sales did not come as a substitute for normal catalog buying, but, for the most part, was a substitute for other forms of buying.

As we approach the 21st Century, every indication is that the printed catalog will continue to hold its own in a world rapidly adjusting to an explosion of computer and electronics technology. Perhaps some major breakthrough will change the public's buying habits—but none appears on the horizon at this time.

In schools throughout the world, the textbook is still the cornerstone of teaching. In spite of the introduction of all kinds of special teaching aids, the entire education system is textbook based. Thus, still another generation of students is being taught to turn to a printed document as the most reliable source of information.

And psychologists tell us there's a sense of security in something you can hold in your hands and "control" yourself. Unless schools teach students to substitute computers and electronics for textbooks, they are likely to continue to leave the halls of education with a demand for printed catalogs as the most comfortable source of information about the products they wish to buy.

Catalogs Throughout the World

While selling by catalogs is more advanced in the United States than in most countries of the world, America doesn't have as much of a lead in this area as it did a decade ago. Countries in Northern Europe have long been catalog oriented. According to some estimates, for example, West Germany posts even higher per-capita mail order buying than in the U.S.

One of the major differences between the U.S. and Northern Europe is that agent selling is more common throughout Europe. Catalogs are sent to "agents," who, in turn, take orders from several others and often handle deliveries and payments. But this is changing rapidly. One major mail order catalog company in England, for example, formerly found its agents handling an average of 18 to 20 customers each time a catalog was distributed. Today, however, their average agent handles only 3.5 customers.

Specialty catalogs are much less common elsewhere. But this, too, is changing. Each year sees a greater number of specialty catalogs being introduced to consumers in many countries.

Major catalog growth is being seen today in Southern Europe and in Asia. As Mom and Pop retailing declines in countries throughout the world, mail order catalogs are finding increasing numbers of willing buyers—just as they have in the U.S. as Mom and Pop retailing has disappeared.

The Key Ingredients
Of Catalog Marketing

2

How Catalog Marketing Is Different

While catalog marketing has elements of both retail selling and direct mail, there are important differences that you need to understand when you set out to create a successful catalog.

First of all, catalog buying differs from retail buying because everything is done "sight unseen." There's no storefront with a door through which you enter. And there's no salesperson to answer your questions (although the increased use of telephone marketing in the catalog field sometimes—but infrequently—puts you in voice contact with someone who can answer questions in addition to taking your order).

Retail buying involves being able to "touch and feel" the merchandise. But in a catalog, the illustrations and copy have to provide a substitute for the touching-and-feeling experience.

And catalog buying is also different from other forms of direct mail. In most cases, responding to a traditional solo mailing (a single offer usually consisting of outer envelope, letter, brochure, and response device) involves an impulse decision. Solo mailings are most often read and considered when they are received, and responses come in a bell-shaped curve, quickly building to a peak and with all but a handful of responses coming within about three weeks.

Catalog buying, on the other hand, seldom involves immediate response. The response curve generally has a much less predominant peak and a long "tail" with responses coming in for many weeks.

When catalogs are received, they're most often treated more like magazines than like promotional mailings. Recipients read through them, looking to see what's new . . . what's different . . . what will fulfill dreams. But little buying is done during this "editorial reading." Instead, catalogs are "filed" for future reference.

In most homes, offices, and institutions, there is generally a single "catalog file." As catalogs are received and reviewed, they're added to this "file." Then, when something triggers a buying impulse, the catalog buyer goes to his or her "file" and searches out those catalogs that are remembered as containing merchandise that can fulfill that buying impulse.

The Importance of Memorability
Thus *memorability* becomes a key ingredient in creating a successful catalog. It's important that your customers and prospects not only remember your catalog, but remember what it contains.

In many cases, there may be a LIFO principle involved—last in, first out. The last catalog received may very well be what triggers a buying impulse . . . and that catalog may get the order—unless the buyer remembers your catalog and takes the time to go to the catalog "file" and search it out.

To obtain this kind of memorability, a catalog needs a distinctive personality. If it seems just like other catalogs, there's little incentive to make a special effort to search it out.

In Advertising 101, you probably studied USP—what Rosser Reeves called the Unique Selling Proposition so essential in marketing individual products. Catalogs, too, need a USP—in this case, a Unique Selling *Position*. This is usually a single, frequently emphasized factor that quickly distinguishes your catalog from others that may offer the same type of products. The catalog USP may be established by your design, copy style, product mixture, pricing, or something else which makes your catalog different. (This highly important ingredient in successful catalogs is discussed in greater detail in Chapter 3.)

A Graphics Medium
Another way catalogs differ from other types of direct mail is that catalogs are basically a graphics medium. Catalog buyers look at the pictures first. Then, if they find they are interested in a product, they

Figure 2-1
Catalog Response Curves

Response to most solo mailings comes in just three weeks and follows the traditional bell-shaped curve that builds more slowly and continues for six months or more—or until response to a subsequent catalog takes over. In a very short season, a catalog may produce a bell-shaped response curve.

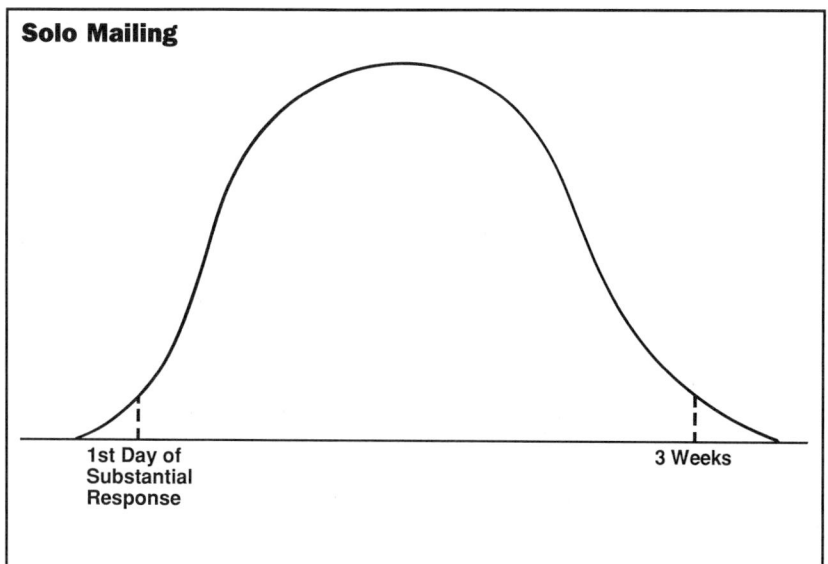

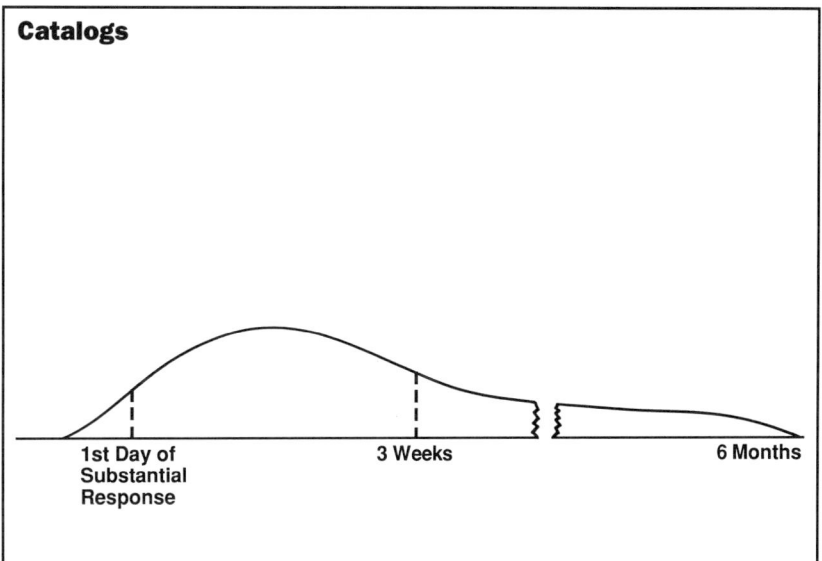

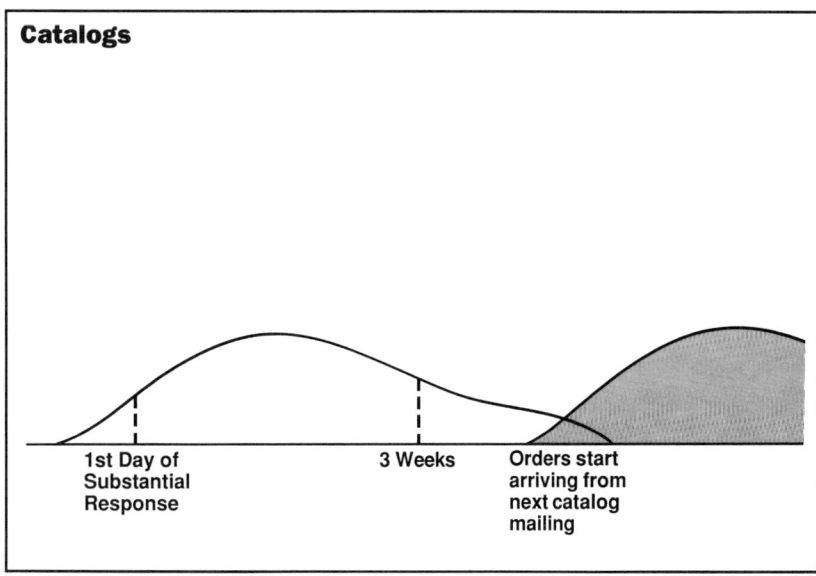

will read the copy to learn things which the pictures fail to tell them. Few catalog readers look at the copy first—even the headlines. They go from picture to picture and then read copy only about the items which are of special interest.

Most other direct mail is a "copy medium." In fact, direct mail (excluding catalogs) is the only advertising medium in which you write the copy first and then design a layout to accommodate the copy. In all other forms of advertising—including catalogs—you usually create a design and then "fill the holes" with copy.

This is not to say that both direct mail and catalogs don't need good design *and* good copy. But in direct mail, if you keep the same copy and change from one good design to another good design, you seldom see major changes in response. If you keep the same design and change the copy—perhaps a new headline, a new lead paragraph, or a new offer—you frequently gain a substantial increase in response.

Catalogs are just the opposite. Start with good copy and good design, and change from one good copy block to another good copy block, and you seldom see any change in response at all. But keep the same copy and change the design—a new photograph, new page design, or perhaps different pagination—and you can see major changes in response.

Help for Catalog Buyers

Catalog buyers like lots of help. One reason many of the best catalog buyers turn to their catalogs is that they don't like to "shop." If they did, they would probably be in their cars heading for the nearest retail store that carries what you're selling.

If you have a page full of similar items and each is treated the same, buyers quickly get confused. They don't want to have to read every block of copy and then decide for themselves which is just right to fit their needs. Instead, they want you to tell them which of these items you recommend.

And they don't want to have to struggle to find items in your catalog—they want it organized like a good store. In my own catalog consulting experience, I've found that the quickest way to improve an ailing catalog is frequently just to do a better job of organizing merchandise into easily remembered "departments." This not only makes it easier for the buyer to find items of special interest, but aids in establishing memorability for a catalog. It's easier to remember that a catalog contains an assortment of a particular type of merchandise than that it contains a specific item.

(For additional details on ways to help the readers of your catalog, see Chapter 6, Organizing Your Catalog.)

The Four Key Words

Four key words are important to consider before you can really begin creating a catalog. They represent the starting point in your relationship with the audience to whom the catalog will be sent.

Each of these words has to be preceded by a common adjective—"perceived"—because what may actually exist is not as important as the way the audience perceives things to be.

Availability

The first of these key words is availability—perceived availability. Does your audience feel that the products you are offering are more readily available from you than from someone else?

While a product or service may be readily available from a local merchant, this becomes a major competitive advantage only if the potential buyer is aware of this fact and thus determines it would be easier to purchase from a nearby source than from a catalog.

Consider the Brookstone catalog, which boldly proclaims it has "Hard-to-Find Tools." Actually, many of the tools that Brookstone sells—or similar tools which will do the same jobs—are available through local hardware merchants. But they're the type of things the merchant keeps in those bins under his counters or back in the stockroom "just in case somebody asks for them."

Thus the reader of a Brookstone catalog perceives such tools to be truly "hard to find" . . . and Brookstone has had steady and profitable growth serving buyers who have come to depend on its catalog rather than local merchants as a source for tools and, as Brookstone often adds, "Other Fine Things."

Of course, almost every product—or a satisfactory substitute—is generally available to those who are willing to take the time to shop around in stores or other catalogs. But there is a constantly expanding market of people who feel they have better uses for their time than "shopping around." Thus, if they discover something in a catalog which appears to be unique and not readily available through some source with which they are already familiar, this registers in their minds and gives a catalog a special advantage over others.

Catalogers have developed lots of special techniques to encourage their customers to perceive their products or services as being unique and thus not easily available elsewhere—exclusive colors, designs, and packaging . . . special combinations of products . . . attractive and easily understood credit plans . . . early introduction of new and improved products . . . and a variety of other effective techniques which traditional retailers have been reluctant to adopt.

The "exclusive" is an important selling element for many cata-

Figure 2-2
Perceived Availability

Brookstone boldly proclaims its catalogs have "Hard-to-Find Tools." Some items could be found locally but not given preferred display. When readers see them in the catalog, they assume they are more readily available from Brookstone. Copyright © Brookstone. Used with permission.

logs. Often a catalog marketer develops a special graphic device to identify products that, in the form being offered, are available only through that catalog.

Eddie Bauer, for example, uses a special signature. Copy in its catalogs explains:

> **This signature appears throughout the catalog to identify products available only through us . . . items produced by us in our own facilities or manufactured for us to our exacting specifications.**

When customers see a product they like that carries the special Eddie Bauer logo, they can make a quick decision on whether to order it or not. Since this product is available exclusively from Eddie Bauer, there's no reason to delay a decision and shop around.

Often just using the word "exclusive" is an advantage. Experience has shown that such a word—when used in a meaningful way—frequently increases sales of products so identified.

Authority

The second key word—and probably the most important for a catalog marketer—is perceived authority: What gives you the right to say what you're saying and expect to be believed?

Every successful catalog has some kind of authority. It may come from the product assortment itself. It may be due to the geographi-

Figure 2-3
Offering "Exclusive" Products

Eddie Bauer uses its signature logotype "to identify products available only through us...." When readers see a product they like with the Bauer signature, there's little reason to delay a buying decision and "shop around." Copyright © Eddie Bauer. Used with permission.

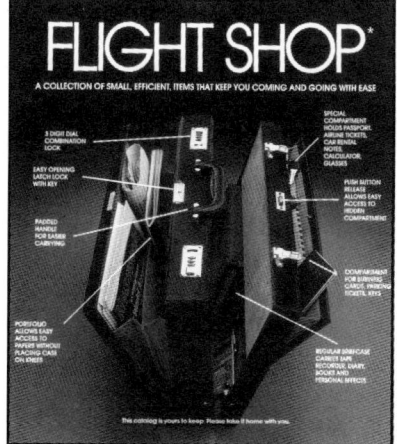

**Figure 2-4
Perceived Authority**

Catalogs distributed aboard airlines frequently feature luggage. Airlines, of course, are "the ultimate authority" on durability of luggage, making their catalogs a logical buying source for such items. Copyright © TWA. Used with permission.

cal location of the catalog company. It may come from known activities of the catalog marketer in other fields. Or perhaps the catalog is built around the personality of an individual.

A good example of how perceived authority directs how a catalog communicates with an audience is those catalogs you find in the seatbacks of most airlines. They carry the name of the airline on the cover, but in most cases they aren't really the airlines' catalogs at all. The majority of them are catalogs of K Promotions, a catalog marketing company in Milwaukee, Wisconsin.

But to the reader, these catalogs carry the authority of the airline whose name appears on the cover. In most of these catalogs, you'll find many items of luggage. When the copy in one of these catalogs says a piece of luggage is "durable," the writer can stop right there. Airlines are the ultimate authority on the durability of luggage—they know more about smashing it up than anyone else. So when they say it's durable, they don't need to say much more.

But suppose your authority is based on being a manufacturer of pantyhose, and you want to sell luggage. If you simply claim it's durable, you aren't anywhere yet. You must give full details about the materials used in its construction . . . cite laboratory tests . . . include testimonials . . . or do something else to make up for your lack of authority on this type of merchandise.

Actually, customer testimonials are a very important element in building authority. Many catalogers fill their pages with dozens of testimonials—not just to fill space, but because they've found these testimonials help to sell products.

Ever wonder why so many catalogs seem to waste so much space on seemingly ego-centered editorial material about the companies, the facilities and the people behind them? It's not just an ego trip in most cases, but rather a carefully calculated program of building authority in the minds of their customers to encourage buying with confidence. And such space is far from wasted when it eliminates the need for a lot of backup copy for each item in the book.

And when catalog marketers feel they lack the proper authority, they aren't hesitant to enlist the support of outside organizations or individuals instantly recognized as authorities in areas related to the merchandise or services being sold.

One of the best examples of how effective this technique can be comes from Germany, where there are three big general merchandise catalogs—Quelle, Otto, and Neckermann. For many years, Neckermann was much like the old Aldens and Spiegel general merchandise catalogs in the United States. It used the theme "Neckermann Makes It Possible," meaning that you could buy more from Neckermann because it featured low-cost products. Neckermann was acquired by a large European retailer, and the new owners wanted to move Neckermann into a more upscale market—particularly in the fashions area. But how does someone with authority in "cheap" products suddenly acquire authority on better-quality, more stylish products?

Neckermann didn't try to do it internally. Instead, it enlisted the help of a German fashion authority in Paris, Jurgen Michaelsen. It engineered a special publicity program to make sure everyone in Germany became acquainted with Jurgen Michaelsen and then used him throughout its catalogs whenever there was a need to talk with authority about upscale fashion merchandise.

Value

The third key word is value—perceived value. And this is a frequently misunderstood word. Value doesn't just mean the lowest possible price. It has to be the right price for the particular audience to whom the catalog is designed to appeal.

In general, mail order catalog buyers tend to position themselves in one of three basic value categories. At one time Sears used the terms *Good, Better,* and *Best* to describe the value level of its products. And those same words are good descriptions of the three basic value categories of catalog buyers:

- *Good*. These buyers are always looking for a bargain. They respond readily to "sale" and discount catalogs.
- *Better*. These are the customers who look for the best combination of price and value.
- *Best*. There are always some who want to feel they've bought something a bit better than similar items owned by their friends, relatives, neighbors, and co-workers.

Figure 2-5
Perceived Value

Breck's uses an easily understood value concept: customers receive substantial savings if they place their orders in advance. Copyright © Foster & Gallagher. Used with permission.

Figure 2-6
Specials-of-the-Month

Quill makes monthly mailings of special sale catalogs, with selected items offered at deep discounts when items are ordered before the end of the month. Copyright © Quill. Used with permission.

The basic audience of any given catalog will generally be composed of buyers who have positioned themselves within one of these three basic value categories. They will generally concentrate most of their mail order buying from catalogs within a single category.

It's very difficult for a catalog to create an image of regularly carrying merchandise in more than one of these value categories. (This is not to say a Best catalog can't have special presentations of remainder items at Good pricing—but it is important to establish a basic image of just a single value category.)

It is best to keep an open mind about specific pricing when starting a catalog. Unlike the majority of retail stores, which establish specific markups for each category of products they sell, successful catalogers do a lot of price testing and let their customers help them pick the "right" price for products.

Whenever pricing tends to differ from normal, it's important to have "an easily understood reason why." One of the best examples of how important this can be is the Breck's catalog, which sells Dutch bulbs to American gardeners.

Breck's has been able to capture a substantial market share of the bulbs shipped from Holland to America each year with an "advance sale" technique. Most Dutch bulbs are sold in the fall at planting time. But Breck's sells them in the spring with an annual sale that ends on July 31; the bulbs are shipped from Holland to arrive at proper planting time in the fall. Copy explains that by taking orders early, Breck's is able to consolidate orders for quantity buying and gets first pick of the best bulbs from Holland's annual bulb harvest. This not only gives the customers superior quality bulbs but makes it possible to offer them at substantial discounts—an "easily understood reason why."

Another good example of sale pricing in catalogs is the technique used by Quill Corporation—America's largest mail order seller of office equipment and supplies. Quill has regular semiannual catalogs with approximately 400 pages. But the bulk of Quill's sales come from monthly 60-page sale catalogs, with selected items available at deep discounts.

In this case, the "easily understood reason" is that the deep discounts are good only for a given month. Sale items are highlighted in each of the monthly catalogs and given special item numbers that reflect the deeply discounted prices. To take advantage of the special prices, the customer must use the special item numbers and order before the end-of-the-month expiration date.

Quill has made buying almost a game for its customers. If they find they will need a resupply of certain items, they will await the first-of-the-month arrival of Quill's sale catalog (and since Quill regularly features many commonly used items among its monthly specials, customers will almost always find something on sale each month which they want to order). Then, when they order those items, it is natural to add on other items they need at that time.

Some other "easily understood reasons why" prices may be different from normal include the following:

- The items are manufactured by the catalog marketer, so there are no broker costs to be absorbed.
- Out-of-season items are being offered to reduce the catalog marketer's warehousing costs.
- The catalog marketer has made a volume purchase.
- It's a traditional sale period (e.g., January "white sales").
- Items are remainders, available in limited quantity.
- Introductory prices are being offered to help establish the demand for a new item.
- Special values are being offered to entice a prospect to become a first-time customer.
- Last year's models are being liquidated to make room for newer merchandise.

Special credit plans can also be an important part of establishing a special "value" relationship with customers. While the prices of merchandise in American Express catalogs don't represent special values in themselves, the fact that American Express cardholders can acquire the merchandise immediately and pay for it in monthly installments without any finance charges gives the company a very special value positioning.

Price testing is often an important part of successful catalog operations. Rather than simply using standard markups for each category of merchandise, many catalogers make tests of different price points. Then they establish the "right price" for a given item based not only on which price pulls the greatest number of orders, but on which price produces the greatest total net income when volume is multiplied by the profit per item sold.

Satisfaction

The fourth key word is perceived satisfaction. Since catalogs most often require dealing with an audience "sight unseen," it is necessary to make customers feel they aren't going to have any hassles in dealing with you.

That's where a catalog's guarantee of complete satisfaction becomes so important.

Catalog guarantees aren't anything new. The first recorded

guarantee was used back in the days of Colonial America by Benjamin Franklin, who distributed a catalog of books which could be bought by mail. His famous guarantee:

> **Those persons who live remote, by sending their orders and money to said B. Franklin, may depend on the same justice as if present.**

Most of today's mail order guarantees are based on one Sears has been using for many years:

> **Whatever you buy at Sears, you have the right to use it for a reasonable time before you determine it is satisfactory and decide to keep it. If you decide it is not satisfactory, return it to us at our expense. We will do whatever is necessary to correct the cause of your dissatisfaction. If we can't satisfactorily provide a remedy, or if you request a refund, we will refund your full purchase price including any appropriate delivery charges, finance charges and applicable taxes.**
>
> ***Our Pledge of Fairness:*** **If, after you have decided to keep your purchase, it doesn't give you the service or performance you reasonably expect of it and there isn't a specific written warranty on the item that will satisfactorily correct the problem, please let us know. We want to make an adjustment that you will consider fair.**

Figure 2-7
Perceived Satisfaction

The mail order guarantee is essential in convincing buyers they can buy "sight unseen" without taking a risk. The most famous of mail order guarantees is one that has been used for many years by Sears. Copyright © Sears. Used with permission.

Most catalogers, however, state their guarantee in fewer words, as does this guarantee from Ambassador:

If for any reason (or no reason at all) you are not completely satisfied with the design, color, workmanship, size or material of any product you buy from Ambassador, simply return it to us within 30 days of receiving it, and we will refund the purchase price promptly—or, if you desire, replace the product you bought free of charge. What's more . . . if you should feel, at any time, that your purchase is not giving you the service you expected it to, just send it back to us and we will either refund the price you paid for it, or replace the product without charge . . . whichever you prefer.

Unfortunately, when lawyers and comptrollers get their hands on a guarantee, they usually want to build in a lot of restrictions for fear some customers will try to rip off the company. Experience has shown, however, that a restrictive guarantee seldom results in fewer requests for refunds or replacements than a wide-open guarantee. Meanwhile, you've lost the promotional value of a guarantee that tells customers they can order from you without worrying about what will happen if they are dissatisfied with what they receive.

The ultimate in no-hassle guarantees comes from Lands' End. It says:

Guaranteed. Period.

Figure 2-8
The Ultimate Guarantee

Just two words: Guaranteed. Period. That's Lands' End's guarantee. Copyright © Lands' End, Inc. Reprinted courtesy of Lands' End Catalog.

But the customer's perceived satisfaction doesn't start and end with the guarantee. Smart catalog marketers are very selective in the merchandise they offer to help quiet any fears customers might have about potential dissatisfaction. In fashions, for example, they often purposely select styles which don't involve critical fits . . . colors which reproduce well and are easily envisioned from printed illustrations . . . and copy which not only romances the product but carefully spells out details that, if misunderstood, could result in dissatisfaction.

Of course, just creating a guarantee and printing it in your catalogs doesn't mean much unless you back it up with good customer service. Profits in catalogs are made by getting previous customers to buy frequently—and dissatisfied customers don't come back for more.

These four words are the starting point. You can't really select the right merchandise, design a catalog presentation, write any copy, or decide when and to whom to mail unless you clearly understand your relationship with your market in each of these areas.

What It Takes to Start a Mail Order Catalog

Five key factors are involved in evaluating the potential for starting a mail order catalog.

Products

It takes unique products to make a catalog stand out from competition. If potential customers already have a source for the products you plan to present, there's no reason to change buying sources.

And you need substantial margins for profit. As a general rule, you should have at least three times markup on the majority of products if your anticipated average order will be $35 or less, and two times markup if your order will be between $35 and $75. If your average order will be over $75, some products might carry a slightly lower markup.

Be prepared for failures on a substantial number of the products you pick for your first catalog. Sales results will quickly tell you what kinds of products your customers want to buy from you. And when you find out, quickly remove all "losers" from your future catalogs. As a general rule, even after you've discovered what types of products your customers want from you, you'll probably find one-third of the products in a catalog will be profitable, one-third will just break even, and one-third will be losers.

If you just carry the same products as others or have to look to outside vendors when others already have similar proprietary products available to them without middleman costs, your chances for catalog success are slim.

Authority

Why should someone feel you are the "right" source for what you plan to sell? There should be something which instantly communicates to potential customers that you, more than someone else, should become their preferred source.

Perhaps you are the creator of the products . . . maybe you have developed a reputation in something that implies you know more about the kinds of products in your catalog than others might know . . . maybe you are located in an area considered the right place to find the kinds of things you plan to sell . . . or perhaps your name is so well known that people already have a desire to have some special relationship with you.

However, if you don't already have some kind of authority, it may take several years to establish enough authority to be competitive against those who do have an accepted authority base.

An important thing to recognize is that what you perceive to be your authority may be limited to those you are already serving in some way and may mean nothing to others to whom you'll have to mail your catalog if you hope to produce enough sales to be profitable. Many major retailers, for example, have made the mistaken assumption that because they are a household word in the markets where their stores are located, and their peers in retailing circles recognize them as leaders, consumers throughout the country will instantly recognize their name and the local reputation they have been able to achieve. Unfortunately, the best-known retailer in Massachusetts may be almost completely unknown in Arizona.

Mailing Lists

Do you already have a list of confirmed mail order catalog buyers—or will you have to start from scratch in building your list?

While it seldom, if ever, appears on the balance sheet, the mailing list is the key asset of a mail order catalog business. You can have the greatest products, the best prices, and the most beautiful catalog—but they're all for naught if you don't have the right mailing list.

Just a list of names doesn't mean much. In any given universe, fewer than half of the people are likely to buy from *any* mail order catalog—and it's too costly to send catalogs to people who won't even consider buying.

You can advertise to get catalog requests—but that's costly. You can rent the use of others' lists of catalog buyers—but so can everyone else. But if you have exclusive access to a list of people who are known to desire the kinds of products you plan to sell and have already demonstrated their willingness to buy sight unseen from catalogs, you are already a step ahead of potential competition.

Facilities

Do you already have facilities to process orders, make shipments quickly, maintain computerized files, and provide efficient customer service . . . or do you have to develop such facilities from scratch? Obviously, you have some major economic advantages if you can utilize facilities which require only cost-sharing.

It is important to recognize that successful mail order catalogs are built upon fast turnaround—generally a maximum of 48 hours from the time an order is received until shipments are on their way to the customer. And similar short turnaround is essential for good customer service operations as well.

Will your facilities permit this kind of dedicated service, or will you have to set up completely separate facilities for your mail order catalog?

Staff

Do you have people who know and understand catalog marketing? While you can obtain outside services to perform almost every catalog operation from selection of merchandise through catalog development, order processing, and fulfillment, most successful catalog businesses perform most of their work internally.

Because of the rapid growth of cataloging, there is a severe shortage of experienced personnel. So if you already have an internal staff that can do much of the work, you have a competitive advantage over others.

It is important to recognize that catalog marketing is different from other forms of marketing since you have to deal with customers sight unseen. And that requires very special skills. Designers and writers, for example, may be the world's best when it comes to working within other marketing disciplines, but lack the knowledge of how to create a mail order catalog which produces profitable response.

Or perhaps your advertising agency handles your regular advertising with outstanding results. Unfortunately, however, few agencies have experienced catalog personnel on their staffs, and when they try to apply the techniques which work well for space advertising and other types of direct mail to catalog creation and production, they most often end up with a catalog which fails to win out against competition.

You may not have built-in strengths in all five of these essential areas—but it is recommended you have some advantage over competition in at least three of them if you hope to have a real chance to become an important entry in today's competitive catalog world.

There are three other factors which many people consider even more important—and they certainly are of extreme importance—but if you are lacking in strength in the five factors just mentioned, strengths in these three are not likely to overcome your deficiencies.

Money

Starting a new catalog requires a lot of money. You can't just create a simple catalog, send it to a few thousand addresses, and start making money right away. It takes a minimum of three years just to know if you have a viable catalog or not.

It takes a year to do the initial testing. To determine the right product mix . . . to find out which lists are most likely to respond ... to work out the bugs in order entry, packaging, shipping, and customer service.

Then, the second year, you are ready to go to work to capture as many first-time buyers as possible. But it takes a third year to determine the most important factor you'll need to know to properly evaluate your future catalog potential—how many of those first-time buyers are willing to buy from you again.

So you'll need financial backing to provide support for at least three years while you're waiting to find out if you really have a viable catalog. Hopefully, there will be some income rolling in during those three years, but if you're counting on catalog income to pay the bills you probably won't have nearly enough to accomplish the all-important task of developing a substantial customer base.

There's a basic formula to cataloging:

PROSPECTS = COSTS

CUSTOMERS = PROFITS

In other words, you *invest* money to attract first-time buyers and produce *profits* by selling to your established customers. If you are making money from mailing to prospects, chances are you are not mailing enough catalogs.

As a general rule, customers will respond three to five times more readily to catalogs than will even good lists of prospects who have never bought from you before. So it's important to develop a list of your own catalog customers just as soon as possible. And that takes lots of money.

Bright Idea

Many think all it takes to be successful in the catalog field is to come up with a bright idea. Unfortunately, what seems to be your bright idea is probably something that has already been tried before and found unprofitable. You think it's a bright idea because you don't see it being used by anyone else. But there are a lot of truly bright people in catalog marketing, and they've already evaluated thousands of seemingly bright ideas—and have already market-tested many of them. You don't see them being used because they failed careful evaluation or testing.

A few years ago, I was quoted in a *Time* magazine article about catalogs. As a result, I got dozens of phone calls—many of them from people who thought they had just come up with a bright idea for a new catalog. Interestingly, over half of them had the same idea. They would go to leading stores in the United States or throughout the world and have each store pick out its best product; then these products would be featured in a single catalog, and the orders would be fulfilled by each of the stores. If there ever was an idea that has been tried over and over again—and always without success—this was it. But, because my callers hadn't seen such a catalog, they thought they had hit on the greatest idea since L.L. Bean started selling Maine Hunting Boots.

If you think you have a bright idea, spend lots of time evaluating why other catalog marketers aren't already doing just what you're thinking about doing.

Bright ideas are important. The most successful catalogs involve a lot of bright ideas. But, even if you have come up with a truly new and unique idea, you still need strength in the other areas already mentioned.

Desire

Then there's the matter of really wanting to be in the catalog business. It takes a lot of dedicated effort to create and maintain a successful catalog business. It won't succeed if you fight it all the way.

That is what's happened to a lot of retailers who have taken a stab at producing mail order catalogs. For years, mail order has been considered "the enemy" by retailers. So it's like joining the enemy camp when they decide they had better see if they can't expand their business by mailing out direct response catalogs. Most often, the management of these retail stores, deep down, doesn't really have a desire to be in the catalog business, and as a result, it doesn't provide the support those responsible for the catalogs need to be able to succeed.

Ten Ways to Win... or Lose... In Today's Highly Competitive Catalog World

3

Everyone, it seems, wants to get into the catalog business. Big companies, small companies, entrepreneurs, venture capitalists, get-rich-quick dreamers and little old ladies whom everyone has told, "You have such great gift ideas, you should start your own catalog."

They may have been reading some of the many articles in newspapers and magazines about "the wonderful world of catalogs." All too often, these articles concentrate on the rags-to-riches stories of people such as Lillian Katz, who started the Lillian Vernon catalog on her kitchen table, or Richard Thalheimer, who started his The Sharper Image catalog by placing a few ads in magazines to sell joggers' watches.

Or the young girl out in Podunk who created a brand-new widget, added a few interesting products from her father's general store, told about them in a simple little catalog she sent to 1,000 personal friends, and found her mailbox filled with so many orders she had to hire all of the neighborhood kids to help her pack the boxes and cart them off to the local post office.

Nice scenario. Except it fails to mention the whole thing cost her twice as much as the income it generated, and she's now working as a waitress in a local diner to raise the funds to pay off the loan her uncle gave her to help launch her on her way to fame and fortune in "the wonderful world of catalogs."

There *are* many opportunities to create successful new catalogs today. And there will be increased opportunities tomorrow. But the successes will be the result of hard work and application of the basic principles of catalog marketing, not just of someone's bright idea and the desire to turn that idea into a catalog business.

What constitutes the major elements of success and failure in the catalog field? For a national catalog conference, I analyzed more than 1,000 mail order catalogs, both successes and failures, and was able to identify 10 basic factors that spell the difference between success and failure.

The Right Thinking

One of the key things you find in every successful mail order catalog is a blending of two important attitudes. First of all, there is an entrepreneurial spirit throughout the entire organization. There's an openness to new ideas, a willingness to explore previously uncharted avenues of opportunity. Although it's difficult to describe in concrete terms, there's a sense of adventure that continues long after a catalog has been established.

It's also important to have direct marketing thinking, a recognition that you're dealing with people who have never met you face to face and have to trust you when you promise to fill their orders.

Many new catalogs are started by entrepreneurs whose past experience has been in retailing. And they continue to think like retailers. But dealing with a sight-unseen audience is far different from dealing with the same kinds of people face to face. Successful cataloging calls for different product selection and presentation. It forces you to counteract your inability to deal directly with customer questions and concerns at the moment they arise by supplying answers in advance.

And once you've attracted new customers, direct marketing thinking is an absolute must. Bill Baker of Baldwin-Cooke, a successful business-to-business catalog, talks about the importance of "hugging your customers." That's direct marketing thinking.

A Unique Selling Position

One element that distinguishes all of the successful mail order catalogs is that they've been able to establish a USP—a unique selling position that distinguishes them from other catalogs in the marketplace. Every cataloger must battle for a share of the consumer's mind, attempting to be remembered as *the* source from which to buy specific kinds of products.

Far too often, a new catalog tries to capitalize on the success of existing catalogs by copying their product selection, presentation techniques, list selections, and/or copy style. But in all of those 1,000 catalogs I studied, I was unable to find a single example of a "copycat" catalog that did any more than simply survive. Not one of them was able to win out over the catalogs it had copied, particularly if it copied catalogs that had already gained a share of customers' minds with clearly recognized unique selling positions.

To gain a share of mind, a catalog should be number one in something *meaningful* to its customers. Everyone, for example, claims to have quality products. There's nothing unique in that. But catalogs that have been able to communicate *how* their products (or services or prices or offers) are superior to those of others manage to survive and grow.

There are many different ways to establish a unique selling position for a catalog. Here are some examples.

The Sharper Image

Dozens of catalogs have tried to copy the distinctive character of the successful The Sharper Image catalog. But all have failed to achieve Richard Thalheimer's unique blending of innovative products, distinctive layout, very descriptive copy, and—the key element in creat-

Figure 3-1
Creating a Unique Selling Position

Richard Thalheimer created a unique selling position for The Sharper Image catalog through distinctive layout style, extensive use of high chroma colors in photographs, and relatively long narrative copy. Copyright © The Sharper Image. Used with permission.

ing a USP for The Sharper Image—unique photography, with original blue and magenta lighting. In spite of all of the attempts by others to be a The Sharper Image copycat, there's no question which is The Sharper Image catalog in any catalog file.

Neiman-Marcus

About 30 years ago, the great Dallas department store Neiman-Marcus hit upon a USP which has made its annual Christmas mail order catalogs the most eagerly awaited—and best remembered—of the thousands of gift catalogs which bombard catalog buyers each fall. It's the annual His & Hers gift.

The idea is so powerful it receives annual coverage by newspapers, magazines, radio, and television (and was even the subject of a full book by Stanley Marcus). Reporters spend weeks trying to get a scoop on what will be featured in each year's Neiman-Marcus Christmas catalog . . . and it's always the first catalog getting attention when it arrives in customers' mailboxes (and probably the best remembered of all gift catalogs that go into the catalog file). It's also the most often stolen of all catalogs, according to postal authorities in Chicago (which led Neiman-Marcus to start sending its Christmas catalogs in plain envelopes—a technique which normally results in reduced response for almost all other catalogs).

Among the clever His & Hers gifts Neiman-Marcus has offered have been airplanes, Chinese junks, hot air balloons, camels, Egyptian mummy cases (one of which arrived in the United States with a mummy still inside), hovercrafts, buffalos, dirigibles, ostriches, robots . . . and, for that couple who already has everything, His & Hers bombproof vaults in the Utah mountains.

Quill Corporation

At the other end of the scale is one of the most successful of all business-to-business catalogs. Quill's USP is discount prices—office supplies at prices substantially below those paid in the typical store. So all of Quill's presentations—and it mails catalogs of one kind or another several times each month—put primary emphasis on the amount of money you can save by buying from Quill.

No fancy layouts . . . big, bold prices printed in red . . . dotted line borders around special offers . . . special "blasts" to highlight the amount which can be saved . . . etc. Quill doesn't ignore such important marketing factors as its no-risk guarantee, speedy shipments, outstanding customer service, and helpful advice. But these are given a backseat to its USP of low prices.

Smithsonian

Products with a direct connection to something on exhibit in the various museums and galleries of the Smithsonian Institution provide a distinctive USP for the catalogs distributed by America's "national attic." There's an obvious relationship between each item in every catalog and the Smithsonian itself.

Copy in a typical catalog explains:

> **On these pages you'll find handsome reproductions, adaptations and other beautiful and useful items that reflect the rich diversity of the Smithsonian. As the world's largest complex of museums, art galleries and research facilities, it encompasses the vast and varied elements of America's cultural, social, scientific and artistic heritage.**
>
> **Historical and educational information is provided on a Smithsonian card included with most products or on our packaging. All income from our catalogue supports our chartered educational purposes and activities.**

To enhance this USP, every item carries two prices—a regular price and a special price for Smithsonian members.

Sheplers

Sheplers describes itself as "The World's Largest Western Catalog," and to maintain that USP, this Wichita, Kansas, company avoids the

Figure 3-2
No Frills

Discount prices are the unique selling position for Quill. Major emphasis is given to the amount of money which can be saved by ordering office supples from Quill Corporation. Copyright © Quill. Used with permission.

Figure 3-3
Maintaining a Consistent Image

Sheplers' USP is "The World's Largest Western Catalog." To maintain this image, it limits its product selection to items with a direct connection to "The West" and chooses models who reflect that image. Copyright © Sheplers. Used with permission.

temptation to include items in its catalog which its customers might buy but which have no obvious Western orientation.

In keeping with the Western feel of its catalog, Sheplers avoids using models who might appear in high fashion catalogs. Instead, Sheplers' models look as though they were found down in the corral or on a Nashville country and western show. And you'll find a lot of straw and weathered wood in the settings used for photography.

Breck's

Breck's, the largest supplier of Dutch bulbs for American gardeners, uses a "Direct from Holland" theme as its USP. Copy emphasizes the fact that Breck's has a full-time staff in Holland that selects bulbs for shipment to America:

> **Ordering from Breck's is like having your own personal buying agent right in Holland. Breck's staff of experts spends the entire year in Holland selecting fine Dutch bulbs guaranteed to grow and bloom in American gardens—a job we've been doing successfully since 1818.**

To support this special USP, Breck's frequently includes photos of Holland in its catalogs and utilizes design techniques to give the catalog a "Dutch look."

L.L. Bean

America's largest specialty catalog, L.L. Bean, is just about as well known throughout the country as Sears. And sticking with a clearly defined USP has helped it maintain a loyal customer audience for many years.

L.L. Bean catalogs have a distinctive appearance—one which has gradually changed from year to year, but with never a question that an old friend has arrived each time a new L.L. Bean catalog arrives in a customer's mailbox. This "not quite old-fashioned, but not quite modern" design enhances Bean's established reputation as a reliable supplier of quality items for outdoor use. Copy frequently is used to help maintain this image. A typical example follows:

> **A "blown seam" or blister can ruin an otherwise enjoyable trip into the wilderness. Durable, proper fitting footwear is essential for any outdoor activity. Our Product Research and Testing Department recently conducted an extensive hiking boot testing program, covering a wide range of hiking footwear styles.**
>
> **Experienced backpackers on our staff as well as hikers and mountaineers from Alaska to the Swiss Alps fully tested these boots in the field. Footwear quality criteria included construction, support, traction, durabil-**

ity and, most importantly, proper fit. **The hiking boots in this catalog were evaluated and judged to provide excellent performance in all categories by our testers. To help you determine the boots that will best meet your outdoor needs, we have listed recommended uses with each boot.**

These are just a few examples of how a handful of American catalogs have been able to establish a unique selling position. The key thing is to find something someone else isn't doing and then use that as a starting point for building a convincing USP.

Involvement of Management

Another factor that distinguishes the winners from the losers is the extent to which top management is involved in catalog operations. Over the years, I've had contact with thousands of different catalog organizations, and I'm still amazed by the degree to which everyone, from the CEO down, is involved in the day-to-day operations of every profitable catalog.

If you like to delegate and then go fishing, the catalog business is not for you.

If you are easily bored by mailing lists, product selection, looking at press proofs, checking the shipping line to see that products are being packed with care, analyzing sales printouts line by line, handling difficult customer service situations, and all the other minutiae essential to a catalog business, why not consider acquiring a McDonald's franchise?

When you take a look at some of the catalog failures, you discover they were started as a hobby, rather than as a business. Someone probably thought it would be great fun to make the rounds of trade shows and vendors to pick products and to work with the artists and writers to create a beautiful catalog, then leave the nitty-gritty to hired hands. It just doesn't work that way.

Another reason for several of the failures was the catalogers' tendency to go on an ego trip. As soon as their catalogs got a little applause, they hired press agents and spent more of their time running around giving speeches and reading their press clippings. Meanwhile, their businesses had to run themselves.

In this same vein, there's all too often a desire to start changing things once they become old hat. Successful catalogers, however, recognize that it's what they're doing *now* that's attracting their customers.

As pointed out previously, the basic formula of catalog marketing is that Prospects = Costs; Customers = Profits. In other words,

TEN WAYS TO WIN...OR LOSE.../3

**Figure 3-4
Maintaining a Reputation**

L. L. Bean knows how to maintain a loyal customer base. While Bean has updated its catalog design from year to year, there's always a touch of "Down East." Copyright © L. L. Bean. Used with permission.

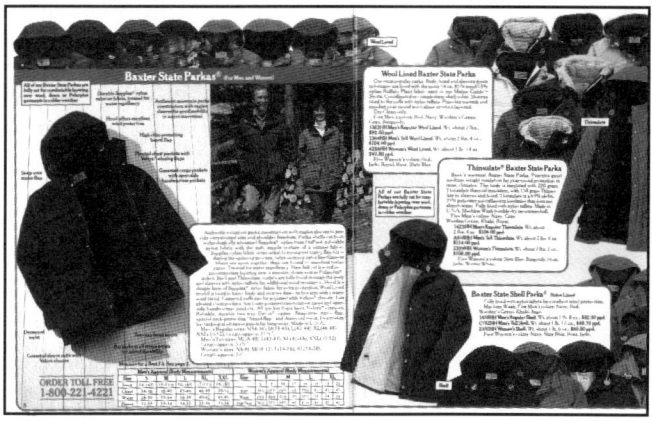

you spend money (sometimes far more than you get back) to make a prospect buy from you for the first time. Profits come when you can go back to satisfied customers and get them to buy again and again. When you change too much, you turn your old customers into prospects again. Instead of an "old friend" coming to call, the revised catalog is a "stranger," and you have to resell your customers on buying from you. That costs money and is a drain on profits.

Successful catalog marketers are willing to stick with what's working, even when it is boring to them. Of course, when what you're doing isn't working anymore, it's important to change. But don't change simply for change's sake alone.

Long-Range Strategy

There are few instant successes in the catalog field. As mentioned previously, you should allow at least three years before you can fully evaluate the potential of a new catalog.

And since you invest to bring a new customer into the fold, it takes time to make back those dollars that have been invested. While some catalog marketers work on five- or ten-year plans, most seem more comfortable working on a three-year basis.

One of the terms you hear over and over again in the catalog field is "the lifetime value of a customer." This represents the amount of profit you can expect an individual customer to generate while remaining an active buyer. My suggestion is that you make such calculations on a three-year basis. This involves considering the gross profits you can reasonably expect from the merchandise the customer is likely to purchase from you during that time, less the costs of catalogs you will be sending to the customer during that period. Once you know that figure, you can make a reasonable judgment about how much can be spent to bring an individual from a list of prospects onto your customer file.

One of the problems many retailers have faced when they've tried to join the catalog revolution is an unwillingness to establish a separate catalog operation. They have someone create a mail order catalog, but they fail to back up the catalog with dedicated merchandise, special fulfillment, and customer services, as well as a way to measure its true effectiveness. When they don't immediately find extra black ink at the bottom of their financial statements, they assume the catalog is a failure. Actually, the failure was a lack of direct marketing thinking, coupled with the absence of long-range strategy.

A Willingness to Gamble

Len Carlson, who created the highly successful Sunset House catalog many years ago, notes that he and his contemporaries succeeded by using the "sweaty palms method." They knew that not every product they selected was going to sell and that many of the new promotional devices they dreamed up wouldn't work. But they were willing to gamble.

Although we live in an age when highly complex research and evaluation programs are what drive many of the most successful companies in the *Fortune* 1,000, the majority of successful catalogs are driven by an old-fashioned gambler's instinct. This, of course, goes hand-in-glove with entrepreneurial thinking. I've read the books and listened to the speeches about the wonders of all kinds of predictive prepromotion research and don't doubt their value in the broad world of commerce. But I can't overlook the simple fact that the vast majority of profitable mail order catalogs continue to operate primarily by the "sweaty palms method."

Expecting losers is a part of the game. The successful catalogers average between 20 and 33 percent losers among the products included in each catalog. They don't cry over them. They just eliminate them from the next catalog and spend their time seeking more products like the winning catalog items.

And they know you have to give new products a try or you'll just find yourself standing still. You expect to have losers and simply accept them as one of the elements of a successful catalog business.

But if you've spent your life in a business where *any* loser is a symbol of failure, it's difficult to change clothes and become a gambler. Yet a catalog of nothing but "safe" products is most often a dull catalog—and dull catalogs are most often unprofitable catalogs.

Trying to mix a philosophy which accommodates gambling into a highly structured business is difficult at best. It's like having an ugly duckling in the flock. Rather than make adjustments to accommodate the misfit, it's easier just to abandon him or find a foster home. This may explain why so many of America's large corporations that tried catalogs later sold them to someone else or simply abandoned them, even though they may have proved profitable.

The Right Product Selection

Just because you like certain products, and just because there are products people are buying from someone else, doesn't mean they're the right items for your catalog. What's important is that your audience wants to buy those products from *you*. That's something successful catalogers fully understand.

A catalog is not primarily a medium for changing needs into wants or for convincing people they should want to buy specific products from you. Every catalog has an authority level that communicates to an audience that it is the right source for certain products. Making sure all of its products fit within that authority level leads to a stronger catalog, one positioned to lead customers to think first of that catalog as the logical source for specific kinds of products.

Listening to customers is a way of life for the successful cataloger. The secret is to let your customers decide which products your catalog should carry. An important rule: Trade on your winners and say good-bye to your losers.

Every catalog, then, becomes a product testing vehicle. If your customers tell you they don't want to buy a new product from you or don't want you to continue to carry an older product, listen carefully. Sales records tell no fibs.

It's almost impossible to take a loser (a product your customers have failed to support with their orders) and turn it into a winner. You may be able to turn a marginal loser into a marginal winner by presenting it in a different way. But when you have an out-and-out loser, call in the undertaker!

When you have a winner, though, you may be able to make it an even bigger winner by new presentation. Or you can boost sales in future catalogs by presenting more products like those your customers have told you they really want to buy from you.

**Figure 3-5
Exclusive Products**

Lillian Vernon has survived and grown when most novelty merchandise catalogs (once the largest of all specialty catalog categories) have disappeared. One reason: page after page of exclusive products. Copyright © Lillian Vernon. Used with permission.

© COPYRIGHT 1991 DARTNELL CORPORATION

Successful catalogers follow a set of very simple but important guidelines in choosing products for their catalogs. They try, where possible, to feature "exclusive" products. An exclusive may be only marginally different from similar products found elsewhere, but even a little difference can increase sales. Perhaps you can supply the product in different packaging, in a different color, with your own special identification, in a unique combination with other products, at a different price point, or in some other way that permits you to say it's exclusive with you. Such identification suggests to the buyer, "Don't look elsewhere. If you want this product as we have presented it, it's available only from us."

It's also important that all products fit your catalog's image. Products that don't seem to fit confuse the customer. And confused customers usually turn to another source to do their buying.

The Importance of Mailing Lists

The cornerstone of any direct marketing business is the mailing list. But not just any mailing list. The *right* mailing list.

Catalog buyers are different from other buyers. Unlike retail buyers, they must visualize, because they can't touch and feel the actual merchandise. A good catalog list is heavy on "visualizers."

Also, contrary to response to solo mailings, most catalog purchases are not made on an impulse basis. When a catalog is received, it is given an editorial reading. Consumers see what's new, what's different, what will fulfill their dreams. While some buying is done at that time, their favorite catalogs are saved until a special buying occasion arises. Thus a good catalog list is heavy on "savers."

Most mail order buyers tend to do the bulk of their buying in one of three categories, which parallel the Good, Better, Best product presentation used for many years by Sears. The Good buyer is always looking for a bargain. The Better buyer wants the best combination of price and value. And then there are the Best buyers, who are always looking for something a little bit better than their neighbors have. Thus a good catalog list is composed of buyers in the right "value" category for your products.

There's also the matter of lifestyle. The right list for your catalog will have consumers whose lifestyle is most closely related to the products you offer.

Winning catalogers spend considerable time developing lists with just the right combination of visualizers-savers-value-lifestyle. This often means doing something more than simply renting a lot of lists from other catalog mailers. The most successful companies have a whole host of list development techniques that they use regularly to keep their customer files active and growing.

Another element in the success of the winners is the amount of attention they pay to list segmentation. They recognize that no list is merely a single list, but contains categories and subcategories. And each of those segments responds differently to various promotions. By carefully analyzing each category (including everything from ZIP Codes and original sources to buying patterns and types of products bought), the winning catalogers are able to tailor mailings to true prospects and eliminate others, thus keeping mailing costs to a minimum and profits to a maximum.

An Open-Door Organization

The flow of ideas throughout a catalog operation is vital to its success. Too often, companies inhibit new ideas by an attitude that says, in effect, "We're already better than anyone else" or "We can do no wrong" or "It's company policy" or "We tried it before and it didn't work." Even if you bring in new management at the top and young hard-chargers at the bottom, if there are still contented old-timers in the center, their complacency can thwart any innovative change in the company.

This has been especially true in established organizations, such as retailers and package goods companies that have tried to integrate catalog selling into their marketing mix. If everything that might make a catalog work is perceived as a threat by entrenched middle management, the catalog has a much smaller chance of success.

A classic example of how closed minds can kill a catalog operation is what happened to the catalog that really started America's love of mail order buying—Montgomery Ward.

I can well remember being on a program with a Ward's executive at the first Retail Advertising Conference in Chicago back in the early fifties. Ward's speaker gave a glowing report about the manual the company had created. It spelled out exactly how each product should be presented on the pages of Ward's catalogs.

"As a result," he said, "we have been able to create the most beautiful catalog in the world. The only thing we haven't been able to understand is how Sears, with a catalog just a couple steps away from the outhouse, is able to outsell us."

A former Sears man in the audience had a quick answer. "Sears," he said, "is smart enough to know the customer is in the outhouse when he's reading it."

The answer got a laugh—but it also pinpointed one of the big differences between Ward and Sears. Ward was internally oriented, while Sears was externally oriented.

© COPYRIGHT 1991 DARTNELL CORPORATION

The catalog manual was just one of the legacies of long-time chairman Sewell Avery, who established many policies in the World War II era that prevented Ward from keeping pace with the times and preparing for the future.

Eventually Avery was deposed, and Ward brought in top management people from the outside and added some young hard-chargers to the organization. But right there in the middle was what insiders often called the "Sewell Avery Dam." The middle management people Avery left behind had become so imbued with the idea that Ward's could do no wrong, they refused to permit new ideas to move up or down the organization.

No input of money—first from Container Corporation of America and then from Mobil—could provide enough grease to get those rusty wheels moving.

Montgomery Ward wasn't the only catalog that failed due to closed doors and closed minds. Much the same thing has happened in dozens of other companies. During the sixties and seventies, a host of package goods companies decided to get into the mail order catalog field by either acquiring established mail order catalogs or starting their own. Then, toward the end of the eighties, almost all of them decided to get out of the catalog business.

Why the sudden change? I'm convinced it was primarily a matter of conflict in personalities. Most major corporations have a rigid staff-and-line structure. They operate with committees, which most often move slowly and carefully to protect individuals from having to take direct responsibility for specific decisions. These slow-moving committees also tend to create a barrier which closes the door on input from others—unless they prepare detailed reports which can be studied and discussed by a committee.

But successful mail order catalogs are more often highly entrepreneurial businesses where everyone's input on an informal basis is welcomed and quick decisions are common.

The fast-moving entrepreneur, however, is a bastard child in the typical corporate structure. And he is told to step aside and await an eventual decision by the committee.

Catalog-Oriented Personnel and Facilities

It's important to recognize that catalog selling requires special talent and special facilities. It's extremely difficult to try to mix orientations.

Creative personnel who are a whiz at other forms of advertising often fail when it comes to producing a good catalog. Usually they're oriented to single messages that have to meet other single messages head-on and compete for attention and response. A good catalog, on the other hand, requires an intelligent combination of attention-getting copy and design and the blending of messages, so that every item in the catalog has an equal opportunity to do its selling job.

Merchandise buyers are often in competition with other merchandise buyers, since many organizations measure their buyers' performance on a comparative basis. In a catalog, however, teamwork is important. If one department "steals sales" from another department, the winners don't get brownie points. They get fired. The total must be more important than the parts.

And the "merchant"—the buyer—must take a back seat to the "merchandiser." Merchants are responsible for locating new products with a lot of potential. But their role stops at that point, and the merchandisers—those whose job it is to figure out the best merchandise mix and how to present it to the catalog audience—take over. This area alone constitutes one of the major differences between successful catalog companies and those that have fallen by the wayside.

Facilities, too, must be catalog-oriented. Manufacturers who are used to shipping by the dozen or gross can seldom make the transition to picking and packing items one by one. Retailers who have developed efficient systems for local deliveries are sometimes at a loss when it comes to preparing merchandise for economical shipment all over the country. Telephone order systems designed to handle one item at a time get snarled with multiple-item orders. Customer service that has been managed effectively by each department falls apart when it has to be centralized. Credit clearance systems that operated routinely under previous conditions go haywire when they have to clear orders quickly from all over the country and also catch rip-off artists who have a whole host of tricks up their sleeves. Receiving departments that had to deal with only a handful of returns coming back in the original cartons, with all shipping documents intact, are overwhelmed when they start receiving merchandise returned in a grocery store bag, with nothing other than a return address on the back of the package. Computers that were efficient in handling financial records become ineffective when they have to cope with mailing lists.

And so it goes throughout an organization that decides to produce a new mail order catalog. Facilities and staff must become catalog-oriented, in response to the very different requirements of catalog selling, for the catalog to be a winner.

Emphasis on the Back End

Far too few new catalogers recognize the importance of all that happens *after* the catalogs go to the post office. But that's where the real successes are made and where the biggest failures occur.

Unfortunately, too many organizations fail to recognize that every contact with a customer is a *marketing* opportunity. Often everything that occurs after the catalogs are mailed becomes the responsibility of those departments within a company that may consider customers "their enemy." Operational personnel often believe their operations would run more efficiently if they didn't have to deal with "difficult customers." Financial people often find their lives complicated by customers who do things that lead to unbalanced books. Data processing departments find that customers create problems for their computers. The efforts of such people are measured on how efficiently they run their departments, so they strive to get *rid* of customers who reduce department efficiency.

I'm not suggesting that marketing management should be in charge of everything in a company, but "marketing thinking" must be instilled throughout the entire organization of a catalog marketer. The successful catalogers develop systems that enable marketers to monitor every point of customer contact.

While it may be operationally efficient to batch orders and level out peaks and valleys, one of the key elements in catalog selling is instant response. As a general rule, any customer request—be it an order or an inquiry—should be turned around within 48 hours. Impossible, say the losers. Absolutely necessary, say the winners—many believing that even 48 hours is too long.

Catalog winners add a marketing touch to every package. There is no better time to sell customers on wanting to buy from you again than at the moment they've just received one of your packages. All of the little things that help make opening that package an enjoyable event tend to build customer loyalty and, therefore, future profits. Among the losers were many who simply turned this important responsibility over to low-paid shipping clerks, while the marketing people went on to concentrate on their next catalog.

The winning catalogs never stop selling. They look for every opportunity to offer something new and exciting to their customers, such as package inserts, statement enclosures, or solo mailings between catalogs. And they constantly recognize the value of the telephone in building a personal relationship with customers. They remember that "hugging customers" is important.

Investing for Customers: Building and Maintaining A Database for Your Catalog

4

Database vs. Mailing List

The hot word in catalog marketing these days is *database*. While, in most cases, catalog marketers simply use *database* as a synonym for *mailing list* (you get a better salary if you say you're working on a database than you would get if you only worked on a mailing list), there is a whole new science in creating a true database for a catalog.

Even though the term *database* came with the use of computers for list segmentation, catalog marketers have long been collecting and recording various pieces of information to help identify the ways in which one group of customers is different from another group. Long before computers, catalog marketers were taking advantage of the 60 notches they could put on the edges of Addressograph plates to record customer information. And then there were the old McBee Keysort cards with holes which could be notched so when you inserted a rod through a particular hole, certain cards would fall off the rod because that hole had been notched.

These and other similar methods provided a start for catalog list segmentation. But because they required time consuming manual operations, they could only be used in a limited way and most frequently were used only by large mailers. And, with just a few exceptions, the information recorded came only from internal records and the use of external overlays was impractical.

Today, progressive catalog marketers have developed extensive databases which not only contain detailed information about each customer but also take advantage of the thousands of different external databases. These external databases can be used as overlays to make sure that catalogs are mailed to all of the best prospects and, perhaps more importantly, to make sure that those not likely to buy are eliminated from catalog mailings.

Basic Mailing List Information

The first information about customers which is included on a catalog database is the basic information found on regular mailing lists.

Name

First of all, of course, is the customer's name. The field used for the name should be long enough to include the full name and any desirable prefixes and suffixes. Abbreviating a customer's name tends to destroy any semblance of a personal relationship, which is an important part of maintaining good customer relations.

While prefixes are no longer as important as they may have been in years past, they may be very important if you plan to use any personalization in special messages added to the catalog. For many years, mailers simply used either a male (Mr.) or female (Ms.) prefix. Unfortunately, women's rights advocates came along and "stole" the Ms. prefix from the mailing list field and it no longer is a "safe," noncontroversial female prefix. Although many women today have strong objections to being addressed as "Ms.," many others prefer it.

In most cases, the easiest solution is simply to eliminate the use of prefixes. But, if you're planning to use personalization, it may be necessary to ask your customers to tell you which prefix they prefer to have you use.

Address

The address entry may include multiple addresses. The primary address will normally be the postal address for mail delivery. A secondary address often is a UPS shipping address which varies from the postal delivery address. In addition, there may be separate ship to/bill to addresses.

Postal Code

While the ZIP Code is an integral part of the address, it may be maintained separately for list segmentation purposes.

Phone Number

It has become increasingly common to include telephone numbers in a customer database. In addition to their value for telemarketing and customer service follow-ups, telephone numbers can help with credit screening. Many catalogers have discovered that customers who volunteer their telephone numbers when requested on order forms seldom turn out to be rip-offs. Therefore, credit limits can be increased for these customers, reducing costs of credit screening.

Sex

Many catalog marketers do what is called "sexing a list"—identifying whether a customer is male or female. This is one of the most frequent segmentation factors when selecting lists for catalog mailings. Included in this segmentation category also may be the specific prefix for which the customer has indicated preference: Mr., Ms., Mrs., Miss, Dr. While mailing addresses will not necessarily include a prefix, this detail can be important if personalized messages are used for catalog wraps or enclosures.

Age Group

While few catalog marketers identify the actual age of a customer in their data files, they often enter an "age group" identifier.

Mail Preference

This entry is an absolute must for today's catalog marketers. It identifies those who have requested that they be excluded from mailings and/or that their names be eliminated before a list is rented to others. When such requests have been received from customers, it is essential to suppress such names before mailings are made to rented lists. In addition, many catalog marketers utilize the Mail Preference Service (MPS) list developed by the Direct Marketing Association. This includes the names of those who have notified DMA they wish to be excluded from all advertising mailings. (The MPS list also includes those who have asked to receive more advertising mail—particularly catalogs.)

Business, Professional & Industrial Lists

Business-to-business catalog marketers normally carry additional mailing list information in their databases. The entries, of course, vary depending on the nature of the products being sold and the types of audiences to whom the catalogs will be sent.

Company Name

This most often is the name by which the company is identified in telephone and other directories.

Company Address

In some cases this will differ from the address being used for addressing catalogs to individuals (such as their home addresses). If so, it is usually carried in the database as an additional entry.

The majority of business-to-business catalog marketers prefer to send catalogs to an individual's business address. As a general rule, it is best for mailings to reach recipients in the environment where they will normally be "thinking about" the products being promoted.

Headquarters/Branch

A common database entry is to indicate whether the company address represents the company's headquarters or a branch location.

Credit Rating

A basic business-to-business database entry is often the credit rating of the company involved. While this may be internally generated, it more often comes from one of the credit reporting services such as Dun & Bradstreet.

Standard Industrial Classification

The U. S. Government has established a series of Standard Industrial Classification (SIC) numbers which are used to identify the basic business of a company. The majority of business-to-business catalog marketers include at least a primary SIC number for each of its customers—and many also include secondary SIC numbers. Since most business and industrial databases are organized by these SIC numbers, including them on a business-to-business catalog database makes it easier to utilize external overlays when making list selections for catalog mailings.

Bill To/Ship To

Since many companies require different billing and shipping addresses than those used for catalog mailings, it is important to capture this information on the database.

Company Size

The size of a company is often a determining factor in developing a business-to-business catalog mailing list, so at least one of three basic size identifiers is included in the database.

- *Personnel Size*—the number of employees.
- *Sales Size*—the annual sales volume of the company.
- *Facility Size*—the number of square feet or some other comparative measure of a company's offices, warehouses, factories, or other facilities.

In addition to information about each company, a business-to-business database often contains details about the role of a given individual on the catalog list.

Title. The title given to the position an individual holds is important because it generally is more permanent than the person who carries that title at any given moment. In some cases this is listed first when addressing catalogs to encourage mailroom personnel to deliver it to the right office, even if the individual whose name is on the list is no longer there.

Function. In addition to job titles, business-to-business databases often include a "function" entry. Titles can often be misleading. Consider, for example, "Director of Communications." What does it mean? In some companies it may be someone in the personnel department or, perhaps, a public relations director. In other companies, it may be used to designate the advertising or sales promotion manager. In still other companies, it may be someone in charge of telephone equipment. By having a function identifier for each name on the list, it's much easier to make sure you're sending your catalogs to those who will be interested in the products you have to offer.

Purchasing Responsibility. In many business and industrial companies, it's important to get catalogs into the hands of multiple individuals. These generally fall into three basic groups, and the data file should identify which part of the buying process each individual represents:

- *Specifier.* These are the people who make the initial decision to buy a product and who frequently specify the source from which it should be bought. Most often if an item costs $50.00 or less, the specifier, alone, is involved in the purchase.
- *Approver.* As the cost of an item increases, there often are additional individuals in a company who must approve a purchase. The number of "approvers" tends to increase as costs increase. The most common "breaking points" are $50.00, $100.00, $500.00, $1,000.00 and $5,000.00. (Which, of course, explains why so many catalog marketers purposely set their prices just below one of these "breaking points.") While many of those on the approval ladder may not be interested in catalogs, it's important to direct promotions to them so they will be less likely to suggest a different vendor.
- *Buyer.* In many companies, someone other than the specifier may

actually do the ordering. It may be the office manager, a purchasing agent or someone else. Most often, these actual buyers maintain separate catalog files and, thus, it is important to include them on catalog mailing lists.

Creating a Customer Profile

The first step in building a catalog database which goes beyond just basic mailing list information is to create a profile of existing customers. While some companies include hundreds of different bits of information in their customer databases, most hold this information to a more manageable number of categories.

First Order Information

Create Date. The first piece of information usually entered into a customer database is the so-called "create date"—the date on which the name originally entered the file.

Source. Next comes the "source"—where the name came from. This may be the mailing list which was used for the catalog or another mailing which produced the first order; the particular publication in which an ad appeared that brought a catalog request; the store where the customer first made a purchase, or any other source.

By combining Create Date with Source, you can usually identify the specific offer which first attracted the new customer.

Offer Type. This is the type of introductory offer which converted the prospect into a customer. It indicates whether the response came with a so-called "hard" offer, which involved no special incentives, or a "soft" offer which involved a special discount, premium, sweepstakes or some other inducement. While the combination of Create Date and Source often provides this information, there are times when multiple approaches are being used and it is helpful to carry this information as a separate entry.

Order Method. This is how the customer placed his or her first order—by mail, phone, at a store, through a salesperson, etc. Also included may be whether this was a multiple-item order or a single-item order and whether it was a gift order or a self-purchase.

Payment Method. This refers to how the customer paid for that first order—cash, credit card, house credit, etc.

Interestingly, catalogers have found that customers with a similar profile in these five areas frequently act like one another as long as they remain on the list. Thus, when analysis of a test mailing is made, and you find strong response from a group with a similar first order profile, you can select all others with that same profile and expect to obtain a profitable response by mailing to the entire group.

RFMR Profile

Back in the Depression Days of the thirties, there came a point when Aldens, the big Chicago mail order catalog company, only had enough money to mail catalogs to half of its customers. The big question was which half should get the catalogs. The answer was provided when the late George J. Cullinan developed the RFMR method to profile Aldens' customers. It provided the solution to Aldens' dilemma and has become the basic method of catalog customer profiling ever since. RFMR involves three specific entries which are constantly updated in a customer's profile.

Recency
This indicates the date of the customer's most recent purchase. Customer files frequently are segmented into recency purchase groups of approximately six-month intervals.

Frequency
How many times in a given time period has the customer made purchases? While the time period differs from company to company, the most commonly used period is the past 24 months.

Monetary
This is the total dollar amount of purchases made during the time period used for Frequency. Dividing the number of orders during that period into the total dollars spent, of course, yields the average order amount. Some catalog marketers also include the amount of the largest single order in this data entry.

Ratio
That last "R" in RFMR stands for "Ratio." All of the RFMR entries are not of equal value, so it is necessary to establish a ratio for customer evaluation purposes. When George Cullinan first developed the RFMR formula, he said that the three ingredients in the formula controlled 90 percent of the reasons why customers repeat at a certain sales volume. Of the factors, he said, Frequency accounted for 50 percent; Recency, 35 percent; and Monetary, 15 percent. As other companies started using this customer profiling method, there was a general trend toward giving greatest emphasis

to Monetary. But today, Recency—the so-called "Hot Line" names—most often get extra emphasis. Each catalog, however, has to create its own ratio, based on careful analysis of its own experience.

The use of the RFMR customer profiling method isn't limited just to consumer mail order catalogs. Jerome B. Osherow, a St. Louis direct marketing expert, tells, for example, of a small paint manufacturer who had built up his customer list to 16,000 names over the year, but had a list which was encumbered with names of firms which had bought a few gallons as long as five years before and had never purchased since.

The list was analyzed on an RFMR basis, using a point system. For recency, a customer who purchased within the past year was given 5 points for Recency. If the last purchase was two years ago, the customer got 3 points, then 2 points, 1 point and 0 if a purchase hadn't been made in more than four years. Frequency was handled in a similar way, and a point was awarded for each $100 in sales to establish the Monetary value.

Then the point value for each customer was calculated and all customers with less than 18 points were eliminated from the list. Customers ranging in value from 19–50 points were set up as a "regular" customer list, and customers with point values of above 50 were segregated into a "prime" list. Using this RFMR method, the total list count was reduced to just 6,200.

Other Considerations

Some marketers include the following indicators.

Seasonality. The seasons in which customers have bought in the past is often maintained as an indicator of the potential profitability of future catalog mailings. Some customers simply purchase from a catalog during the Christmas gift-buying season. Others may concentrate their buying in some other season. Thus, this information can help to screen out names with little potential for sales from a given catalog.

Last Transaction. Some catalog marketers include special details about the most recent transaction in their customer data files. This could include record of payment, any change of address, record of correspondence, etc.

Length of Time on the File. Another helpful piece of information to maintain on customer files is the length of time a name has been on the file. While this information may be extracted from the Create Date entry, it is often helpful to carry it as an additional entry.

Lifestyle Indicators

Robert Kestnbaum, often considered the world's foremost authority on catalog list analysis and segmentation, recommends expanding the RFMR formula by the addition of the types of purchases a customer has made. He calls his formula FRAT—Frequency (which he considers the most important element), Recency, Amount of Purchase and Type of Purchase.

Products Purchased

Perhaps the best indicator of customer psychographics—their lifestyles—is the products they buy. What they've bought in the past is usually a good indicator of what they are most likely to buy in the future.

For database purposes, it's usually not practical to record each individual item purchased (although this often is necessary for customer service files). Instead, most catalog marketers record purchases within a relatively limited number of product categories. As a general rule of thumb, about 10 categories are about all that are practical for mailing list segmentation.

Within these categories, however, may be a number of subcategories. For example, there may be a basic category for purchases of men's clothing. But within this category may be subcategories for the "value" of purchases—for example the good, better, best value indicators previously discussed. Or, perhaps, there may be subcategories for outerwear, work clothing, dress clothes, accessories, etc.

Some catalog marketers, however, have developed techniques to utilize hundreds of different product purchase entries. One major department store, for example, has over 2,000 different product categories in its database and regularly uses this information to make specialized mailings. Included, for example, is a record of those who purchase specific brands of designer merchandise. When a new shipment from a special designer of women's clothing is received, "first-opportunity" mailings are made to those who previously have purchased this designer's labels. For high-ticket items, they even offer to send a limousine to pick up the customer and bring her to the local store to inspect the new arrivals. For most catalogers, however, so many product entries are unmanageable.

While a single purchase may be a useful lifestyle indicator, most catalog marketers look for product purchasing patterns. Often a single purchase can be misleading. For example, there may have been the purchase of a baby's crib. This might easily be interpreted as a lifestyle indicator of "a new mother." But it might just as easily be a grandmother or the buyer for a group of co-workers who have purchased a gift for a mother-to-be. But if the crib purchase is followed by other items for a new baby, chances are you have identified someone who will have a continuing interest in products for a young household with a newborn.

A lot of experimental work is being done to use product purchase information to identify different lifestyles. One women's fashion catalog, for example, is keeping track of color preferences, wanting to determine if those who regularly buy warm, cool or neutral colors are different enough from one another to suggest developing separate catalogs for each audience.

In addition to lifestyle information garnered from specific product purchases, the type of offer which has produced sales can also be valuable. Some people respond more readily to "hard sell," while others react best to a softer approach. Some respond to special promotions such as premiums, sweepstakes and discounts, while a KISS approach ("Keep It Simple, Stupid") has greater appeal to others.

Screening Codes

A very important part of any catalog database are special screening codes which are used to suppress certain names to make sure they don't receive future catalogs.

Credit Code

Almost every catalog database has a credit code which identifies customers with a poor record of payments. This may include a number of categories such as no-pay, slow-pay, one-time credit problem, and multiple credit problems etc.

Customer Service Code

Another very important suppression code is an identifier of people who cause "back end" problems. They may score very high on an RFMR scale, but they end up costing the company money, rather than generating profits.

One of the most frequent types of buyers whose names you may want to suppress are those who keep ordering merchandise, but constantly return it for credit, refund or replacement. Such buyers can be a serious drain on profits, particularly for catalogs which offer a "free bonus" with every order.

Then, there are those who constantly bombard customer service personnel with mail or phone calls. While their numbers may be small, the cost of handling their accounts can be enormous. Often, these problem customers are so obvious, customer service personnel can quickly give you their names and addresses without even looking them up.

Another group which can represent losses for a catalog business are those which constantly move from one address to another. Just updating the mailing list and handling forwarding of orders can wipe out any potential profits from their orders.

You might ask, Why not just remove these suppression names from your database? The problem is twofold. First of all, if you take them off the list and can't identify them, they often get right back on the list again. Second, this suppression code is important in deleting unprofitable names from the outside lists you rent.

Overlays

In addition to information on the customer database, catalog marketers often use external databases as overlays in making selections for catalog distribution. Today, there are literally thousands of different external databases available to catalog marketers. Government bodies, for example, offer many different databases which frequently are used for catalog list segmentation. Often the information included on these databases is broken down by five-digit ZIP Codes, which makes them ideal overlays for catalog marketers' databases. The Bureau of Census, for example, offers more than 1,000 different categories of information, all easily extracted in ZIP Code sequence, which are often used by catalog marketers.

Many publishers, mailing list compilers and computer service bureaus have developed special databases which are ideal as catalog database overlays. Typical of the available overlay information used by catalog marketers are:

- Auto Registration Lists
- Organization Membership Rosters
- Product Ownership (from warranty card registrations)
- Family Income Categories
- Education Level
- Type of Dwelling
- Number of Family Members
- National Origin
- Hobby Interests
- Other Demographics
- Other Psychographics

These overlays often include extensive detail for each individual, family or address. When it comes to Type of Dwelling, for example, the external database may include such things as:

- Dwelling Unit Size
- Length of Residence
- Whether the Home Is Owned or Rented
- Home Value
- Age of Dwelling Unit
- Size of Lot
- Style of Home

Postal Code Segmentation

Probably the most common use of outside overlays to select addresses for catalog mailings is what is commonly called "ZIP Deciling." Several organizations offer a special service which enables catalog marketers to analyze response to their previous mailings and then utilize this analysis, on the basis of relative response from different ZIP Codes, to select the geographical areas of greatest potential profitability for future catalog mailings.

Since previous response within any individual five-digit ZIP Code may be insignificant, a technique called "ZIP Clustering" is utilized. This involves creating a profile of each of the approximately 39,000 five-digit ZIP Codes in the U.S. by using information available from the Bureau of Census and other sources. Then, ZIP Codes with similar profiles are clustered and previous response is analyzed cluster-by-cluster.

The name "ZIP Deciling" comes from the often used practice of ranking ZIP clusters from 1 to 10 based on their sales potential. Many catalog mailers eliminate addresses in all except their top clusters. On a general basis, it has been discovered that the top decile usually is 40 to 60 percent more responsive than the average of the total list, and the top decile often is 300 percent or more better than the bottom decile.

Actually, five-digit ZIP Codes may be too large and heterogeneous for effective list analysis. They were originally developed for the convenience of mail delivery and not for statistical analysis purposes. A single five-digit code area may easily include everything from highrise luxury apartments to slums and farming areas.

So smaller statistical units based on census data are often used. These include block groups, census tracts and enumeration districts.

An even more practical base for catalog marketers may be postal carrier routes, but little outside list overlay information is available on this basis.

Most frequently, outside service organizations such as the major consumer mailing list houses and computer service bureaus provide ZIP Deciling and other list analysis services. In addition, there are a number of specialized lifestyle research and analysis services such as National Demographics & Lifestyles (NDL), Demographic Research Co., CACI and Claritas Corp.

One of the first to enter the field was Claritas, which offers a service called PRIZM. Claritas coined the term "geodemography" to describe its use of census demographic and socioeconomic data to provide identification for five digit ZIP Codes and other census areas. They came up with 40 neighborhood types or clusters and gave each of them an easily remembered nickname. Some of these include: Back Country Folks, Blue Blood Estates, Blue-Collar Nursery, Bunker's Neighbors, God's Country, Hard Scrabble, Marlboro Country, Money and Brains, Old Brick Factories, Urban Gold Coast, Young Influentials and Young Suburbia.

Each of these geographical clusters has a distinctive personality (thus the unusual nicknames). Using the ZIP Codes of these clusters as an overlay is particularly useful in making selections from outside lists.

Another frequently used selection program is The Lifestyle Selector created by NDL, which maintains a "lifestyle inventory" of 57 activities and interests of a substantial portion of the U.S. population. Much of the information for this database was acquired by questionnaires attached to product warranty cards included with various types of products. Over 14 million of these questionnaires are processed by NDL each year.

The Lifestyle Selector list is used not only as a catalog mailing list in itself, but enables catalog marketers to use it as an overlay to create a detailed profile of the customers on their internal databases.

A frequently used database for business-to-business catalogs is the Business Leaders file of McGraw-Hill. It consists of over 1.5 million executives who subscribe to various McGraw-Hill business publications and offers a variety of different items of information about each company and the role of individual executives.

This is just one of a vast number of external overlays which are available to business-to-business catalog marketers. In addition to other publishers, various U.S. Government, state and local agencies have computer files which are available for database enhancement.

How to Build a Mailing List

If you're starting a new catalog, you'll most likely have to build your mailing list from scratch. There are four basic ways to do so.

- Compile the List Yourself
- Have List Compiled by a List Compiler
- Exchange Lists with Another Direct Marketer
- Rent the Use of Someone Else's List

Compile Your Own List

A company or organization can compile its own mailing list if it has unique source data. The sources may be lists of past customers, lists of one's own credit card holders, responses to mailings or advertising, records of sales call reports, attendance at trade show exhibits, visitors, warranty card registrations, or other internal records.

While many mail order catalogs start by running newspaper or magazine ads which invite potential customers to request a catalog, this is often more costly in the long run than simply mailing catalogs to outside lists.

Have a List Compiled for You

If a list is to be compiled from external sources such as telephone directories, membership rosters, business and industrial directories or other sources that are universally available, it is more common to use the services of organizations called "list compilers."

Companies specializing in list compilation are generally more proficient at developing mailing lists than nonspecialists. As specialists they can do the job more efficiently. There are generally multiple data sources for most lists, and it takes specialized knowledge to determine which of these sources is more reliable. For example, any directory has a certain amount of out-of-date information, and it takes specialized knowledge to know which sources are more up to date than others. However, these compiled lists most often lack one vital piece of information—evidence that the people on them are known mail order buyers. Therefore, such compiled lists are used only infrequently for catalog mailings.

Exchange Lists

One way to obtain a mailing list is to exchange lists with others. At one time this was a "no-no." A mailing list was considered very private property, and direct marketers would go to great lengths to make sure nobody else ever had access to their mailing lists. Today, however, the exchange of mailing lists—even between direct competitors—has become common practice.

It has come to be recognized that there is no such thing as a "private list." If someone wants to reach the people whose names are on your list, there are alternate ways to reach them. It may require more time and effort, but it can be done. So why not take advantage of the opportunity to gain access to those on someone else's list through exchanges?

No money changes hands in the process. It's just a name-for-name exchange: "I'll let you mail to 10,000 of my buyers if you will let me mail to 10,000 of your buyers."

Rent the Use of Someone Else's List

The most frequently used lists in the mail order catalog field are lists of those who have already taken the same kind of action you want people to take in response to your mailing.

Many companies rent their mailing lists to others for specific purposes. This is often a most important source of income for such companies. In fact, some companies in direct marketing lose money on their product sales; but they build such a valuable mailing list they can rent it over and over and not only make up for losses on product sales, but end up with an overall profit.

The basic difference between a "compiled" list and a "rental" list is that the names on a compiled list are people who *are* something while the names on a rental list are people who have *done* something—something specific such as having bought a product, made an inquiry, attended a trade show, or taken some other action which makes them different from others. Because the names on rental lists represent people who have taken some specific action, you are better off mailing to them to encourage them to repeat this type of action . . . rather than mailing to a list of "unknowns" hoping you can get them to take, for the first time, the action you seek.

The Cost of Rental Lists

The cost of renting lists varies. Compiled lists generally are less expensive than lists of people who have taken some specific action. And, when it comes to these action-identified lists, there are generally three types offered for rental.

Hot Line Names. These are people who have taken the action most recently. Unfortunately, there is no specific definition of "hot line." Sometimes it will mean those who have taken the action within the past 30 or 90 days. In other cases, it may mean those who have taken the action within an entire season. In all cases, it is important to ask the list owner to provide specific information on the time period involved. These lists are highly sought after since they have two important advantages—they're the most up-to-date lists available, so you can obtain a higher percentage of "deliverables" . . . and they contain names of people who, for one reason or another, are "in the mood" to buy things now.

Actives. These are the names of people list owners consider their active customers, subscribers, donors, etc. This list may or may not include the so-called hot line names, but it represents those who have taken the action for which they're being identified recently enough to be considered among the group most likely to repeat the action. In the catalog field, this is usually a two- or three-year period.

Inactives. These are people who once took the action but are no longer taking it. (In the publication field, these are known as "expires.") These names generally do not respond as well to catalog mailings as lists of "actives," but are often more responsive than any compiled list.

The average rental fee for a list of active catalog buyers runs $65–$80 per thousand names. As a general rule, you have to pay $10–$20 more per thousand for hot line names, and considerably less for inactive names. It's important to recognize, however, that this payment is a rental fee—you're not buying these names.

- You are renting the names for one-time use only.
- You don't have the right to remail these same names again, unless you arrange another list rental and pay for a second use. Any responses you receive, however, can be added to your own list, and you have the right to remail these names as many times as you wish . . . and you can even rent these names to others. (While this is most often true in the United States, it may not hold true in other countries.)
- You rent a list for mailing within a specific time period, and you don't have any right to hold on to the list for mailing at some future date. Most often, the owners of lists will not make their lists available for rental to others during periods when they're planning to make their own mailings . . . and many times they will not make the same names available during the same time period to two direct competitors.
- You rent a list to make a specific offer . . . and you don't have the right to make any other offer without first getting specific approval from the list owner.

The Relative Value of Outside Lists

All outside lists don't have the same value. Some lists might perform 10 to 20 times better than other lists. So seeking the right lists for rental, purchase, or exchange becomes an important part of any direct marketing business.

There are three primary areas where one list will differ from other lists.

Kinds of Products or Services

The first thing you look for is a list that involves the same kind of products or services you plan to offer. Often this doesn't mean exactly the same kind of products or services, but those that indicate the same general lifestyles.

For example, you may be planning to mail a catalog featuring outdoor clothing. Most likely, those who are already selling outdoor clothing will consider you a direct competitor and, thus, won't rent their names to you. They might be willing to exchange names of buyers, but if you are just starting a business, you don't yet have sufficient buyers to make a name-for-name exchange viable.

So you look for other lists indicating the kinds of people you want to reach—perhaps buyers of skiing equipment, backpacking equipment, tents, boats, fishing rods, or shotguns.

Value Category

The second thing you look for is a list of buyers who fit your "value category." Mail order buyers tend to make most of their mail order purchases in the same value category.

At one time, Sears labeled most of its products by one of three value categories—*Good, Better, Best*. These same three titles fit most mailing lists.

- *Good* buyers are always looking for "a bargain." They respond readily to "sale" prices and special discounts.
- *Better* buyers seek the best combination of price and value.
- *Best* buyers want something a little bit better than their neighbors, co-workers or friends have.

It's not just a matter of how much money someone spends. Many lists are identified by "average unit of sale." But that can be misleading. You may, for example, have a list identified as containing those who have spent an average of $50 per purchase. But a $50 book will generally fall into the "best" category, while a $50 fashion garment will likely be only in the "good" category.

Type of Action

The third and most important consideration is the action that led the name to the list in the first place. Your chances of success are greatest if you can mail to people who have already responded to the same stimuli you plan to use.

All of the people in any given universe do not necessarily respond equally to the same things. Take any given universe—all of the residents of a city or town . . . all of the members of a club or organization . . . all of those who enjoy a particular hobby.

Generally, only 50 percent of those in that universe will be "mail-oriented"—that is, likely to respond to mailings of any kind. The other 50 percent may be skeptical of mailings or unsure of how to take action by mail, or maybe they just don't like to deal with anyone "sight unseen."

But, of those who are mail-responsive, about 25 percent will respond more readily to catalogs, while 25 percent will respond more readily to "solo mailings"—the kind of mailing that comes in an envelope and generally offers only a single product or a group of closely related products. Thus, out of a given group of mail-oriented people, only 50 percent respond equally to both catalog and solo mailings.

There are also those who are responsive to "hard sell" and those who respond more readily to "soft sell"; those who respond to big, splashy graphics and those who respond to more quiet, sophisticated mailings.

As a result, you want to concentrate on those who have already given evidence they "like" the kinds of mailing you are planning to use.

The key idea in selecting a mailing list is what I call "Mail Smart"—to reach the maximum number of people most likely to have an interest in the product or service you are promoting . . . who make purchases in the same value category . . . and who have given some indication they respond to the kind of mailings you plan to use . . . and eliminate mailings to those portions of a universe less likely to respond.

To put it in simple terms: concentrate on *prospects* rather than just *suspects*.

Eliminating Duplication

You want to do everything possible to make sure the same person doesn't get two of the same catalogs on the same day. A very common term in the mailing list field is "merge/purge." It makes possible the elimination of duplicate mailings to the same name when two or more lists are being used.

This involves putting all of the lists on magnetic tape and then running them through a computer program that compares one list against the others and identifies all names that appear to be similar by using selected numbers and characters—a "match code." Here's a typical match code:

44136 WIT C 351 PR 2

Mr. Charles J. Winter
12351 Prospect Road
Cleveland, Ohio 44136

"44136" is the ZIP Code. The "WIT" comes from the first, second, and fourth characters of the family name. The "C" is the first character of the given name. The "351" is the last three digits of the address numeral. The "PR" comes from the first two characters of the street name. Then there is a check digit, which is determined by the number of characters remaining after the last extraction from the family name. Since the "T" in Winter was the last extraction, there are two remaining characters—thus the check digit is "2."

Mailing List Security

Since mailing lists represent such a valuable property, special steps have to be taken to protect them from unauthorized use when they are rented by others. It might seem easy just to duplicate a tape containing someone's list and then keep using it over and over again. But, before a list is sent to renters or their service bureaus, dummy names are seeded onto the list. These will be unique names used for this purpose only; thus, whenever a mailing is received with this dummy name, it is immediately known that it came from the rented list.

Actually, list theft has not turned out to be a major problem for most direct marketers. Most cases of list theft have been internal rather than external—employees "stealing" the list for their own use or to sell to others. But with proper seeding of lists—with no two people knowing all of the dummy names—the thieves are usually quickly caught.

Sources of List Information

With so many lists to consider—and changes coming daily—keeping abreast of the list field is a demanding task. Fortunately, catalog marketers have a lot of help available to them.

First of all, they have a regularly published directory to which they can turn to review the possibilities. Standard Rate & Data Service, Inc. (3004 Glenview Road, Wilmette, Illinois 60091) publishes *Direct Mail List Rates and Data,* a comprehensive listing of thousands of lists available for rental, with regular updates.

In addition, mailing list brokers can provide list cards with complete details about individual lists and available segmentation. Most lists are rented through a mailing list broker, who handles all details of the rental transaction.

Even though mailing list brokers provide services primarily to the list user, they receive their compensation in the form of a commission paid by the mailing list owner. Today's mailing list broker maintains extensive computer files filled with reams of valuable information about thousands of lists—not just what's available, but analysis of how those lists are being used by others.

Compilers of lists also provide list users with detailed catalogs of the hundreds of lists they have available for rental.

Thus a catalog marketer can stay well informed about mailing lists. But, even with all this help, it takes great skill to make initial list selections, analyze results, and then apply this analysis to choose just the right list segments to obtain the most profitable response.

List Service Organizations

Catalogers utilize a number of different types of service organizations to help find, acquire, and process mailing lists.

List Brokers

The key outside service organization utilized by catalogers is the list broker. The broker handles the details of list rental transactions. A report from the Direct Marketing Association explains:

> List brokers can be defined as independent agents whose primary function is to arrange rental and addressing transactions between list users and list owners. Brokers represent the list owners, and the commission that they receive for their services usually is 20% of the amount the mailer pays [although in recent years a smaller commission—particularly on large rentals—has become more common]. The commission is deducted by the broker before payment is forwarded to the list owner.
>
> It should be pointed out that activities often overlap in the list business. Some brokers not only arrange for the rental of lists owned by other companies, but they also may do compilation work or buy outright certain lists they can make available for rental.
>
> Although this may seem confusing, in the course of working with list organizations, you are likely to find that each has its own particular specialty. And very often you may decide that it is wise to deal with certain organizations for specific types of lists.

It is the list broker's job to keep abreast of all developments in the list field. Most brokers have an experienced staff that is always searching for "new" lists, more detailed information about known lists, ideas that will help catalogers use their lists more profitably, and anything else to improve the effectiveness of catalog mailings.

While any professional mailing list broker can arrange rentals of well over 90 percent of all lists available, many catalogers prefer to work with two or more list brokers in order to get as many viewpoints as possible on list rental possibilities. In the long run, however, most catalogers utilize the services of a maximum of three list brokers so they can develop a close relationship that leads to a better understanding of the catalogers' needs and requirements.

It is a paradox, perhaps, that while most of the work list brokers do is for the mailing list users, they are paid by the mailing list owners. Nevertheless, the Direct Marketing Association suggests mailing list users should expect the following services from list brokers:

- **Finds New Lists.** The broker is constantly seeking new lists and selecting for your consideration ones which will be of particular interest. In fact, brokers spend a great deal of their time encouraging list owners to enter the list rental field.
- **Acts as Clearing House for Data.** The broker saves you valuable time because you can go to one source for a considerable amount of information, rather than to many sources which may or may not be readily available.
- **Screens Information.** The broker carefully screens the list information provided by the list owner. Where possible, he or one of his representatives personally verifies the information provided by the list owner. (Today, most list brokers maintain a comprehensive mailing list database, which often contains specially screened information.)
- **Reports on Performance.** The broker knows the past history of many lists and usually knows the performance of ones which have previously been used by other mailers. [Often these performance reports are based primarily on observations of who rents which lists how often. Even if a list broker has learned actual response statistics, such information is generally considered confidential.]
- **Advises on Testing.** The broker's knowledge of the makeup of a list is often valuable in determining what will constitute a representative cross section of the list. Obviously, an error in selecting a cross section will invalidate the results of the test and possibly eliminate from your schedule a group of names that could be responsive.

- **Checks Instructions.** When you place an order with a list owner through a broker, he and his staff double check the accuracy and completeness of your instructions, thus avoiding unnecessary misunderstandings and loss of time.
- **Clears Offer.** The broker clears for you in advance the mailing you wish to make. He supplies the list owner with a sample of your piece or a description of it, and by getting prior approval minimizes the chance of any later disappointments.
- **Checks Mechanics.** The broker coordinates with the list owner the necessary mechanics of the list rental transaction, checking instructions to make sure the rental list will be supplied in the specific format required.
- **Clears Mailing Date.** When contacting the list owner, the broker checks on the mailing date which has been requested and asks that it be held open as a protected time for you.
- **Works out Timing.** The broker arranges either for material to be addressed or to have labels or computer tapes sent to you or your designated service bureau or mailing house at a specific time, thus enabling you to maintain your schedule of inserting and mailing.

While list brokers are generally expected to perform all of these services for list users, it should be recognized that several of them might involve a considerable amount of expertise, time, and effort. It is important to remember that the list broker's compensation is just a small percentage of the amount that will be paid for a list rental, and that commission may not cover extensive extra effort—particularly if you are planning to rent only a minimum number of names. In such cases, it is only legitimate for a list broker to request separate compensation for any "extras" you might request.

Finding a good list broker—one who understands your specific needs and provides all of the help you require—is not necessarily an easy task. While they can arrange rentals of all types of lists, list brokers generally tend to specialize in certain types of lists. Seek out a list broker with extensive experience in handling the types of lists you plan to use.

Your fate will be primarily in the hands of the person from the list brokerage organization with whom you will have personal contact. So it is important to seek out those who readily understand your needs and consistently provide the exact service you require.

One good way of finding the "right" list broker is to ask the advice of other catalog marketers—particularly those in your own geographical area. Brokers' representatives usually work within specific geographical areas, so even if the list brokerage firm itself has the experience you need, it won't do you much good unless the representative in your area can serve you adequately.

List Compilers

Mailing list compilers tend to specialize in either consumer lists or those for business and professional markets. While list compilation may be part of a list broker's operations, it is usually treated as a separate business.

While list compilers can create a list specifically for the use of an individual mailer, most lists are precompiled in the expectation that they are going to be of interest to many users. It is more common to simply rent precompiled lists each time they are to be used, rather than buy them for multiple uses. By renting a compiled list when you actually need it, you will be able to take advantage of all efforts the compiler makes on a regular basis to keep each list up to date.

Compiled business and professional lists are derived from a variety of sources such as telephone directories, business and industrial directories, membership rosters, and government records. Mailing list compilers frequently use multiple sources to keep their lists complete and current.

Many of the compiled consumer lists used by catalogers come from one of three major national compilers—Reuben H. Donnelley, Metromail, and R.L. Polk. These big compilers have lists covering 85 percent or more of all the households in the United States, with a vast variety of segmentation information that permits the selection of highly specialized lists.

In addition there are a number of compilers, such as The Lifestyle Selector, who have developed lifestyle lists. These lists are often used for database overlays as well as for actual mailings.

List Managers

This title is something of a misnomer, since these organizations don't actually "manage" lists. Instead, most serve primarily as the "promotion manager" for list owners. Their basic job is to promote the use of rental lists.

In some cases, list managers may provide additional assistance, such as that outlined in DMA's *Fact Book on Direct Marketing:*

> One who, as an employee of a list owner or as an outside agent, is responsible for the use, by others, of a specific mailing list(s). The list manager serves the list owner in several or all of the following capacities: list maintenance (or advice thereon), list promotion and marketing, list clearance and record keeping, collecting for use of the list by others.

In many cases, list management is one of the services offered by list brokers. But, like list compilation, it is considered a separate business.

List Consultants

Another business service found within some list brokerage firms is a separate list consulting function. This takes on many shapes and can involve providing expert advice on everything from how to compile a list internally and how to provide for useful segmentation to working to convince a reluctant list owner to make a list available for rental or exchange.

In many cases, this is the service a list broker offers when commissions from list rentals can't cover the costs of all of the different things requested by a list user.

There are, of course, many independent list consultants, most of whom tend to specialize in list analysis, list segmentation techniques, and/or developing computer programs for mailing list compilation and maintenance.

Service Bureaus

With the coming of ZIP Codes in the mid-sixties and the need to add them to mailing lists quickly, computer service bureaus found an instant market among catalog marketers. Since that time these bureaus have expanded their services into all areas of mailing list compilation, segmentation, maintenance, merge/purge, carrier route sorting, and other list-related activities.

Many catalogers utilize service bureaus for all of their mailing list activities, rather than trying to do the work internally.

Mailing Houses

In the days before computers, these organizations were more commonly known as "letter shops." Today, however, that simple name scarcely covers the complexity of the work they do.

Often mailing houses include most of the services offered by service bureaus; in fact, the name sometimes is simply a synonym for service bureau. Usually, however, they provide additional services involved in the actual preparation of catalogs for delivery to the post office—affixing mailing labels, sorting, bagging, etc.

Friend-Get-a-Friend

Next to the list of a catalog marketer's own list of customers, the most valuable list is often one made up of names furnished by those customers.

Many catalogers regularly ask customers to supply names of friends whom they feel will be interested in receiving a copy of their catalog. This should not be confused with "member-get-a-member" or "customer-get-a-customer" programs, wherein a customer is asked to solicit an order. In friend-get-a-friend programs, it is simply a matter of asking for names to which catalogs can be mailed.

When there is an actual sale involved, the customer who has become an "agent" for the catalog marketer is rewarded with a cash commission or a merchandise bonus. But in friend-get-a-friend programs, incentives are seldom offered. Catalog marketers have generally found that they get a better quality of names without offering incentives, since many customers may send in unqualified names just to get the reward offered. Without incentives, there may not be as many names provided, but the conversion quality of the names is generally higher.

It usually doesn't pay to request too many names. When multiple names are supplied, a cataloger may choose to mail catalogs only to the first two or three names on the list. Most people, it seems, don't know more than two or three people like themselves.

One of the best places to request friend-get-a-friend names is on the back of order envelopes. (One of the worst places is often the back of the order form—many people, it seems, don't bother to turn over an order form and look at the other side.) Typical of the way friend-get-a-friend names are requested is the message on the back of reply envelopes used by Spring Hill Nurseries:

> **Spring Hill is delighted to offer you this opportunity to obtain America's finest nursery stock. If you have friends who also enjoy shopping from the comfort of their homes, please fill in their names, addresses and ZIP Codes. We'll be happy to send them a free copy of Spring Hill's catalog.**

Mailing Lists — The Cornerstone Of Catalog Marketing Programs

Mailing lists are not something a catalog marketer can simply turn over to a staff of buyers and statisticians. Since mailing lists are the cornerstone of a direct marketing program, they call for constant attention from everyone in a catalog marketing organization. Managements of most catalog marketing companies spend more time and effort on mailing lists than they do on any other single function. And everyone else involved in direct marketing must pay special attention to the mailing list.

Copywriters can't write their best copy unless they have a thorough understanding of who will receive the catalogs.

Designers can't tailor their designs for greatest effectiveness unless they know who will be seeing the catalogs.

Product buyers can't select the right products unless they know who will be asked to buy them.

Everyone in catalog marketing needs to be a list specialist, in addition to whatever other duties they may have.

The mailing list is the cornerstone of every catalog marketing program and is worthy of every minute spent gaining an understanding of "who's out there . . . and how to reach them."

The One Constant: Change

A list, however, is never static. While the degree of change will vary depending on a variety of factors, all lists have some degree of change from day to day.

Age, for example, is an important factor. The younger the audience, the greater the change. Young audiences move more frequently than older audiences and change their buying habits more often. The older the audience, the less the change. (Right up to the ultimate list—the tombstones in a cemetery. Never any deletions . . . just a few additions each year.)

Overall there will be a 17 percent change of addresses on the average customer list each year. In a five-year period, over half of the people on the average consumer mailing list will be living at a different address than the one at which they were living five years earlier . . . and this doesn't take into consideration those who have moved more than once during that period or changes due to deaths, marriages, new citizens, and many other factors.

Telephone numbers change an average of 22 percent each year.

And the greatest change takes place on business lists—as many as 56 percent of the names change each year. A high percentage of direct marketing is done on a business-to-business basis—and it is important to be able to reach the specific individual who can buy or specify the kind of product or service you are trying to sell, not just the company itself. That can be extremely difficult, since people keep changing jobs.

McGraw-Hill Publishing Company has studied changes of address that show up each year on the circulation lists for its paid circulation magazines. Out of every 1,000 names it found 343 new names had shown up; 65 had new titles, usually representing changes in buying responsibilities; and 157 had shifted to new locations within their own companies or had moved to other companies in their field. This means only 435 out of every 1,000 remained in the same position at the same location with the same company from one year to the next.

© COPYRIGHT 1991 DARTNELL CORPORATION

Obviously such changes mean that keeping a mailing list up to date is a very demanding, and often costly, job. But it's a very important one, since a direct marketing program is only as good as the mailing lists that are used.

Eight "Usually Reliable Truths" about Mailing Lists

Nobody wants to mail to people who aren't interested in what is being offered . . . and the more ways you can find to delete nonrespondents before you mail, the more successful a catalog marketing program becomes.

Many factors go into list segmentation. Bob Stone, one of direct marketing's leading authorities, cites eight "usually reliable truths" that can be applied to list segmentation:

1. Direct response lists will usually outpull compiled lists—people who have done something rather than just people who are something. Most catalog marketers seldom use names from compiled lists unless not enough direct response names are available.
2. Customer names will outpull prospects or names from outside lists. If they don't, there's good indication something is terribly wrong with your business—you've somehow been disappointing your customers, and they aren't coming back for more.
3. People over 35 years of age generally are more responsive to mailings than those who are younger. While even teenagers have become increasingly responsive to direct mail, older audiences have had more experience dealing with offers that come through the mails and thus are more comfortable in responding.
4. People who live in rural areas respond more readily to many direct mail offers than those who live in cities. Many products or services, of course, aren't as readily available to rural residents, and direct marketing provides a handy way to acquire them. This "truth" can be misleading, however. Many kinds of products and services find a more responsive audience in urban areas. Collectibles, for example, often are more popular among those who live in cities, and many magazines and books prove to be more popular in urban markets than they are in rural markets.
5. "Hot line names"—people who have responded most recently—are likely to be the best names available. There are two reasons for this. First, all of these names are up to date; thus, there are fewer undeliverables. Second, these are the people who are "in the mood" to buy now.
6. Those who have bought more than once in a year or a season will outpull those who have made only a single purchase. These, of

course, are the people who make it a "habit" to respond to mailings.

7. Any list will differ from other lists on a geographical basis. The geographical pattern of names on one list will be different from the ZIP-by-ZIP breakdown of another list which otherwise might appear to be similar.

8. Finally, each list will also vary on a seasonal basis—the season during which names originally came onto the list—and seasonal selectivity can be a very important factor in choosing list segments for specific mailings. Most gift purchases, for example, are made during the fall and early winter months, while during January, February, and March, people are more frequently buying things for their own use. Thus, if you are looking for gift orders, you like a list heavy with names acquired from September through December.

Circles of Convenience

A technique originally developed by retailers is the basis for list selection in direct marketing. It's called "circles of convenience."

For many years, retailers thought their basic market consisted of everyone living within a concentric circle—all of those living an equal distance from their place of business. It might be those within five blocks . . . five miles . . . or 500 miles. But, whatever the distance, they thought they had an equal chance to make customers of everyone within that circle.

But that theory was put to the test. Retailers took maps of their areas and put pins in the locations where present customers lived, and they discovered some interesting things. They found, for example, when there were natural barriers such as rivers or express highways, people who lived on the other side of these barriers tended to go away from the barrier to do their shopping, rather than crossing it. If there was a school within the circle, people tended to go toward the school rather than away from it. If there was a shopping center within the circle, people tended to gravitate toward the shopping center.

As a result, when retailers charted where their customers were actually located, they seldom found them in concentric circles around their stores. Instead, they fell into irregular patterns—patterns which came to be called "circles of convenience."

The significance of these findings was important in planning direct mailings. If you could mail to those living within the areas where others had found it convenient to shop at your store, you were more likely to get response than if you simply mailed to everyone in a concentric circle around the store.

The idea has its counterpart in catalog marketing. Direct marketers determine who is buying from them now . . . and then search for more people like those buyers. The odds of success are greater if you concentrate on developing additional customers just like your present customers, rather than expending your efforts trying to cultivate new markets.

Selecting Products for Your Catalog

5

Products to a catalog are like an engine to a car. Nobody would want a fancy automobile—even with the slickest design and the most luxurious interior—if it had a lawnmower motor under the hood.

Unfortunately, too many catalogs put almost all of their emphasis on presentation and give only secondary attention to product selection. Catalog consultant Bill Nicolai hit the nail on the head: "One sometimes gets the feeling from attending seminars and reading articles that the goods we sell by mail are a minor detail, or perhaps a loosely related adjunct, to our catalog business. We get so wound up in the 'tricks' of successful presentation or the 'techniques' we use in finding names we can mail to, that we forget that *what* we sell—the merchandise—is the only reason we are in business at all."

Finding good products for a catalog is considerably more difficult than selecting merchandise to be sold in a retail store. A retail merchant can select an item with little advance thought on how it will be presented. If experience seems to indicate an item will appeal to the store's clientele, the merchant places an order and puts the item on display.

If it sells briskly, additional quantities can be ordered and put on sale when they arrive. If it isn't on display for a while, store customers naturally assume it isn't currently available. And it can be reintroduced when additional supplies are available.

If it doesn't sell as planned, the store has multiple options. It can be given extra shelf facings, moved to a special display space, featured in a window, promoted on store banners, advertised in newspapers or broadcast media, or, perhaps, offered at a different price point.

But before merchandise is selected for a catalog, a number of details must be considered:

- Where will it be positioned in the catalog?
- Can it be properly shown with a single photograph?
- Can it be adequately described in a limited number of words?
- What will be the right price point? Once the catalog has been printed, that's the price with which you'll have to live for an extended period.
- Can the vendor provide a prompt resupply if the orders keep rolling in faster than expected? Customers who see the item in a current catalog naturally expect it to be in stock and available for prompt shipment.

When an item goes into a catalog, that's it. It either sells or it doesn't sell. Most often, you don't get a second chance. This is why it's so often difficult to recruit merchandise buyers from retail organizations to do the buying for catalogs—it takes different types of personalities.

Buyers, Rebuyers, and Merchandisers

Catalog buying often differs from traditional retail buying, where one individual or a single staff is responsible for nearly everything related to a specific type of merchandise. In most catalog companies, on the other hand, buying, rebuying, and merchandising often become separate functions.

The saying is that in retail stores "the merchant is king." Merchandise buyers are called "merchants," and they usually have almost complete control over the merchandise category for which they are responsible. They evaluate all available products, select items, issue the purchase orders, determine price points, decide how the merchandise will be presented within the store, maintain inventories, determine when markdowns should be made, and control the destiny of every item from start to finish.

But in catalog companies, it is common to find these tasks divided at least three ways. And the merchant is no longer king. That royal role goes not to those who select the merchandise, but to those responsible for how it will be presented in the catalog—the "merchandisers."

Even buying and rebuying are frequently separated. Buyers are creative types with inquiring minds who scour the market to locate unique and innovative products. They present their finds to the merchandiser (often the top catalog executive) and then head back out to find more new products.

It is the merchandisers who play the key role. They evaluate the products located by the buyers and make the final decision on what will be featured in each catalog. They determine where and how the product will be presented, decide what the price point will be, and forecast how many units will be required to fill orders.

Meanwhile, the rebuyer takes over. While catalog buyers are creative types (and often are rather weak on paperwork and details), catalog rebuyers are in-house types who love handling fine details. Buyers make it a point to be friendly to everyone who may have potential products for the catalog. But rebuyers can be more hardhearted. They twist arms to get special price breaks. They keep on top of vendors to make sure products are delivered on time. They maintain a day-to-day watch over inventory levels. They deal with production and distribution personnel within vendors' organizations on a no-nonsense basis.

This separation of responsibilities capitalizes on the unique personalities of three different types of personnel: the traveling buyer with friends in every port, whose primary role is to search out and find new products; the stay-at-home rebuyer who's great on paperwork and twisting arms to get the best deal; and the creative merchandiser who knows how to narrow down product selection to create the best mix in the catalog and present each item for maximum sales.

Where to Find Products

Locating new products for catalogs is an ongoing task. Most catalogs change a substantial number of merchandise units for each new issue. Fashion catalogs may require nearly complete change from issue-to-issue. Giftware catalogs average about 50 percent change. Even in fields where there is relatively little new each year, the average catalog will change at least 20 percent of its merchandise each time around just to keep things interesting for customers.

There are three primary ways to locate new products.

Trade Shows and Fairs

One of the primary ways to find new products is by attending trade shows and fairs. It takes a lot of stamina to walk aisle after aisle, keeping an eye out for something new and interesting. But it's an important part of every cataloger's business life.

While the shows and merchandise fairs to be attended will vary, depending on the product mix in a catalog, a high percentage of catalogers can regularly be found at the National China, Glass and Collectibles Show in Washington, which kicks off the trade show season each January. Then, month after month, there are shows held throughout the country. Some of the most heavily attended by catalogers include the Variety Merchandise Show in New York, the Premium and Incentive Shows in both New York and Chicago, the National Hardware Show, the National Housewares Show, the International Jewelry Trade Shows, and the big Consumer Electronics Shows held annually in both Las Vegas and Chicago.

A smaller show that draws a lot of catalogers is the National Mail Order Merchandise Show in New York, which is devoted entirely to merchandise for mail order. Then there are a host of gift shows in various cities throughout the United States and abroad. (All of the business magazines devoted to catalogs and direct marketing regularly carry listings of these and other shows.)

Smart catalogers know the newest items are often hidden from view during trade shows, and they've learned to develop a special relationship with exhibitors so they can request a sneak preview of what's "under the counter" and soon to be available. Just going from booth to booth to pick up readily available literature usually isn't worth the effort. Most of it, in fact, ends up in hotel wastebaskets to lighten the suitcase when heading back home. But asking the right questions often reveals something really worthwhile.

In many of the shows, there is a "hidden corner" where new exhibitors find a spot after the "regulars" have reserved all of the key traffic locations. Searching out these newcomers often proves worthwhile and turns up that very special new product before other catalogs are able to locate it.

In addition to the annual trade shows in the United States, there are many international trade fairs throughout the world that are a must for many catalogers. These special shows often draw large crowds, and it takes early planning to book travel and lodging.

Merchandise Centers

In many of the major cities of the United States—especially New York, Chicago, Dallas, and Atlanta—there are year-round displays of merchandise in both individual manufacturers' showrooms and big merchandise centers.

For catalog buyers, New York City is often considered "just one big showroom"—particularly for clothing, toys, jewelry, gifts, and imports. Chicago is noted for its Merchandise Mart, Apparel Center, and Furniture Mart. In Dallas you'll find the Home Furnishing Mart, Trade Mart, World Trade Center, clothing marts, and even a unique facility called the Infomart, featuring computer hardware and software. Atlanta has its Merchandise Mart and Apparel Mart.

Since many of these merchandise centers are off limits to the general public, it is advisable to arrange admittance in advance.

Trade Publications

Another valuable source for new product ideas is regular reading of various trade publications. Thousands of them are published regularly, and if you don't already have a publications directory in your own office, you'll find one in any large library.

Progressive catalogers make it a point to read at least a dozen of these publications every month and respond to hundreds of the ads offering information or samples of new products. While many of these publications include a "bingo card" (a reply card you can use to request literature from multiple advertisers), responses can often be slow or nonexistent. If you come across items of real interest, it is generally wise to write or call these advertisers individually.

Keeping an Open Door for Vendors

New product ideas do simply "walk in the door"—if you keep it open. Encouraging vendors to come to call often pays off since they are more likely to save really special ideas for those who they consider their friends.

Many catalog companies set aside certain days as an "open house" for vendors. Others keep vendors posted on when they will be in their areas so they can arrange special meetings.

Also, make sure your name gets on vendors' mailing lists. Don't just wait for it to happen. Write vendors to tell them of your special interests and *ask* to be placed on their mailing lists.

Review Other Catalogs

If there's one thing smart catalogers read more often than trade magazines and the mail they receive from vendors, it's the catalogs produced by others—and not just those produced by their direct competitors. Lots of interesting new products show up first in some offbeat catalog. Just seeing a new item, however, seldom indicates who produced it. You often have to order the merchandise to determine its source. Placing catalog orders has an additional benefit. Since catalogers often rent or exchange lists of their customers, you'll soon be receiving additional catalogs and have additional sources for locating products.

The task of carefully reviewing hundreds of different catalogs can be overwhelming at times. A good technique is to assign the review of specific catalogs to key personnel (and, perhaps, give them an allowance so they can make small purchases to ensure that they continue to receive catalogs). These reviewers are expected to report regularly on everything they see that's new and different.

Visit Stores

It isn't just catalogs that introduce you to new merchandise. It's also a good idea to make it a regular practice to visit stores both in your area and elsewhere. And don't just visit the big malls. You're more likely to find interesting new products in neighborhood stores.

A good idea is to tack a day onto your out-of-town trips and devote it to visiting local stores. This is particularly important if you're traveling abroad. Allow an extra day to visit local department stores. Take the escalator to the top and work your way down, floor by floor.

The great retail and mail order merchant Stanley Marcus says that he often finds more interesting things in retail store windows than in manufacturers' showrooms. He advises all buyers to pound the pavements of foreign shopping areas. His theory is that most good shopkeepers put their newest and most unusual merchandise on display to attract customers. They take special pride in offering such merchandise and are often pleased when an American notices it and comments on it. Often they are only too happy to reveal the source of the merchandise to a visitor from abroad, who they feel will not be in competition with them.

And while you're out in stores, take time to visit with both customers and store personnel. Ask them what's new and get their opinions on products you're considering for your next catalog.

Invite Your Customers to Help

An often overlooked source for new product ideas is a catalog's own customers. Encourage them to suggest new products. You'll not only uncover a lot of ideas you may be overlooking, but anytime customers volunteer to lend you a hand, they feel they've become "part of the family" and are likely to buy from you more frequently than before.

Invite Employee Participation

Your merchandise buyers aren't the only employees who can discover new products for your catalog. All employees should be encouraged to regularly keep an eye open for anything new and different. Some catalog companies even offer special rewards for every employee suggestion, with a bonus if the product is selected for the catalog.

The Importance of Unique and Exclusive Products

The most important characteristic of a good catalog product is that it should be something truly unique—and, if possible, an exclusive product available only from you. Catalog readers love to discover something they never have seen before. While they may not buy that specific product, it tends to reinforce your catalog in their minds and encourages them to give special attention to your future catalogs.

The ultimate example of unique and exclusive products is Neiman-Marcus's annual His & Hers gifts, which were mentioned in Chapter 3. Even though there have been years when none of the intriguing His & Hers products—ranging from Chinese junks to a pair of camels—have been sold, they make the arrival of Nieman-Marcus's annual Christmas catalog a very special event.

The importance of being the first to introduce something is demonstrated by these His & Hers gifts. While dozens of other catalogs have tried to adapt the idea (including Sakowitz, Neiman-Marcus's archcompetitor in Texas, which came up with ideas such as a swimming pool in the shape of Texas, filled with Perrier water, and the opportunity to have your own backyard amusement park built by a Disneyland designer), most of the Johnnies-come-lately are ignored while America focuses its attention on the annual Neiman-Marcus Christmas catalog.

But publicity isn't the main reason for featuring unique products in catalogs. If all a customer sees—or expects to see—in a catalog is a presentation of familiar products, there's no reason to spend time looking through it each time it arrives. Instead, it will likely be simply set aside for possible ordering later. Meanwhile, a competitive catalog arrives and offers something new and different. It gets extra attention and thus will more likely be remembered when it is time to order.

Just as Neiman-Marcus doesn't necessarily expect to sell all of the His & Hers gifts it features, many other catalogs often include intriguing products simply to make each issue of their catalogs more interesting to recipients. Such products don't have to be something expensive. Sometimes, for example, all it takes is a good copywriter to convert a routine product into an intriguing attention-getter. Some years ago, Early Winters simply added a unique guarantee to a pair of boot socks and not only created catalog excitement but produced a 100 percent increase in sales for what would otherwise be just a common, ordinary product.

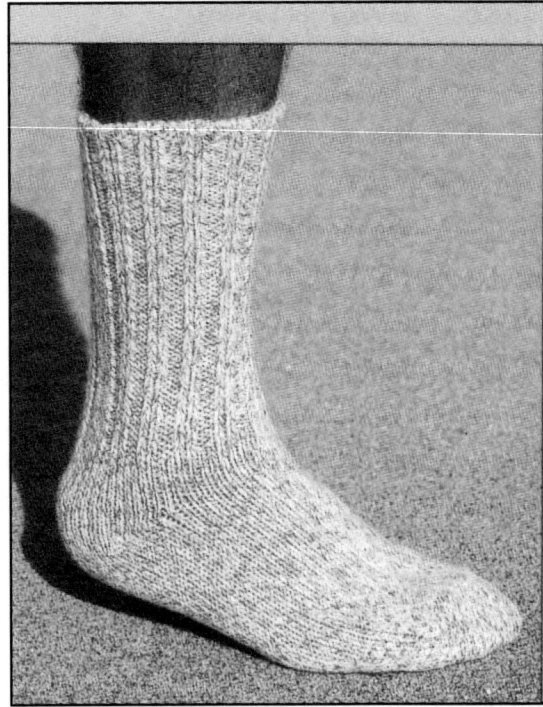

**Figure 5–1 (above)
Unique Guarantee**

Early Winters added this "1,000 Mile Guarantee" to a pair of boot socks and saw sales soar. Copyright © Early Winters. Used with permission.

**Figure 5–2
An Effective Combination Offer**

An attractive package converts a self-purchase item into a sales-producing gift. Copyright © Foster & Gallagher. Used with permission.

Early Winters' socks were guaranteed for "one year or 1,000 miles of wear—whichever came *last*." Bill Nicolai even went so far as to include a "mileage record" with each pair of socks they shipped.

Unique packaging can also turn a common product into something unique. Norm Thompson, for example, took an assortment of wildflower seeds, put them in a decorative can, and offered them as "Meadow in a Can."

Joy and Murray Hall started Ambassador International with a single product—a ladies' handbag with a number of special features. Then, year after year, they kept adding new features to this basic product to keep it fresh and interesting until it became the "Everything Bag." Even though lots of others tried to copy Joy and Murray's idea, they always ended up with "last year's product," while Ambassador had a new version that provided a cornerstone for their catalogs.

Exclusive Products

Another way to make your catalog stand out from the competition is to feature "exclusive" products—things that are available nowhere else.

Actually, exclusives don't have to be all that different from similar items. But when catalog shoppers come across something of interest which they are told is an exclusive, they tend to think, "I like what I see here, and the price seems right; why bother to waste my time looking anywhere else?"

There are many ways to take a basic product and convert it into something exclusive. One of the quickest ways is to change the packaging.

Breck's, for example, adds special packaging to a unique combination of products to create its exclusive "Dutch Treat" gift collection. Ten each of 10 different varieties of Dutch bulbs are shipped in a decorative box—which converts an "ordinary" product, normally purchased only by gardeners for their own use, into something which can be sent to others as a gift—and thousands of buyers take advantage of this special opportunity each year.

Histacount, which supplies printed stationery items to professional audiences, was just another source until it created exclusive designs for the traditional symbols used to identify different professions. This added an exclusive touch to the letterheads, envelopes and business cards it offered and helped make its catalog different from dozens of competitors.

Other simple ways to convert an ordinary product into an

Figure 5–3
Exclusive Designs

Norm Thompson made its stationery different from the competition by offering designs created from original watercolors—and then offering the framed originals as well. Copyright © Norm Thompson. Used with permission.

Figure 5-4
Office Products for the Home

Reliable, "The Office Supply People," recognized the emerging home office market and created "HomeOffice," a catalog of products functionally related to their business-to-business counterparts, but geared to a more design-conscious consumer. Copyright © Reliable Corporation. Used with permission.

exclusive include offering it in a different color or adding a decal or appliqué. Think of all of those ordinary golf shirts with an alligator, fox, lamb, or some other animal; or all of those uniquely decorated tote bags.

Identifying exclusives in a catalog is as important as telling catalog recipients what is new. "New" and "exclusive" are two of the three most important words in cataloging (the other is "free," which never seems to lose its magic).

Many catalogs adopt a special graphic device to identify each of their exclusive items. It is often their logotype, or a variation of their logotype. Or it may be some other symbol, which is reserved for identification of exclusives. Johnny Appleseed, a women's fashion catalog, for example, uses a bright red apple. Other times, a catalog will simply insert the word "Exclusive" in bold type somewhere in the copy about the item.

Product Innovation

While product uniqueness and exclusivity are two of the most important ways to keep buyers interested in a catalog, it isn't necessary to constantly search the world over to find unique and exclusive products. Often you can take existing products and add something extra to give them a unique quality and make them yours exclusively.

Here are 25 basic ways to convert a conventional product into something uniquely your own.

1. **Change Audience.** Perhaps you have a product originally intended for office use. How about offering it for use in the home? Reliable combined selections from its office supplies catalog and created a new catalog for the home office.
2. **Modify.** Take a standard product and make it an exclusive by adding your own special touches. Gucci added red and green stripes to conventional items and was able to sell them as "exclusives" at higher prices.
3. **Add New Uses.** Early Winters took a Japanese lunchbox and offered it as a watertight container for outdoorsmen. Gardenway suggested a kitchen-utensil carousel would be useful for tools in the workshop.
4. **Magnify.** Offer the item in a larger size. Think Big is a whole catalog of giant-size products.
5. **Minify.** You can also reduce the size and offer a miniature. The Franklin Mint had great success selling a series of medals featuring the presidents of the United States. Then it reduced the size of the same medals and had another success selling Presidential Mini Medals.
6. **Add Features.** Consider the famous Swiss Army Knife. Here's a single product which has become a popular product for a wide variety of different catalogs thanks to the addition of special-use features for each audience. What can you add to a product which will make it of special interest to your customers?
7. **Add Quantity.** Why sell just one when you can sell a combination? One of Breck's best-selling catalog items is a 120-Day Flowering Collection featuring 17 different kinds of Dutch bulbs.
8. **Subtract Quantity.** Does your product normally sell in large lots? Why not give your customers a chance to try the product by offering single samples? Quill, for example, normally sells pens and markers by the dozen. But to introduce a new line of colored markers, Quill offered a bargain six-pack, with one of each color.
9. **Add a Color.** Everyone else offers the product in red and blue. Make it special for your customers by offering it in green and yellow. At one time, Ambassador had great success with a relatively common handbag by offering it in a unique purple color.
10. **Change Sexes.** Remember those Franklin Mint presidential medals? They sold primarily to a male audience. So they offered a matching series featuring America's first ladies and had a product with unique appeal to women. Think of all of the men's fashion

items which have been adapted to appeal to females, and of the women's jewelry items which have been adapted to appeal to males.

11. **Change Materials.** Speaking of the Franklin Mint, it was responsible for creating the modern-day boom in collector's plates. All of its original collector's plates were etched silver. But to attract additional collectors, these were followed by plates of china, porcelain bisque, crystal, pewter, gold plate, stained glass and other materials.

12. **Change Form.** The Country Store found lots of buyer interest in a charming photograph of a little farm boy. So it offered the farm boy as a figurine.

13. **Change Packaging.** This is perhaps the easiest of all ways to give a product unique qualities. Gump's took a popular brass egg paperweight, added a leather pouch, and had an instant winner.

14. **Adapt.** Many catalogers have attached a gold chain to unique items—ancient coins, military emblems, shards of antique pottery, etc.—and offered them as jewelry.

15. **Add a Service.** Many catalogers offer unique gift wrapping or expedited delivery. Lands' End offers a variety of special gift-related services.

**Figure 5–5
Change Product Form**

Spinoffs of a popular product can be of interest to your customers. Country Store, a catalog for farm wives, found tremendous interest in posters featuring a photograph of two little farm boys. They created a figurine of the two lads, which proved so popular they created another dozen figurines based on the same characters. Copyright © Reiman Associates. Used with permission.

6 ways we can help your gift giving.

1 Order as late as Dec. 21 and we'll get it there.

That's right—Lands' End Express orders can be placed as late as December 21. The cost for this special service is just $6 over our usual $3.50 shipping charge. And our regular $3.50 shipping service will get it there for Christmas too, if you order by December 17.*

3 "Your gift's in the mail."

There's no guesswork or worrying involved—once your gift is on its way, we'll let you know by mail. Immediately.

5 A Christmas "warning."

Friends and family have itchy fingers? Tell us about this particular problem when ordering a gift, and we'll attach a particularly clever "Don't open 'til Christmas" sticker. Bound to stop even the sneakiest of sisters.

We feel that you—a devoted Lands' End shopper—deserve a freebie. Just order any gift from our catalogue and we'll enclose a gift card gratis, complete with your own message.

6 And if you're really at a loss...

Our Gift Certificate is easy to use!

Always a convenient gift, because anyone who receives a Lands' End Gift Certificate can redeem it by ordering over the phone!

It's available in any amount you specify, adorned with ribbon, and accompanied by our latest catalog, and each new issue for six months.

2 We solve your gift-wrapping problems.

For just $5, we'll wrap your gift in tissue. Seal it with a sticker. Place it in a festive box. Even top it with a matching bow. Last, but not least, we'll seal it in polyfilm to avoid scratches en route.

*Dec. 17 & Dec. 21 dates apply to in-stock items. Monogrammed or inseamed items take an extra day.

Figure 5–6
Add a Service

Offering a special service can help make catalog products of greater interest to customers. Lands' End, for example, offers festive gift wrapping, cards, and stickers. Copyright © Lands' End, Inc. Reprinted courtesy of Lands' End Catalog.

16. **Combine.** Combine items in a unique way, and you can have an attention-getting "new" product. Spring Hill Nurseries, for example, took several perennial plants common in Elizabethan England and offered them as an "English Cottage Garden." A number of office suppliers have combined letterheads, envelopes, invoice forms, business cards and other imprinted items and offered them as a "starter kit" for new businesses.

17. **Split Up.** Just as you can combine items, you can also split up items normally sold as a unit and offer them separately. Ambassador, for example, took the wallet and key case normally included in its Everything Bag and offered them as separate products.

18. **Change Offer.** Lots of possibilities here. Fingerhut is famous for its installment payment plans. And one of the most popular offers of all is the "Two-Fer"—two of an item at a reduced price. Haverhill's goes a step further, offering "a third one free" when you buy two of an item.

19. **Reintroduce.** Take a look at popular items of the past. They may be "new" today—either in appearance or use. Reliable offered a number of professional office items for home office use. They were not only functional, but offered a unique decorator's touch.

Figure 5–7
Combine Products

Combining several products into a single offer often produces increased response for a catalog. Here, for example, Spring Hill Nurseries combined eight different varieties of perennials into an English Cottage Garden Collection. Copyright © Foster & Gallagher. Used with permission.

20. **Get 'em into the Act.** Inviting buyer participation is a good way to build stronger customers. Horchow sells memberships in a "V.I.P." club, assuring members not only of receiving every Horchow catalog, but of a multitude of other benefits such as product discounts, free gift wrapping, special offers, and even their own special telephone order-taker. Other catalogs, such as The Sharper Image and The Drawing Board, offer frequent buyer programs similar to the frequent flyer programs of the airlines, with points which can be redeemed for merchandise.
21. **Personalize.** Almost any item can be personalized with a name or initials to make it stand out from nonpersonalized items. This is something often sought by gift purchasers. By offering a host of personalized items, Miles Kimball keeps customers coming back year after year. Lillian Vernon is another that continually adds unique interest to common products through personalization.

Figure 5–8
Reintroduce

Reliable reintroduced standard office products into the home office market. Copyright © Reliable. Used with permission.

Figure 5–9
Personalize

One of the easiest ways to add a special touch to a catalog product is to offer it personalized. There's even a complete mail order catalog—Initials—that offers nothing but personalized items. Copyright © Initials. Used with permission.

22. **Add Fun.** Sometimes a sense of humor helps give products a unique touch. Hog Wild!, for example, made gift candies unique by molding them in the shape of a pig (and, of course, calling them "Pig Mints"). And its golf shirts don't have alligators; they have pigs.

23. **Join a Trend.** Capitalize on the latest craze by giving your products a special touch. When Gorbachev's glasnost captured the headlines, The Sharper Image offered Russian Army Watches. Telescopes attracted special interest for Edmund Scientific when Halley's Comet was due to come into view. A winning television show, a popular movie, a best-selling novel, a new fashion trend—all offer opportunities to give conventional items a new look.

24. **Change Countries.** Spiegel was able to build renewed interest in a wide variety of products by issuing special catalogs featuring merchandise from Ireland, Italy, and Scandinavia. The Franklin Mint had a big success with a special St. Patrick's Day medal made of Irish silver.

**Figure 5–10
Add Fun**

The kind of humor that can lead to distinctive mail order products is in "The Pork Avenue Collection" catalog of Hog Wild! It features products with "a touch of pig." Copyright © Hog Wild! 1986. All copyright and trademark rights reserved.

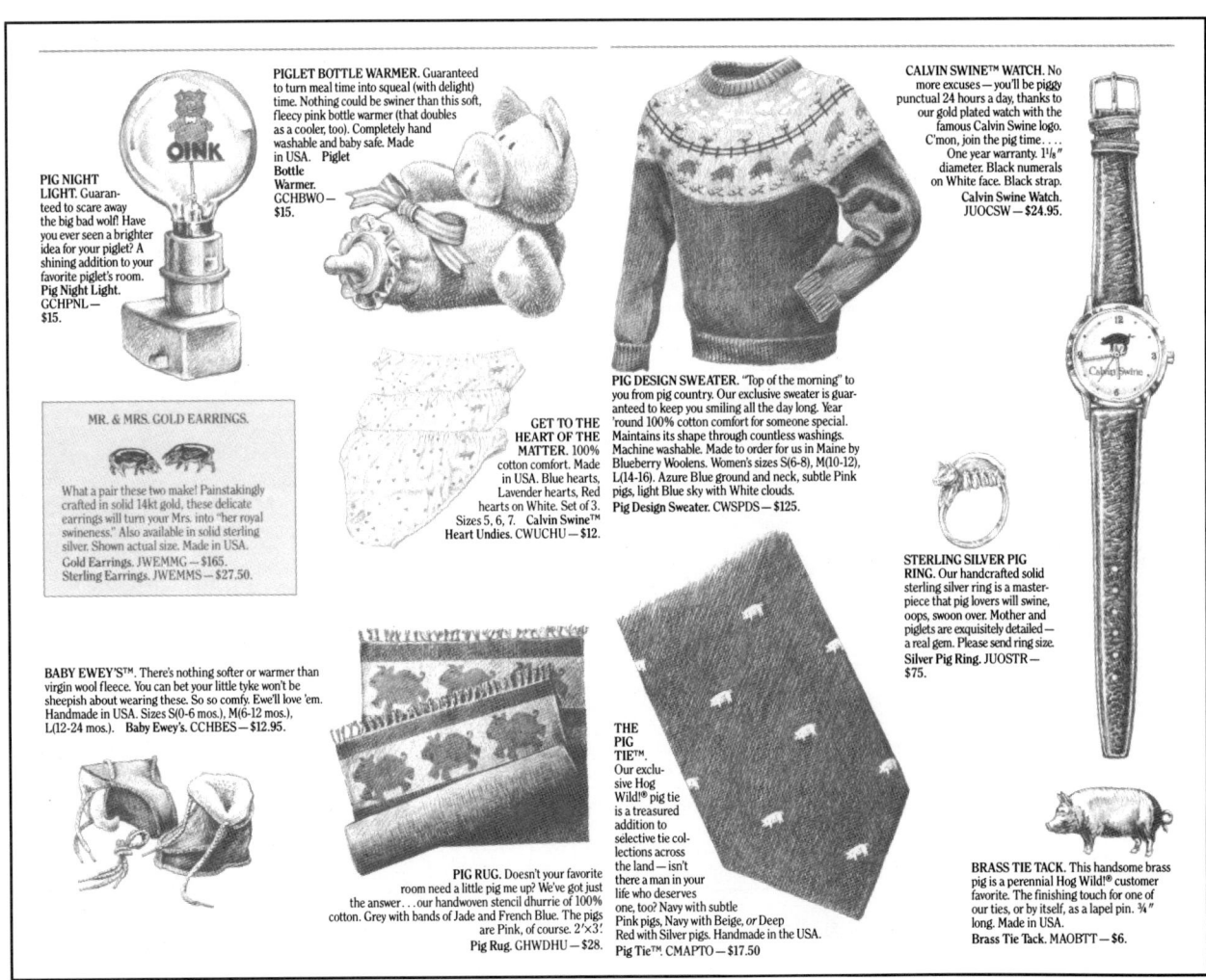

25. **Add a Celebrity.** American Beauty Roses increased interest in a new rose by naming it "Peggy Lee." Sears boosted sales of sporting goods by using baseball great Ted Williams as a spokesman. Spiegel had Candice Bergen select all of the products for a last-minute Christmas gift catalog.

Figure 5–11
Change Countries

American mail order buyers show special interest in products with a foreign origin. For example, Spiegel developed this 36-page catalog devoted to products from Sweden, Norway, Denmark and Finland. Copyright © Spiegel. Used with permission.

Figure 5–12
Add a Celebrity

A product can attract special interest when its presentation is tied in with a celebrity. American Beauty Roses, for example, named a new rose for singer Peggy Lee. Copyright © Foster and Gallagher. Used with permission.

© COPYRIGHT 1991 DARTNELL CORPORATION

How to Select Good Mail Order Products

Len Carlson, who created the Sunset House catalog, which was the world's largest specialty catalog company until low-ticket catalogs became uneconomical due to rising costs of printing, paper, and postage, created a 34-point checklist which is still one of the best guides to selecting products for all types of mail order catalogs.

1. Is there a perceived need for the product?
2. Is it practical?
3. Is it unique?
4. Is the price right?
5. Is it good value?
6. Is the markup sufficient?
7. Does it have broad appeal?
8. Are there specific smaller segments of my list that have a strong desire for the product?
9. Is it new? Or, will my customers perceive it to be new?
10. Will it photograph or illustrate interestingly?
11. Are there sufficient unusual selling features to make the copy exciting?
12. Is it economical to ship? Too fragile? Odd-shaped? Too heavy? Too big?
13. Can it be personalized?
14. Are there any legal problems to overcome?
15. Is it safe to use?
16. Is the supplier reputable?
17. Will backup merchandise be available for fast shipment on reorders?
18. Does my mother (wife, brother, husband) like it? [Somewhat tongue-in-cheek, Len adds, "If so, it probably should be discarded." But this is an important caution. Just because you and your family like something doesn't mean it's right for your catalog audience. If you're in love with a product, you may be wearing blinders and fail to recognize how others will react.]
19. Might returns be too huge?
20. Will refurbishing of returned merchandise be practical?
21. Is it, or can it be, packaged attractively?
22. Are usage instructions clear?
23. How does it compare to competitive products?
24. Will it have exclusivity?
25. Will it lend itself to repeat business?
26. Is it consumable (for repeat orders)?
27. Is it faddy? Too short-lived?

28. Is it seasonal for mail order selling?
29. Can an add-on product make it more distinctive and saleable?
30. Will the number of stockkeeping units (sizes and colors) create inventory problems?
31. Does it lend itself to multiple pricing?
32. Is it too readily available in stores?
33. Is it like an old, hot item that guarantees its success?
34. Or is it doomed because similar items failed before?

Another good set of guidelines for product selection was included in Roger Horchow's interesting book, *Elephants In Your Mailbox* (Times Books, New York, 1980). [This is one of three outstanding books telling about personal experiences in cataloging. I recommend reading all three, both for enjoyment and because they're filled with important tips on how to create successful catalogs. The other two are by Stanley Marcus: *His & Hers:—The Fantasy World of the Neiman-Marcus Catalogue* (Viking Penguin, New York, 1982) and *Quest For The Best* (McGraw-Hill Publishing Co., New York, 1985).]

Even though the Horchow Collection features products at the opposite end of the scale from those which were in the Sunset House catalogs, it is interesting to note the many similarities between the Carlson and Horchow checklists. Here's Roger Horchow's list.

- Is it a good value?
- Will it give us enough profit?
- Is it a straightforward, honest item?
- Is it of good quality? (We want to protect the customer, first of all; but, also, we don't want to have to take a lot of merchandise back because it is poorly made or of inferior material.)
- Is it easy to pack and ship? (I should say, can it be made to fit, we have to pack and ship lots of things that aren't *easy*.)
- Is there a lot of competition on the item? (We don't like to copy others.)
- Will it be understood from a photograph? (Stationery, for example, does not sell well from photographs.)
- Is it a sensible item or would it be used just to create a sensational image? (We don't do any "His & Hers" type offerings for glamor only; we leave that to others.) [An interesting comment since Roger Horchow not only was associated with Neiman-Marcus before starting his own business but, after writing his book, sold the Horchow Collection to Neiman-Marcus.]
- Have we had anything like it before to which we may compare sales potential?

- If not, is it worth trying?
- Will it be exclusive to the Horchow Collection?
- If it is not exclusive, where else will it be sold?
- How long will we be allowed to have the item before it is sold to the general market?
- If it is clothing, will there be a size problem, or will one size fit all?
- Can we explain how it fits, or works, in our copy or over the telephone? (We simply can't say, "Oh, you'll just have to try it and see.")

Roger Horchow has one special technique he uses regularly in evaluating potential products for his catalogs. He asks himself to whom he would likely give this item as a gift. If he can't think of someone, the item doesn't get space in the catalog.

The 10 Key Factors in Selecting Catalog Merchandise

In my catalog seminars, I offer my own checklist of what I consider the 10 most important factors in selecting catalog merchandise.

1. **Is it wanted from YOU?** Just because there is demand for a product doesn't necessarily mean that your customers want to buy it from you. This has a lot to do with one of the key words I explained in Chapter 2—"authority." No matter how hard you try, you will never be able to convince even your best customers that you are the logical source for everything.

    Sears is respected by its customers as an authority in areas such as tools and appliances. But it has never been able to get customers to accept it as an authority on fashions. Penney's, on the other hand, has great authority on many kinds of soft goods, but it had to give up on automotive accessories and finds its catalog buyers going to Sears for tools.

    Whenever considering a new product, be sure to ask yourself if your customers are likely to make you their first choice if they want to purchase that item.

2. **Is it "priceable"?** By that I mean, can you offer it at a price which seems "right" to your customers and still make a profit for you?

    In catalog selling, the average order size will play a major role in determining how much markup a product must carry. While "keystone" pricing is standard in many retail stores (i.e., doubling your cost price to get your selling price), this probably won't be sufficient if your average orders are $35 or below. While some very popular products may be profitable with a two-time markup, you'll need a lot of other products with at least a three-to-one markup. Keystone may prove to be a good average markup if your orders are in the $35 to $75 range. But you probably won't want to consider smaller markups until your average orders start moving beyond the $75 level.

But markups alone are just one of the pricing factors you must consider. You'll need to offer a range of price points—particularly if you have a gift catalog. And you'll have to consider inventory costs. Highly seasonal items, for example, may have to be warehoused from one season to the next—and the carrying cost of the inventory and storage may reduce their profitability.

3. Is it "presentable"? Can you use a single photograph to present the item in your catalog? Can it be described fully with a limited number of words? Or is it a "touch and feel" product—something customers must see "in the flesh" and handle before they can determine if they want it?

Keep in mind that every square inch in your catalog must generate the costs of producing that square inch, plus something left over for the profit column. Can you afford enough square inches for an adequate product presentation?

4. Is it "orderable"? There are many items which simply can't be ordered in the spaces on a catalog order form. You need more information from the customer than can be fitted into the space available.

And even if you think everything necessary can be fitted onto the order form, will your customer have confidence in ordering? I hate to think of how many catalog orders have been lost because customers just weren't sure they would get exactly what they wanted if they simply provided you with the information you required on your order form. (We'll discuss the whole subject of order forms in detail in Chapter 10.)

5. Is it "shippable"? While modern packaging methods make it possible to safely ship almost anything these days, that doesn't mean you can do it profitably. (And even if it can be shipped, will your customers *believe* you can get it to them without damage?)

You'll have to consider the sizes and shapes of cartons in your basic inventory. Anything which requires an odd-shaped carton is not only likely to cost more to pack and ship, but could easily disrupt your fulfillment operations.

One of the factors to include when evaluating a new item is whether it will come in a reshippable container, or you will have to repack it before it heads to the customer.

Weight is another important consideration—particularly if you will be basing shipping and handling charges on the dollar amount of the order (the most common method used by consumer catalogs to recover shipping and handling costs). Ten pounds of nails and one feather pillow may bring in the same amount for shipping and handling, but it will obviously cost a lot more to get those nails to the customer.

6. **Is it "receivable"?** When your customers open your packages, will they feel they have received something every bit as good as what they expected? It's easy to oversell an item in a catalog, making it look and sound better than it really is. This may pull a lot of initial orders. But it can prove a disaster in the long run. You'll not only get lots of returns, but you'll also end up with a lot of customers who will never again believe what you say in your catalogs and will be lost to you forever.

7. **Is it "usable"?** Can the customer immediately put the product to use after unpacking it, or will there be lots of questions to answer? Good assembly, use, and care instructions are a must in mail order. (And beware of simply using those created by the vendor—particularly if you've sourced the product abroad. Far too often, these prepackaged instructions were created or translated by people who already know a lot about the product and assume everyone else has the same starting point. Before ever shipping an instruction sheet, have it read by some of the least-educated people in your company and see if they can follow the directions without having to ask questions.)

I know I'm not alone in an experience I had some years ago. I had purchased a three-piece toy kitchen appliance set for my youngest daughter's Christmas present. The copy in the catalog had said, "Assembles easily in minutes." I should have known better, but after we put my daughter to bed on Christmas Eve, I unpacked the set and began the assembly. Two hours later, I was still having no luck with the first of the three items, so I convinced an engineer friend to come over and help me. Three hours later, the two of us finally managed to complete assembly of that first unit—the other two had to wait until the Christmas rush was over. That was over 30 years ago, and I've never made another purchase from that catalog!

When calculating product costs, always keep in mind postsale customer service costs. If customers are going to keep calling for advice about the product, your customer service costs will wipe out any profits you may have made.

8. **Is it "refurbishable"?** Expect merchandise returns. That's a normal part of catalog marketing. But how much will it cost to refurbish those returned items and put them back into your inventory?

9. **Is it "extendable"?** Is this an item that, once purchased, will lead to repeat orders? Can you sell the customer accessories and supplies?

10. **Is it in "the correct image"?** This is a key question to ask. You can ruin a good catalog by trying to load it with lots of products unrelated to your basic image. Watch out, in particular, for products not in keeping with your catalog's basic quality level. They can easily confuse your customers—and confused customers quickly look for another catalog from which to order . . . or head for the nearest store.

    Many catalogs have failed as a direct result of forgetting who they were. They'd get excited about every new product that showed up and squeeze it onto their pages. Pretty soon, they ended up with a catalog without a unique personality—and their customers were heading elsewhere.

Have a written guideline establishing the parameters for product selection—and stick with it!

The Ultimate Authority—Your Customer

Once a catalog has been published, forget everything you *thought* you knew about product selection. Your customers will quickly tell you what they want to buy from you—and what they don't want to buy from you.

One of the biggest reasons for catalog failures is that the entrepreneur and the buyers fall in love with favorite items of merchandise they've selected for the catalog. When an item doesn't sell as expected, they shout, "You used a bad photograph" . . . "You wrote poor copy" . . . "You put it on the wrong page." So the item is kept in the catalog. A new photo is shot, new copy is written, the item gets a special spot in the next catalog. And the inventory continues to gather dust on the warehouse shelves.

© COPYRIGHT 1991 DARTNELL CORPORATION

It's almost impossible to convert a "loser" into a "winner," regardless of how much creative effort is applied. By giving it a lot of special attention, a loser may break even or produce marginal profits, but in 99 percent of the cases, you'll be better off carefully analyzing the products your customers prefer and spending your time finding more like them, rather than devoting your effort to "saving" your personal favorites.

# Organizing Your Catalog

6

Think of your catalog as a store in print. How does your favorite store organize its merchandise? Chances are, it groups related merchandise in logical categories so you'll have a good idea of where to go to find a given item whenever you visit the store.

This same basic form of organization is important in catalogs. Whenever you have enough products to create a product category, they should be grouped together in your catalog.

Over the years, I've heard many marketers insist that if they made products easy to find, customers would just skip from one favorite section to another and ignore everything in between. That may seem logical, but it flies in the face of the actual experience of thousands of catalogers.

In nearly 30 years of working with hundreds of catalogs both in the United States and abroad, I've never seen a case of too much organization. In fact, I've found departmentalization of merchandise has been the single most effective technique in increasing the profitability of weak catalogs.

Too often, a catalog is organized by who buys the merchandise or where it is located in a warehouse. One of the gift catalogs on which I was asked to assist had traditionally assigned each merchandise buyer a specific number of pages. Each buyer was assigned the responsibility of dealing with all vendors in a specific geographical area, rather than being assigned a merchandise category. As a result, similar items often appeared in different parts of the catalog. For example, three different buyers had located decorative miniature trees, which were scattered throughout the catalog. By combining them onto one spread, total sales for the decorative trees increased 300 percent.

While sales increases of 300 percent are unusual, you will generally find greater sales for any given category of merchandise if all items are grouped in the same section of your catalog.

Even when you don't have enough of any one category of merchandise to create a meaningful department along the lines of what you might find in a retail store, there are other ways to group merchandise for maximum effect. You can group it by color . . . by how it is used . . . by seasonality . . . by price points . . . by users' sex . . . by users' age group . . . and in many other ways.

As we pointed out in Chapter 2, "memorability" is a key factor in catalog success. Your catalog is likely to get an "editorial reading" well before any orders are placed. And it is important for customers to come out of that editorial reading with a lasting impression of your catalog—not only who you are, but what products you offer. If you've departmentalized your merchandise, readers are more likely to remember that your catalog offers a given category of products; thus they are more likely to return to it when it's time to purchase such products.

We also pointed out that catalog buyers are "lazy" buyers. They don't want to have to go to a lot of effort to locate products. If you make it difficult for them, they'll simply seek out a competitor's catalog where things are organized for them.

Indexes and Tables of Contents

Any discussion of catalog organization invariably leads to the question of whether or not to include an index. My suggestion is that unless you have a very large catalog, you should consider a table of contents listing your basic product categories, rather than an every-item index.

In my experience, I've found those most likely to use a detailed index are your own staff and your competitors. Your customers are perfectly happy with a less detailed table of contents.

One of the problems with an every-item index is that you are likely to use a different language than your audience. If they look for "their" word and don't find it in the index, they are likely to assume you don't carry that item, even though you may have listed it using "your" word.

I recall a classic research project I conducted some years ago for a leading automobile manufacturer. An argument had developed between the engineers and the marketing department about what should be included in the owner's manual that goes into the glove compartment of each new car. So they called for outside research to determine what new car owners really wanted in their manuals.

We interviewed 5,000 owners of that make of car—100 in each of 50 different markets. What was interesting was that in each of those 50 markets, the most-asked-for item was the same: "How much gas does the gas tank hold?"

That information was already included in their owner's manuals. But it was listed under "Fuel Capacity" rather than "Gas" or "Gas Tank," and the owners hadn't thought to look for it under that heading.

If you do decide on an index, it is a good idea to have an outside indexer, who isn't handicapped by your internal language, create the listings for you. But in most cases, all you'll really need is a table of contents—something you should be able to create internally.

It isn't necessary to devote valuable selling space in the front of your catalog or opposite the back cover to a table of contents or index. Just put it in some less valuable space and tell your customers where to find it.

A helpful device to make it easy for your customers to locate merchandise in your catalog is an "edge index." There are several variations of this device. The most common is a solid color bar bleeding off the edge of each page. Then, even before a catalog is opened, a reader can identify the location of each category of merchandise simply by looking at the colors bleeding off the trimmed edges of the pages.

Pictorial indexes can also be useful. Inmac, a computer supplies catalog, provides a good example of this technique. Inmac uses a third of page 3 of its catalogs for a table of contents, with a black-and-white line drawing assigned to each merchandise category (Peripherals, Cables & Accessories, Printer & Plotter Supplies, Workstation Furniture & Accessories, etc.). At the upper corner of each page, one of these symbols is printed. By fanning the catalog, a reader can quickly locate each category of merchandise.

How Many Pages Should Your Catalog Have?

As a general rule, the more pages your catalog has, the more business you will do. But it's important to add a big "if"—if you have enough additional items with strong appeal to your audience to fill more pages.

The typical consumer mail order catalog averages 10 items per

Figure 6–1
Pictorial Indexes

An excellent device to make it easy for customers to find products in a catalog is a pictorial index. Inmac, for example, carries a table of contents on page 3 of its catalog, with a symbol for each product category. These symbols are then shown on the upper corner of each page so a reader can quickly locate each product category. Copyright © Inmac. Used with permission.

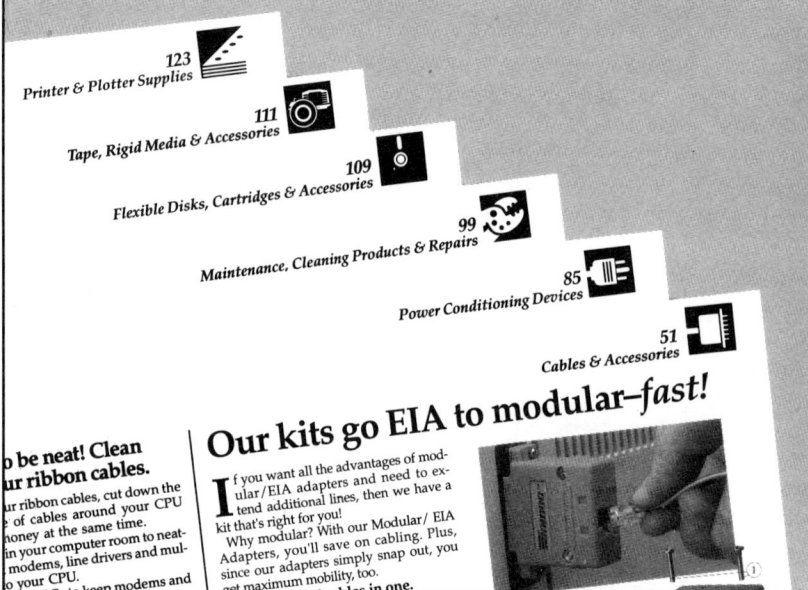

Complete index on next two pages		
	New Products	3A-15
	Productivity Boosters	16-19, 192-202
	Data Communications	20-46
	Cables & Accessories	47-81
	Power Conditioning Devices	82-93
	Test & Monitoring Devices	94-96
	Maintenance, Cleaning Products & Repairs	97-101
	Flexible Disks, Cartridges & Accessories	102-109
	Tape, Rigid Media & Accessories	110-117
	Printer & Plotter Supplies	118-146
	Security & Antistatic Products	147-152
	Workspace Maximizers	153-159
	Workstation Furniture & Accessories	160-191
	Ordering Information	203

spread—5 per page. Since printing economies usually call for increasing page counts in minimum increments of eight pages, you'll have to ask yourself if you have at least 40 products of merit to justify additional pages.

Frequently, the average number of line items ordered and the average order amount don't change greatly as you increase page count, but the total number of orders often increases. The larger the catalog, the more likely it will be "significant" to recipients.

Since ordering often doesn't start until many days after a catalog is received, it is important to have your catalog look as if it's worth saving. If your catalog is too flimsy, it may be quickly discarded rather than saved. As a rule of thumb, I advise most clients to seek out enough strong products to fill at least 20 pages—a 16-page body plus 4 cover pages. You can sometimes increase the weight of paper to make a smaller catalog seem significant; but unless you're offering products which can't be found in any other catalog, it's difficult to start a catalog with fewer than 100 products.

The Importance of Spreads

It's important to remember that readers seldom look at catalogs one page at a time. Instead, they view each two-page set of facing pages as a single unit—*if* merchandise is presented in spread format. Regardless of whether your readers go from front to back or back to front, their eyes almost always gravitate first to the right-hand page. If you've organized your catalog on a page-by-page basis, rather than spread by spread, there's a tendency for readers to concentrate attention on just the right-hand pages, often ignoring left-hand pages.

I've had new clients tell me their right-hand pages "always pull better," so they put all of their most popular merchandise on those pages and consign "also-rans" to left-hand pages. When I review their catalogs, I invariably find they've laid out their catalogs page by page. When these catalogs are redesigned with spread layout, there is always an increase in total sales for the two pages.

Creating Eye-Flow

The key to a good catalog spread design is establishing strong eye-flow—a planned path for readers to follow. Eye camera studies have shown that, without anything in the design to lead the eyes in an alternate pattern, the majority of readers will enter a spread at the upper right corner of the right-hand page. Their eyes will then flow in a sideways U pattern, downward and to the left, just barely crossing the gutter at the center of the two-page spread. Then the path turns back toward the right and exits the spread at the bottom center of the right-hand page.

There are several ways, however, that you can change this "automatic" eye-flow.

Focal Point

First of all, you can offer readers an obvious point of initial focus. If you use a strong graphic device somewhere on the spread, it is only natural for the eyes to quickly leave the upper right-hand corner and be drawn to this "bull's-eye."

The most obvious focal point is an illustration which is considerably larger than others on the same spread. Or it can be an illustration featuring high intensity colors. Even a large area of "white space" can quickly attract the eye.

If there is just a single illustration with people in it, that illustration is likely to act as an eye magnet. In Chapter 7, you'll find a listing of other design elements which get preferential viewing and thus are important in establishing eye-flow.

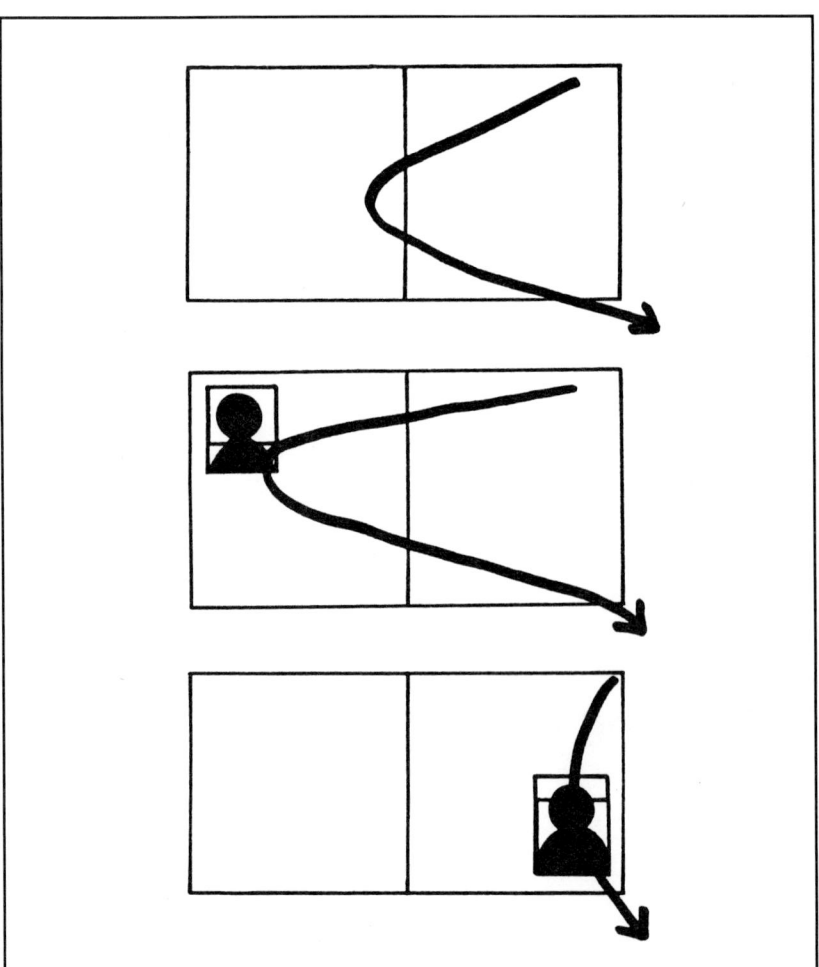

Figure 6–2
Catalog Eye-Flow

Eye camera studies have shown that the average catalog reader looks at the upper right corner of a two-page spread in a catalog. Then, if there aren't graphic elements which divert the eyes, the normal eye-flow is down and to the left, moving slightly across the center of the spread and exiting at the bottom right corner. When a dominant graphic element is positioned on the left page, the eyes will be drawn toward it and then move across the spread before exiting at the bottom of the right page. On the other hand, if a dominant graphic element is positioned at the bottom of the right page, eyes normally flow directly to it and there is a strong tendency to ignore items elsewhere on the spread.

Figure 6–3
Using Gaze Motion Effectively

These two examples show how gaze motion can hurt or help the presentation of merchandise on a catalog spread. In the top example, the model is looking off the spread. Thus, a reader is likely to follow her eyes away from the merchandise and on to the next spread. In the example below, the eyes of the doll are pointing left, encouraging readers to take a look at the remainder of the merchandise on the spread. Copyright © QVC. Used with permission.

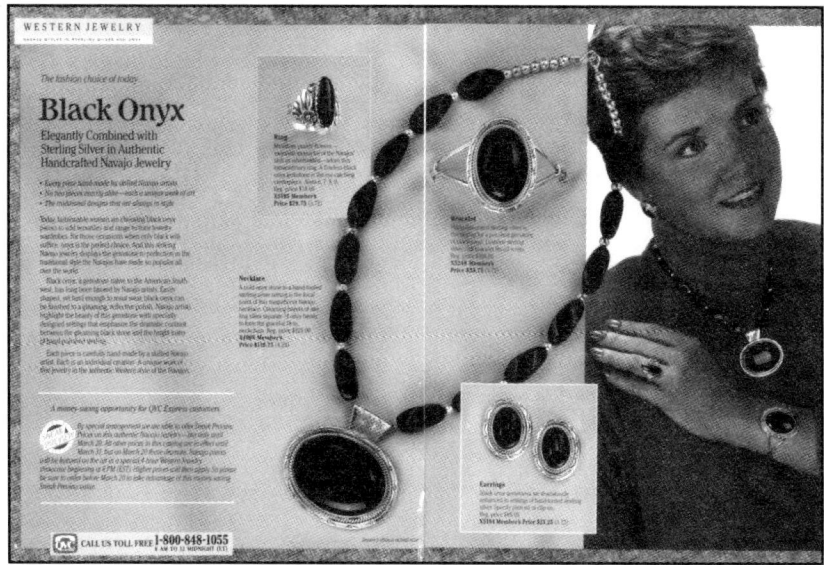

Figure 6–4
Focal Point

A dominant illustration—particularly one featuring a person—serves as an "eye magnet," drawing the eyes from the entry point at the upper right corner of a spread. Copyright © QVC. Used with permission.

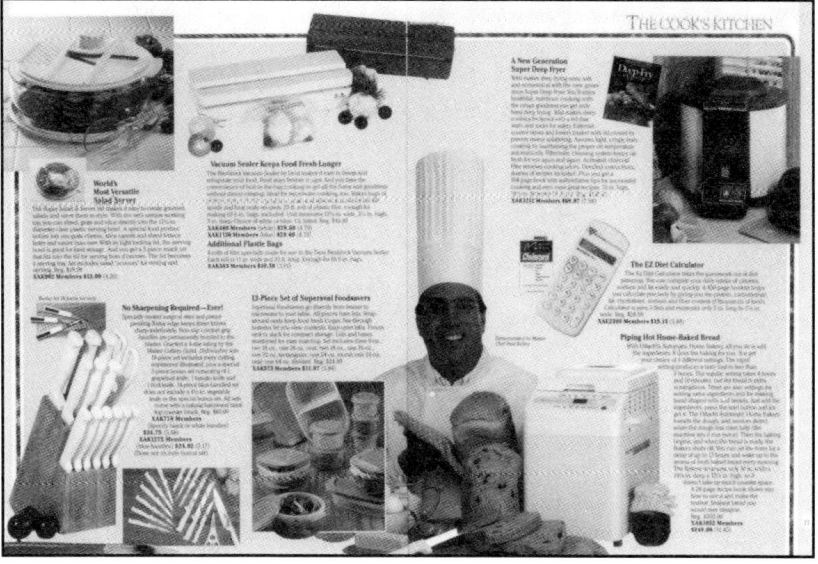

Gaze and Structural Motion

Two types of motion can be utilized by catalog designers to establish eye-flow: gaze motion and structural motion.

Anytime there are eyes in an illustration, the reader automatically looks to see what those eyes are looking at. It's a subconscious reaction but plays a major role in determining what reading path a catalog buyer will follow.

If you have a fashion model in the upper right-hand quadrant of a catalog spread with the eyes looking off the page, the reader is likely to follow those eyes and turn to the next spread without taking time to look elsewhere. But if the model is looking to the left, the reader's eyes will flow in that direction and begin a reading path that can encompass everything else on the spread.

The second kind of motion is structural motion. Anything that tends to "point" will create an involuntary reaction leading the reader in that direction. Perhaps the best example is a shoe. A reader's eyes will automatically move in the direction the toe of the shoe is pointing.

Some products are static in themselves. But by tilting the product, you can stimulate eye movement in the direction of the tilt.

What's so important about creating eye-flow? It helps to lead a catalog reader through all of your merchandise presentations, rather than just concentrating on those which quickly capture the eye. We'll discuss this subject in greater detail in the following chapter.

Figure 6–5
Gaze Motion

It's a natural reaction to look wherever a person's eyes are focused. Note how all three people in this QVC Express catalog are looking directly at the bread maker. Thus, a reader's eyes are immediately drawn to the product being offered for sale. Copyright © QVC. Used with permission.

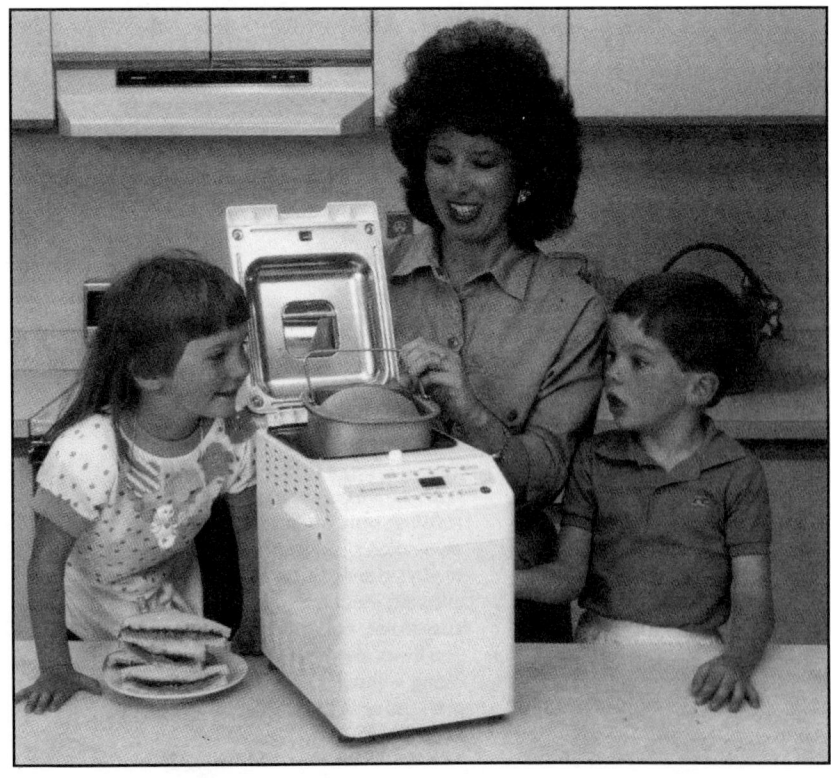

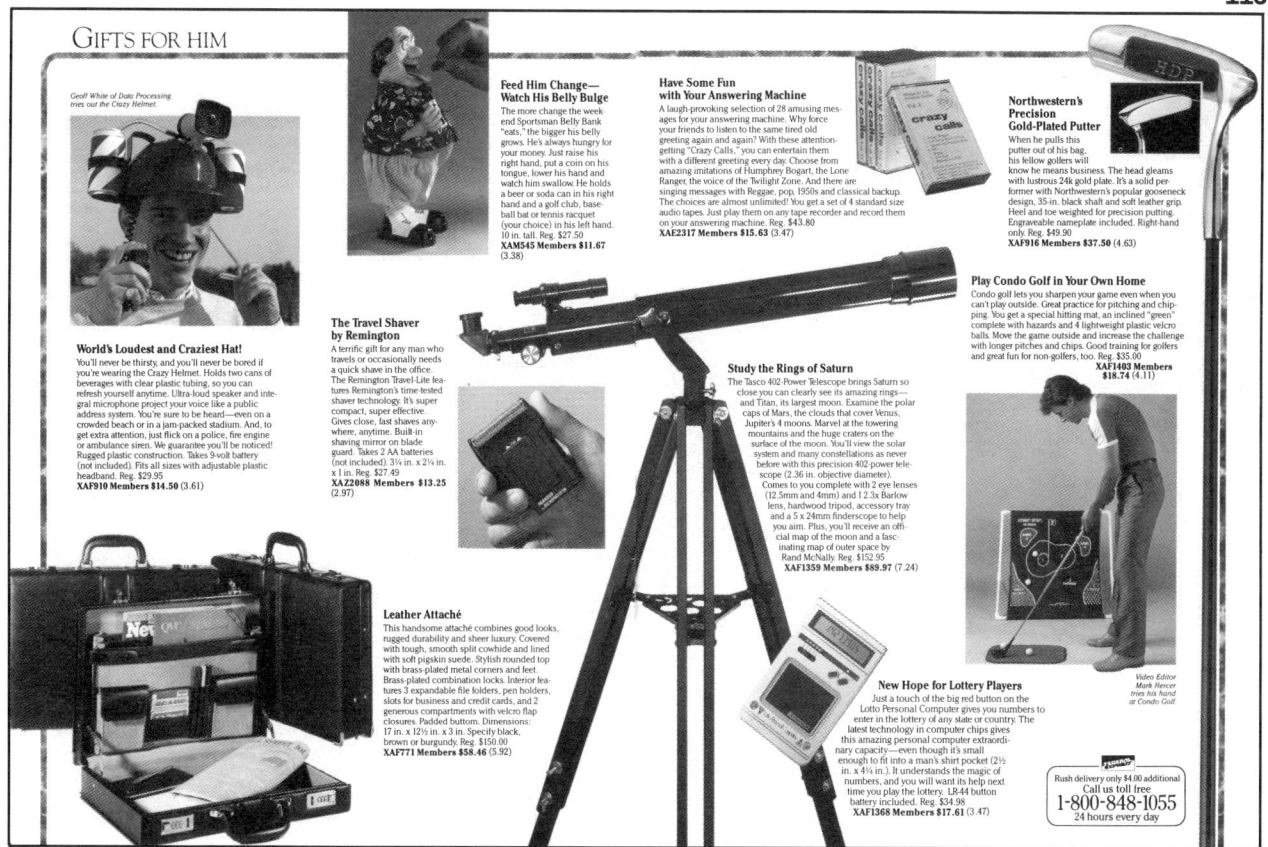

**Figure 6–6
Structural Motion**

Note the structural motion of the telescope in the center of this spread. It strongly points to the right, pushing the eyes in that direction and away from other merchandise on the spread. Copyright © QVC. Used with permission.

Establishing Starting Points

As we've pointed out, a catalog will almost always sell more of a category of merchandise if all of the items in that category are grouped together in one area of the catalog. But beware of presenting all items equally. That not only leads to a dull catalog, but generally reduces total sales for that merchandise category.

A good catalog is a *selling* vehicle, not simply a *reference* book. Customers *want* your advice. If you are carrying 10 steam irons and treat each of them equally, the customer is often confused. Smart catalogers select one of the 10 and give it special treatment, saying, in effect, "If you don't know which one to buy, we *recommend* this one."

The most frequently used visual device to give the reader a starting point in merchandise selection is devoting more space to a selected item. But you can also highlight an item with special design treatments.

Which item you select will depend on a variety of factors. Most often, the item to be featured will be the one most likely to appeal to the majority of buyers who would be interested in that category of merchandise. On the other hand, it may be chosen because it is the newest, because it has special attention-getting features, or because the brand name of the manufacturer carries respect. If there is a wide range of price points, it is quite common to feature an item with a midprice point. At other times, an item will be featured because there is excess inventory to be sold or because that item has the greatest profit margin.

Developing Catalog Continuity

As we noted previously, a catalog is "a store in print." A consistent image is evident in most successful retail establishments. Except for a handful of discount operations and some food and drug chains, successful stores generally develop their own signage, with a consistent type style and sign format. As you move from one department to another, you "feel at home."

This same consistency is an earmark of a good catalog. You should develop specific parameters for page and spread design; pagination; typefaces; promotional blurbs; category identification; use of color; handling of headlines, body copy, and ordering information; etc.

If you jump from one style to another, you breed confusion about your image in your customers' minds. And customer confusion leads to reduced response.

It isn't just between the pages of a single catalog issue that continuity is important. Perhaps even more important is maintaining

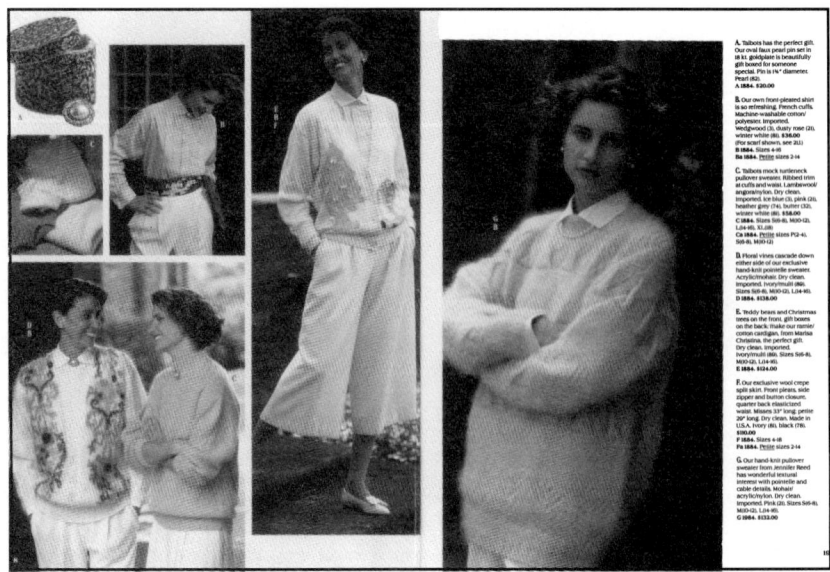

Figure 6-7
Giving the Reader a Starting Point

Talbots regularly offers its customers a wide variety of choices for each category of merchandise. On many pages it selects one item of merchandise and features it so the reader will have a starting point. It is saying, in effect, "If you're confused about where to start, here's our recommendation." Copyright © Talbots. Used with permission.

continuity from one catalog to the next. It's important to remember the basic catalog formula: Prospects = Costs; Customers = Profits. When you change presentation formats, you can turn profitable customers into less responsive prospects who need to be resold on doing business with you.

This isn't to suggest you shouldn't modernize your catalog presentation techniques as the marketplace changes. But it should be done gradually, rather than overnight. A good example of gradual change is provided by today's leading American specialty catalog—L.L. Bean.

From the very beginning, L.L. Bean has had its own unique style of presentation. There have been many changes over the years (see Figure 3-4), but there never is a question that "an old friend is coming to call" whenever an L.L. Bean catalog arrives.

A classic example of how a change in format can confuse loyal customers happened some years back when Sunset House was sold by Len Carlson to the Broadway-Hale stores. Len had created a unique format for the original Sunset House catalogs, with a variety of low-ticket products, each presented in relatively uniform picture-caption format. And, sticking with this format, Sunset House had become the world's largest specialty catalog of its day.

But the new owners decided "everyone was tired" of the old-fashioned format Len Carlson had been using so successfully over the years and the time had come to "modernize" the catalog. Unfortunately, they chose to do it in one giant step. They abandoned the tried-and-proven uniform picture-caption format and featured a number of items at higher price points. Few would question that the new format was more pleasing to the eye.

But they forgot one important thing—Sunset House's millions of customers were buying because they *liked* the old format. They weren't the ones demanding something new. And they proved it by ignoring the "new" catalog which had arrived in their mailboxes.

Fortunately, Sunset House learned their lesson quickly and returned to the established Sunset House style, with just simple modernization. And Sunset House continued to be a customer-pleasing—and profit-producing—catalog for many more years until rising production and postage costs spelled doom for the majority of the low-ticket novelty merchandise catalogs.

There's an old axiom that when you get sick and tired of your advertising, it's about the time outsiders just start to notice it. This is certainly true of catalogs. Most often, catalogs are changed simply because the people producing them are tired of doing the same old thing, without bothering to find out if customers are looking for something new and different.

Figure 6–8
How to Lose Customers and Get Them Back

It's important to remember that your present customers are buying from you because they like your catalog. Sunset House had become the world's largest specialty catalog of its day with the type of presentation shown at the right. When ownership changed, it was decided to "modernize" the catalog (illustration below). Price points went up, the presentation was made more lively...and customers stopped buying. Fortunately, the radical design change lasted only briefly. By reverting to the format customers had shown they liked, Sunset House returned to profitability for several more years. Copyright © Sunset House. Used with permission.

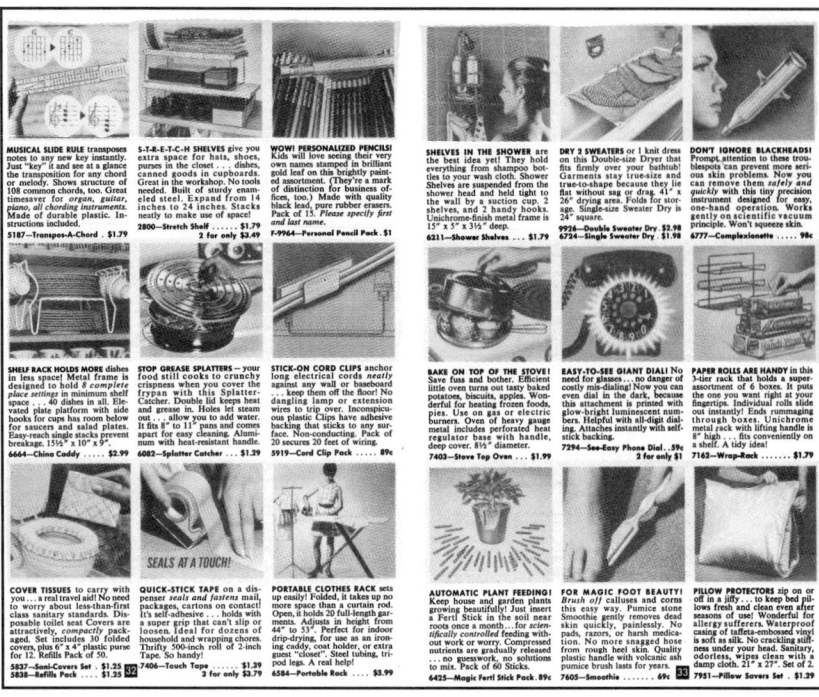

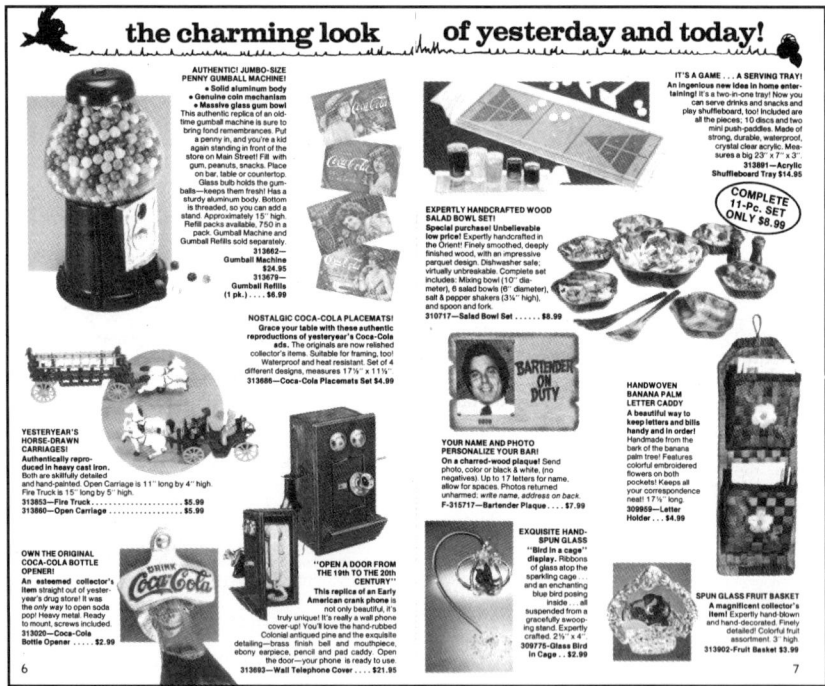

When Should You Change?

While change for change's sake alone is not recommended, there are times when a catalog should make changes. A time for change is when your marketplace changes. It's important to constantly monitor the composition of your buying audience. If you start seeing a different composition of buyers, it's probably an indication that there are new opportunities awaiting you.

Your first consideration should probably be to explore the possibilities of creating an additional catalog to serve growing segments on your list. Often, however, this is uneconomical. Therefore, you may want to consider making gradual revisions to both your product selection and presentation techniques to increase your appeal to new buyers, without sacrificing your appeal to your established customer base.

A number of computer supplies catalogs, for example, developed their basic audience by serving the needs of owners of IBM PC's and compatible computers. But as Apple's Macintosh computers grew in popularity, more and more Apple owners began showing up on buyer lists.

The obvious question was whether to create entirely new catalogs to serve the Apple market or simply add additional Macintosh-related items to the regular catalogs. Both techniques were used successfully. But the more common was to simply expand existing catalogs and add special messages for each segment of the audience, highlighting new products of special interest to each.

Developing Change of Pace

While catalog continuity is important, too much emphasis on continuity can result in dull catalogs—and dull catalogs are often unprofitable catalogs.

Every spread in a catalog shouldn't look just like every other spread, with just the products changed. Some catalogs look like a row of telephone poles stretching down a dull and dreary highway.

Browsing through a newly arrived catalog is not unlike driving down an interstate highway. You can get "highway hypnosis." You're just driving along and don't really see anything of interest—until you come to an abrupt change of scenery. Then you sit up and take notice.

It's just as easy to get "catalog hypnosis." You keep turning pages, and before you know it, you've reached the end of the catalog and nothing has really registered in your mind. But some variety in your spread layouts will help to capture readers' attention. In particular, using a variety of different techniques to present unique and interesting products will heighten readers' interest in your entire merchandise presentation.

It is particularly important to emphasize the beginning of each new category of merchandise. While readers may not have been especially interested in the section they've just passed through, it's easy just to keep moving along unless there's something to say, in effect, "Wait a minute! We have something different for you to consider now."

Magalogs and Catazines

As the number of specialty catalogs proliferated and the frequency of distribution of many catalogs increased, new interest was created in the use of magazine techniques to create a new look for each catalog.

I have to confess to being the language culprit who, when I was editing magazines back in the 1950s, introduced a new word, "Magalog," to describe that odd couple—the combination magazine and catalog. Even then the idea wasn't new. I don't have historical records to show when the idea first came onto the scene, but there is evidence this hybrid product has been around for over a century.

Some time later, I coined another new word, "Catazine," to describe a variation on the Magalog—the use of magazine editorial techniques for merchandise presentation in catalogs.

There is an important difference.

In the so-called Magalog, an attempt is made to *disguise* a merchandise-selling catalog as a magazine, with the thought that you can get readers involved in the stories behind a company and its products before asking them to send in orders.

While a newly issued Magalog frequently receives a lot of attention, I know of no case where it has proven successful over an extended period. It does offer an interesting way to introduce a new catalog, but it seldom has lasting power. In fact, Magalogs have won awards in competitions, only to be quickly discontinued or replaced by a forthright catalog.

The Magalog technique, however, may continue to be used with success to introduce an established catalog to new markets. Such presentations are not intended as a regular bill of fare, but as an opportunity to say the kinds of things an audience needs to know before accepting a new source from which to do their mail order buying.

I've used this Magalog technique on a number of occasions over the years, but once the catalogs had been introduced, editorial material was quickly dropped and product selling presentations got maximum attention.

Simply using long copy to describe catalog merchandise doesn't make a catalog a Magalog. The classic example of this technique was the Products That Think catalogs published by Joe Sugarman. Joe is an ace copywriter, and he used his always intriguing copy to convert what might otherwise be a routine product into something unique. He often used as many as two copy-packed pages to sell a single item. That was his style. But never for a moment did he suggest there was any reason for reading the copy other than to sell the product. His catalogs may have looked like Magalogs, but they were definitely Catazines.

In a Catazine, it is very apparent right up front that the objective is to sell something. But by using magazine-type techniques, it's possible to make one catalog stand out from another. Catazine techniques are the catalog sweepstakes of today.

Back in the heyday of the novelty merchandise catalogs such as Sunset House, Foster House and Spencer Gifts—the big circulation specialty catalogs of 20 years ago—there was a basic problem. Catalogs were mailed frequently, but there was little change in merchandise from one catalog to another. So how do you make each catalog fresh and appealing? The answer then was to feature sweepstakes, which could be made new and interesting each time a catalog was mailed, even though the catalogs themselves had few changes.

Sweepstakes have lost their luster for most catalogs today, but today's specialty catalog leaders have a problem just like the one that faced yesterday's novelty merchandise catalogs. Lands' End and The Sharper Image, for example, mail catalogs monthly with little change of products from one to the next. So to make the merchandise look fresh and interesting, these (and many other catalogs) adopt editorial presentation techniques. They photograph the merchandise in different settings or with different props . . . they approach copy

**Figure 6–9
Long Copy Classic**

The catalog which really introduced long, editorial-style copy to the consumer market was Joe Sugarman's Products That Think. The use of long narrative copy was logical since customers had been acquired through first time purchases in response to long-copy editorial-style publication ads. Copyright © JS & A. Used with permission.

from many different angles... and they use variety in pagination... plus an assortment of special, but not dominating, editorial features.

A third type of catalog-magazine combination is used primarily by catalogs that carry a relatively high cover price and are intended to be retained for buying over an extended period. One example is the comprehensive catalog of Colonial Williamsburg. It combines reference material on colonial American furnishings with a complete presentation of Williamsburg reproductions.

Colonial Williamsburg asked $8.95 for each catalog. And therein lies a problem. Once a prospect has laid out such a princely sum for a catalog, he or she isn't likely to buy another copy for a number of years—particularly when there are very few new products added from one year to the next. But prices do change, and it's important to encourage customers and prospects to obtain the latest catalog.

This was the problem Colonial Williamsburg tossed at me some years ago. My solution was to add editorial reference material which could be changed from issue to issue. Thus, even if products remained pretty much the same, a catalog could become "new."

Another kind of Magalog continues to survive—but its primary purpose is not to generate direct response orders. This is the type of Magalog published regularly by stores such as Harrods in England and Hermes in France. Several American department stores have also published similar Magalogs. These beautifully produced maga-

Figure 6–10
Refreshing a Catalog

Even though there were few product changes, Colonial Williamsburg wanted to give its catalog a fresh look each year. To accomplish this, they introduced new editorial features in each issue. Copyright © Colonial Williamsburg. Used with permission.

zines do feature many items of merchandise which you can order by mail or phone, but they are primarily designed for image building and to generate store traffic. (And they often have an additional profit-making benefit for the stores, since advertising space can be sold to vendors.)

There are occasions when a true editorial product can be useful to supplement catalogs. Lands' End, for example, uses an effective "who we are" booklet, which it sends along with its latest catalog to fulfill catalog requests generated by publication advertising. It's a 16-page black-and-white picture story tracing Lands' End's history from its original 1963 yachting supply store in Chicago's old tannery district to the 40-acre cornfield in rural Wisconsin from which it serves millions of mail order customers today.

A key feature of the Lands' End booklet is a listing of the eight "Principles of Doing Business," which are the backbone of Lands' End's success story.

An equally effective image-building catalog editorial supplement was distributed some years ago by Carl Forslund & Sons. It was a spectacular picture-story booklet, "Fine Furniture Begins at Seven," which was filled with heartwarming photographs of the first day the late Carl Forslund's seven-year-old grandson visited the Forslund furniture "manufactory" in Grand Rapids. It demonstrated for customers Carl's pride in both his business and his family—the cornerstones of his successful mail order business. It was mailed ahead of Forslund's annual catalog and effectively created special interest for the catalog to come.

It should be noted that both the Lands' End and Forslund booklets were separate pieces—not Magalogs with image-building editorial and merchandise-selling presentations competing for the customer's attention.

Effective Catalog Design

7

Beware of Art Directors!

I say that somewhat facetiously since art directors are a vital part of any catalog team. A catalog is primarily a design medium—if the product presentations don't attract attention, few will stop to read the copy.

But good art directors tend to have a strong creative ego and often are anxious to win the applause of their peers. They love to win awards in art directors' competitions. And all too often, an award-winning catalog fails in the most important competition of all—winning sales!

Unique design techniques most often win art directors' awards. But in a good catalog, the techniques of presentation must take a backseat to the merchandise. When design techniques get special attention, the merchandise gets less attention, and the catalog rings up fewer sales.

This isn't to suggest every catalog should have sterile design. The best catalog art directors successfully use innovative presentation techniques to direct increased attention to the merchandise and, at the same time, create a distinctive appearance for the catalog.

But while innovative presentation techniques that give your catalog a distinctive look are desirable, it is important to establish a basic style for your catalog and weave innovations into the established format. You will want to establish guidelines on selection of typefaces, basic page and spread formats, use of space and color, how and when models should be used, use of repeated design devices (e.g., those to identify new or exclusive products), placement of ordering information, etc.

Selection of Typefaces

While copy is secondary to illustrations in a catalog, typographic styling is an important part of your design. Some of the basics of typography should influence your selection of typefaces.

The first thing to remember is how almost everyone was taught to read. As children, Americans learned to read from left to right and from top to bottom. Copy, for the most part, was in black on white. And most early reading involved a "reading crutch." That crutch was found in so-called Roman typefaces—type with serifs, which create a line to hold the eye while reading.

Today many art directors prefer sans serif faces; the most popular being **Helvetica**. While there is nothing wrong with sans serif type, a little bit can go a long way. The problem is the absence of those little feet on letters—the serifs—which provide that line to hold the eye. Since a serif line is missing in sans serif typefaces, it is necessary to add extra white space between each line to create a line of white space, so the eye won't slip from one line to the next while reading. And because you have to add that extra white space, you end up having to reduce the amount of copy you can fit into a given amount of space.

While catalogs with only a minimum amount of copy can be less concerned with the selection of typefaces for body copy, those using longer copy should give special attention to some readership research studies which have been conducted in recent years.

The most important studies were conducted in Australia to determine how different typographic treatments affect comprehension of editorial material. These studies, conducted by Colin Wheildon, publications editor for Australia's National Roads and Motorists Association in Sydney, were oriented toward magazine readership, but the results can be applied equally to long-copy catalogs.

More than 200 readers were presented with a series of one-page magazine articles in different formats and then tested to determine how presentation techniques affected the comprehension of what they had read.

For example, one group of the articles was set in a conventional Roman typeface with serifs (eight-point Corona on a nine-point body), while others were set in the most popular sans serif type (eight-point **Helvetica** on a nine-point body). There were groups of articles in each typeface with the body copy set flush left and right; flush left, ragged right; and flush right, ragged left.

While the use of sans serif typefaces has become widespread in Australia, just as it has in the United States and Europe, the tests showed reading comprehension drops drastically when sans serif faces are used for body copy—from 67 percent comprehension of copy set

Preferred Setting — Roman Type
(12 pt. Times Roman, 1 pt. leaded)

Most everyone learned to read using a crutch — the serifs on Roman types such as this example set in 12 pt. Times Roman. Because the serifs provide a base line, there is little tendency for the eye to slip from one line to the next while reading. When additional space is introduced between lines, copy appears more difficult to read.

Wrong Setting — Roman Type
(12 pt. Times Roman, 6 pt. leaded)

Most everyone learned to read using a crutch — the serifs on Roman types such as this example set in Times Roman. Because the serifs provide a base line, there is little tendency for the eye to slip from one line to the next while reading. When additional space is introduced between lines, copy appears more difficult to read.

Wrong Setting — Sans-Serif
(12 pt. Helvetica, 1 pt. leaded)

Many catalog art directors prefer using a sans-serif type such as this example set in 12 pt. Helvetica. Because there are no serifs to hold the eye while reading, there is a tendency to slip from line to line unless additional space is used between lines to create a line of white space.

Better Setting — Sans-Serif
(12 pt. Helvetica, 6 pt. leaded)

Many catalog art directors prefer using a sans-serif type such as this example set in 12 pt. Helvetica. Because there are no serifs to hold the eye while reading, there is a tendency to slip from line to line unless additional space is used between lines to create a line of white space.

Figure 7–1
Roman vs. Sans Serif Typefaces

While sans serif typefaces have grown in popularity among catalog art directors, research studies indicate such typefaces often create reading difficulties, particularly when there is too little line spacing. Comprehension of copy set in sans serif type can be improved by introducing "a line of white space" between each line of copy. On the other hand, traditional Roman typefaces have serifs which create a base line to hold the eye while reading. When additional line spacing is used with Roman types, copy often appears more difficult to read.

flush left and right in Roman serif type to just 12 percent when the same copy was set flush left and right in Helvetica sans serif.

Ragged copy also resulted in a drop in comprehension. In contrast to the 67 percent comprehension level of Roman type set flush left and right, comprehension dropped to 38 percent for Roman type set flush left, ragged right, and way down to 10 percent for Roman type set flush right, ragged left.

Although some designers insist italic type is "hard to read," there was little drop in comprehension (only to 65 percent from 67 percent) when an italic version was substituted for regular Roman type (both set flush left and right).

Copy Set Flush Left & Right

Reseach studies show that copy set flush left and right has much higher comprehension than copy set either flush left, ragged right, or flush right, ragged left. While this may not be particularly important in relatively short catalog captions, it deserves special attention whenever longer copy is used.

Copy Set Flush Left, Ragged Right

Reseach studies show that
copy set flush left and right
has much higher comprehension
than copy set either
flush left, ragged right,
or flush right, ragged left.
While this may not be
particularly important
in relatively short
catalog captions,
it deserves special
attention whenever
longer copy is used.

Copy Set Flush Right, Ragged Left

Reseach studies show that
copy set flush left and right
has much higher comprehension
than copy set either
flush left, ragged right,
or flush right, ragged left.
While this may not be
particularly important
in relatively short
catalog captions,
it deserves special
attention whenever
longer copy is used.

Figure 7–2
Ragged Typesetting Reduces Comprehension

According to the research studies conducted by Colin Wheildon, comprehension is best when type has been set flush left and right. Compared to a 67% comprehension level for flush left and right, comprehension drops to 38% when type is set flush left, ragged right, and to 10% when type is set flush right, ragged left. While this may not affect most short catalog captions, it can be an important factor when longer copy is used.

In another of Wheildon's studies, he tested what happened to comprehension when boldface type was used. In this case, articles set in regular Times Roman scored a 70 percent good comprehension, which dropped to 30 percent when the same material was set in Times Roman Bold.

Another important typographic consideration for body copy is the width of the type measure. As a general rule, avoid line lengths which are wider than two alphabets of the type you are using. In Wheildon's studies, 38 percent found copy wider than 60 characters "hard to read." But, even more important, another 22 percent said they *wouldn't* read such copy.

A type measure that is too narrow is also to be avoided. Columns with fewer than 20 characters of type were disliked by 87 percent of Wheildon's readers. As a general rule, avoid body copy which is set less than 10 picas wide.

Typefaces for Headings

You have a wider choice in typefaces for headings. While you'll get the greatest comprehension of what your heading says when it is set in upper and lower case letters of a Roman typeface (92 percent in Wheildon's studies), comprehension drops only two percentage points when you use upper and lower case sans serif type (90 percent). But you'll experience a substantial drop in comprehension if you use all capital letters—71 percent for Roman type; 59 percent for sans serif type.

The poorest comprehension comes when you use cursive or script as a heading typeface. (See Table 7–1 for a comparison of various heading typefaces.)

Table 7–1
Typeface Selection and Headline Comprehension

In the copy comprehension studies conducted by Colin Wheildon, it was discovered that the typeface used for headlines can affect the comprehension of what the headline says. While the use of upper and lower case Roman letters provides maximum comprehension (92%), there is only a slight drop when upper and lower case sans serif typefaces are used (90%). The use of all upper case letters results in a serious drop in comprehension. The greatest drop, however, occurs when cursive or script types are used.

Table 7-1   Headline Comprehension

Roman Upper & Lower Case	92%
Sans Serif Upper & Lower Case	90%
Roman Italics Upper & Lower Case	86%
ROMAN ALL CAPS	71%
SANS SERIF ALL CAPS	59%
ITALIC ALL CAPS	57%
Cursive or Script Upper & Lower Case	37%
CURSIVE OR SCRIPT ALL CAPS	26%

Reverse Copy

Remember your audience grew up reading black on white. Whenever you reverse type out of a black or color background, you're introducing an uncomfortable reading experience. Every one of the participants in the Australian tests expressed a dislike for reverse type.

In one of Wheildon's studies, which showed an average 70 percent good comprehension of type printed in black on white, none of the subjects scored good comprehension when body copy was set in white on black. In fact, 88 percent showed poor comprehension of what they had read (or tried to read). (See Table 7–2 on the opposite page for more complete scores on reverse typography as reported by Wheildon.)

And tests by U.S. catalogers have shown reverse type can reduce response. Williams-Sonoma reviewed three years of actual experience and discovered it had been experiencing a 33 percent decrease in sales on the same products whenever it presented catalog copy white on black, rather than black on white.

Figure 7–3
Reverse Type Reduces Sales

When Williams-Sonoma analyzed sales results of items which had been presented with reverse type in one catalog (below) and positive type in another catalog (opposite page), they discovered that copy in black on white produced 33% more sales than when copy was white on black. Copyright © Williams-Sonoma. Used with permission.

Table 7-2
How Reverse Type Affects Comprehension

According to the Wheildon studies, comprehension drops drastically when body copy is printed in reverse — white on black.

Table 7-2   Body Text Printed in Reverse

	Comprehension Level		
	Good	Fair	Poor
Text printed in black	70%	19%	11%
Text printed white on black	0	12	88
Text printed white on PMS 259 (deep purple)	2	16	82
Text printed white on PMS 286 (French blue)	0	4	96

While there are times when reverse typography can add a touch of elegance to a catalog presentation, it should be used sparingly—particularly if your catalog is going to be read by older audiences. Visual difficulties often increase for those 40 years of age and older. As they start to read white on black, the characters become blurred. Knowing this, older readers are likely to simply avoid such copy.

A Bake two delectably crisp, European-style waffles in just 90 seconds in the **Electric Belgian Waffle Iron**. Thermostat holds proper baking temperature after a 10 minute warm-up. Cast aluminum grids with chromed steel housing and heat-resistant handles. 13½" x 10" x 5" H., made in USA by Vitantonio. Instructions and recipes included. #64-30395 Regularly $55.00 **Special Price $44.00**

In a hurry? We offer rush delivery. Please see order form.

B Bake charmingly shaped muffins easily and quickly in the non-stick **Harvest Muffin Pan**. An authentic facsimile of an early American piece, it is made of heavy cast iron and has eight molds in the form of vegetables and fruit. Coated inside and out with Ironclad™, a non-stick silicone finish, the pan has scrolled handles and a lip around the edge to prevent spills. Molds are 2" diam. x 1" D.; pan is 7½" x 15" overall, made in USA. Recipe included. #64-89425 $17.50

C Use our **Croque Monsieur® Toasting Iron** from France to make shell-shaped grilled sandwiches on top of the stove in an instant. Line the iron with buttered bread and add ham and Gruyère cheese, cooked bacon with tomato, or sliced apples and apricot jam. Great for breakfast, lunch and midnight snacks. Of cast aluminum, it measures 8" x 4¾" and is 13" long including heatproof handles. Recipes included. #64-01339 Regularly $21.00 **Special Price $18.00**

D English tin plated mince or **Jam Tart Plaques** have shallow indentations (⁵⁄₁₆" deep by 3" across) for making "correct" tea tarts — delicate, of sweet pastry, and without too much filling. We have teamed the plaques with a set of **Crinkle Cutters** — the largest is for cutting the pastry. Recipes included. The set: two 9-tart plaques and 3 cutters, 2", 2½" and 3" diameter. #64-50138 $8.50

E Cartwright & Butler Traditional Mincemeat is made in the time-consuming, old-fashioned way. Rich and mellow, with plump vine fruits and almond halves mixed with lashings of brandy, it really is a cut above the rest. It makes memorable mince tarts that taste the way they should. Prepared in small batches under the supervision of Marion Cartwright. This limited production of 2½ lb. jars is being made especially for Williams-Sonoma. Recipe for Mince Tarts included. #64-144105 $17.50 ⓔ

F Harney & Sons, Ltd., Purveyors of Fine Teas, is a small family concern located in Salisbury, CT. They still believe that the old ways are the best ways, so they buy only the best teas, blend and package in small quantities to insure freshness, and use tin canisters to seal in tea flavor. **Harney's Earl Grey Tea** is delicately scented with oil of bergamot (a distinctively aromatic citrus), and 8 oz. will provide, when properly brewed, more than 100 cups of delicious tea. 8 oz. tin. #64-77453 $8.00

G-J The original Jena Glass Works, founded in Jena near Leipzig nearly a century ago, was the first to introduce borosilica glass, the very thin fireproof glass originally made for laboratory use. Their award winning teapot and handled tea glasses have been featured in exhibitions throughout the world for both design and function.
G Jena Glass Teapot has a perforated removable central tube for steeping tea leaves. When tea is steeped to your taste, remove the tube. 44 oz. cap., 7" H. #64-88047 $23.00
H Glass Warming Stand holds a standard warming candle (included). 5¾" diam. x 3¼" H. #64-88039 $9.00
J Matching **Jena Tea Glasses** show off the clear amber of properly brewed tea to perfection. 8½ oz. cap. Set of six #64-134163 $12.00
Special Set. Teapot and Warming Stand. #64-134833 Regularly $32.00 **Special Price $25.00**

Type in Color

Over the years, your audience has learned to be comfortable with copy printed in black. Whenever you substitute another color for black, you can expect diminishing comprehension.

Wheildon's studies, for example, showed comprehension scores ranging from a high of 51 percent to a low of 10 percent when colored inks were used for body text, rather than black on white (70 percent). (See Table 7–3.)

While the use of colored inks for catalog headings is quite common, there was one interesting discovery in Wheildon's studies which had not previously occurred to designers. He found that when high intensity colors, such as magenta, hot red, hot orange, or lime green, were used for headlines they drew increased attention for the heading, itself, but the comprehension of *body* text suffered. (See Table 7–4.)

Eye camera studies provide a clue for this somewhat surprising drop in comprehension. High chroma colors act like a magnet for the

Table 7–3
How Color Affects Comprehension

Readers are most comfortable reading black type. When colored ink is used for body type, comprehension suffers.

Table 7-3 Body Text Printed In Colored Ink

Ink Colors	Comprehension Level		
	Good	Fair	Poor
Text printed in black	70%	19%	11%
Low intensity color (PMS 259 — deep purple)	51	13	36
Medium intensity color (PMS 286 — French blue)	29	22	49
Muted color (PMS 399 — olive green)	10	13	77
High intensity color (cyan or warm red)	10	9	81

Table 7-4
Relationship of Headline and Body Copy

One of the most interesting things to show up in the Wheildon studies of typography was how a headline in a high chroma color can affect comprehension of body copy. A bright heading can act like an "eye magnet" — it keeps pulling the eyes away from the body copy, resulting in a drop in comprehension.

Table 7-4 How High Chroma Headline Colors Affect Comprehension of Body Copy

Ink Colors	Comprehension Level		
	Good	Fair	Poor
Black Headlines	67%	19%	14%
High Chroma Colors (hot red, hot orange, lime green)	17	19	65
Low Chroma Colors (deep blue, dark green, purple, plum)	52	28	20

eyes. They keep drawing eyes away from the body copy as it is being read, resulting in a loss in reading continuity. Comments by those who participated in the Wheildon studies confirm this finding—64 percent said they found the color intruding while they were trying to read the text. Another 12 percent said they felt the same effect as when an obtrusive light or an overbright color television picture distracted the eyes.

Background Tints

We emphasize again: your audience learned to read black on white. When a color is used as a background behind type, there is often a decline in comprehension. Pastel tints of a color often can be used

Table 7-5
How Color Background Affects Comprehension

Colored backgrounds can also affect copy comprehension.

Table 7-5 Body Text Printed on Background Tints

Ink Colors		Comprehension Level		
		Good	**Fair**	**Poor**
Black on Process Blue (cyan) tint	10%	68%	24%	8%
	20%	56	21	23
	30%	38	19	43
	40%	22	12	66
PMS 259 (deep purple) on own tint	10%	50	14	36
	20%	32	10	58
PMS 286 (French blue) on own tint	10%	27	16	57
	20%	12	10	78
Process Blue (cyan) on own tint	10%	6	7	87
	20%	nil	2	98
PMS 399 (olive green) on own tint	10%	8	8	84
	20%	2	6	92
	30%	0	3	97
Black on PMS 399 (olive green) on own tint	10%	68	26	6
	20%	53	21	26
	30%	32	19	49
	40%	22	13	65

safely. But as the intensity of the background increases, the comprehension of what's being read decreases. Color on color is even worse. (See Table 7–5.)

There's even a problem when black type is printed on a tint of black. (See Table 7–6.) As the background tint percentage increases, comprehension drops—and it drops dramatically with just a 10 percent increase in background.

Past experience has taught many readers that it is more tiring on their eyes when they have to read type printed on a colored background. Older readers, for example, often have found it difficult to read type on warm-colored backgrounds (e.g., reds). So they often avoid such copy when it appears in a catalog.

Cool-color backgrounds (e.g., blues and colors with blue in them) present a dual problem. Not only have many readers learned that such copy is tiring on their eyes, but you may have a problem with your printer. There's a "visual chemistry" that takes place when black ink is printed atop a blue background. The black often disappears into the blue. I've found this phenomenon unpredictable—there doesn't seem to be any way to know in advance how much your black copy will stand out from any background of blue.

The greatest reading difficulty, however, occurs when type is printed against a patterned background, such as being surprinted on a photograph. And readability really hits rock bottom when type is reversed out of a photo.

Many times, readers won't even notice that there is copy to be read when it is combined with a photo. And even if they do see it, they tend to avoid reading it.

Table 7–6
Comprehension: Black on Gray vs. Black on White

Even black on a gray tint can result in lower comprehension than black on white. While a light gray (10% of black) doesn't affect comprehension greatly, just an additional 10% of background tint produces a drastic drop.

Table 7-6   Body Text Printed on Grey Tints

	Comprehension Level		
	Good	Fair	Poor
Black on white	70%	19%	11%
Black on 10% black	63	22	15
Black on 20% black	33	18	49
Black on 30% black	3	10	87

EFFECTIVE CATALOG DESIGN / 7

Functional Use of Color

Today we live in an age of color. We see it used everywhere. Even newspapers, which lived for centuries with just black ink and white paper for editorial content, are now heavily saturated with color.

Catalogs too often splash color everywhere, whether it is needed or not. But color should be used like Tabasco sauce—a little bit can go a long way.

This doesn't mean you should avoid use of full-color illustrations of your products. Whether to have a full-color catalog or not will depend primarily on the types of products to be presented. If color is necessary to show your products realistically and help your readers make buying decisions, by all means, you should have a full-color catalog. But if you are selling nuts and bolts or automobile tires, chances are you will do just as well with black-and-white illustrations.

One important caution: be sure your colors are realistic. Flesh tones, in particular, are very important. If skin tones on your models come out blue, green, or purple, for example, you're immediately suggesting to your readers that they shouldn't believe the colors in your product illustrations. Whenever you are presenting something which your audience will recognize as being right or wrong from a color standpoint, take extra pains to get those items as close to the real thing as possible.

But it's the miscellaneous use of color which often presents the greatest problem. If you "waste" color on unimportant things, you no longer have it available to use as a functional tool when necessary. You may need color to separate one category of products from another; to highlight special prices; to emphasize new items; or, perhaps, to connect related items. If you've already used every color in the rainbow for something else, a special color is no longer viable for such special purposes.

Space as a Design Element

All too often, catalogs have what I call "engineer's layout"—a uniform amount of white space is used to separate every item: the illustration, captions, the heading, the body text, price lines, etc. As a result, each of these becomes a single element to the reader's eye. And the more elements you have on a page or spread, the busier it appears. And "busy" layouts create the impression your catalog is hard to read.

An illustration and its caption, for example, should be separated by less space than that used to separate this total unit from other similar units. There should never be a question of which caption goes with which illustration.

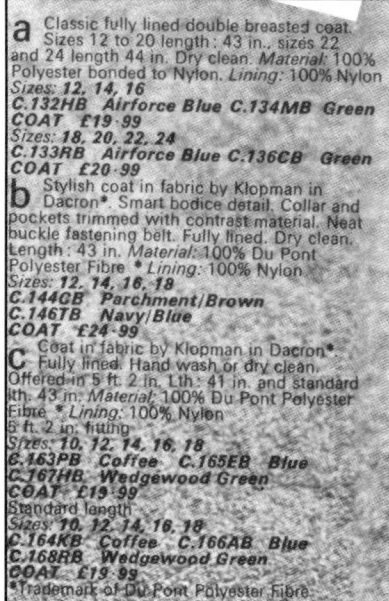
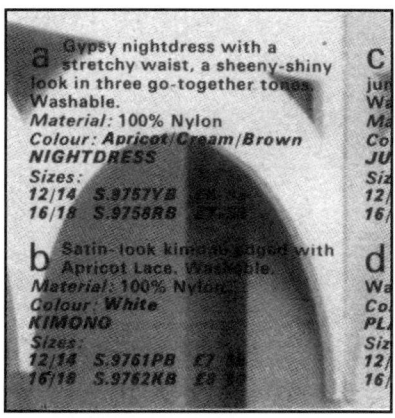
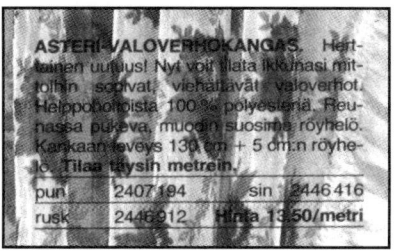

Figure 7-4
Avoid Type Surprinted on Illustrations

Type printed atop an illustration with a distracting pattern is extremely difficult to read, and many times, readers don't even notice copy has been printed there. Type in the middle box ran into a problem when it was printed atop deep shadows. The almost totally unreadable type in the last box describes the floral pattern atop which it is printed.

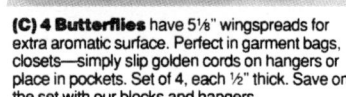

American Cedar!
The best natural moth-repellent adds a fabulous woodsy fragrance.

Native Cedar Safeguards Your Fine Woolens, Ends The Worry Of Chemicals. Chases moths, fleas and silverfish away naturally and safely. No costly repellents to buy—cedar lasts forever, and a light sanding renews the aroma. Quality-crafted in the U.S.A. with smoothly finished edges—won't snag.

(A) 12 Cedar Blocks tuck into drawers, pockets, shelves and trunks, keep clothing and linens fresh and free from mildew. 4x2x½" thick. Great natural room deodorizers, slip under furniture in musty, stuffy areas. Set of 12, ours alone.
564322   Genuine Cedar Blocks. 1 Set $10.98

(B) 2 Aromatic Cedar Hangers—all the benefits of a cedar closet at a fraction of the cost! Large 17" size is sturdy for fur coats and men's suits, the 14½" dowels hold pants crease-free. Lacquered, brass-plated steel hooks. Set of 2.
524522   Genuine Cedar Hangers. 1 Set $9.98

(C) 4 Butterflies have 5⅛" wingspreads for extra aromatic surface. Perfect in garment bags, closets—simply slip golden cords on hangers or place in pockets. Set of 4, each ½" thick. Save on the set with our blocks and hangers.
505722   Cedar Butterflies. 1 Set $9.98

Buy The Whole 18-Pc. Set And Save $9.00. 12 cedar blocks, 2 hangers and 4 butterflies, for complete storage protection.
457722   Entire Cedar Collection $22.00

Deodorize Smelly Sneakers And Shoes...Overnight! Stinky Pinkys™ are sacks of minerals that absorb foot odors—put one in each sneaker, leather shoe or boot at night to ensure fresh-smelling footwear in the morning. They'll last indefinitely if, every 3 months, you put them in the sun for a day. Helps prolong shoe and sneaker life. Set of 2—8x3¼". U.S.-made.
560822   Stinky Pinkys™.
1 Set $5.98
2 Sets $10.98

Adjustable Belt And Tie Rack hangs 'em neatly, keeps 'em tangle-free, easy to select. Bars lock into the horizontal position, or swing down if space is limited. Sturdy solid pine has warm walnut finish—5 non-slip rods hold up to 40 ties, 6 solid brass hooks secure belts. Made to my specifications: 20x4", bars extend to 8½", fold down to 3½" deep.
682222   Convertible Belt and Tie Rack $19.98

CHARGE IT! 914-633-6300

Figure 7–5
Placement of Captions

This page from a Lillian Vernon catalog illustrates several effective methods for handling captions. The group of related-product pictures at the top of the page had alpha identifiers, while other items had individual captions. Note how captions were linked to the proper photograph by placing the captions close to the pictures, with white space used to separate each picture-caption unit. In the product at the lower left of the page, the caption was wrapped around the dual pictures, making the two photos and the caption an integrated unit. Copyright © Lillian Vernon. Used with permission.

Captions

For maximum readership, it is best to have individual captions for each product illustration in a catalog. And as a general rule, captions should be placed below or to the right of the product illustration.

The normal eye flow is down and to the right. You'll seldom go wrong when catalog copy is placed below an illustration, since that's where the average reader will look for it. The secondary position is to the right of the illustration unless there are compelling gaze or structural motion elements in the illustration which lead a reader's eyes in another direction.

One of the greatest errors in catalog presentation is to place a headline *above* an illustration. Since readers will look at illustrations first and then just naturally move down and/or to the right, headings above pictures are often completely overlooked. Such headline placement is particularly bad when the headline is above the picture and the caption is below the picture. Asking a reader to first "look up" and then "look down" results in substantial loss of readership and reduced comprehension.

In the interest of saving space, many catalogs group captions together, rather than attaching them to individual product illustrations. Then alpha or numeric identifiers are attached to each product illustration, with corresponding letter or number codes added to the catalog copy.

Over the years, catalog buyers have learned to accept this space-saving design technique; and, while it is seldom as effective as having individual picture-caption units, it permits presentation of more products in a catalog and can prove to be cost-effective.

When using this technique, it is advisable to have illustrations and copy on the same page and in an easily understood sequence. As a general rule, it is best to start the identification sequence in the upper left and move first to the right and then from top to bottom. One way to make it easy for a reader to mentally connect pictures and captions is to use each page number as a prefix (e.g., 26–1, 26–2, 26–3, etc., or 26-A, 26-B, 26-C, etc.).

And speaking of page numbers, every page in a catalog should carry an easily found page number. Many buyers like to jot down page numbers as a reminder of items they wish to give further consideration. Always position your page numbers in a consistent manner. The preferred location is either at the center bottom or at the outside bottom of each page (to the left on left-hand pages and to the right on right-hand pages). And by all means, use even numbers for left-hand pages and odd numbers for right-hand pages. That's what newspapers, magazines, and books have taught readers to expect, and flying in the face of experience may confuse a buyer.

Don't Give Readers an Excuse to Stop

There's a lesson catalog designers can learn from other direct marketers and magazine designers: Don't give readers an excuse to stop reading.

In direct mail, the basic rule for multipage letters is never to end a page with a period. That's a too easily accepted invitation to stop reading, rather than move on to the next page. The ideal page ending is the middle of a hyphenated word, so the reader automatically moves to the next page to complete the word.

In magazines, designers use what has come to be called the "Continuous Circle" technique (a strange title since a circle, by its very nature, is "continuous"). The basic idea is to encircle all copy which is intended to be read continuously within a continuous line. (See Figure 7–6.) Whenever there is an element, such as a heading or illustration, which interrupts reading, the reader must make a decision about where to go next—something which often isn't obvious. In such cases, an alternate decision—to simply stop reading—is often the choice.

In the Wheildon studies, several different styles were tested to evaluate the effect of different layout techniques on reader comprehension. A basic layout with a picture at the top of the page, a headline immediately below the picture, followed by three uninterrupted

Figure 7–6
The "Continuous Circle"

When you have long copy, it's important to avoid giving readers a natural opportunity to stop reading. There should be no distracting elements breaking up the flow of copy. Designers use a technique called the "Continuous Circle" to check readership flow. It involves drawing a continuous line around all of the copy which is intended to be read continuously. In the JS&A Products That Think catalog spread shown here, note how all illustrations are positioned outside the "Continuous Circle" (which we have added) so one paragraph flows into the next without interruption. Copyright © JS&A. Used with permission.

columns of copy (Figure 7–7) resulted in 67 percent thorough comprehension. But when the headline was inserted halfway down the same body matter (Figure 7–8), comprehension fell to just 32 percent.

While these studies obviously have more direct application to catalogs with long copy, the basic principles of uninterrupted eye-flow can be applied to any catalog style. The eye-flow starts with the product illustration. If the picture creates the desire for more information, the flow will move first to a picture caption, then to a separate headline relating to that specific item (if it wasn't a part of the picture caption), and subsequently to any other copy about that item. Anything which interrupts this eye-flow sequence will reduce reader comprehension.

Figures 7–7 and 7–8
Breaking Up Copy

In the Wheildon studies of copy comprehension, it was discovered that moving the headline from just below a top-of-the-page illustration and inserting it within the body copy at the center of the page resulted in a drop of body copy comprehension from 67% to 32%.

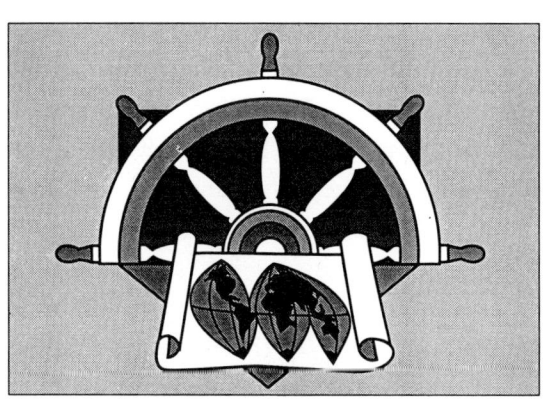

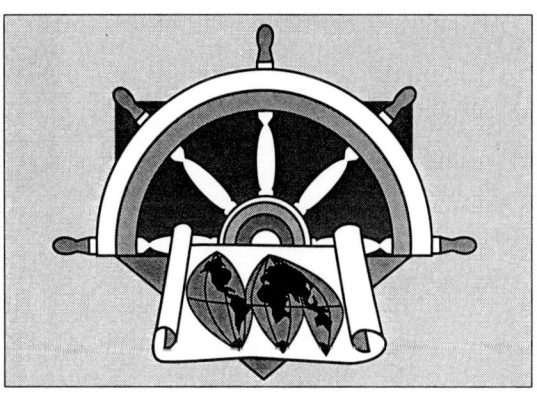

Tips for More Effective Catalog Design

While Colin Wheildon was conducting his readership comprehension studies down in Australia, another research project with special importance to catalogs was in progress in Europe. Professor Siegfried Vogele, dean of the Institute for Direct Marketing in Munich, Germany, developed an improved version of the eye camera to measure eye-flow on catalog pages and spreads.

Eye camera technology is extremely complicated, but the essence of the technique is the ability to follow the precise movement of a subject's eyes as he or she reads a catalog. At the same time, other cameras study body language and hand movements to determine the subject's emotional reactions.

Although any individual study has only marginal significance, Professor Vogele has had the opportunity to analyze several thousand eye camera studies involving dozens of different catalogs. And from his research has come a number of highly significant findings which are important in creating more effective catalog design.

Basic Eye-Flow

Professor Vogele found that catalog readers have a consistent eye-flow pattern. Regardless of whether they read a catalog from front-to-back or back-to-front, the eye gravitates first to the upper right-hand corner of a spread. Unless there are design elements which "pull" the eye in another direction, most readers follow a sideways U viewing pattern, moving downward and to the left. The eyes just barely cross the center gutter margin onto the right-hand page before reversing themselves and exiting at the bottom right of the spread. (See Figure 7–9.)

On the other hand, if there is a dominant graphic element elsewhere on the spread (Figure 7–9), the eyes will be pulled toward it and then start moving to the normal bottom right-hand spread exit point.

The worst layout is one with a dominant graphic element at the bottom right of the spread. The eyes move there immediately and exit before giving attention to other items on either page of the spread.

Illustrations

No graphic element plays a greater role in determining the pattern of catalog readership than the illustrations. Before any word of text is even noted, eyes are attracted to photographs and/or drawings. But Professor Vogele's eye camera studies showed that every illustration doesn't have equal "drawing power." Here are some of his findings:

- Large pictures get attention before smaller pictures.
- Color pictures are noted before black-and-white pictures.
- A sequence of pictures will be noted before individual pictures.
- Action illustrations will be seen before still pictures.
- Pictures with people in them will be looked at before pictures of products.
- Portraits will gain attention before full pictures of people.
- Photos with a close-up of just a portion of a portrait normally are noted before full portraits.
- Eyes will most often be the first thing upon which a reader focuses.
- Most often, a larger group of people will gain attention before a smaller group.
- Children will gain attention before adults.
- Outline illustrations will generally be noted before square halftones.

Copy

Professor Vogele's eye camera studies also offer clues to the most effective methods of handling headings and text matter in catalogs (but it is important to remember that his studies involved eye-flow only and made no attempt to evaluate comprehension of copy).

Figure 7–9
Basic Eye Flow

In the eye camera studies conducted by Professor Siegfried Vogele, it was found that readers normally first look at the upper right corner of a spread. Their eyes then move down and to the left, just crossing the gutter between the two pages before moving down and to the right, exiting the spread at the spread's lower right.

- Copy within a border will be read before "open" text.
- Short paragraphs will be given greater attention than longer paragraphs.
- There is a tendency to read short words and short lines before longer words and longer lines.
- Numbers are noted before longer words.

Shapes

Another interesting finding of the Vogele eye camera studies was that 80 percent of readers will go to a vertical shape before a horizontal shape. Even more eye-compelling is a diagonal shape.

Circled areas are generally noted before square-cornered areas and closed shapes are most often observed before partially open shapes.

Bursts get immediate attention, but generally the attention is of very short duration. (Vogele also found that such dramatic elements can often be distracting since they have a tendency to keep reattracting the eyes, drawing them away from copy.)

Other Observations

As a result of his testing, Professor Vogele offers some basic suggestions. First of all, he calls attention to what he labels the "Law of Proximity." Whatever is closer to an item, he says, will be perceived as related to that item. Thus, as we have pointed out previously, it's important to place captions as close to pictures as possible. The Vogele eye camera studies underscore the importance of placing captions below or to the right of an illustration, not above or to the left.

He also warns that one element can affect how other elements are perceived. In the seminars which he conducts throughout Europe, he uses a simple illustration to underscore this point.

Note in Figure 7–10 how changing the shape of the mouth changes the perception of the eyes. As an example of how this can be applied to catalogs, he suggests that introducing an eye-compelling "burst" into a layout can change the total image of that spread.

Figure 7–10
The Power of a Single Element

Introducing one eye-compelling design element can change the entire image of a spread.

Grid Layouts

An important catalog designer's tool is the grid layout. While many designers will start out insisting that forcing them to use a standard grid for layouts will stifle their creativity, it often works in the opposite way. Once freed from having to create a unique layout for every spread through the use of standardized grids for "ordinary" pages, the designer can concentrate creative energies on those situations where special design techniques will make a major difference in catalog presentation.

The highly simplified grid layout (Figure 7–11) shows the basic technique. First of all, allowances are made for page margins and areas for any repeated elements such as page or spread headings. Then each spread is divided into a number of equal units. Thus, when illustration-copy units are created, they conform to one or more of the grid units.

This makes it possible to move units from one place to another on the spread and to pick up complete units from one catalog to the next. The grid technique can be particularly valuable when quick replacement of an item is necessary.

Figure 7–11
The Grid Layout

While this is a highly simplified grid layout, it shows the basic principle. Each spread unit is first broken into the two individual pages, with space required for outer and gutter margins indicated. Next, space for a heading is indicated (if headings are normally used). Then each page is given an equal number of vertical columns, which are divided into equal-size units. While we've used a nine-unit-per-page grid for illustration simplicity, it is more common to divide each column into a greater number of units.

Most catalog grids will have far more than nine units to a page. Usually a grid starts with either two or three vertical columns per page. Then these vertical units are divided into equal horizontal segments, each from one to three inches high.

In many catalogs more than one grid is required. Different categories of products, for example, may call for different grids. There may be one grid for clothing; another for appliances. There may be a grid for long-copy presentations; another for short-copy spreads.

The best rule of thumb to follow when using grids for a catalog is to insist that designers follow the basic grids *unless* there is a specific, identifiable reason for departing from them—not because the designer wants to create something different just to be different.

Writing Catalog Copy

8

While copy is secondary to the illustrations in a catalog, it plays a vital role. It's like the salesperson's "close."

The basic role of copy in a catalog is to answer questions which remain unanswered after a buyer has been attracted to a product illustration.

The best guide to writing effective catalog copy I've ever seen was developed many years ago by Eleanor Bishop for the old Kaleidoscope catalog. Copy for Kaleidoscope, like many catalogs, was written by freelancers, and each was provided with the following guidelines:

Kaleidoscope Copy Guidelines

The distinguishing characteristics of Kaleidoscope's copy are that it is

1. Strong on benefits
2. Literate
3. Smooth flowing

After reading a number of catalogs, you'll be able to dissect any given copy block into the following components.

The Head

Whether it is a play on words, a literary allusion, a reference to a universal experience or a simple alliterative phrase, the head serves as the "hook." Its function is not unlike the old speech giver's ploy of saying, "Sex," and then, "Now that I've got your attention . . . ." But even within this clearly defined function, the head must lead to a benefit—if not state one. A good pun that does not lead to a benefit serves only the copywriter's ego. The head should always be analyzed carefully for any negative connotation. Don't use a literary allusion unless you're sure of its meaning.

The Beneficial Sentence

This follows the head and most often begins with a strong verb and an implied "you," that is, an imperative sentence. It can also be a conditional sentence that states the need in the "if" clause with the benefit in the "then" clause. This is almost always a complete sentence, never a noun or verb phrase.

The Descriptive Sentence

Here's where you tell what the thing is and why it is so special. One warning: the supplier himself doesn't always know the primary benefit or important descriptive fact of his own product. Remember that there *is* a photograph, so you don't have to describe everything about the item; but you do have to wax enthusiastic in the description and help supplement the photograph. Once again, try to use a complete sentence.

The Statistics

Here's where you give the facts, Ma'am, just the facts. You can, and should, use noun phrases here.

Some extras

If there's room, and the item warrants it, you might want to add *a Sandwich* (a restatement of the benefit with a little extra oomph, perhaps even a little hyperbole) or *a Zinger* (a short and snappy variation on the Sandwich—always terribly clever).

In addition to knowing the elements of the style, the following might be helpful:

- Try to learn what has sold well in the past. It will help you understand *who* the customer is.
- Aim a little above your customer. She doesn't understand French but wishes she did. If you give her a French phrase she can easily figure out, she'll think she's neat and like Kaleidoscope for the compliment.
- For heaven's sake, don't get kinky. The Kaleidoscope customer is not Marissa Berenson!

- Use a dictionary—spelling counts.
- Work in spreads so you don't end up repeating the same phrase three times on one spread.
- Touching and feeling the samples helps. The more you know about the merchandise, the better the copy.
- Use old headlines and even old blocks of copy when possible. Nobody cares that you "copied," and it helps lighten the load.

Take a close look at the nine items on a single page of a Kaleidoscope catalog (Figure 8–1). Copy averages only 35 words for each item, but does an excellent job of supplementing photos. Here's the copy for each item:

A. GATHER UP THE GOODIES. When it's time for a picnic, our bright yellow picnic pack is ready to go! Complete tableware for four picnickers—plates, bowls, flatware, and serving pieces—fit neatly together to form a 9" square pack. 35 polypropylene pieces in all.

B. TAME THE DRAGON. This 25-ft.-long kite takes off by itself and soars to the heights of fantasy. So easy, a child can fly it! So much fun, grownups won't give it up. Made of strong, safely non-conductive parachute nylon. Won't breathe fire! [Note the Zinger at the end.]

C. COUNT ON CANVAS — for casual good looks and exceptional durability. Our handsome natural canvas tote—with brown leather trim—is versatile too. It folds over to become a clutch! 12" x 15", with outside zipper pocket.

D. FANCIFUL FISH, handscreened in Chinese blue, give your 10 $1/2$" x 16" canvas tote a fashionable Far East flair! Carries a lot, goes anywhere! [Don't assume the benefits are obvious—tell them it carries a lot and goes anywhere.]

E. FAIR WEATHER FRIEND. This pretty handprinted tote is designed for get-up-and-going when the weather says, "NOW!" Carries all your gear, unzips to become a comfy 24" x 72" padded mat. 100% cotton. 18" x 24" zipped. [Less than 40 words, but all that are needed to tell what the photo doesn't show.]

F. ASHTRAYS ASTRAY? Our colorful deco-design stacking ashtrays are always handsomely at hand. Gift-boxed set of eight enameled in red, green, camel and white. [Note how many of the headings use alliteration to add a bit of spice to this relatively busy page.]

G. YOU'RE A NATURAL. Enhance your adventuress look with a cossack tunic of 100% raw silk from Mainland China. The oatmeal shade goes with everything! With Mandarin collar, V-slit neckline, buttoned cuffs, and wear-

A. GATHER UP THE GOODIES. When it's time for a picnic, our bright yellow picnic pack is ready to go! Complete tableware for four picnickers — plates, bowls, flatware, and serving pieces — fit neatly together to form a 9"-square pack. 35 polypropylene pieces in all.
Picnic pack, #5215, 20.00 (1.65)

B. TAME THE DRAGON. This 25-ft.-long kite takes off by itself and soars to the heights of fantasy. So easy, a child can fly it! So much fun, grownups won't give it up. Made of strong, safely non-conductive parachute nylon. Won't breathe fire!
Dragon kite, #5209, 30.00 (1.75)

F. ASHTRAYS ASTRAY? Our colorful deco-design stacking ashtrays are always handsomely at hand. Gift-boxed set of eight enameled in red, green, camel, and white.
Deco ashtrays, #5267, 10.00 (1.45)

G. YOU'RE A NATURAL. Enhance your adventuress look with a cossack tunic of 100% raw silk from Mainland China. The oatmeal shade goes with everything! With Mandarin collar, V-slit neckline, buttoned cuffs, and wear-if-you-wish self belt. S,M,L.
Silk tunic, #5203, 48.00 (1.75)

C. COUNT ON CANVAS — for casual good looks and exceptional durability. Our handsome natural canvas tote — with brown leather trim — is versatile too. It folds over to become a clutch! 12"x15" with outside zipper pocket.
Canvas tote, #5016, 18.50 (1.45)

D. FANCIFUL FISH, handscreened in Chinese blue, give our 10½"x16" canvas tote a fashionable Far East flair! Carries a lot, goes anywhere!
Oriental fish tote, #5217, 20.00 (1.45)

E. FAIR WEATHER FRIEND. This pretty handprinted tote is designed for get-up-and-going when the weather says "NOW!" Carries all your gear, unzips to become a comfy 24"x72" padded mat. 100% cotton. 18"x24" zipped.
Tote-mat, #5205, 48.00 (1.75)

H. PANAMA HATS COME FROM CHINA. That's where this sun-shading chapeau was handwoven of sea grass. One size fits *any* pretty head. And it goes anywhere — *always* looks great.
Handwoven hat, #5125, 6.00 (1.25)

J. AT THE RAINBOW BAR. The happy hour couldn't be happier when the drinks are served in these brightly striped handpainted *triple* old-fashioneds. You'll feel better even before the first sip. 17-oz. capacity, set of six. Dishwasher safe.
Rainbow stripe glasses, #5015, 16.50 (1.85)

if-you-wish self belt. [Note how product details are woven into copy to create a readable paragraph.]

H. PANAMA HATS COME FROM CHINA. That's where this sun-shading chapeau was handwoven of sea grass. One size fits any pretty head. And it goes anywhere—*always* looks great. [In this case, italics for "always" provided a quick benefit emphasis.]

J. AT THE RAINBOW BAR. The happy hour couldn't be happier when the drinks are served in these brightly striped hand-painted *triple* old-fashioneds. You'll feel better even before the first sip. 17-oz. capacity, set of six. Dishwasher safe.

Features vs. Benefits

The first key point in Eleanor Bishop's Kaleidoscope guide—*strong on benefits*—is too often overlooked by catalog writers, yet it's the single most important aspect of strong catalog copy.

Nick Samstag, longtime genius behind promotional mailings for Time, Inc., once reported on a series of tests which were conducted to determine *when* people read advertising in *Time* and *Life*. It was discovered people only read the copy in ads when they recognized they were in the market for what was being advertised.

For example, people will look at the pictures of new cars, but only read the copy when they are in the market to buy a new car—unless, of course, they are "car buffs" who read everything about cars. There's a lesson here for catalog copywriters.

Emphasis should be placed on benefits, not features, of a product. This is particularly true for headings. Far more people will be interested in almost any benefit than will be interested in any given feature. Thus a benefit in a head will encourage readership of the rest of the copy.

An outstanding example of strong benefit-laden heads in a catalog can be found in Inmac, a computer supplies catalog. Here, for example, are just a few of the "strong-on-benefits" heads in a single Inmac catalog:

Assemble a premium sound cover yourself in just 10 minutes—& save at least $90!

Gain accuracy & speed! Replace your old keyboard for as little as $59.95!

Turn your publications into works of art with Inmac Scanners & free imaging software.

Avoid costly setbacks. Back up hard disks easily & automatically with this 40MB tape drive system!

Figure 8–1
Strong on Benefits
(opposite)

Being strong on benefits is the single most important aspect of effective catalog copywriting. Kaleidoscope uses smooth-flowing, clever copy to sell its products. Copyright © Kaleidoscope. Used with permission.

Mini, mountable switch saves space & budget bucks. Lets you share any device!

Increase productivity! Now up to 6 users can share 1 parallel printer without leaving their PCs!

Laser Print Switch ends long waits for print runs & Auto CAD plots.

Don't play games! Our data buffers win back valuable time from your long print runs.

Affordable, adaptable Ethernet: The wiring's already in your walls!

Now sharing files between PCs & Macs doesn't have to be a pain in the neck! TOPS is the affordable way to network PCs with Macs.

Be safe, not sorry! 3-part system completely solves the problem of what to do with all those cables!

Save space and key in comfort! Tuck your keyboard into one of our low-cost Keyboard Keepers.

European-styled Free Float Monitor Arm takes up as little space on your desk as your coffee cup.

Input faster! Keyboard templates keep commands at your fingertips.

But it isn't just Inmac's heads that are strong on benefits. Consider Figure 8–2.

DESIGN YOUR IDEAL WORKSTATION NOW, ADD TO IT LATER.
DATAMASTER MODULAR FURNITURE GROWS WITH YOU!
It's a pretty simple idea. You know what you want in a workstation—you decide what goes into it.

Which is why DataMaster modular furniture gets you organized better than other office furniture. It lets you design your workstation to fit your exact needs by choosing exactly the furniture you want.

And as your career takes off, you can expand your DataMaster simply by adding more modules and accessories.

THE DATAMASTER FORMULA:
COMFORT + ORGANIZATION = EFFICIENCY.
Choose from three basic DataMaster modules for the arrangement that works best for you! Our 26 $1/2$" high workstation puts your worksurface at a comfortable height for keying.

Our desk modules measure 29 $1/2$" high from floor to worksurface. Perfect for flow-charting, report writing and other non-keyboard work.

Or, choose our Adjustable Keying Desk module. It gives you desk-height convenience and a computing ease in one workstation.

WRITING CATALOG COPY / 8

All modules use a cantilevered support system—you enjoy unrestricted side-to-side movement with lots of floor space underneath.

Roomy 30" deep tops (in your choice of widths) ensure more than enough worksurface for PCs, monitors, modems and coffee mugs.

And no matter how you look at your DataMaster, you won't be looking at cables. Knockout wiring ports in the modesty panels keep them safely hidden.

HOW A GOOD IDEA GETS EVEN BETTER.
Pre-drilled holes in all DataMaster workstations make adding accessories fast and easy.

Add overhead storage risers to keep manuals, reference materials and documents conveniently out of the way.

Or add drawers and clear your worksurface of papers, pens and file folders.

Of course, with a DataMaster workstation, you can add accessories now . . . and add them later as your needs change.

QUICK SHIPMENT. EVEN QUICKER ASSEMBLY.
Order your workstation before 3:30 p.m. and it's on its way to you . . . today. They're a snap to assemble, too. All you need is a screwdriver, wrench and about 40 minutes.

You'll also be pleased to know that DataMaster workstations are con-

Figure 8–2
Integrating Features and Benefits

Tying features and benefits into the same statements can create strong copy.
Copyright © Inmac. Used with permission.

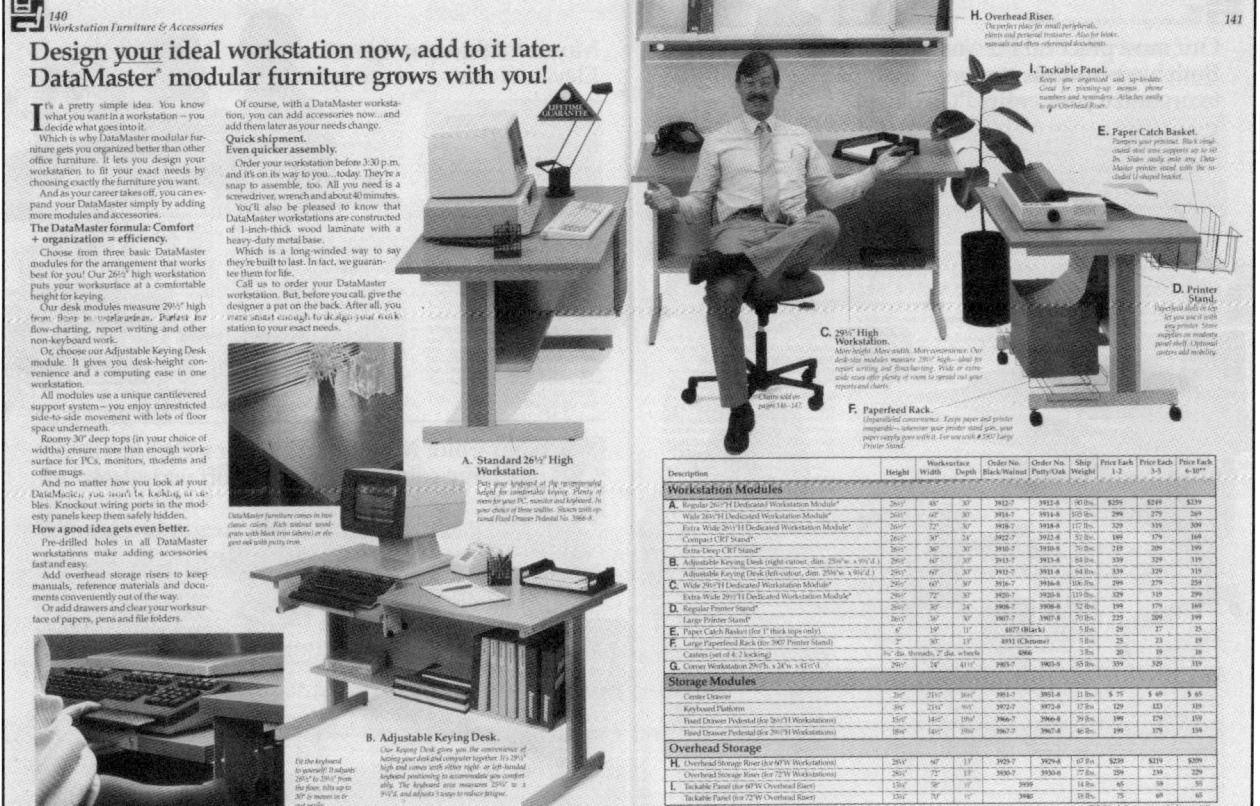

> structed of 1-inch-thick wood laminate with a heavy-duty metal base.
>
> Which is a long-winded way to say they're built to last. In fact, we guarantee them for life.
>
> Call us to order your DataMaster workstation. But, before you call, give the designer a pat on the back. After all, you were smart enough to design your workstation to your exact needs.

Notice how the benefits of each feature are cleverly woven into each paragraph of this relatively long copy. Even dimensions are turned into benefits (26 $\frac{1}{2}$" high workstation—a comfortable height for keying; 29 $\frac{1}{2}$" high desk modules—perfect for flow-charting, report writing; 30" deep tops—more than enough worksurface for PCs, monitors, modems, and coffee mugs.)

Benefits for the Consumer

Of all the benefits-oriented copy I've collected over the years, my two favorite examples both came from a British catalog—Scotcade. The first presented a new product called the Goblin Teasmade:

> The idea of waking up to a nice hot cup of tea every morning is so appealing, it's hardly surprising that the Goblin Teasmade is so popular.
>
> At the recommended price of £44.71, it's got to be worth every penny. At the Scotcade price of just £33.95, plus post and packaging, you'd have to be an insomniac to turn it down.
>
> Actually, the name "Teasmade" is a bit misleading, because it makes coffee too.
>
> But whichever you prefer, it's incredibly simple to work. You just put water in the kettle, tea or coffee in the pot, set the alarm, and forget about it.
>
> The next thing you know, you're gently woken up by the buzzer, the bedside lights are on, and there are four freshly made cups of whatever you fancy sitting there waiting for you. With enough hot water left in the kettle for two more. There's even a detachable tray included so you won't spill anything on the bed.
>
> The whole thing is operated by a single master switch. It controls the bedside lights, the luminous clock, the alarm buzzer, and the kettle itself. And if you happen to wake up early, there's even a special "Tea Now" position which overrides your previous setting.
>
> Send for your Teasmade now, and it'll arrive at your door within 21 to 28 days, complete with a year's guarantee from Goblin.
>
> And if you're not completely happy with it, all you have to do is return it to us within 30 days.
>
> We won't ask questions, we'll simply refund your money in full.

Another outstanding example of Scotcade copy utilizes a technique which can be adapted by every catalog copywriter—the "which means" technique *(note the examples, to which we have added italics)*. This copy promoted the Original Russell Hobbs Automatic Electric Kettle:

> **The Russell Hobbs was the first kettle that you could switch on and forget about, because it switched itself off automatically when the water boiled.**
>
> **Now, predictably, it's the biggest-selling electric kettle in the U.K. at a recommended price of £19.97. The Scotcade price of £13.95 (plus p&p) makes it even more attractive.**
>
> **It boils three pints of water in something like four minutes.**
>
> **It's made from solid stainless-steel, *which means it's tarnish-resistant*.**
>
> **It's BEAB approved, *which means it's safe*. It's guaranteed for 12 months, *which means you're safe* (there are over 70 Russell Hobbs service agents in the U.K.).**
>
> **And, of course, the fact that it switches itself off automatically *means that you save electricity and it can't boil dry*.**

Whenever you have a feature to present, write "which means" after it and see what fits. If you can't come up with a worthwhile benefit, chances are the feature is unimportant.

Benefits in Headings

The ideal place to bring out the benefits of a product is in the heading. A consumer catalog which regularly stresses benefits in its headings is Brookstone. Consider these examples:

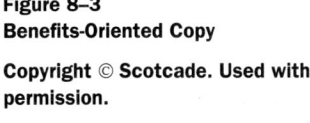

Figure 8–3
Benefits-Oriented Copy

Copyright © Scotcade. Used with permission.

Figure 8–4
The "Which Means" Technique

One effective way to tie benefits and features is to state the feature and add "which means." Your benefit should follow logically. Copyright © Scotcade. Used with permission.

For its power caulker:
> **The Faster, Less Tiring Way To Caulk**

For a wireless wall light:
> **Put In The Lights The Builder Forgot**

For a heat tape:
> **Self-Regulating Heat Tape Puts More Heat Where Pipes Are Coldest**

For weather stripping for a door:
> **Seal Your Front Door As Tight As Your Refrigerator Door**

For a refrigerator brush:
> **Cut Energy Bills And Increase The Life Of Your Refrigerator**

For a compact fan:
> **Compact Fans Move Hot Or Cold Air Where You Want It Most**

For a fireplace grate:
> **Get More Heat And Slower Burning From Your Fireplace**

For a move-about ladder:
> **You Don't Have To Get Off The Step Ladder To Move It**

For a faucet extension:
> **Make Your Hard-To-Reach Spigot More Reachable**

For a shoehorn:
> **This Extra-Long Natural Shoehorn Saves You From Bending**

Long Consumer Catalog Copy

The all-time master of long copy for consumer catalogs is Joe Sugarman. The spread illustrated in Figure 8–6 is from one of his early Products That Think catalogs. Note the heavy emphasis on benefits in the first half of the copy.

> **The telephone is changing. And the new JS&A Tridar Phone will change your concept of telephone design. Here's what we mean:**

**Figure 8–5
Stressing Benefits in Headings**

**Note how Brookstone introduces a specific benefit into each of its catalog headings.
Copyright © Brookstone. Used with permission.**

NO MORE CRADLE.

Who says a phone needs a cradle? The new JS&A phone has a button. When the phone rings, you press it to answer.

NO MORE HANDS.

When you talk on our phone, you have a choice. You can either pick it up, or you can leave it on your desk. If you leave it on the desk, you answer by pressing the "on" button, and the Tridar turns into a hands-free amplified speaker phone.

NO MORE STRAINING.

If the kids are screaming in the background or your secretary is typing nearby, just pick up your JS&A Tridar, and your phone switches automatically from a speaker phone to a conventional phone. You can also adjust the integrated volume control to make listening easier in either mode—perfect for the hard-of-hearing.

NO MORE EMBARRASSMENT.

Who says you can't put a hold button on a single-line phone? Just press the hold button on the Tridar, and the red LED light blinks on and off while you tell your kids to quiet down or your secretary to get a report.

NO MORE DIALING.

The new Tridar operates on any touch-tone line. A new system is being

Figure 8–6
Matching Benefits and Features in Long Copy

Note how benefits are stressed early in this copy and how the editorial style describes features that match those benefits. Copyright © JS&A. Used with permission.

developed which will permit touch dialing even on rotary-dial lines at no additional expense. You should first check with your phone company to see if your phone lines accept touch-tone operation. If not, we will be happy to take your order for the rotary version when it becomes available.

NO MORE HANG UPS.
You don't have to hang up a phone to disconnect a call. Just press the "off" button.

Picture this. The Tridar phone rings. (There are two loudness levels to this very pleasant electronic sound.) You walk up to the phone, press the "on" button and say "hello." The party at the other end requests to talk to somebody else in your home. You say, "Hold for one minute."

You then press the "hold" button and call the other person to the phone. Look how simple that was. You never picked up the phone, you never had to cover the mouthpiece while you called the other party, and your caller appreciated not hearing the clunk of your phone as you placed it on your desk.

SPACE-AGE STYLING
The Tridar is perfect for patients because they can lie in bed and talk hands-free. The phone is perfect for the hard-of-hearing or for people in loud environments who need extra volume when listening. The dual volume control adjusts both the hands-free phone and the earphone to just the right loudness level.

You couldn't own a more dramatic or handsome-looking phone than the Tridar. Its sleek, space-age styling and its white finish with black inset panel look great on any desk, in any room, for any occasion.

Another great catalog copywriter is Ron Zimmerman, whose sparkling copy helped make Early Winters a catalog success in the early 1980s. Like Joe Sugarman, he had the ability to weave benefits into a catalog narrative. Here are two examples of his unique copy style.

KEEP A COOL HEAD . . . HAT SHADES YOUR EYES, HELPS SAVE YOUR NECK.
No wonder desperate men can't wait to join the French Foreign Legion. It gives them the chance to wear the suavest sun hat that ever blocked a ray.

Two elegant "tails" keep burning rays off your neck, and actually scoop air in to cool you as you walk. In scorching weather, dip the tails in water for a cooling compress that beats the driest sirocco.

Our Sahara Hat's broad, shapable bill is angled just right to shade your eyes without obstructing your view of the oasis shimmering on the horizon.

And the $2\,^1/_2$-oz. Sahara Hat is 100% light, breathable cotton. It crushes to fit easily in pack or pocket, and rides light on your head from sunup to sundown.

You don't have to enter the Legion to enjoy their famous hat. Order yours today.

ULTRALIGHT, PACK-ANYWHERE RAFT PUTS YOU ON MOUNTAIN LAKES.
Now any lake you can hike, bike, or climb your way to, you can float and fish in our Ultralight Raft.

For day trips or long treks, it's the lightest, most compact lake-going vessel ever.

20-OZ. RAFT PACKS SMALL.
An incredible 20 ounces light, the entire craft weighs less than a single paddle of other "lightweight" rafts. And its 4x10" packed size fits easily in your backpack or daypack.

Roll it out on shore and the stuff sack becomes a unique air pump. Attach it to the raft's one-way valve, push air in, and in minutes you're out on the lake—not out of breath. A special spigot (included) turns the stuff sack into a handy water bag, too.

BUILT TOUGH TO LAST.
The raft is handmade of heat-treated, urethane-coated nylon. Unlike heavy-gauge vinyls, this tough fabric won't crack and weaken in the cool water of mountain lakes, so it not only travels lighter, but lasts longer, too.

It's the perfect size for you and your camera and fishing gear. The tapered design keeps you riding steady, lets you lean back and relax without tipping.

You can stake out a secluded campsite on the far side of the lake, reel in a meal, and watch morning come to the mountains.

Order your Ultralight Raft and test it—at no risk to you—for 30 days.

You'll discover even familiar areas take on a whole new look when you're floating free, surrounded by water and towering peaks.

Figure 8–7
Weaving Benefits into Long Copy
(below and on opposite page)

Note how this long-copy style incorporates benefits throughout editorial descriptions of features. Copyright © Early Winters. Used with permission.

Making a Common Product Unique

Another advantage of concentrating on benefits is that you can tailor copy to your specific audience and often make a common product seem uniquely your own. Another Early Winters example illustrates this point. The Leatherman combination tool has been offered by dozens of different catalogs, but never better than in the Early Winters presentation illustrated in Figure 8–8. Both the body copy and the illustration call-outs concentrate on benefits.

> Goes anywhere, does so much.
> **FIVE-OUNCE TOOLCHEST TAMES MOST ANY TASK.**
> This is a toolchest you can hold in your fist, stash in a band-aid box, or slip in your jeans pocket. But it won't stay in storage long. It's designed so cleverly, works so smoothly, it just may replace your regular pocket knife.
>
> **SO INGENIOUS, IT'S HARD TO PUT DOWN.**
> Don't blame us, we're warning you: Our Pocket Toolchest [note the use of an "exclusive" name] may send you into a fix-it frenzy . . . at home *and* on the trail. [Adding "on the trail" helps tailor the copy to Early Winters' basic audience of outdoorsmen.]
> Its ingenious design and exceptional strength will delight how-to wizards. And those used to meeting emergencies with paper-clips and table knives will find that its 10 useful tools inspire a new and satisfying sense of preparedness.

Ultralight, pack-anywhere raft puts you on mountain lakes.

Now any lake you can hike, bike, or climb your way to, you can float and fish in our Ultralight Raft.

For day trips or long treks, it's the lightest, most compact lake-going vessel ever.

20-oz. raft packs small.

An incredible 20 ounces light, the entire craft weighs less than a single paddle of other "lightweight" rafts. And its 4X10" packed size fits easily in your backpack or daypack.

Roll it out on shore and the stuff sack becomes a unique air pump. Attach it to the raft's one-way valve, push air in, and in minutes you're out on the lake—not out of breath. A special spigot (included) turns the stuff sack into a handy water bag, too.

Built tough to last.

The raft is handmade of heat-treated, urethane-coated nylon. Unlike heavy-gauge vinyls, this tough fabric won't crack and weaken in the cool water of mountain lakes, so it not only travels lighter, but lasts longer, too.

It's the perfect size for you and your camera and fishing gear. The tapered design keeps you riding steady, lets you lean back and relax without tipping.

You can stake out a secluded campsite on the far side of the lake, reel in a meal, and watch morning come to the mountains.

Order your Ultralight Raft and test it—at no risk to you—for 30 days.

You'll discover even familiar areas take on a whole new look when you're floating free, surrounded by water and towering peaks.
Includes raft, stuff sack, spigot, and repair kit. Not for use in rough water, high wind, or whitewater.
Dimensions: 11X36½X69"; 16X50½" inside.

Ultralight Raft   Wt. w/ stuff sack: 20 oz.
No. 40-6560 . . . . $199.95

Ultralight Paddles   Two sturdy, 3½-oz. paddles of rigid, vinyl-covered urethane. 5¾X10¾X⅜"
No. 40-6561 . . . . $14.95

You're likely to find the Pocket Toolchest—engraved free with your name [an added benefit helped make this an "Early Winters Exclusive"]—the single most versatile five ounces you own, and maybe the most fun!

BUILT TO TOUGH MILITARY SPECS.

Pick it up. A ruler etched on the handles lets you start work before you even open it up. Make your measurement, then unfold it. Just look at all it holds!

Pivot the tool you need from the handle. Then fold the handles together to lock the tool safely in place. The Pocket Toolchest gives you the sure grip and balance of a full-size tool.

The tools are crafted to military specs of alloyed stainless steel, and heat-treated to give you a lifetime of dependability.

Order a Pocket Toolchest soon. You'll be thoroughly pleased you had the foresight to order this one little item that goes anywhere, and does so much.

The illustration call-outs also are benefits-laden (the underscores are added to show how naturally benefits have been woven into the copy):

Figure 8–8
Making a Common Product Unique

Concentrating on all specific benefits can give a sense of individuality even to a common product. Copyright © Early Winters. Used with permission.

- Leather carrying case rides on your belt.
- Sturdy pliers give you a needle-nose, curved inner jaw, wire cutter & fishhook remover.
- Razor-sharp, rust-free 2 3/4" blade handles your cutting jobs with ease.
- Handles fold together to safely lock each tool in place. You enjoy the sure grip & balance of a full-size tool.
- 8" ruler lets you size up the job.
- Smooth-action can opener pops the top off bottles, too.
- Small screw driver has 1/16" tip for eyeglass joints, precision work.
- Handy awl/punch makes leather work and belt repairs a snap.
- Large screwdriver has 5/16" tip for steady turning.
- 2 1/4" file to shape parts, smooth edges, sharpen blades, even saw wood.
- Phillips screwdriver opens radio, other appliances.

Adding the Personal Touch

Another method of giving catalog copy uniqueness is by writing in a highly personal vein. This can backfire, however. If the copywriter's ego gets in the way, the tendency is to write the copy to enhance his or her reputation and, in the process, ignore many of the things the reader really needs to know to make a buying decision.

This is particularly true when the writer tries to be humorous. One of the most difficult things to use successfully in catalog copy is humor. If done well, it can both be entertaining and entice the audience into wanting to know more about the product. That's fine if there is enough space to provide both humor and selling copy.

But what is funny to the writer may easily lay an egg with the majority of readers. It takes a very special skill—seldom found even among professional catalog copywriters—to write humorous catalog copy that sells. Just because your staff laughs at the copy you've written, don't be deceived. They're being paid to laugh at your jokes. It's best to test humorous copy on a wide variety of different types of readers and make sure it appeals to all of them before putting it in print.

The J. Peterman Company

Humor in copy is one of the primary things which establishes a unique personality for The J. Peterman Company. This unique catalog of informal wearing apparel substitutes color drawings for the usual photographs found in catalogs. But what makes it highly distinctive is the light-hearted tone of the copy.

Typical is the message labeled, "Philosophy," which introduces the catalog (See Figure 8–10):

> **People want things that are hard to find. Things that have romance, but a factual romance, about them.**
>
> **I had this proven to me all over again when people actually stopped in the street (in New York, in Tokyo, in London) to ask me where I got the coat I was wearing.**
>
> **So many people tried to buy my coat off my back that I've started a small company to make them available. It seems like *everybody* (well, not everybody) has always wanted a classic horseman's duster but never knew exactly where to get one.**
>
> **I ran a little ad in the *New Yorker* and the *Wall Street Journal* and in a few months sold this wonderful coat in cities all over the country and to celebrities and to a mysterious gentleman in Japan who ordered *two thousand* of them.**
>
> **Well, the coat *is* magnificent. Simple, functional, handsome, extremely well made, affordable and yes, romantic.**
>
> **I think that giant American corporations should start asking themselves if the things they make are really, I mean really, better than the ordinary.**
>
> **Clearly, people want things that make their lives the way they wish they were.**

Copy for the Peterman catalog products—presented one product per page—maintains this light-hearted tone. Consider the spread in Figure 8–9:

> **GABLE. Clark Gable was this guy who had just returned from a war.**
>
> **No idea what to do with his life.**
>
> **Needed a job. Almost broke.**
>
> **Next thing I know, he wants to spend his last dime on an incredibly expensive necktie.**
>
> **I was 9 years old at the time. But sitting in a darkened theater, watching Clark about to spend his last dime on a tie . . . well, he was making me plenty nervous. Up to that time, I thought Clark Gable knew his way around.**
>
> **There was no way to stop him. Thirty-five dollars, out the window. On a stupid tie. I even remember him calling it a "sincere" necktie. Some kind of grown-up joke, I guess. I didn't get any of it.**
>
> **Instantly he got the job. Well, it was just a movie. He was a good talker, though. And he looked smooth. The tie wasn't so bad either. But thirty-five dollars? No job is worth that.**
>
> **Quietly luxurious Italian silk tie. It was "sincere" then, even more so now.**
>
> **Colors: old-money blue, old money-maroon. Gable wore one or the other. We'll never know which. The movie was black and white.**
>
> **Price: $35. We pay shipping.**

WINTER SILENCE. Put on this handsome soft snuggly red nightshirt and almost immediately you'll hear the silence that always precedes the beginning of a snowfall.

You could pretend you're doing it for the children.

And that wouldn't be entirely fictitious, would it? (Besides, the children won't be the only ones who hear it, either.)

And if at this place and at this time you don't happen to have a mess of children (or none at all) and you don't have a fieldstone fireplace either, then you'd better get one of these bright-red soft nappy nightshirts right away.

You might even consider getting two of them.

Optimism never hurts.

Classic Nightshirt. Tab collar. Placket with 4 soft rubber soccer-shirt buttons. Shirttail hem. Soothing cotton flannel in a pure unmistakably true red.

Sizes: (unisex) S, M, L, XL.

Price: $35. We pay shipping.

One of the advantages of using this informal approach is that is makes it easy for a copywriter to convert features into meaningful benefits. Consider, for example, this Peterman copy to sell a wallet (Figure 8–11):

THE RIGHT STUFF. The shops in Zurich, or on upper Madison or on old Bond Street . . . the kind of shops where you have to ring a buzzer to get inside, have wallets these days made of ostrich, sea snake, lizard . . . and once in Hong Kong I actually saw wallets made from chicken feet . . . all costing so much that once you buy one you have nothing left over to put in them.

Accordingly, I now wish to draw your attention to something different: a wallet made of a baseball mitt. This is not a joke.

Stop and think about that wonderful dark pocket of leather in the middle of a baseball glove, lovingly used and punished for half a lifetime. Is it wearing out? Is it ready to throw away? No, it's just quietly getting better.

This wallet is made out of *that* leather: baseball-glove leather. Centercut, Beautifully cut and sewn and made to last and made to darken; made to be with you for a long time.

Regular billfold size, 6 credit card pockets, 2 inside pockets, full-length compartment for bills, lined throughout.

Handsome, simple, hard to argue with.

Price: $62. We pay shipping.

My favorite piece of Peterman copy, however, is used to sell canvas shirts:

ROCKING THE BOAT. There's no question that your rights to wear a shirt like

Gable.

Clark Gable was this guy who had just returned from a war.

No idea what to do with his life.

Needed a job. Almost broke.

Next thing I know, he wants to spend his last dime on an incredibly expensive necktie.

I was 9 years old at the time. But sitting in a darkened theater, watching Clark about to spend his last dime on a tie...well, he was making me plenty nervous. Up to that time, I thought Clark Gable knew his way around.

There was no way to stop him. Thirty-five dollars, out the window. On a stupid tie. I even remember him calling it a "sincere" necktie. Some kind of grown-up joke, I guess. I didn't get any of it.

Instantly he got the job. Well, it was just a movie. He was a good talker, though. And he looked smooth. The tie wasn't so bad either. But thirty-five dollars? No job is worth that.

Quietly luxurious Italian silk tie. It was "sincere" then, even more so now.

Colors: old-money blue, or old-money maroon. Gable wore one or the other. We'll never know which. The movie was black and white.

Price: $35. We pay shipping.

Winter Silence.

Put on this handsome soft snuggly red nightshirt and almost immediately you'll hear the silence that always precedes the beginning of a snowfall.

You could pretend you're doing it for the children. And that wouldn't be entirely fictitious, would it?

(Besides, the children won't be the only ones who hear it, either.)

And if at this place and at this time you don't happen to have a mess of children (or none at all) and you don't have a fieldstone fireplace either, then you'd better get one of these bright-red soft nappy nightshirts right away.

You might even consider getting two of them. Optimism never hurts.

Classic Nightshirt. Tab collar. Placket with 4 soft rubber soccer-shirt buttons. Shirttail hem. Soothing cotton flannel in a pure and unmistakably true red.

Sizes: (unisex) S, M, L, XL.

Price: $35. We pay shipping.

To order call toll free 800-231-7341
8 AM to 10 PM (EST) weekdays and weekends.

FEDERAL EXPRESS rush delivery $6.50, see p. 2

Figure 8–9
Humor in Copy

The J. Peterman catalog copy maintains a light-hearted tone.
Copyright © The J. Peterman Company. Used with permission.

Philosophy.

"People want things that are hard to find. Things that have romance, but a factual romance, about them.

I had this proven to me all over again when people actually stopped me in the street (in New York, in Tokyo, in London) to ask me where I got the <u>coat</u> I was wearing.

So many people tried to buy my coat off my back that I've started a small company to make them available. It seems like everybody (well, not <u>everybody</u>) has always wanted a classic horseman's duster but never knew exacly where to get one.

I ran a little ad in the New Yorker and the Wall Street Journal and in a few months sold this wonderful coat in cities all over the country and to celebrities and to a mysterious gentleman in Japan who ordered <u>two</u> <u>thousand</u> of them.

Well, the coat <u>is</u> magnificent. Simple, functional, handsome, extremely well made, affordable and, yes, romantic.

I think that giant American corporations should start asking themselves if the things they make are really, I mean really, better than the ordinary.

Clearly, people want things that make their lives the way they wish they were."

The right stuff.

The shops in Zurich, or on upper Madison or on Old Bond Street...the kind of shops where you have to ring a buzzer to get inside, have wallets these days made of ostrich, sea snake, lizard...and once in Hong Kong I actually saw wallets made from chicken feet...all costing so much that once you buy one you have nothing left over to put in them.

Accordingly, I now wish to draw your attention to something different: a wallet made out of a baseball mitt. This is not a joke.

Stop and think about that wonderful dark pocket of leather in the middle of a baseball glove, lovingly used and punished for half a lifetime. Is it wearing out? Is it ready to throw away? No, it's just quietly getting better.

<u>This</u> wallet is made out of <u>that</u> leather: baseball-glove leather. Centercut. Beautifully cut and sewn and made to last and made to darken; made to be with you for a long time.

Regular billfold size, 6 credit card pockets, 2 inside pockets, full-length compartment for bills, lined throughout.

Handsome, simple, hard to argue with.

Price: $62. We pay shipping.

Figure 8–10 (top)
Philosophy

Figure 8–11 (bottom)
The Right Stuff

Copyright © The J. Peterman Company. Used with permission.

Rocking the Boat.

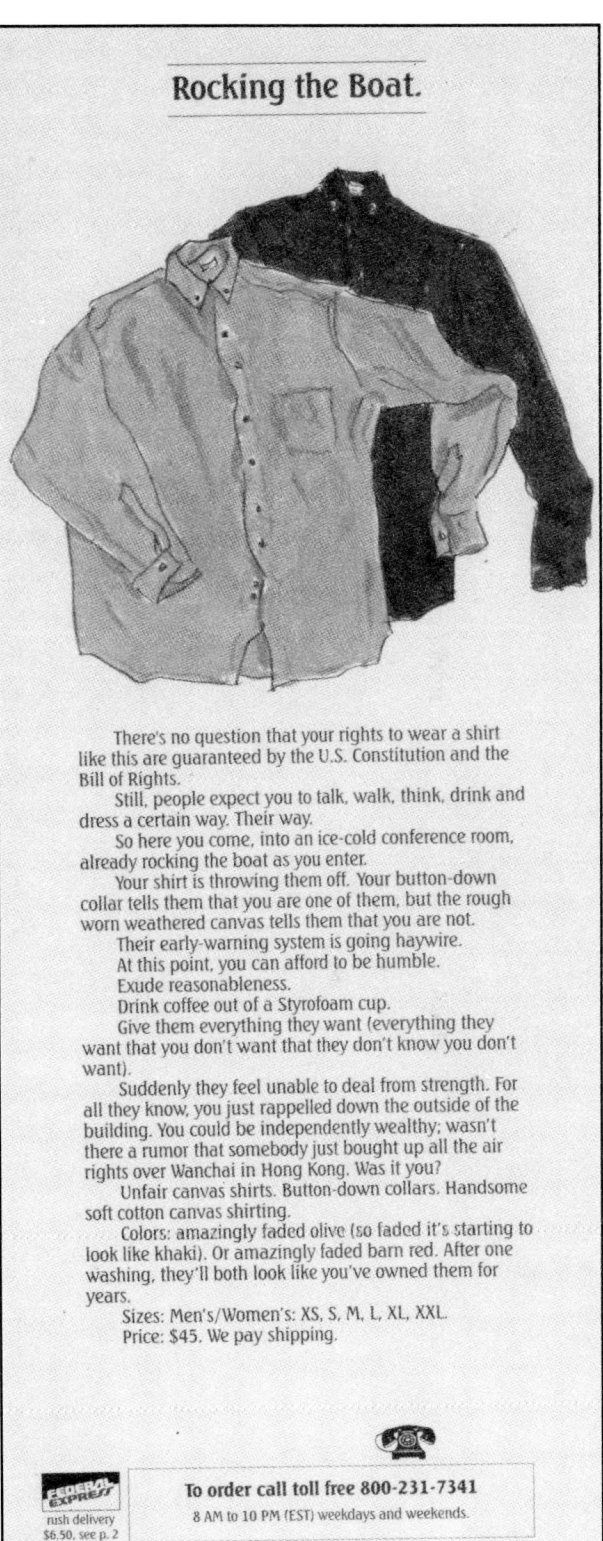

There's no question that your rights to wear a shirt like this are guaranteed by the U.S. Constitution and the Bill of Rights.

Still, people expect you to talk, walk, think, drink and dress a certain way. Their way.

So here you come, into an ice-cold conference room, already rocking the boat as you enter.

Your shirt is throwing them off. Your button-down collar tells them that you are one of them, but the rough worn weathered canvas tells them that you are not.

Their early-warning system is going haywire.

At this point, you can afford to be humble.

Exude reasonableness.

Drink coffee out of a Styrofoam cup.

Give them everything they want (everything they want that you don't want that they don't know you don't want).

Suddenly they feel unable to deal from strength. For all they know, you just rappelled down the outside of the building. You could be independently wealthy; wasn't there a rumor that somebody just bought up all the air rights over Wanchai in Hong Kong. Was it you?

Unfair canvas shirts. Button-down collars. Handsome soft cotton canvas shirting.

Colors: amazingly faded olive (so faded it's starting to look like khaki). Or amazingly faded barn red. After one washing, they'll both look like you've owned them for years.

Sizes: Men's/Women's: XS, S, M, L, XL, XXL.

Price: $45. We pay shipping.

To order call toll free 800-231-7341
8 AM to 10 PM (EST) weekdays and weekends.

FEDERAL EXPRESS
rush delivery
$6.50, see p. 2

Figure 8–12
Rocking the Boat

Copyright © The J. Peterman Company. Used with permission.

this are guaranteed by the U.S. Constitution and the Bill of Rights.

Still, people expect you to talk, walk, think, drink, and dress a certain way. Their way.

So here you come, into an ice-cold conference room, already rocking the boat as you enter.

Your shirt is throwing them off. Your button-down collar tells them that you are one of them, but the roughworn weathered canvas tells them that you are not.

Their early-warning system is going haywire.

At this point, you can afford to be humble.

Exude reasonableness.

Drink coffee out of a Styrofoam cup.

Give them everything they want (everything they want that you don't want that they don't know you don't want).

Suddenly they feel unable to deal from strength. For all they know, you just rappelled down the outside of the building. You could be independently wealthy; wasn't there a rumor that somebody just bought up all the air rights over Wanchai in Hong Kong. Was it you?

Unfair canvas shirts. Button-down collars. Handsome soft cotton canvas shirting.

Colors: amazingly faded olive (so faded it's starting to look like khaki). Or amazingly faded red. After one washing, they'll both look like you've owned them for years.

Sizes: Men's/Women's: XS, S, M, L, XL, XXL.

Price: $45. We pay shipping.

Carl Forslund

Another excellent example of writing copy with a personal touch was done by the late Carl Forslund, whose furniture catalogs were "must" reading for thousands of dedicated catalog buyers for many years. The catalogs had strong emphasis on the dedication to quality of the Forslund family and frequently opened with pictures of the entire family. This led to frequent family references in the catalog copy.

THE BRIDGET LEE WASHSTAND

Mr. & Mrs. F have two of our Bridget Lees (made only by us). One in Grand Rapids in Mr. F's cluttered bedroom, the towel bars hold a mess of ties, the drawers—"junk." The shelf holds all the shoe shining gear and the top, everything left over. Then the other, the original (and it is hard to recognize that it is, as our replicas are so close to the old one), is up at Drummond Island. The top holding all "the Happy Hour" glasses and bottles—the shelf, Mrs. F's cook books and . . . Bridget is quite at home in both places.

THE UTILITY LEE

Grandpa Lee proudly brought the original of this folding sewing table home to Grandma from a Country Auction years ago . . . and it became Grandma's most treasured article. It has so many uses: for sewing, for teas, for buffets and informal TV snacks; or put two together for luncheons and supper parties. It folds away to just 4 inches to tuck in a closet and is so much more attractive and sturdy than an ordinary card table. Solid cherry, spool turned, tapered legs; strong metal device for folding the legs. In our durable, rich, deep toned Forslund Cherry or Light Buckwheat Honey. The top is 36 inches x 18 inches, 25 $\frac{1}{2}$ inches high (just right to pull up to a comfortable easy chair) and it closes to 4 inches thick. We pay the express to you. Such a grand gift . . . such a good buy.

While this copy was written by Carl Forslund himself, personal-style copy can be written by professional catalog copywriters as well. To maintain a consistent image, however, requires special effort. A stylebook is a must. It should include copious examples of copy written by the personality whose style is to be copied.

If the personality is fictitious, it is advisable to create a mythical biography which will enable the copywriter to visualize the individual he or she is representing. One direct marketer even had a portrait painted of his company's mythical spokesperson, and framed prints were hung in each copywriter's office.

Before the Writing Starts

Most of the hard work of catalog copywriting occurs before a single word is put to paper.

Review Old Copy

The first step is to review previous catalog copy written about this product or similar products—including a study of results.

While it may hurt the creative ego of some copywriters, there is no need to rewrite catalog copy that is working. Nobody—at least nobody in the audience you want to reach—cares if you use old copy again and again.

Of course, one of the difficulties with reusing old copy is the boss who doesn't feel a copywriter is earning his or her keep if every word isn't new. But smarter bosses recognize one of the real tests of a good copywriter is the willingness to utilize tried and proven copy regardless of who originally put the words together.

David Ogilvy once said, "One of the greatest wastes in advertising is to do away with copy which is still working." And it's important to remember the often-repeated truism that when you start getting bored with an advertising message, that's about when the audience starts to notice it.

It's also important to remember that a catalog customer is not "the same person" from day to day. The way customers are thinking and the things in which they are interested when a new catalog arrives are often quite different than they were when a previous catalog was received. Thus the old copy will most likely be "new" to them—and if it's really good copy which has worked in the past, it should continue to do a selling job each time around.

White Mail

Another important first step is to expose the copywriter to the "white mail" received by a catalog.

White mail is any correspondence other than orders or payments received from customers. Here is where the copywriter will learn the language used and most easily understood by the customers. When you use customers' language, rather than the copywriter's own language (or the language used within a catalog organization), the whole process of communication is improved.

If you don't get much white mail from your customers, it's easy for a copywriter to pick up a phone and talk with a handful of typical customers. Try to describe the product and listen for the questions the customers ask. (And you'll get a side benefit, too. When you ask customers to help you solve problems, you develop a special relationship with them and research has shown that such customers not only buy more from you in the future, but remain loyal customers for a long time.)

Competitors' Copy

Another early step is to make a thorough review of how competitive catalogs describe the same or similar products. You won't want to copy others—just the opposite. Look for a new approach with ways to give your customer a reason to buy from you rather than the other guy.

Gather the Facts

The next step is to gather all research material for each spread and review it carefully. Good catalog copy should have a flow, and this can be broken if you constantly have to go and seek out elusive facts before you can continue with your writing.

By putting together all of the information you need, studying it thoroughly, and fixing the key points in your mind before you begin writing you can concentrate on the writing itself and won't be sidetracked by having to seek out facts you need.

I've made it a regular practice to develop "copywriter's packets" which provide ready reference on all the products and services with which I've had to deal. You'll find an outline of the ideal contents of a copywriter's packet on pages 169–72.

When it's time to write copy for a catalog spread, I simply gather all of the copy packets for the items to appear on that spread and give them to the copywriter. Thus he or she can start writing immediately after reviewing the contents of each packet.

It's easy for a secretary or clerk to prepare the copy packets and maintain them on file so they'll be ready and waiting when the writing is to be done. This is very cost-efficient, since the hourly rate of good catalog copywriters is generally considerably higher than that of secretaries and clerks.

The Starting Point

All of this has been preliminary to actually writing a word of the copy. But now it's time for action, and that always starts in just one place. If there's one absolute rule for catalog copywriting, it is *Always Write The Order Form First!*

The order form is the copywriter's target. Writing copy without an order form as a target is like trying to be a sharpshooter by simply shooting bullets against a blank wall and then drawing circles around the places where the bullets hit. Nobody ever won a rifle championship that way, and you can't expect championship catalog copy unless there is an order form at which to aim.

All copywriters should have a copy of the catalog order form staring them in the face as they write. There will, for example, be only so much space available to write a description of the product, and the copywriter must make sure that the copy includes a description which will fit into that space.

Another area where it is easy for a copywriter to go wrong is in handling quantities. The copy may be talking about a set of four items. But when customers have to fill out the order form, they can easily be confused, wondering whether to put in "1" for "1 set" or "4" for the number of items in the set.

A copywriter also has to be very careful about other numbers. Quite often there are both a model number and a stockkeeping number. If both are included in the copy, without telling the customer which to use, many of the orders may arrive with the wrong number.

You'll often hear order entry people say this is really not a problem since they can easily match up the product description with the price, even if the customer has substituted a model number instead of the stockkeeping number. But one thing an order entry person can never tell you is how many people failed to send in an order because they were confused about how to fill in the order blank. Customer confusion probably results in more lost sales than any other single reason. Customers don't want to "look dumb," so they'll order from someone else rather than take a chance if they are even slightly confused about how to place an order with you.

Editing Copy

The natural tendency of copywriters is to want to jump up from the typewriter, word processor, or writing pad when the copy is completed and rush over and read it to a colleague. That's the worst possible way to evaluate the effectiveness of a piece of catalog copy.

When you read to someone, you put the emphasis where you intend it to go. But you can't read your copy to every catalog recipient. And your colleagues know only too well the problems you've had to face in writing copy and will tend to be overly sympathetic if you don't quite overcome a difficult communications hurdle.

The Hat Trick

The best way to get an evaluation of your copy is what is called the "Hat Trick"—put on your hat, get out of the office, take the copy to someone who doesn't know a thing about the product, and have that person read the copy back to you.

Listen carefully to where he or she puts the emphasis . . . and even more carefully to any questions he or she wants you to answer to help explain what the whole thing is all about. If there are still questions, the copywriting job isn't over.

The Cross-out/Write-in Test

Another good test of catalog copy is to cross out every reference to your company and its product and write in the name of your competitor and their product. If the copy still fits, there's still a lot of rewriting to be done.

A good catalog copywriter should be able to come up with copy points which your competitor couldn't say (or hasn't said) about that product. That's what often identifies the true professional in catalog copywriting—the ability to instill a uniqueness in the copy which encourages a prospect to want to order it from *you*.

Take a look back at Ron Zimmerman's copy for Early Winters' Pocket Toolchest illustrated on page 157. Here was a common item offered by dozens of others, yet this copy converted it into what appeared to be an Early Winters' "exclusive."

The Committee

Someone once observed that a camel was a horse that had been created by a committee. And all too often, copy that has been subjected to the blue pencils of a committee is about as graceful as a camel when the job calls for a sleek racehorse.

So, after the committee has done its collective damage, it's time to send the copy back to the copywriter for a final rewriting. That doesn't mean the writer can ignore the committee's no-nos and must-musts. But the writer can start from the beginning again and interweave the changes into a smoothly flowing unit.

COIK

Someone in government, where acronyms are the order of the day, came up with COIK as a way to describe copy which is difficult to understand:

COIK = **C**lear **O**nly **I**f **K**nown

That's an acronym which should be pasted on every catalog copywriter's wall.

Too often catalog copy is written so that it can be fully understood only if the audience knows as much about the subject as the copywriter—and that seldom is the case.

There used to be a saying that you should write for the 12-year-old mentality. That's dangerous today, however. The 12-year-olds know too darn much. Instead, it's suggested you write for the college freshman . . . and eventually the chairman of the board will be able to figure it out.

Seriously, however, it is important to keep the knowledge level of the catalog audience clearly in mind. A good rule to follow:

> Don't overestimate the knowledge of the audience . . . but don't underestimate their intelligence.

In other words, don't "write down" to your readers, but make a special effort to remember just how much previous knowledge they are apt to have about the product being described.

The Copywriter's Packet

Research and copywriting are two separate tasks, even though they may be performed by the same individual. However, regardless of who does the prewriting research, it's a good idea to maintain a continuing file of background information which can be utilized over and over again whenever promotion copy is needed for the same product or service—or even as a starter file for similar products or services.

Such a file is particularly important for catalogs since there is an average of 80 percent pick-up of products from one catalog to the next. Once good copy has been created and proven to work, there's no reason to rewrite it unless there's important new information about the product. Usually, it's just a matter of fitting the old copy into the copy space available in the new catalog and avoiding any conflicts with similar items which now appear on the same spread.

My personal preference for copy packets is to keep all of the information in indexed ring binders, with the latest material always added to the front of each section. Then, when it's time for the writing to begin, the material is ready and waiting.

Here are some of the things which should be included in a copywriter's packet.

Old Copy

Include all previous copy used to describe this product, no matter how long ago it was used. It's helpful to clearly identify which copy worked well in the past. And it's even more important to identify copy approaches which failed, so they won't be repeated.

Results from Previous Catalogs

This will help identify which styles of copy are most effective. And if the results can be broken down by audience segments, you'll be able to identify the best prospects for the item.

Competitors' Copy

Be aware of what others are saying about the same product—or at least the same type of products. This isn't to suggest you should copy what others have said. In fact, you'll generally obtain much better results if you can find a way to make a point which is uniquely your own. But it is important to be fully aware of the competitive environment your copy will face.

Vendors' Data

Have the vendor of the product provide as much information as possible. Don't expect vendors to know all of the benefits of their products or even the key selling points. They're often too close to the forest to see the trees. But there's no reason to reinvent the wheel. Anything you can get from a vendor means just that much less time you'll have to spend researching.

If the product comes in a package with information on it, it's a good idea to include a reproduction of the package information in the packet. If there are printed inserts in the package, make sure they are included in the copy packet. And if there are instruction sheets, how-to-assemble directions, etc., make sure they too are included.

An often overlooked source of good background material is the vendor's customer service department. Often these departments will have special letters and enclosures loaded with helpful reference material.

Specification Sheet

There should be a standard specification sheet for each type of product included in a catalog. This will provide spaces for information such as dimensions, weight, colors, type of packaging, materials, when the product was first introduced, how it is packaged, country of origin, warranties which cover the product, etc. This information should be provided by the merchandise buyer—or, if the product has been created internally, by the product manager or others who know most about the item.

A key part of this specification sheet should be answers to these key questions:

- How does this product differ from similar products?
- Why should a customer buy this product rather than something similar?

In addition, this sheet should identify the key benefits of the product and its Unique Selling Position (USP)—and it's my belief no product is worthy of catalog presentation if it doesn't have an identifiable USP.

It's important to establish a policy that every detail must be completed on the specification sheet before a copy packet goes to a catalog copywriter.

Editorial Reference

Every editorial mention of the product should be clipped on a regular basis and added to the copy packet. This should not only include newspaper and magazine articles, radio and TV scripts, and other "published" material from outside sources, but also anything produced internally within the vendor's or your own organization, including engineering reports, customer service reports, transcripts of focus group sessions, press releases, etc. (The more background a writer has before starting to write, the better the chance he or she will come up with a truly distinctive approach which will help sell more of the product or service.)

Sales Records

The copy packet should contain all records of previous sales of the product. All too often, the writer is left out of discussions concerning sales results from previous catalogs, yet they are essential to a full understanding of how best to create words which will help sell the product.

Customer Comments

This is perhaps the most important item of all. A copy of every letter and record of customer service phone calls concerning the product should be added to the copy packet as they are received.

Tom Collins's Checklist:
What Good Catalog Copy Should Provide

Thomas L. Collins, one of America's all-time great copywriters, offered this useful checklist during an advanced catalog seminar at New York University.

1. Information (basics about product)
2. Immediate benefit (the promise)
3. Ultimate benefit (the "promise of the promise")
4. Uniqueness (exclusivity)
5. Product advantages/features in order of priority
6. Empathy (requires product visualization)
7. Wish fulfillment
8. Vicarious experience
9. Proof of promise
10. Clarity
11. Readability
12. Conciseness
13. Authority
14. Completeness
15. Competitiveness (why your offer is better)
16. Appropriateness (of copy to your catalog's image)
17. Explanations (of any product features needing clarification)
18. Prospect orientation
19. A "handle" ("the right name/the big idea")
20. Uses of the item
21. Value to the customer
22. A personalized approach
23. Conversational tone
24. Provocativeness (stimulation to buy)
25. News (or newness of item, if appropriate)

Twenty Questions to Ask about Your Catalog Copy

If there's a "Copy Chief" in the world of direct marketing, it's Hershell Gordon Lewis. He suggests playing an old parlor game, 20 Questions, to evaluate catalog copy.

1. Do you know who reads your catalog?
2. Is your copy pitched specifically toward the biggest reader group?
3. Do you tell the catalog recipients repeatedly why they should buy from you?
4. What about your product descriptions motivates the reader to buy?
5. Do you repeatedly use sentences longer than 12 words? **Long sentences slow down the reader's comprehension, especially in narrow copy blocks.**
6. Does your description match the illustration?
7. Does your description cover deficiencies in the illustration such as relative size, colors, or descriptions of each possible use?
8. If you have a "welcome" letter, is it just a bunch of words or is it genuine salesmanship?
9. Is your copy peppered with "in talk" the average reader might find incomprehensible?
10. Can someone unfamiliar with a new product visualize a reason to buy it from your description?
11. Is your order form simplified, easy to fill out?
12. Does the catalog cover excite the reader?
13. Have you cleansed your copy of egomania and megalomania? **Part of [the writer's] job is to avoid dislocating the corporate arm by using it to pat the company on its own back.**
14. Do you pepper your copy with "spot" testimonials, bonus gifts, 800-number reminders, or early-bird discounts? **Excitement doesn't end with the front cover. Any catalog has holes. Fill those holes with inducements; who knows when the urge to order something will strike?**
15. Does your copy stroke the reader by saying, "Only you"?
16. Does your catalog project an image, and does your copy match that image?
17. Is your copy timely, tied to the season or period of issue?
18. Do you write in the active rather than the passive voice?
19. Are you sure you've selected the key selling point for each item?
20. Are you positive your catalog has no product descriptions you could have written more vividly if you'd had more time or more information?

Catalog Hot Spots, Covers, and Wraps

9

Covers and Other Hot Spots!

All positions in a catalog don't have equal value. There are a number of "hot spots" which generally produce increased sales. They have special selling potential for one or both of two reasons:

- Because they indicate that you feel what is being shown has special merit.
- Because these pages are seen more frequently than other pages in a catalog.

The average catalog has eight primary hot spots:

1. Front cover
2. Back cover
3. Inside front cover (Page 2)
4. Pages 3-4-5
5. Inside back cover
6. Center spread
7. Pages facing order form
8. Pages facing any other insert

If your catalog has 16 or fewer pages, chances are only the front and back covers will turn out to be hot spots. And if your catalog has 100 or more pages, you may be able to introduce more than the eight basic hot spots through the use of special design techniques.

Front Cover

There's nothing more important to a catalog than its cover. The cover gets more attention than any other page, and whatever you present on the cover generally sells considerably better than it would sell on any other page in the catalog.

I'm a strong believer in the idea of using a catalog cover to sell something specific. Many catalogers, however, are so strongly concerned with "image" that they concentrate on simply producing "pretty picture" covers. To my mind, a pretty picture cover that doesn't also sell a product most often is evidence of an unimaginative art director. There are literally hundreds of different ways to create image-building covers built around your products.

As a general rule, I've found that a product featured on a front cover produces at least double the sales it would have generated if it were simply presented in the same amount of space anywhere else in the catalog (other than another hot spot).

The technique I've found to work best features a product on the front cover with a caption telling the reader that information about it will be found on page 2. Then, on page 2, I prefer to show either a reproduction of the cover or another illustration of the product along with the selling copy. While there may not be enough space for another illustration, it is very important to clearly identify the copy as "the cover special," instead of leaving it to the reader's imagination.

If space isn't available on page 2 for a product description, the cover caption can direct the reader to some other spot in the catalog. This, however, may encourage a reader to turn immediately to that page and overlook what's being presented in the pages preceding it.

It is usually preferable to select items for presentation on the front cover that will appeal to the majority of those who will receive the catalog. Midprice points are generally best. And whenever possible, feature a new item, which will suggest that your entire catalog likely contains things the recipients haven't seen before. This, of course, stimulates catalog readership.

One reason cover presentations are so important is that they have a combination of both of the advantages of a hot spot. First of all, more people see your cover than any other single page in a catalog. Plus, when a product is shown on a front cover, you're saying, in effect, "This is the most important thing we have to offer to you."

When selecting a cover design, remember that your catalog is "a store in print," and the cover serves as both your storefront and your display window. It establishes your identity and can telegraph the catalog's contents. It should be a cover which "sticks in customers' minds," so they will be able to locate it quickly among the catalogs they've saved when they're ready to order merchandise.

Figure 9–1
Using Covers to Lead into Editorial-style Presentations

Copyright © Lands' End. Reprinted courtesy of Lands' End Catalog.

Continuity in catalog covers is important. Since your best prospects for orders from any given catalog are those who have purchased from past catalogs, each issue of your catalog should be recognized as coming from you. But since a catalog's cover will be the most remembered thing about any issue, it's important to have a cover change each time you mail to the same audience—even if the contents of the catalog haven't changed. If customers see an "old" cover, they are likely to assume they've already considered everything that catalog has to offer and throw it away or set it aside without giving it an "editorial reading."

A substantial number of direct marketers mail several copies of the same catalog—particularly to their best customers—during a single season. Although there are seldom changes to any of the body pages, each mailing sports a new set of covers. An analysis of response shows subsequent mailings, while seldom producing a response as high as that of the first mailing, result in enough additional sales—*if there is a change of covers*—to more than justify the added expense.

Changes in the body of the catalog—particularly the introductory pages—can produce increased response, but that increase seldom is great enough to justify the added cost of catalog body changes. While customers are quick to recognize a repeated cover, the catalog body itself often seems "new," since the things in which a customer is interested change from day to day. What grabs their attention when another catalog arrives is likely to be different from what was of interest when the first catalog was received.

If you are going to mail just one first-of-the-year catalog, the best mailing drop date is probably early in January. This avoids the extremely heavy catalog mailing period immediately following Christmas, but still gets your catalog in the hands of buyers while they're in a mood for self purchases.

If you will be distributing two of the same catalog, with just cover changes, the first should go into the post office in time to be distributed as soon after December 26 as possible, with the second mailing scheduled to arrive about February 1.

For three-time distribution, the usual pattern is

1. Late December
2. February 1
3. March 1

For four-time distribution, it is quite common to move the first two mailings closer together, possibly with the first catalog distributed to only your best customers so it will arrive just ahead of Christmas, rather than after Christmas. However, a more common pattern is

1. Late December
2. Mid-January
3. Mid-February
4. Mid-March

Multiple gift catalog mailings most often follow a Labor Day to November sequence, although recent years have seen more early and late catalog mailings.

If just one gift catalog is to be distributed, it will probably work best if it is received early in October.

If two of the same catalog will be distributed, the normal pattern is to mail the first one so it will arrive shortly after Labor Day. (Labor Day is the most frequent change-of-lifestyles period—summer activities are over; kids are back in school; and preparing for the Christmas holidays is beginning.) Then the second catalog is usually dropped to arrive in mid-October.

For three-time gift catalog distribution, the usual sequence is

1. Early September
2. Early October
3. Early November

Four-time gift catalog distribution tends to vary a lot. Many direct marketers try to get a jump on the season by mailing the first gift catalog in August, and then follow up with mailings in late September, late October, and mid-to-late November.

Back Cover

The second most important hot spot in a catalog is the back cover. This is true for three major reasons:

- Sometimes a catalog is placed face up; other times, face down. So the back cover gets increased visibility.
- While most people read a catalog from front to back, a substantial number of catalog recipients read from back to front. Thus for many, the back cover can be almost as important as the front cover.
- From past experience, catalog readers have discovered that back covers are frequently used to feature special merchandise . . . so they suspect you're telling them that back cover products have some special merit.

Ever since printers began offering jet-ink imaging for catalogs, the opportunity has been available to imprint personalized messages on each catalog. While relatively few catalogers take advantage of the opportunity to create a personalized message for each reader, those who have used this method have seen substantial increases in sales.

There are a number of different systems available for jet-ink imaging individual messages on catalogs. A typical system permits adding a 50-character-per-line, six-line message both on the back cover and on an order form bound into the catalog. This is in addition to a 30-character, six-line address in each location.

These messages are added during the catalog binding process. While the printing quality usually leaves much to be desired, they still have high impact. Most catalogers, however, simply use a standard message (which could just as easily have been printed during the regular press run) for all catalogs.

A good example of the use of individually personalized jet-ink messages on back covers is shown in the Breck's catalog (Figure 9–2). The basic personalized message for catalogs sent to active customers reads:

> WE'RE HAVING A GREAT SPRING HERE IN HOLLAND AND YOU'LL FIND THIS SUPER VALUE CATALOG FILLED WITH INCREASED SAVINGS ON BULBS TO PLANT THIS FALL IN THE [RECIPIENT'S LAST NAME] GARDEN. SPECIAL FREE BONUS IF YOUR ORDER TOTALS $25: 8 RED ESTATE TULIPS TO ADD DUTCH BEAUTY TO YOUR [TOWN] GARDEN!

Another message was developed for those who had made their first purchase from Breck's the preceding year:

> THANK YOU, [NAME OF RECIPIENT], FOR ORDERING FROM BRECK'S LAST YEAR. TO SHOW OUR APPRECIATION, WE'D LIKE TO SEND YOU 8 ESTATE TULIPS TO PLANT IN YOUR [TOWN] GARDEN. THEY'LL BE YOURS ABSOLUTELY FREE WITH ANY ORDER OF $25 OR MORE FROM THIS CATALOG. SEND NO MONEY. ORDER NOW AND SAVE AS MUCH AS 50%!

Figure 9–2 (opposite)
Jet-Ink Personalization

The availability of jet-ink imaging has made it easy to add personalization to catalog mailings. Typically, a catalog can have an 80-character, six-line message on both the back cover and on inside page. Breck's used 30 characters per line to create the mailing address, with the additional 50 characters used to create a six-line personalized message on both the back cover and the reverse side of the order form. Copyright © Foster & Gallagher. Used with permission.

FREE BONUS
8 Red Apeldoorn Tulips

There's a very special bonus awaiting you when you order bulbs from Holland during Breck's 1990 Advance Sale. With every order of $25.00 or more, we'll include eight of our finest Red Apeldoorn Estate Tulips absolutely FREE! These fine Darwin Hybrids bloom brightly in mid-spring with large scarlet blooms on strong, sturdy 24" stems.
E14282 Apeldoorn Estate Tulip Bonus
8 Top Quality Bulbs   **FREE**
with any order of $25.00 or more.

FREE! Breck's Exclusive
Dutch Bulb Handbook

Breck's experts in Holland have created a Dutch Bulb Handbook filled with tips on how to plant and care for your bulbs. Available nowhere else. Yours FREE with every order.

BRECK'S Instant Credit
Breck's Credit Already Established
For amount, see special message on the back of the order form in the center of this catalog.

SEND NO MONEY
All bulbs may be inspected and approved after they arrive direct from Holland at fall planting time before any payment is required.

BRECK'S – Like Having Your Own Personal Dutch Bulb Buying Agent Right in Holland

Our low sale prices are made possible by our ability to coordinate orders well ahead of shipping season. By making early commitments to growers we get first choice of their finest bulbs and gain volume discounts – savings we pass along to you. Ordering from Breck's is like having your own personal buying agent right in Holland. Our experts spend the entire year in Holland, selecting fine Dutch Bulbs for American gardens – a job we've done successfully for 172 years. Breck's standards are so high only 1 in 20 bulbs grown in Holland each year qualifies for shipment to our customers in America. Even gardeners right in Holland can't obtain fresher, healthier, better quality bulbs.

SAVE AS MUCH AS 50%!

A SPECIAL MESSAGE FROM HOLLAND

BRECK'S
U. S. Reservation Center
6523 North Galena Road
Peoria, Illinois 61632

BULK RATE
U.S. POSTAGE
PAID
BRECK'S

RESIDENT OR

```
****************5-DIGIT 19395

MR. T EHTEN
P O BOX 46
1433 JOHNNYS WAY
WESTOWN          PA 19395
```

```
JOIN THE THOUSANDS OF MONEY-WISE PENNSYLVANIA
HOMEOWNERS WHO SAVE AS MUCH AS 50% BY ORDERING
DUTCH BULBS FROM BRECK'S. SEND NO MONEY. PAY AFTER
BULBS ARRIVE DIRECT FROM HOLLAND AT FALL PLANTING
TIME FOR WESTOWN. ORDER NOW. GET FREE
BULBS TO ADD BEAUTY TO THE EHTEN HOME.
```

172 Years of Serving American Gardeners

Breck's has been serving American gardeners since 1818. Our staff of Dutch Bulb Experts in Holland provides on-the-spot buying services which enable American gardeners to obtain cream-of-the-crop bulbs from the top crops of leading Dutch growers. No other organization offers so much experience in knowing the various growing conditions throughout the U.S. and applying this knowledge to the selection of bulbs which can be fully guaranteed to grow and bloom in your garden year after year. And by taking Advance Sale orders well ahead of shipping season, Breck's receives maximum quantity discounts – savings we pass along to you.

SEND NO MONEY
Pay After Bulbs Arrive Direct from Holland

You don't have to send a single penny when you order prime quality Dutch Bulbs from Breck's. The bulbs you order will be individually selected by Breck's skilled Dutch Bulb Experts in Holland. Each bulb is professionally inspected and then cured in special facilities right in the heart of Holland's bulb-growing area. When it nears proper fall planting time for your area, the bulbs you've ordered are once again inspected, cleaned and carefully packaged by experts. Then your package is placed in a special temperature-controlled container for shipment across the Atlantic to the port nearest your home. Breck's handles all customs clearances and checks to make sure your bulbs have sustained no damage during their voyage from Holland. Then your package is rushed to you by fast overland transportation so your bulbs arrive in fresh, healthy ready-to-plant condition. You'll have full opportunity to inspect and approve every bulb before you'll be asked to pay a cent.

BRECK'S GUARANTEES SPRING BEAUTY

ORDER WITHOUT RISK
Satisfaction Fully Guaranteed

There's no risk when you order from Breck's. Satisfaction fully guaranteed. If, for any reason, you're not completely pleased with your bulbs upon receipt, after planting or once they grow and bloom, all you have to do is write Breck's anytime before July 1, 1991. We'll send full refund, replacement or exchange – whichever you prefer. No questions and no quibbling. You, and you alone, will be the judge! This no-risk guarantee is backed by Breck's 172 years of service to American gardeners. Millions of American gardeners have learned that ordering cream-of-the-crop Dutch Bulbs from Breck's is the ideal way to bring Dutch beauty to their yards and gardens.

SAVE AS MUCH AS 50% ON HOLLAND'S FINEST BULBS FOR PLANTING THIS FALL!

```
SPECIAL MESSAGE FOR MR. T EHTEN

BRECK'S 1990 ADVANCE SALE OFFERS BIG SAVINGS ON
BULBS TO ADD BEAUTY TO THE EHTEN HOME.
ORDER DIRECT FROM HOLLAND. SAVE UP TO 50%! EVERY
BULB GUARANTEED TO BLOOM IN WESTOWN.
ORDER NOW AND GET 8 BIG RED APELDOORN TULIPS FREE!
```

BRECK'S INSTANT CREDIT
Send No Money. Pay After Your Bulbs Arrive Direct From Holland This Fall.

Credit Authorized:
$100.00

```
EA52918294-193  EA0199H4 18
MR. T EHTEN
P O BOX 46
1433 JOHNNYS WAY
WESTOWN          PA 19395
```

The credit amount shown above has already been authorized. If you wish to place an order for a larger amount, expedited clearance will be extended.

EA

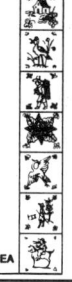

© COPYRIGHT 1991 DARTNELL CORPORATION

This personalized message was used for inactive customers:

WE'VE MISSED SEEING THE [RECIPIENT'S LAST NAME] NAME AMONG THE ORDERS WE'VE SHIPPED TO [STATE] FROM HOLLAND. WE'VE GOT SOME EXTRA SPECIAL VALUES THIS YEAR FOR YOUR [TOWN] GARDEN PLUS A GREAT FREE BONUS—EIGHT OF OUR FINEST TULIPS. SEND NO MONEY. ORDER NOW AND SAVE AS MUCH AS 50%!

Another personalized message was used for promotion to known gardeners who had never bought from Breck's:

ORDER DIRECT FROM HOLLAND AND SAVE AS MUCH AS 50% ON PRIME QUALITY DUTCH BULBS TO BEAUTIFY YOUR [TOWN] HOME. SEND NO MONEY. PAY WHEN BULBS ARRIVE AT PROPER FALL PLANTING TIME FOR [NAME OF COUNTY] COUNTY. ORDER NOW AND GET FREE BULBS FOR THE [RECIPIENT'S NAME] GARDEN.

Yet another version was used for promotion to other outside lists:

JOIN THE THOUSANDS OF MONEY-WISE [STATE] HOME OWNERS WHO SAVE AS MUCH AS 50% BY ORDERING DUTCH BULBS FROM BRECK'S. SEND NO MONEY. PAY AFTER BULBS ARRIVE DIRECT FROM HOLLAND AT FALL PLANTING TIME FOR [TOWN]. ORDER NOW. GET FREE BULBS TO ADD BEAUTY TO THE [RECIPIENT'S NAME] HOME.

For lists of new homeowners, this version was substituted:

WELCOME TO YOUR NEW [TOWN] HOME! AS A WELCOMING GIFT, WE'D LIKE TO SEND YOU 8 FREE ESTATE TULIPS. THEY'LL BE YOURS ABSOLUTELY FREE WITH ANY ORDER OF $25 OR MORE FROM THIS SPECIAL CATALOG. SEND NO MONEY. PAY AFTER BULBS ARRIVE DIRECT FROM HOLLAND AT FALL PLANTING TIME FOR [STATE].

(As you will note, all personalization elements in these messages were automatically generated by information appearing in the mailing address. The name of the county in which the recipient lives can be determined by readily available software programs which identify counties simply by reading the ZIP Code.)

To have a supply of catalogs ready to fulfill catalog requests, a nonpersonalized message was jet-ink imaged on a quantity of the catalogs, to which a mailing label would be added later:

THANK YOU FOR REQUESTING BRECK'S CATALOG. WE INVITE YOU TO JOIN THE THOUSANDS OF MONEY-WISE AMERICAN GARDENERS WHO SAVE AS MUCH

AS 50% BY ORDERING DUTCH BULBS FROM BRECK'S. SEND NO MONEY. PAY AFTER BULBS ARRIVE DIRECT FROM HOLLAND THIS FALL. SATISFACTION FULLY GUARANTEED. FREE BONUS IF YOU ORDER PROMPTLY.

The cost of personalization such as that shown in these examples is modest—just some extra computer programming charges. Thus, it is surprising that so few catalogs take advantage of this way to increase catalog response.

Pages 2–5

The inside front cover and first few body pages of a catalog are two additional hot spots. Even though a substantial number of readers may start at the back of a catalog, their previous experience tells them they are most likely to find "important" information "up front." After all, that's where they find the most important news stories in their newspapers and the primary feature articles in magazines. And from past experience, they've learned that many catalogs traditionally use front-of-the-book pages to introduce new items and to present products of special interest.

While these pages seldom pull as much increased response as that generated by items featured on the front and back covers, they generally produce a significant number of added sales.

Many catalogs take advantage of the increased readership of the inside front cover to present a special message to "introduce" the catalog. An outstanding example of this technique is the "Culinary Notes from Chuck Williams," which regularly introduce each Williams-Sonoma catalog. These brief letters most often focus on a featured product. Here's an example:

> **I was in Dusseldorf not long ago, arriving on the sort of bleak, windy day that makes you turn up your coat collar and wish that you were somewhere else. Hunting for a taxi, I crossed the square outside the train station, and there was a marvelous sight: a bakery with the window piled high with familar, bee-hive shaped loaves of dark bread, all floury and inviting. Needless to say, I couldn't resist going inside, to be greeted by a round, cheerful lady who was delighted, *Naturlich!*, to show me her husband's old-fashioned brick bread ovens and his stacks of bannetons. Of course, these bee-hive shaped bread-rising baskets are familiar in many parts of France and Germany, and we've been selling them at Williams-Sonoma for years. It's too bad that we can't sell brick ovens—baking tiles are the best we can do! (Leave them in the oven; they really do help promote even, steady baking.)**
>
> **Anyway, that's how the cover of this catalog got started—in Dusseldorf! Bon appetit.**

© COPYRIGHT 1991 DARTNELL CORPORATION

**Figure 9–3
Catalog Letters**

An outstanding example of the way letter messages can build interest for catalogs are the "Culinary Notes from Chuck Williams" which appear regularly on the inside front cover of Williams-Sonoma catalogs. Most often, they tie-in with specific product offerings. Copyright © Williams-Sonoma. Used with permission.

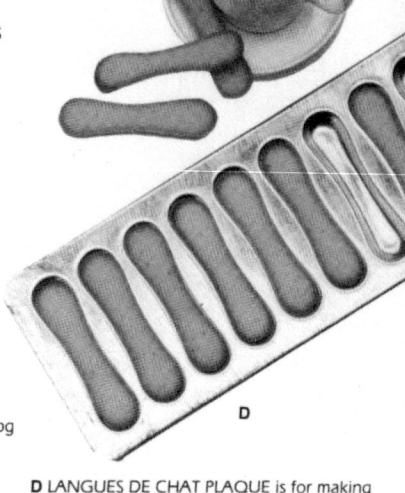

Photos and selling copy for the bannetons and baking tiles were positioned just below this inside front cover letter.

A more typical inside front cover letter is this one from a Lillian Vernon sale catalog:

Dear Friends,

A lot of people never see savings like the ones I've put inside. That's because I don't offer them to just anyone.

You are holding my Private Holiday Sale—only our customers receive it. And when you see the price reductions, you'll have something else to celebrate this holiday season.

The Private Holiday Sale means special Private Holiday Sale prices—up to 75% off! Many items are offered at lower prices than ever. Others are on sale for the very first time—and maybe the last. So take a minute right now to browse through this sale. Pass it along to family and friends too.

It's easy to order. Just use the enclosed form. Or take advantage of our expanded charge-by-phone service: call 914-576-6300 anytime between 9AM and midnight seven days a week, and use any major credit card.

So don't miss out on one of the year's biggest savings celebrations. It's our way of saying "thank you" for shopping with us this year. We'll do all we can to ensure your satisfaction in the coming year, which we hope is a happy and healthy one for you and your family.

Figure 9–4
Typical Catalog Letter

This letter in a Lillian Vernon catalog is typical of the way a person-to-person message can introduce a catalog to readers. Copyright © Lillian Vernon. Used with permission.

Unfortunately, many of these inside front cover letters are simply a bit of corporate bragging, with a "look how great we are" tone. Instead of being oriented to what's important to the reader, they are simply institutional messages which most likely go unread.

Hershell Gordon Lewis offers this rule:

> If, in your letter, the word "we" appears before the word "you" appears, chances are just about 100 percent that your intra-catalog letter has less apppeal to the recipient than it could have and should have.

He further suggests that a letter can justify its space if it transmits any *two* of these messages:

1. Here's a hard, specific benefit of doing business with us.
2. Here's either a deal or the names of items you can't get anywhere else.
3. Here's a genuine reason to feel confidence in us.
4. Here's why we are different from everyone else.
5. Here's our unique selling position.

Inside Back Cover

Both the inside back cover itself and the page facing the inside back cover also generate increased response. I'm not sure just why this happens (perhaps it is because a substantial number of catalog buyers start reading from back to front), but after analyzing thousands of catalogs over the years, I have found that the inside back cover pages most frequently show up as the fifth most important hot spot.

Center Spread

Next in order as a sales-increasing hot spot is the center spread of catalogs which are saddle-stitched (with the staples protruding into the center of the catalog). The staples serve as a "divider." No matter how quickly you may flip through the pages of a catalog, you're almost sure to "hit" the center spread. Thus each time the catalog is read, the items on the center spread get special attention.

Pages Facing the Order Form

The order form in a catalog is like the cash register in a store. That's where you most often find impulse purchase items—flashlight batteries, chewing gum, cigarettes, etc. Most buyers don't go into the store just to buy these items, but decide to add them to other purchases when they see them at the checkout counter.

This same type of impulse buying can be important in a catalog. While anything on pages adjacent to the order form gets hot spot treatment, these pages are particularly effective when they include items that can be added as last-minute thoughts when the order form is being filled out.

In most catalogs, the order form is bound into one of two already established hot spots—the center spread or inside the back cover. While it helps if you can position the order form in a non-hot spot position, this is often impractical. But at least you can recognize the importance of placing impulse items adjacent to the order form. (For more information about order forms, see Chapter 10.)

Other Inserts

Anything bound into a catalog tends to "index" the catalog at that point. As readers go through a catalog, they automatically hit pages which face the insert. And this produces added attention for those pages.

Spring Hill Nurseries, for example, inserts a reply envelope between printed signatures of its catalogs. [See Figure 9–5.] It is inserted between the staples so that half of the envelope appears in the front half of the catalog, the other half of the envelope in the back half of the catalog. No matter how you flip through the catalog's pages, you automatically hit these two hot spots—and items appearing on the pages facing the envelope regularly produce increased sales.

Figure 9–5
Creating Additional Hot Spots

Additional hot spots can be created in a catalog through the use of inserts, such as a reply envelope. No matter how quickly someone may thumb through the catalog, they automatically find themselves giving special attention to the spreads where the envelope is positioned. Copyright © Foster & Gallagher. Used with permission.

Other catalogs have a binding stub on their order forms. Usually the order form (often with an attached envelope) appears somewhere between printed signatures in the back half of the catalog, while the stub, used for special copy, creates a hot spot in the front half of the catalog.

Other frequently used bind-ins include discount coupons, friend-get-a-friend catalog request cards, new product listings, a quickly found table of contents, etc.

Additional Hot Spots

If you have a catalog of fewer than 100 pages, these eight primary hot spots are about all you can use. But with larger catalogs, you can create additional hot spots in a number of ways.

One of the most popular methods is "stopper pages." Browsing through a catalog is not unlike driving down an express highway. You get "highway hypnosis." You just keep driving along without really seeing the surrounding country. But when you come to a stop sign, all of a sudden you notice your surroundings.

In larger catalogs it's easy to get "catalog hypnosis." You thumb through the pages, and after the first few pages, you find yourself just turning the pages without really stopping to see what's there. But when you come to one of the "stopper pages," your attention is arrested. You not only pay special attention to that page, but to the

**Figure 9–6
Stopper Pages**

One way to fight "catalog hypnosis" is to use stopper pages. Quelle, Europe's leading general catalog, has 1,000 or more pages, and regularly inserts stopper pages every 30 pages or so. Quelle even uses the word "stop" on each one. Copyright © Quelle. Used with permission.

page facing it, and likely to the next few pages as well, as you resume your trip through the catalog.

Another way of adding hot spots to a larger catalog is to use divider pages—something special to indicate when you change from one merchandise category to another. These become somewhat like additional covers. The items featured on these pages frequently produce added sales because you have said, in effect, this merchandise is of special importance.

One warning, however. Remember the folk tale of the little boy who cried, "Wolf!" so often, nobody paid any attention when the wolf really showed up. If you use too many stopper or divider pages, they lose their attention-demanding value.

Catalog Wraps

Many catalogs use outside wraps both as a way of creating a new "cover" for additional mailings of the same catalog, and as a way to add special messages for special audiences.

Special wraps may be used for answering catalog requests; to explain why another copy of the same catalog is being sent; to highlight sale events or special prices; to direct attention to sections of a catalog of special interest to each audience; to support local retail outlets; and, most commonly, as a "kicker."

The kicker wrap is used to reactivate customers who are about to be dropped from the catalog mailing list. The word "kicker" comes from the thought expressed by such wraps—"we're going to kick you off our list unless you buy something." Often, by using this technique, you can recapture the latent buyers on your file—especially if some special offer is made to get them to buy again.

Personalized Wraps

Catalog wraps are most effective when they are personalized for each recipient. While nobody is fooled into thinking a personalized catalog has been created especially for him or her, there's a built-in mail order magic which results from personalization. What personalization does is say to the recipient, "You were *specially selected* to receive this catalog."

And it works! When personalization is done effectively, it almost always produces a substantial boost in response for a catalog. When catalogs sent to customers carry personalized wraps, they frequently boost response as much as 30 to 35 percent. While personalization to prospects generally produces less of a lift in response, I've seen many cases where the increase is in excess of 25 percent.

Just adding the customer's name in a number of places on the wrap

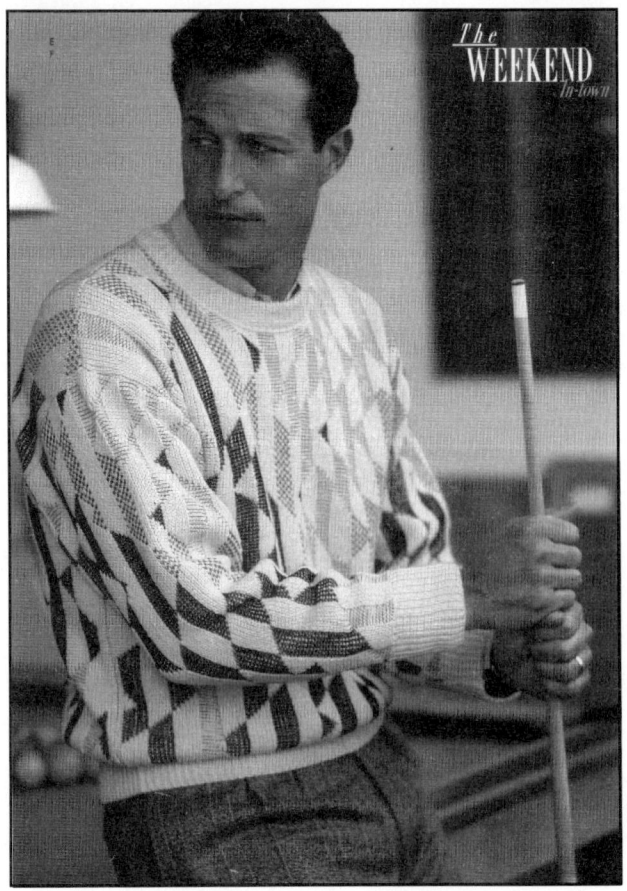

Figure 9–7 (opposite)
Divider Pages

Spiegel uses divider pages to introduce each type of merchandise in its big catalogs. Copyright © Spiegel. Used with permission.

is seldom enough to produce a major increase in response, although even that small amount of personalization often more than pays for itself. But creating a personalized letter or another narrative with multiple personalizations is most effective.

Here are three examples of wraps I've created over the years which have produced a substantial increase in response.

Quill Corporation Although personalized wraps are more common on consumer catalogs, the wrap shown in Figure 9–8 demonstrated that personalization can also be extremely effective in business-to-business prospecting. (While, as the illustration shows, boldface type was used in a number of areas on the wrap; in the copy below we have used an italic and an underscore to clearly identify areas of personalization.)

> **WE WANT TO GIVE YOU A FREE GIFT JUST FOR GIVING US A CHANCE TO PROVE HOW MUCH WE CAN SAVE FOR**
>
> ### *SIMONETTI & SULL*
>
> Last year, *18,202* money-wise organizations in *New Jersey* enjoyed big savings on their office supplies and equipment. And they received super-fast service as well!
>
> In the *Newark area* alone, there are *5,508* buyers who take advantage of the savings and superior service we offer here at Quill Corporation of Lincolnshire, IL.
>
> "But that's *800* miles away," you may be saying.
>
> We're well aware of your concern. That's why we're making a special offer to encourage you to discover how Quill's unique service wipes out the problems distance might seem to create.
>
> Just give us a try. Select any of the money-saving offers on office supplies from this Quill Sale Book. We'll process your order within 8 to 32 hours and rush every item direct to your door. And when your shipment arrives in *Bayonne,* you'll find a valuable 4-piece Portfolio Set included absolutely FREE as our way of saying thanks for giving us a try. (Just follow the directions in the bonus coupon above.)
>
> SEND NO MONEY! With a good credit reference (see details on page 16), we'll bill you when your order is shipped and you'll have 30 days to pay. SATISFACTION GUARANTEED!

This personalized memo from Jack Miller, president of Quill, appeared on the back cover of the wrap:

> I would cordially like to invite *SIMONETTI & SULL* to become a Preferred Customer.
>
> Though we are *800* miles away from *Bayonne,* we are as near as your phone or mailbox.

We're proud of the fact that more than 18,202 other organizations throughout *New Jersey* turn to Quill to take advantage of the money-saving offers we provide on quality office supplies and equipment. Yes, our low prices are important, but so is our super-fast service.

Just because we aren't "just down the street" doesn't mean you have to wait to get the supplies you need. We have become America's foremost office supplier not only because of our low prices on quality merchandise, but also because of our ability to process and ship orders in 8 to 32 hours.

I'm so convinced that once you've seen Quill in action you'll become a regular customer that I want to give you a valuable FREE gift just for giving us a chance to prove we mean what we say.

Give us a try. If we don't meet your needs in every way, just send back what you ordered. We'll cancel your bill and you can keep your 4-piece Portfolio Set as our way of saying thanks.

Alongside this back cover memo was a picture and description of the four-piece portfolio set bonus and the famous Quill Customers' Bill of Rights. The inside front cover of the wrap highlighted "12 Special Benefits For You Exclusively From Quill." On the inside back cover were testimonials from customers in all parts of the United

Figure 9–8
Personalized Catalog Wrap

Quill Corporation used this personalized wrap around a copy of its 32-page monthly sale catalog to drive home its sales points to prospective customers. Copyright © Quill Corporation. Used with permission.

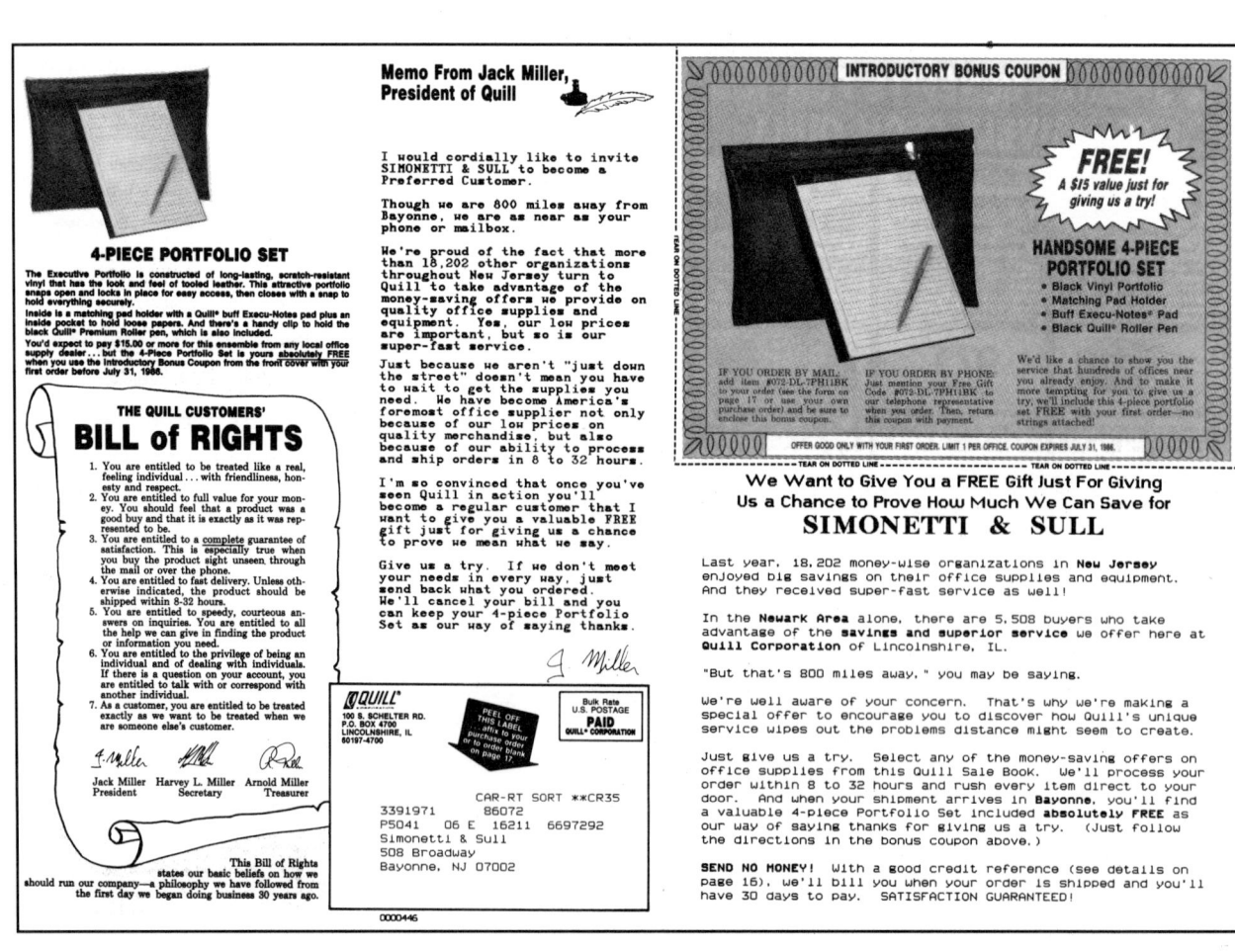

States, plus quotes praising Quill that had been published in five nationally recognized publications.

U.S. General Supply Corp. A prospecting wrap aimed at consumer mail order markets was used by U.S. General Supply. (See Figure 9–9.) Here, heavy emphasis was placed on the recipient's name. Instead of the U.S. General Supply catalog, it became "the [name of customer] Bargain Book."

> **229 top quality tools and hardware supplies at prices far below what you'll find in stores anywhere throughout [town].**
>
> **Save as much as 60% on 97 surplus specials to help stretch the [name of recipient] budget! Free when you order! A heavy duty locking knife for the [name of recipient] tool box.**
>
> **Plus a second free gift for you! A handy trouble light for the [name of recipient] car.**
>
> **For fastest delivery to [city], call us TOLL-FREE at 1-800-645-7077, 24 hours every day.**

The back cover of the wrap featured illustrations of the two premiums with this personalized message:

> **TWO VALUABLE FREE**
> **GIFTS FOR**
> **[NAME OF RECIPIENT]**
>
> **Get two bonus gifts when you order from this [name of recipient] bargain book. You'd pay $15 or more to buy them in any store in the [town] area . . . but they're yours absolutely free with any order!**
>
> **You'll want to keep the deluxe knife handy in the [name of recipient] tool box. Folds to just 4" but opens and locks so its surgical steel blade is ready to take on any cutting task.**
>
> **And when you need an extra light, you'll be glad you have the magnetic light for the [name of recipient] car. Extend the 12' cord and its beam lights up any trouble spot.**

Inside were two personalized flaps. Personalization was done before folding and trimming, and the flaps became what are known as "flag wavers." The imprinted side of the front-of-the-catalog flap repeated the free knife offer with the heading: "A very special free gift reserved for [name of recipient]." Printed copy described the knife, and then there was an added personalized postscript: "You'd pay up to $10 to buy this knife at any store in the [town] area . . . but it's yours absolutely FREE when you order!" The unpersonalized reverse side of this flap pictured and described the magnetic light premium.

Figure 9–9
Extra Personalization Opportunities

U.S. General Supply used a personalized catalog wrap to yield two "flag waver" flaps when catalogs were trimmed. Personalized messages appeared inside both covers. Copyright © U.S. General Supply. Used with permission.

Front of wrap

Back of wrap

Front and back of "flag waver" flap inside front cover

HOT SPOTS, COVERS AND WRAPS / 9

U.S. GENERAL SUPPLY CORP.
100 COMMERCIAL STREET • PLAINVIEW, N.Y. 11803

<u>We don't talk about big savings
just to get your attention . . .</u>

Take a look at the prices inside this Book of Bargains.
You'll quickly discover we aren't just making a lot of
noise about nothing. You really can obtain big savings
when you order now from U. S. General.

We'll be surprised if you can find bargains at any store
in your area which even come close to our special offers.
Consider, for example:

* Deluxe 20-piece <u>X-Acto Knife & Blade Set just $10.99!</u>
  That's $6.50 less than the manufacturer's list price.

* <u>Skil's new Cordless Screwdriver for just 19.80!</u> Others
  charge $27.99 for this absolute must for any workshop
  or toolbox.

* You'll <u>save $43.20</u> on Makita's Versatile 3/8" Variable-
  speed Reversing Drill. Makita's price is $98.00.
  Our's is just $54.80!

* Every catalog seems to be featuring the ever-so-useful
  <u>Mag-Lite Mini-Flashlight</u>. But only U. S. General offers
  it to you at a money-saving price of <u>just $10.80!</u>

* And don't overlook the great buy on our <u>Electronic Stud
  Sensor</u>. Our low price is just $15.95. But that's not
  all. Order now and the manufacturer will give you a
  $2.00 rebate so your actual cost will be <u>just $13.95!</u>

Just those five items alone mean savings of over $60.00
when you order from this U. S. General bargain book.
But that's only a start. There are dozens of other
money-saving values you won't find anywhere else.

And you don't just pay less at U. S. General. <u>You get free
gifts, too!</u> Just order anything from this bargain book and
when your package arrives, it will include two very special
bonuses -- a Deluxe Locking Knife for your tool kit and a
versatile Magnetic Light for your car <u>both absolutely FREE!</u>

And, to top things off, we're even going to give the first
300 customers who mail in an order from this special Book
of Bargains a <u>50% cash rebate!</u>

Get out your pen or pencil right now -- or pick up your
phone and give us a toll-free call at 1-800-645-7077.
With savings like these, you can't lose. You order
without risk! <u>Everything is fully guaranteed.</u>

Steve Harrow
Steve Harrow
Vice President

Inside front of wrap

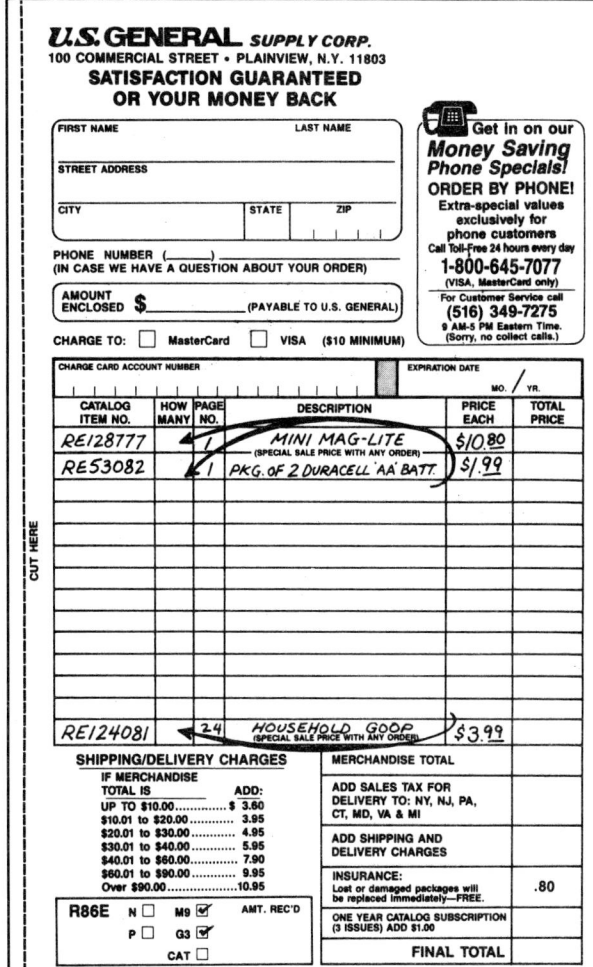

Inside back of wrap

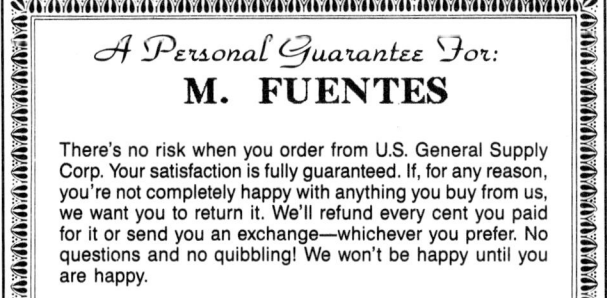

Front and back of "flag waver" flap inside back cover

© COPYRIGHT 1991 DARTNELL CORPORATION

Another flag-waver flap, featuring a personalized guarantee, was positioned atop the order form, which was printed on the inside of the back cover of the wrap. Experience indicates that a personalized guarantee is one of the most effective forms of personalization catalogers can use.

On the back of this flap was a special 50 percent rebate offer to be given to those sending in the first 300 orders from the enclosed catalog.

The inside front cover of the wrap had a letter which introduced U.S. General to the prospect. While it was not personalized, it demonstrates an important technique which is all too often missing from catalogs.

Like all other forms of direct mail, a letter is one of the most effective ways to communicate with a mail order audience. Many catalogs have a simulated letter on a portion of the inside front cover of the catalog itself, but such presentations do not have the impact of a letter in a real letter format. Most often these page 2 letters, accompanied by a picture of the company president, have a "look at how great we are" tone. (I call them the "president's ego trip.") While some are extremely well done and may help to give a catalog a personal touch, they don't substitute for a real letter.

The U.S. General letter, on the other hand, had the basic ingredients of a person-to-person letter. (See Figure 9–9.)

Breck's. Breck's, which is the leading mail order marketer of Dutch bulbs in the United States, utilizes personalized wraps for both prospects and customers. For many years wraps were attached outside the covers of catalogs, but testing revealed that covers are so important to a catalog, the cover impact is lost when it is covered up by a wrap. So wraps were moved *inside* the cover, appearing between the inside front cover and page 3 and between the inside back cover and the last body page. The back page of the wrap contains the order form on one side and a personalized message on the reverse. The back cover carries a die-cut window with the mailing address, which is printed below the personalized message, showing through the window. This permits capturing the address and customer or prospect mailing code when the order form is returned.

Figure 9–10 shows a typical Breck's wrap. At the time these wraps are written, a special mailing address is created to make sure there will be space to accommodate the maximum length in each portion of the address field when the variables of personalization come into play:

Mrs. A. R. Extralongsurname
1234 Downtown Street
South San Francisco,
Yellow Medicine County,
South Carolina 00000

Using this maximum length address, the basic personalized message for active customers reads:

**WE APPRECIATE ALL THE ORDERS
YOU'VE SENT US SINCE [YEAR OF FIRST ORDER],
MRS. A. R. EXTRALONGSURNAME**

**WE LOOK FORWARD TO HELPING
YOU ADD NEW BEAUTY TO YOUR
SOUTH SAN FRANCISCO HOME**

I hope it's as pleasant in South Carolina as it is here in Holland this spring and that you have been enjoying the full beauty of the Dutch bulbs you ordered from Breck's in *[year of most recent order]*.

This is a good time to look around your home in South San Francisco and decide what new varieties you would like to order for planting this fall in The Extralongsurname Garden.

There's a special reason to order now during Breck's 1989 Advance Sale. If you order promptly, we'll include five of our finest Angelique Tulips. They're a $7.33 catalog value, but will be yours absolutely FREE with any order of $25 or more.

No matter how many Tulips you already have blooming in your South San Francisco garden, I'm sure you'll find a number of spots where you'll enjoy these gorgeous pink Tulips.

As one of our Preferred Customers, you don't have to send a single penny to reserve bulbs from Breck's. We want you to inspect your bulbs when they arrive direct from Holland at the proper fall planting time for Yellow Medicine County before you pay a cent.

Your satisfaction is fully guaranteed!

The message on the back cover reads:

**SPECIAL PREFERRED CUSTOMER CREDIT
HAS ALREADY BEEN ESTABLISHED
FOR MRS. A. R. EXTRALONGSURNAME**

One of the nice things about being able to serve our Breck's Preferred Customers like you, Mrs. A. R. Extralongsurname, is that we can offer instant credit on your orders.

This means you can take advantage of the huge savings being offered during Breck's 1989 Advance Sale, yet you don't have to send a single penny when you order bulbs to plant in your South Carolina garden.

A line of credit of $200.00 *[the amount is automatically calculated by computer, based on the size of the customer's largest previous order]* has been established for you. And even if you wish to buy more, your Preferred Customer status means your order can be forwarded to Holland, even before our credit manager authorizes the higher sum.

You'll have full opportunity to inspect and approve every bulb after your shipment arrives direct from Holland at the appropriate fall planting time for Yellow Medicine County before you'll be asked to pay a cent.

Order without risk. Satisfaction guaranteed. If, for any reason, you're not fully pleased with your bulbs when they arrive in South San Francisco this fall, after you plant them in The Extralongsurname Garden, or once they grow and bloom, just write Breck's anytime before July 1, 1990. We'll send a full refund, replacement or exchange—whichever you prefer.

Even though you can obtain a wide variety of Holland's finest bulbs at

Figure 9–10
The Personalized Message

Breck's uses a special mailing address to accommodate the maximum length in the address field. Copyright © Foster & Gallagher. Used with permission.

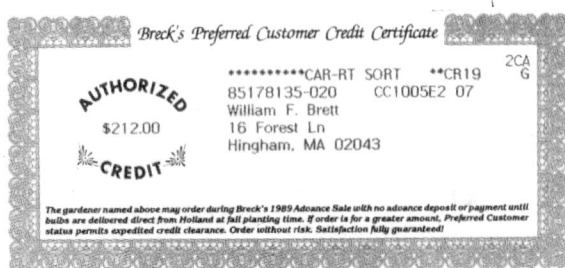

savings of as much as 50% during Breck's Advance Sale, you'll never find fresher, healthier bulbs.

And don't overlook our special bonus—five beautiful Angelique Tulips—a regular $7.33 catalog value—but yours absolutely FREE with any order of $25 or more. They are ideal for planting in <u>South San Francisco</u> and will be a welcome addition to The <u>Extralongsurname</u> Garden.

Appearing below this letter is a Preferred Customer Credit Certificate, again mentioning the amount of credit available, and containing the mailing address which will appear through the window in the back cover of the catalog.

There were several versions of this wrap, with messages changed to reflect the relationship between the customer and Breck's. There were special treatments for those who had ordered just once previously; inactive customers whose names were to be deleted from the mailing list after one more mailing; and prospects who had never ordered previously.

The "kicker" wrap, aimed at inactive customers, read:

**WE'D LIKE TO KEEP SENDING
BRECK'S DUTCH BULB BOOKS TO
<u>MRS. A. R. EXTRALONGSURNAME</u>**

**HERE'S HOW TO KEEP FREE COPIES COMING TO YOUR
<u>SOUTH SAN FRANCISCO HOME</u>**

This Breck's Dutch Bulb Book may be the last one we can send to the <u>Extralongsurname</u> home—unless you've already sent us your 1989 Advance Sale order—or send one soon.

We appreciate having had the opportunity to serve you since [<u>year of first order</u>], but our records show you haven't ordered since [<u>year of last order</u>]. Because our costs have increased greatly, we must cut the number of catalogs we send to America. Our only way to know who's still interested is to check who has placed orders recently.

If you've already taken advantage of Breck's 1989 Advance Sale savings by reserving prime quality Dutch bulbs to plant this fall in The <u>Extralongsurname</u> Garden, your name is already listed to receive future issues.

But if you haven't yet ordered, take a look outside and note the places around your <u>South San Francisco</u> home which will be more beautiful next spring with some of the Dutch flowers in Breck's Advance Sale Bulb Book.

Free Bonus: **You'll receive a special gift if your order totals $25 or more—five beautiful Angelique Tulips.**

For catalogs sent to prospects who had never previously purchased from Breck's, the wrap art remained the same; but completely revised personalized messages were prepared for both the front and the back of the wrap:

**BRECK'S WOULD LIKE TO SEND YOU
A GIFT DIRECT FROM HOLLAND,
MRS. A. R. EXTRALONGSURNAME**

**. . . FIVE BEAUTIFUL ANGELIQUE TULIPS
ABSOLUTELY FREE TO PLANT IN SOUTH SAN FRANCISCO**

Breck's would like to send you a valuable free gift to encourage you to find out for yourself the advantages of obtaining cream-of-the-crop bulbs direct from Holland for planting in The Extralongsurname Garden.

We've reserved a quantity of our finest Angelique Tulips and we'll send you five of these unique bulbs absolutely FREE with any order of $25. (See facing page for details.)

***SEND NO MONEY* . . . Your bulbs will be shipped from Holland at the appropriate fall planting time for Yellow Medicine County and you'll have full opportunity to inspect and approve every bulb before you'll be asked to send a single cent.**

***SAVE AS MUCH AS 50%* . . . By ordering now during Breck's 1989 Advance Sale, you can enjoy big savings on Holland's finest top quality bulbs for fall planting in The Extralongsurname Garden.**

***ORDER WITHOUT RISK* . . . If you're not completely satisfied with your Dutch bulbs when they arrive in South San Francisco, after planting or once they bloom in your South Carolina garden, just write before July 1, 1990. Breck's will send full refund, replacement or exchange—whichever you prefer.**

The opening of the message on the back of the wrap used for prospects was changed to:

Since 1818, Breck's has been supplying American gardeners with Dutch bulbs, and we would like to encourage you, Mrs. A. R. Extralongsurname, to join the thousands of Preferred Customers in South Carolina who take advantage of the savings we offer during our annual Advance Bulb Sales.

One of the advantages of being a Breck's Preferred Customer is that you don't have to send a single penny to reserve Holland's cream-of-the-crop bulbs for planting each year in your South San Francisco garden. We've already established a line of credit of $200.00 *[here the credit limit is established either by buying records of other subsidiaries of Foster & Gallagher, which produces the Breck's catalogs, or by a pre-established limit based on the prospect's ZIP Code]* **for you. And even if you wish to buy more, your Preferred Customer status means your order can be quickly forwarded to Holland, even before our credit manager authorizes the higher sum.**

The importance of offering a specific credit limit was discovered many years ago by Lou Rudin of Spiegel's. His research showed that just telling customers and prospects that credit is available often leads them to question whether the amount of their order will qualify or not—and they hesitate to send in an order for fear it will be rejected because it exceeds the unknown credit limit. Telling them how much credit they have not only makes the wrap more personal, but overcomes their fears about exceeding the credit limit.

While most catalog recipients wouldn't want their credit limit to be exhibited for all to see, by placing this information *inside* the catalog, its privacy is protected.

Is Personalization Right for You?
I've found many catalogers looking down their noses at the whole idea of using personalization like that shown in the preceding examples. "It's just too phoney and unsophisticated," they say. But invariably I've found these skeptics have never tested personalized wraps for their own catalogs. My own experience involves wraps for all types of catalogs—business-to-business, and consumer catalogs ranging from low-ticket bargain catalogs to upscale catalogs drawing orders of several hundred dollars. While the design of the wrap will change greatly depending on the audience, the types of personalization shown in the three examples just presented have worked well for all types of audiences.

The key essential for effective personalization is computerized database information which can quickly be accessed. With a good database, you can build personalization around such items as these:

- Thank you for first purchase
- First anniversary as a customer
- Subsequent anniversaries
- Number of years as a customer
- Suggest repurchasing products
- Reference to other products purchased
- Number of purchases
- Date of first or last order
- Amount of last order
- Reference to a previous catalog
- Geographical references
- Distances involved
- Nearest airport
- Location of nearest store
- Date of telephone contact
- Name of telephone operator

When directing a personalized message to a customer, you're on pretty safe ground if you make mention of any information a customer has "given" to you. In fact, customers often feel flattered that you "see" them as individuals. But when preparing personalized messages for prospects, you have to be much more concerned with what they may feel is an invasion of their privacy. Even though you can obtain lists which may contain highly personal information such as age, income status, number and names of family members, etc., a prospect who has had no direct relationship with you in the past may feel you have no "right" to know such information and show that displeasure by refusing to even consider your catalog.

There are, however, many nonprivate types of personalization which are readily available from outside sources.

- City, county, area, and state, which can be determined from ZIP Codes.
- Mention of weather factors, such as rainfall, average temperatures, drought conditions, etc., which can be obtained on a regular basis from the weather bureau.
- Type of automobile owned—available from a number of mailing list compilers or directly from state license bureaus.
- You can also make reference to airplanes or boats owned—information available from registration bureaus.
- Mention of perceived hobbies or special interests based on list sources such as subscriber lists of specialty magazines or membership in organizations.

There are literally hundreds of external databases with information that can be adapted for personalized mailings. But whatever you use, the main objective will be to convince the catalog recipient that he or she has been *specially selected* to receive your catalog, rather than just being one of millions who may have gotten it by chance.

Checklists for Selecting Merchandise for Cover Presentation

Two leading catalog consultants offer tips on choosing merchandise for presentation on front and back covers of catalogs:

JoVon Tucker on front and back covers:

1. **Topicality.** Is it new? Has it been seen in other catalogs?

2. **Lifestyle.** Does it fill a need? Will it enhance buyers' lifestyles?

3. **Design.** Is it a great design? Does it have a better line or better look than previous vertical products?

4. **Price points.** Is it fairly priced? Does its price fall within an average range of your usual merchandise offering? If it is too high or too low in pricing, discard it as a cover subject, because it will distort the positioning of your entire catalog.

5. **Representation and reproduction.** Will it photograph well? Does it represent the kind of products that you are known for?

Lawson Traphagen Hill on back covers:

1. Merchandise should be representative of the rest of the catalog.

2. If the catalog is for both men and women, then there should be products for both.

3. The products should get customers into the catalog.

4. If the catalog is going to rented lists, the products on the back cover should be proven best sellers.

5. If the catalog is going to buyers, the products should be new, as well as items the cataloger thinks will become the best sellers.

6. The products should be interesting.

One other thought on the back cover: It should probably contain a small amount of institutional selling, something that will express the concept of the business.

Making It Easy to Order

10

One of the mysteries of the catalog world is why so little attention is devoted to one of the most important parts of any catalog—the order form.

An order form, of course, is essential to a mail order catalog—even in these days when in excess of 50 percent of all orders arrive by telephone. For telephone orders, an order form serves as a worksheet, giving buyers a handy place to list the items they want and to record details such as item number, quantity, and price, which are important when placing orders via phone.

Yet in spite of its importance, the order form is often considered simply a "necessary evil." My experience, however, clearly indicates that spending extra time on order form design and copy pays off handsomely. I've seen cases where simple changes in order form design have not only produced increased response, but have boosted the size of the average order as much as 20 percent.

Don't Reinvent the Wheel

One of the biggest order form mistakes a cataloger can make is to try to be "different." It's important to remember that someone else has already trained your customers on how to fill out order forms.

Study your audience. Find out the catalogs from which they are already ordering. Study the order forms from those catalogs. And then use those order forms as models to follow in creating your order form.

Probably more people have filled out Sears, J.C. Penney, and Spiegel order forms than any others. So start your order form review by taking a long, hard look at what these three big mail order companies are doing (See illustrations A, B, and C in the Order Form Portfolio on pages 231–235.)

If you're in the business-to-business mail order catalog field, your starting point might well be Quill's catalog. Many of your customers-to-be are probably found on Quill's customer list, so they are well acquainted with Quill's order form [Portfolio Illustration D].

Make Your Order Form Look Inviting

Nothing will turn off a mail order customer faster than an order form that looks as if you have to be an engineer or an accountant to fill it out.

All too often, those who design catalog order forms start with what is best for internal order fulfillment, rather than with what would make ordering easy for the customer. I've often heard catalogers comment, "If the customer makes mistakes in filling out the order form, we can usually decipher what they want." But there's one thing nobody can tell you, and that is how many *didn't* send in orders because they found the order form too confusing.

All order forms should *start with the customer*. Make it as easy as possible for the customer to fill out the order form, and then make *absolutely necessary* revisions to avoid major headaches for order entry personnel. My theory is that it is less expensive to hire more order entry personnel than to attract more customers.

Of all the catalog order forms I've seen, my favorite for simplicity is the one that has been used for many years by Miles Kimball [Portfolio Illustration E]. It's clean, neat, and inviting. Nothing to suggest that there will be any difficulty in telling Miles Kimball exactly what you want.

On the other hand, take a look at the two-page order form shown opposite in Figure 10–1. It has nearly 20 separate areas to be completed (or at least reviewed) before the order can be completed. Then compare it with the easy-to-use order form of Hammacher Schlemmer [Portfolio Illustration F]. If you had a choice of ordering from the catalogs containing these order forms, which would you choose?

There is a tendency of many catalog marketers to try and combine "how to order" instructions with the order form itself. This is most often a mistake. Keep order forms as uncluttered as possible.

If you need to include "how to order" information, you can place it adjacent to, or on the back of, the order form. The back of the

Figure 10–1
Making It Easy to Order

A complicated order form can scare away even customers who are ready to order. A catalog order form should look easy to use. Compare this complicated ordering device with those shown in the Order Form Portfolio—particularly the one from a Miles Kimball catalog.

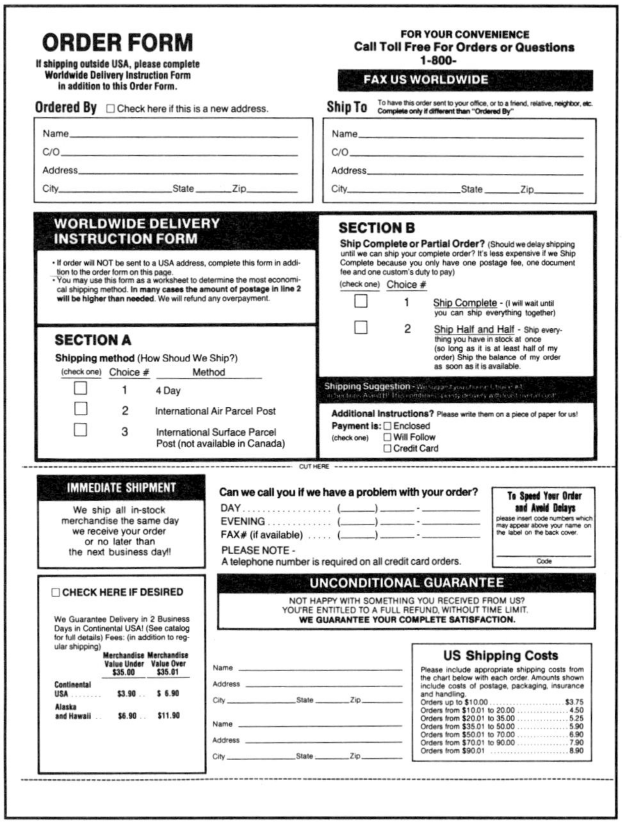

ORDER FORM
If shipping outside USA, please complete Worldwide Delivery Instruction Form in addition to this Order Form.

FOR YOUR CONVENIENCE
Call Toll Free For Orders or Questions
1-800-
FAX US WORLDWIDE

Ordered By ☐ Check here if this is a new address.
Name
C/O
Address
City State Zip

Ship To — To have this order sent to your office, or to a friend, relative, neighbor, etc. Complete only if different than "Ordered By"
Name
C/O
Address
City State Zip

WORLDWIDE DELIVERY INSTRUCTION FORM
• If order will NOT be sent to a USA address, complete this form in addition to the order form on this page.
• You may use this form as a worksheet to determine the most economical shipping method. In many cases the amount of postage in line 2 will be higher than needed. We will refund any overpayment.

SECTION A
Shipping method (How Shoud We Ship?)
(check one) Choice # Method
☐ 1 4 Day
☐ 2 International Air Parcel Post
☐ 3 International Surface Parcel Post (not available in Canada)

SECTION B
Ship Complete or Partial Order? (Should we delay shipping until we can ship your complete order? It's less expensive if we Ship Complete because you only have one postage fee, one document fee and one custom's duty to pay)
(check one) Choice #
☐ 1 Ship Complete - (I will wait until you can ship everything together)
☐ 2 Ship Half and Half - Ship everything you have in stock at once (so long as it is at least half of my order) Ship the balance of my order as soon as it is available.

Shipping Suggestion -

Additional Instructions? Please write them on a piece of paper for us!
Payment is: ☐ Enclosed ☐ Will Follow ☐ Credit Card
(check one)

CUT HERE

IMMEDIATE SHIPMENT
We ship all in-stock merchandise the same day we receive your order or no later than the next business day!!

Can we call you if we have a problem with your order?
DAY ( ) -
EVENING ( ) -
FAX# (if available) ( ) -
PLEASE NOTE - A telephone number is required on all credit card orders.

To Speed Your Order and Avoid Delays
please insert code numbers which may appear above your name on the label on the back cover.
Code

☐ CHECK HERE IF DESIRED
We Guarantee Delivery in 2 Business Days in Continental USA! (See catalog for full details) Fees: (in addition to regular shipping)

	Merchandise Value Under $35.00	Merchandise Value Over $35.01
Continental USA	$3.90	$ 6.90
Alaska and Hawaii	$6.90	$11.90

UNCONDITIONAL GUARANTEE
NOT HAPPY WITH SOMETHING YOU RECEIVED FROM US? YOU'RE ENTITLED TO A FULL REFUND, WITHOUT TIME LIMIT.
WE GUARANTEE YOUR COMPLETE SATISFACTION.

Name
Address
City State Zip
Name
Address
City State Zip

US Shipping Costs
Please include appropriate shipping costs from the chart below with each order. Amounts shown include costs of postage, packaging, insurance and handling.

Orders up to $10.00	$3.75
Orders from $10.01 to 20.00	4.50
Orders from $20.01 to 35.00	5.25
Orders from $35.01 to 50.00	5.90
Orders from $50.01 to 70.00	6.90
Orders from $70.01 to 90.00	7.90
Orders from $90.01	8.90

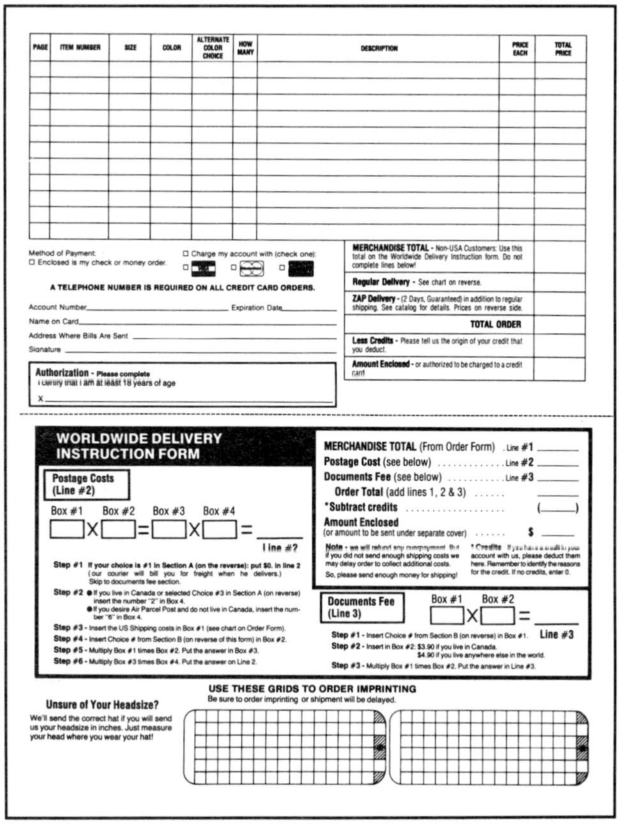

PAGE	ITEM NUMBER	SIZE	COLOR	ALTERNATE COLOR CHOICE	HOW MANY	DESCRIPTION	PRICE EACH	TOTAL PRICE

Method of Payment:
☐ Enclosed is my check or money order.
☐ Charge my account with (check one):
A TELEPHONE NUMBER IS REQUIRED ON ALL CREDIT CARD ORDERS.
Account Number Expiration Date
Name on Card
Address Where Bills Are Sent
Signature

Authorization - Please complete
I certify that I am at least 18 years of age
X

MERCHANDISE TOTAL - Non-USA Customers: Use this total on the Worldwide Delivery Instruction form. Do not complete lines below!
Regular Delivery - See chart on reverse.
ZAP Delivery - (2 Days, Guaranteed) in addition to regular shipping. See catalog for details. Prices on reverse side.
TOTAL ORDER
Less Credits - Please tell us the origin of your credit that you deduct.
Amount Enclosed - or authorized to be charged to a credit card

WORLDWIDE DELIVERY INSTRUCTION FORM
Postage Costs (Line #2)
Box #1 Box #2 Box #3 Box #4
☐ X ☐ = ☐ X ☐ = Line #2
Step #1 If your choice is #1 in Section A (on the reverse): put $0. in line 2 (our courier will bill you for freight when he delivers.) Skip to documents fee section.
Step #2 ● If you live in Canada or selected Choice #3 in Section A (on reverse) insert the number "2" in Box 4.
● If you desire Air Parcel Post and do not live in Canada, insert the number "6" in Box 4.
Step #3 - Insert the US Shipping costs in Box #1 (see chart on Order Form).
Step #4 - Insert Choice # from Section B (on reverse of this form) in Box #2.
Step #5 - Multiply Box #1 times Box #2. Put the answer in Box #3.
Step #6 - Multiply Box #3 times Box #4. Put the answer on Line 2.

MERCHANDISE TOTAL (From Order Form) Line #1
Postage Cost (see below) Line #2
Documents Fee (see below) Line #3
Order Total (add lines 1, 2 & 3)
*Subtract credits ( )
Amount Enclosed (or amount to be sent under separate cover) $
Note - we will refund any overpayment. But if you did not send enough shipping costs we may delay order to collect additional costs. So, please send enough money for shipping!
* Credits - If you have a credit in your account with us, please deduct them here. Remember to identify the reasons for the credit. If no credits, enter 0.

Documents Fee (Line 3)
Box #1 Box #2
☐ X ☐ = Line #3
Step #1 - Insert Choice # from Section B (on reverse) in Box #1.
Step #2 - Insert in Box #2: $3.90 if you live in Canada. $4.90 if you live anywhere else in the world.
Step #3 - Multiply Box #1 times Box #2. Put the answer in Line #3.

Unsure of Your Headsize?
We'll send the correct hat if you will send us your headsize in inches. Just measure your head where you wear your hat!

USE THESE GRIDS TO ORDER IMPRINTING
Be sure to order imprinting or shipment will be delayed.

Hammacher Schlemmer order form [Portfolio Illustration F], for example, carried detailed information in an "Ordering Is Easy" section.

Other examples of how catalogers present "how to order" information separate from the order form are shown in the Order Form Portfolio.

If you feel your customers will need help in understanding how to fill out your order form, you can use the technique illustrated in the Talbots order form [Portfolio Illustration G]. Here, a mythical order form entry is preprinted as a sample to show the customer the information required for each item selected. [I would suggest one change, however. In Talbots' example, they showed "1" for quantity, even though the price extensions were $00.00. My choice would have been to enter "0" for quantity so the customer doesn't become confused, possibly thinking she will receive the listed item as a free gift. Another way of handling this type of illustration is to print it atop a distinctive background screen and have it carry a label such as: "Here's How to Fill out the Order Form—for Illustration Purposes Only."]

Other ways to illustrate how to fill out an order form are shown in the Breck's [Portfolio Illustration H] and Spring Hill [Portfolio Illustration I] order forms. In these examples, a free bonus entry is preprinted.

Ask for Information "as Given"

It is important to coordinate catalog copy with the design and content of the order form. Order forms should *always* be prepared before catalog copy is written. Copywriters should have an order form staring them in the face as they write copy so they will be sure to provide all information a customer will need to fill out the order form . . . and be sure that the information will fit within the space available.

One area which often presents difficulty is the information to request in the typical order form space labeled "Description." There are many times when the full name of an item is just too long for order form purposes. In such cases, it is best to include an abbreviated title in the catalog copy.

The ideal handling of "price line" information for each item in the catalog is to add it at the end of any other copy and follow the exact sequence the order form calls for (Item No., Quantity, Description, Price, etc.).

Another problem area is where there are both model numbers and product identification numbers. You know which is which. But don't assume your customer will necessarily select the right one when filling out the order blank. If possible, do not use model numbers in catalog copy unless they are the same as the item numbers. If model numbers are absolutely necessary for the product description, try to keep them well separated from the item number which the customer will use when ordering.

Avoid Confusion

One of the big problem areas on catalog order forms is handling of "quantity." While the first step may be to use the heading "How Many" rather than "Quantity," this may not be enough in some catalogs.

For example, pillowcases most often come in sets of two. If you simply ask for "quantity," how does the customer know whether to write in "1" for one set of two or "2" because she wants two pillowcases?

Several examples in the Order Form Portfolio illustrate how various catalogers have solved this problem:

Portfolio Illustration D (Quill)
Two separate columns: "HOW MANY?" and "UNIT, Ea., Dz., etc."

Portfolio Illustration H (Breck's)
Column reading "No. of Bulbs," with an explanation above reading "Enter Number of Bulbs." (Experience showed it was important to add the explanation since many of the catalog offers involve collections or mixtures with varying numbers of bulbs.)

Portfolio Illustration I (Spring Hill)
Column headed "How Many," with color-coordinated box above reading "NOTE: When ordering Collections, enter in the 'How Many' column the number of Collections, not the number of items in the Collection."

Portfolio Illustration J (Williams-Sonoma)
Column headed "QTY. 1 Set = 1 Qty."

Portfolio Illustration K (The Chef's Catalog)
Column headed "HOW MANY, Ea., or Set."

Portfolio Illustration L (Fuller Brush)
Column headed "Qty. (Sets count as 1)."

Portfolio Illustration M (Fidelity Products)
Two separate columns: "HOW MANY?" and "UNIT, Ea., Dz., etc."

Don't Expect Your Customer to Be an Accountant

Few customers feel comfortable with mathematics. So don't ask them to do any unnecessary calculating.

Take another look at the Sears order form [Portfolio Illustration A]. At the bottom of the area for listing items ordered is a section for "totals." But note the line above that area: "Fill in spaces below on CASH ORDERS only." Sears, of course, uses computers to calculate all credit orders (and the majority of Sears orders are credit orders). So why ask customers to do the addition unless they want to do it for their own benefit?

J.C. Penney [Portfolio Illustration B] has two separate "totals" areas—one for "Credit Order," which calls for no addition, and another for "Cash Order," calling for calculations.

Keep Shipping and Handling Uncomplicated

One of the order form areas which often gets confusing is shipping and handling charges. The easiest way for the customer, of course, is if you include shipping and handling charges in the basic price of each item of merchandise. While some, such as L.L. Bean [Portfolio Illustration N] and Hammacher Schlemmer [Portfolio Illustration F], still offer "free" shipping and handling, this practice has nearly disappeared.

While "free shipping and handling" can be a marketing plus if heavily promoted, studies of catalog customer behavior suggest it may work to a catalog marketer's disadvantage. Catalog readers generally look at the first price given for an item of merchandise and ask themselves, "Is this the right price?" Then they look at shipping and handling charges separately and ask, "Are these reasonable?" For some unknown reason, consumers seldom seem to add merchandise and shipping and handling charges together in their minds when making an initial decision about items they are considering buying. (Perhaps this is because the average consumer "hates" mathematics and wants to deal with numbers as little as possible.)

The problem of adding shipping and handling charges into the basic price of the merchandise is that this will generally mean the "first price given" will have to be higher than that presented by competitors who charge shipping and handling separately. In reviewing 500 popular consumer mail order catalogs, I discovered only 17 still included shipping and handling in the basic price of each item of merchandise.

There are five basic ways of presenting shipping and handling charges in catalogs.

"Free"

In addition to L.L. Bean and Hammacher Schlemmer, which promote free shipping and handling charges, there are several variations on this theme.

Quill [Portfolio Illustration D] heavily promotes "Free Delivery on Most Quill Orders." Copy explains: "Delivery is usually FREE. If you are located in the contiguous 48 states, we'll pay all shipping charges for you as long as the subtotal (before any taxes) of merchandise shipped to a single address is more than $45. The only exceptions are items described as 'F.O.B.,' for which you will always pay the entire shipping charge."

Memindex [Portfolio Illustration O] uses "Free Shipping" to promote prepayment on orders. A bold box on the Memindex order form states: "FREE SHIPPING when your check accompanies order." In its ordering instructions, Memindex adds, "You can save all shipping, handling, and delivery charges when you include your check with your order. (Next Day and Second Day UPS charges excluded.)"

Current also makes no charge for shipping when orders are prepaid. The summary area on Current's multipage order form [Portfolio Illustration P] states: "Current pays the postage on your shipment when your check or money order is enclosed. If you charge your order, we'll add postage costs (20¢ per item) to your bill." Current does, however, charge a $2.00 "handling fee" on each order.

Order Amount

The most common method of presenting shipping and handling charges is with a table based on the dollar amount of the order. In the portfolio of order forms, you'll see this method used by:

Miles Kimball [Illustration F]
Talbots [Illustration G]
Breck's [Illustration H]
Spring Hill [Illustration I]
Williams-Sonoma [Illustration J]
The Chef's Catalog [Illustration K]
Lillian Vernon [Illustration Q]
The Nature Company [Illustration R]

Per Item

There are times when shipping and handling costs are not directly related to the dollar amount of the order. Thus a standard table with shipping and handling costs averaged is not practical. Many catalogs—particularly those offering upscale gifts—use an alternate method with a per item shipping and handling charge shown in parentheses following the price for each item.

For example, on one Horchow catalog page, there are four items with obvious differences in shipping and handling costs:

- Girl's "dress up" trunk @ $230 with shipping and handling charges of $13.45.
- Remote-control fire engine @ $125 with shipping and handling charges of $13.60.
- Slumber bag @ $70 for toddler-size, @ $115 for youth size, each carrying $7.65 shipping and handling charges.
- Battery-powered Jeep @ $425 with shipping and handling charges of $80.

The Horchow order form has a separate column headed "Packaging, Ins. & Shipping." Imprinted atop this column in light pink type is the legend: "There is no additional shipping charge for identical items (same size and color) shipped to the same address."

Avon Fashions combines a per order handling charge of $1.95 with a separate shipping charge of 75¢ per item.

Weight and Distance

At one time, it was common for mail order catalogs to ask customers to calculate actual shipping charges by including a weight and distance chart. The weight for each item was listed, and customers were required to add up the total weight of their order, determine the distance their shipments would have to travel, and then calculate costs by using a chart in the catalog.

Very few catalogs use this method today. It is still utilized by the "Big Three"—Sears, J.C. Penney, and Spiegel (Portfolio Illustrations A, B, and C), although each of these general merchandise catalogs has a different method for calculating charges.

- Sears has the most simple system of the three. Distance is not a factor. A single table shows shipping costs based on just 11 different categories of total order weights. (As noted previously, Sears doesn't ask customers to do calculations—including total weight and shipping and handling charges—unless they are sending cash with their order.)
- Penney uses a two-zone distance system and shows shipping costs in 51 different total weight categories for each zone. A full page

in the Penney catalog is devoted to a table from which customers can determine by state and/or ZIP Code whether they are in Zone I or Zone II. (Not only is there a full page for the distance chart, but it takes three additional full pages with small type to explain all of the details of Penney's shipping and handling charges.)

- Spiegel has a single chart with three zones, broken down by states, and 11 different total weight categories for each. The Spiegel chart also has two additional columns showing total weight "Spiegel Custom Delivery" charges for two types of expedited shipping—four-day "Express" and two-day "Express Plus." Like Sears, Spiegel doesn't ask those sending charge orders to do totals calculations. Copy below the Spiegel shipping chart says: "Spiegel Preferred Charge or credit card customers. We figure delivery charges for you and add the amount to your account." (In addition to shipping charges, Spiegel also adds a $1.50 per order "handling charge.")

Many business-to-business catalogs also add weight and distance shipping costs. Most often, however, these are not shown anywhere in the catalog. Instead, the customer is either billed for these costs or asked to pay the carrier upon delivery.

One business catalog that does offer a guideline to "estimated truck charges for 150 lbs. or less" is Quill. The Quill catalog has a chart showing estimated charges broken down by both states from which F.O.B. items will be shipped and the state in which delivery will be made. (As noted previously, most Quill shipments are made without added shipping and handling charges.) Copy above the chart explains:

> **Larger F.O.B. items ship by truck. Packages that weigh more than 70 lbs. and measure greater than 130 inches in length and girth (distance around) will have to be sent by truck, because they exceed limits set by UPS. Since all truck items are designated as F.O.B., you will pay the shipping charge on them, regardless of distance or the subtotal price of your order.**
>
> **Truck lines have a minimum freight charge for shipping less than 150 pounds of merchandise originating from the same F.O.B. point. That charge can vary significantly, depending on distance and merchandise being shipped. We suggest you order several items from the same factory to avoid excessive shipping charges. For more clarification or a freight quote, please contact our Order Department for assistance.**

The Drawing Board [Portfolio Illustration T] charges $1.95 for "packing, handling and guaranteed delivery," and then notes "Shipping Charges Additional."

The order form in the Devoke computer accessories catalog [Portfolio Illustration U] says: "All orders are shipped FOB shipping point. For your convenience, we prepay all freight charges (actual) plus add a $3.00 handling charge and add them to your invoice."

Per Shipment

A number of catalogs simply have a standard shipping and handling charge, regardless of the size of the order or the distance it has to be shipped.

Fuller Brush [Portfolio Illustration L], for example, has a single $3.95 shipping and handling charge. Copy explains: "Order as much as you want—your shipping, handling, packing and insurance will still only be $3.95. Items ordered together are not necessarily shipped together."

Lands' End [Portfolio Illustration V] has a single $3.50 charge for "Shipping, Packing, Handling and Insurance." It does, however, offer express shipments at higher rates. Copy explains:

WE SHIP FASTER THAN ANYONE WE KNOW OF.
Usually within 24 hours after receiving your order. (Monogrammed, in-seamed or gift boxed items take a day or two longer.) To your home, or your office. Wherever you like. We want to make shopping as convenient as possible for you.

Our famous fast service is even faster when you choose one of our express delivery options:

(A) Federal Express Standard Air Shipment gets you your order within 3–4 business days.* Cost is an additional: $5 per shipment for Continental U.S. $15 per shipment to Alaska and Hawaii.

(B) Lands' End Express™ Shipment (via Federal Express) gets you your order within 2 business days.* You can pick the delivery day; even Saturday! (The exact day you specify just has to be within a week of your order.) Cost is an additional: $6 per shipment for Continental U.S. $16 per shipment to Alaska and Hawaii.

* If we monogram, inseam, or gift box, please allow 1 additional business day.

Omaha Steaks International [Portfolio Illustration W], whose catalog promotes gift shipments, charges $5.50 per shipment for postage and handling.

Selective Software [Portfolio Illustration S] offers three levels of shipping—UPS Ground, UPS 2nd Day Air, Overnight—with a basic price at each level for shipments with one or two items, and a second price for shipments with three or more items.

Sell Something

The catalog order form is like the cash register in the store. And what do you find adjacent to the cash register in a good retail store? Impulse items! Cigarettes, candy bars, chewing gum, flashlight batteries—the kinds of things you probably didn't come into the store to purchase. But now that you're there, and the items are readily available, you pick them up and add them to the things you came in to purchase.

The same philosophy works for catalog order forms. If you surround the order form with impulse items, you frequently find them being added to the order. And, if you can include selected impulse items as preprinted line items on the order form, you often can get them added to a substantial percentage of the orders.

A good example of this technique is shown in the Spring Hill order form [Portfolio Illustration I]. At the bottom of the order form, two plant foods are offered—an ideal impulse item for buyers of plants, trees, and shrubs. Then, on the order form itself, these two items have been preprinted as line items. To order, the customer simply indicates the quantity desired and enters the prices.

The ultimate order form in attracting impulse business is that of Williams-Sonoma [Portfolio Illustration J]. The order form is $8\,^3/_8$ x $13\,^1/_2$", but folds to just $8\,^3/_8$ x $4\,^1/_4$" to fit Williams-Sonoma's digest-size catalog.

Facing the folded order form, which is bound into the center of the catalog, is an order envelope with a $4\,^1/_4$ x $8\,^3/_8$" full-color back panel featuring, in a typical example, three impulse items—a kitchen hand cream, a liquid glycerine soap, and a special metal polish. In addition, there is a coupon to be used to request that a catalog be sent to a friend.

The envelope unit is tipped to a $4\,^1/_2$ x $8\,^3/_8$" panel with black-and-white line drawings of 12 "service products"—inexpensive items that don't justify regular display space in the catalog itself, but are the kind of items gourmet customers expect to be able to obtain from Williams-Sonoma. Typical items are a French-style bean slicer, several cooking thermometers, and a number of specialty knives.

The $9\,^1/_2$ x $8\,^3/_8$" center spread created by this order form—envelope unit contains six boldly numbered inexpensive specialty items with full-color illustrations.

When the order form is unfolded, the back features another seven boldly numbered inexpensive specialty items with full-color illustrations.

But selling doesn't stop there. On the face of the order form, there's a special panel for ordering herb plants, which are described elsewhere in the catalog. These plants are sold in sets of 6 or 12. But customers have to choose which of 19 herbs they want in their sets. Rather than having the customer use most of the lines on the regular order form just to list the herbs, Williams-Sonoma provides the special ordering panel with a plant list for the customer to check.

But this special herb panel serves two other important purposes. It not only reintroduces the herbs as an impulse purchase item, but reduces the space required to present them in the body of the catalog.

Figure 10–2
Promoting Impulse Sales

Williams-Sonoma effectively utilizes a combination of catalog selling space and its order form to promote impulse sales. Rather than taking a lot of copy space on the spread to list each of the 19 different herbs, copy directs the customers to the order form for additional information. Copyright © Williams-Sonoma. Used with permission.

Handling Supplemental Information

Using a special area for ordering something which is not representative of typical catalog items can be very important in making an order form easy to use. The Williams-Sonoma order form [Portfolio Illustration J] also has a separate area for ordering gifts to be sent to a separate address. This contrasts with a Horchow order form, which includes a ship-to column for each line item. This not only limits the order form to a maximum of five line items, but makes the order form appear less complicated for customers who are ordering only for themselves.

Lillian Vernon [Portfolio Illustration Q] uses two ship-to columns, with space for a separate shipping address, at the bottom of a 14-line area for the customer's regular order. The space for order totals is at the bottom of both direct-ship and ship-to areas. Lillian Vernon uses a table based on total dollars of the order for shipping and handling charges. For split orders, the customer is asked to pay an additional $2.00 for each ship-to address.

A technique used by many gift catalogs is seen in The Nature Company order form [Portfolio Illustration R]. At the far right of each line item is an A-B-C-D-E listing. Elsewhere on the order form are address spaces with alphabetical labels. With this system, the customer can circle one of the five letters at the end of each line and then use the appropriate alphabetically designated address spaces to indicate where these items are to be sent.

Separate order form spaces can also be used for other out-of-the-ordinary items. For example, take a look at The Drawing Board order form [Portfolio Illustration T]. There are three separate areas for item ordering—one for unimprinted items; a second for order forms, checks, and labels; and a third for business cards, letterheads, and envelopes.

On the reverse side of the order form, there are areas for personalization instructions for each imprinted item ordered, plus another separate area for ordering imprinted greeting cards.

A Well-Organized Gift Shipment Order Form

Mauna Loa Macadamia Nuts manages to work in a host of ordering details and yet make the order form (Figure 10–3) look uncluttered and simple to fill out. Everything follows a logical sequence. It is worthwhile studying the details of each area of this outstanding catalog order form.

1. A cut-off date ("Order in Time For Christmas! For normal

shipping, Christmas delivery guaranteed for orders received by Dec. 14.") is given so customers will feel confident that orders can be delivered in time for the holidays.

2. The area for customers to enter their names and addresses includes some special features:
   - While it doesn't show in the illustration, there is a faint blue surprint reading "Please Print." (In too many catalog order forms, this instruction is surprinted in a solid color or a heavy tint. A maximum tint of 20% is recommended.)
   - There are check boxes for prefixes—Miss, Mrs., Mr., Mr./Mrs.—plus an additional box and write-in line for optional prefixes such as Dr. and Ms.
   - There are three separate address lines—Business Address, U.P.S. Address, and Mailing Address. When using U.P.S., it is especially important to give customers the opportunity to provide separate addresses for shipping since U.P.S. can't deliver to post office box numbers. Providing a separate line for business addresses allows entry of special information when a package is to be delivered to a business location.

3. Arrows are used effectively to connect the lines for ordering items to be shipped directly to the customer with the address area above.

4. In the line item area, there is a space for "Name of Gift." Many customers are uncomfortable with just giving an item number, a practice which is quite common on order forms in food gift catalogs. Having customers provide a word description of each item also prevents errors in order entry since it is sometimes difficult to decipher handwritten numbers.

5. Another set of arrows points toward an area for summarizing ship-to gift orders ("Use These Spaces for Gift Shipment to Others Shown Below"). Four lines are numbered to correspond with numbers on the four gift order areas at the bottom of the order form. This summary area has a light pink background to clearly separate it from the area for ordering direct-ship items.

6. Customers are given "Four Ways to Order"—check, Visa, MasterCard and American Express. (Many catalogs have found it advisable to show miniature illustrations of each credit card option.)

7. Four shipping options are offered: Ship Now, For Christmas, Deliver by (date), and Express Air Delivery.

8. The order summary area follows a logical sequence:
   - "Total Amount Merchandise" against a light blue background tint.
   - "Add Shipping & Handling Charge" with instructions to select the right amount from a chart at the right.
   - "Add $10 per Address for Express Air Delivery."

- "State Sales Tax." In this case, sales tax is charged only for Illinois (6 percent) and Hawaii (4 percent) residents. *[The Mauna Loa catalog is a joint venture between Mauna Loa, located in Hawaii, and Foster & Gallagher, located in Illinois. Thus there is nexus [i.e., a physical presence] in only these two states. At this writing, many states are seeking to overturn the National Bellas-Hess ruling by which the U.S. Supreme Court determined that mail order companies were not required to collect sales or use taxes for individual states unless the company had nexus in a specific state.]*
- "Total Amount of My Order."

9. At the upper right-hand corner of the order form is a blue-boxed area "For Office Use Only." This is used by order entry clerks and does not require any action by the customer. The corner positioning makes this information easily observed for reference.

10. Company name *and address*. While this may seem obvious, it is interesting to note the number of order forms which fail to include this vital information on the order form when an addressed envelope is enclosed in the catalog. *(Another all too common error is failing to include a company address anywhere except on the order form. Thus, when the order form has been removed, the catalog can't be used for future orders.)*

11. "From Hawaii With Love." This decorative area ties the order form to the theme of the catalog.

12. Telephone ordering information. A yellow background tint, bold type, and illustrations of telephones call special attention to this detail. *(Many catalog companies prefer to receive telephone orders. Even though there is additional cost involved, it's possible to gain substantial increases in average order size when you have an opportunity to make suggestions to the customer at the time of ordering.)* The use of illustrations of telephones is highly recommended by those experienced in telemarketing. Note the instructions: "Have your completed order form and credit card handy when you call." (Illustrations of the three accepted credit cards are shown.)

13. Just below the request to have your credit card handy when you call is a space for entering the credit card number, expiration date, and customer's signature. There are 16 boxes for the credit card numbers. Using boxes makes it easier to read numbers during order processing.

14. This area also asks for the customer's phone number. Copy reads: "Please include your phone number. We will call only if there is a question about your order." While this does provide phone numbers for customer service calls, it also serves a credit-checking purpose. Experience indicates that there is less of a likelihood the

Figure 10–3
Gift Shipment Order Form

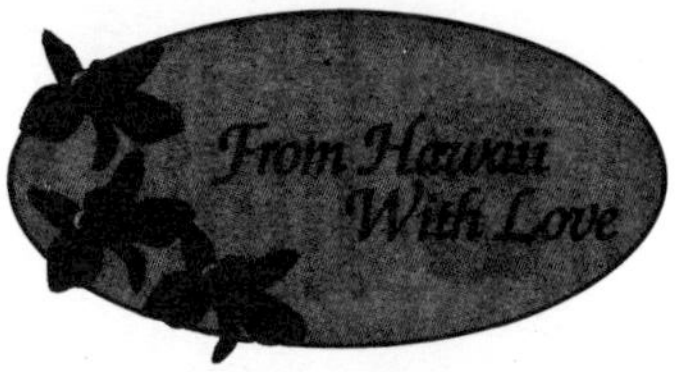

This catalog order form used by Mauna Loa makes it easy for customers to order gift shipments. Copyright © Mauna Loa Macadamia Nut Corp. Used with permission.

order is being placed by a "rip-off artist" or a "deadbeat" when a telephone number is voluntarily given.

15. Shipping and handling chart. This is a highly simplified chart:
    - Up to $25.00—add $4.95
    - $25.01 to $45.00—add $7.95
    - $45.01 to $65.00—add $9.95
    - $65.01 to $85.00—add $11.95
    - Add 10¢ for each $1.00 of purchase over $85.00.
    * Rush—Add $10 per address for Express Air Delivery.

16. "Catalog prices effective until June 1, 1990." How many times have you pulled out an old catalog and questioned whether the prices were still in effect?

17. In the margin at the far left, there's an important message in bold red type: "Order With Confidence. Your Satisfaction 100 percent Guaranteed!" Even if you've stressed your mail order guarantee throughout your catalog, it is good to restate it on the order form.

18. Orders for giftees. There are four numbered spaces at the bottom of the order form, each with address lines, two item order lines, a totals line, and space to request Express Air Delivery. In addition, each of the numbered spaces permits addition of a Gift Message: "A Gift of Aloha from [maximum of 30 characters]". This giftee area has a bold red type heading: "Use These Spaces To Order Gifts To Be Sent To Other Than Your Own Address." Smaller black type adds: "For additional gifts, please enclose information and addresses on separate sheet."

The back of the order form, Figure 10-4, contains details on the uniqueness of Mauna Loa Macadamia Nut Corp. plus detailed ordering information, including:

- How to Order by Mail
- How to Order by Phone
- Delivery in Time for Christmas
- Information about Corporate Gifts
- Express Air Delivery Service for Rush Orders
- Four Ways to Pay
- Shipping and Handling
- Customer Service (including a toll-free number to call and times service is available plus an address for mailing)
- And a *Total* Guarantee of Satisfaction:
  We're confident that every Mauna Loa® gift is of superior quality—so confident, that we offer our no-strings-attached Total Guarantee on every order. If, for any reason, you're not completely satisfied with any item you receive, we'll refund the full price you paid or replace the item—whichever you prefer. Just

return the item to Mauna Loa and we'll act promptly on your request. No questions asked. No quibbling. And no strings attached.

Three disclaimers are added:

- Mail Preference—On occasion, we give others permission to make offers of special merit to our valued customers. If you'd prefer not to receive such offers, just let us know and we'll exclude your name from such mailings.
- Although every precaution is taken, errors in price and/or specifications may occur in printing of our catalog. We reserve the right to correct any such errors.
- Due to warm weather, chocolates are not shipped during June, July, and August.

Figure 10–4
Providing Detailed Ordering Information

Mauna Loa provides detailed information on how to order by mail or phone. Copyright © Mauna Loa Macadamia Nut Corp. Used with permission.

There is also a special impulse item—the Mauna Loa Tee Shirt @ $14.95. "Here's your chance to make a Hawaiian-style hit with the hometown folks, without having to take a Trans-Pacific plane flight!"

Two other similar impulse items are offered on the back of the attached order envelope (illustrated below). One is for Mauna Loa Polo Shirts @ $29.95; the other for "Formal" Sweatshirts, also @ $29.95.

The mailing side of the envelope has a "friend-get-a-friend" coupon, with spaces to request "a copy of the Mauna Loa Macadamia Nut Catalog for the friends you list below."

Figure 10–5
Placement of Impulse Items

Placing impulse items on or adjacent to an order form can help boost order size. These two items were on the back of the reply envelope in Mauna Loa's catalog. Copyright © Mauna Loa Macadamia Nut Corp. Used with permission.

Response Envelopes

The Mauna Loa envelope is not postage-paid. Copy in a stamp affixing area reads: "Affix Postage Stamp Here (Post Office will not deliver without postage)." [Experience of most catalogers indicates it is uneconomical to use Business Reply Envelopes. Those who take the time to search through a catalog to find items they want and then fill out an order form will seldom check first to see if a postage-paid BRE is enclosed. And few ever seem to object to being asked to pay postage to send their order—particularly when a toll-free phone number is given as an option. In several tests where both a BRE and a place-stamp-here envelope were enclosed in a catalog (with the place-stamp-here envelope labeled "Rush Order"), a substantially higher percentage of orders arrived with the customer paying the postage. In the tests I've seen where the two types of envelopes were tested on an equal A-B split basis (with a "Rush Order" label on the place-stamp-here envelope), the bottom line always has favored the envelope where the customer pays the postage.]

Few catalogers question the desirability of including some kind of response envelope in a catalog. This not only appears to produce more orders, but seems to encourage more payments with orders. In European catalogs, order cards are more common than order forms and envelopes. However, American buyers appreciate the privacy an envelope provides. It's not just a matter of not wanting the postman to know what they're ordering; it's also a way of hiding credit card numbers and signatures.

As a general rule, fold-it-up-and-make-your-own-envelope order forms tend to reduce response. When combination order form-envelopes have been tested against separate order forms and enve-

**Figure 10–6
Reply Envelopes**

Note the "Friend-Get-a-Friend" offer on Mauna Loa's reply envelope. Names obtained this way often prove excellent prospects for a cataloger. Copyright © Mauna Loa Macadamia Nut Corp. Used with permission.

Figure 10–7
Catalog Order Cards

European mail order catalogs most often carry a number of order cards, rather than order forms and envelopes. American mail order buyers, however, prefer the privacy an envelope provides. Copyright © Neckermann. Used with permission.

NECKERMANN
BESTELLKARTE

Ich bestelle zu den Neckermann-Bedingungen mit Rückgaberecht gemäß der von mir angekreuzten Zahlungsart. Falls ich keine bestimmte Zahlungsart ankreuze, kann die Ware auch per Nachnahme geliefert werden. Dieser Bestellschein ist selbstverständlich für alle Artikel aus der großen Neckermann-Auswahl gültig.

Bei Kauf auf Rechnung unbedingt ausfüllen!

Ich zahle (bitte ankreuzen)... gegen Rechnung

1 innerhalb 14 Tagen nach Erhalt der Ware

3 in 3 Monatsbeträgen (ab DM 150,-)

5 in 5 Monatsbeträgen (ab DM 200,-)

7 in 7 Monatsbeträgen (ab DM 350,-)

12 in 12 Monatsbeträgen (ab DM 600,-)

Staatsangehörigkeit

Geburtsdatum

Wenn Sie auf Rechnung kaufen und in 3, 5, 7 oder 12 Monatsbeträgen bezahlen, können Sie Ihre Bestellung innerhalb einer Woche schriftlich widerrufen. Den Widerruf richten Sie an: Neckermann Versand AG, Abt. Kundenbetreuung, Postfach, 6000 Frankfurt 1. Zur Wahrung der Frist genügt die rechtzeitige Absendung.

Gegen Nachnahme 0 in einem Betrag direkt an den Zusteller

Unterschrift (Vor- und Zuname)

Bei Zahlung in Monatsbeträgen berechnen wir einen Aufschlag von 0,6% pro Monat auf den Warenwert. Der effektive Jahreszins beträgt max. 14,2% (bei 12 Monatsbeträgen). Näheres auf den Informationsseiten des jeweils gültigen Hauptkataloges. Die Ware bleibt bis zur vollständigen Bezahlung Eigentum der Neckermann Versand AG.

Artikelbezeichnung	Bestell-Nummer	Farb-Nr.	Größe	Menge Meter	Gesamtpreis DM	Pf
GESAMTWERT MEINER BESTELLUNG: (nicht unter DM 50,-)						

ABSENDER K 218 EB o. V.

Kunden-Nummer (falls vorhanden, unbedingt eintragen) 116

Name/Vorname

Straße/Hausnummer

PLZ Wohnort

Damit wir Sie bei eventuellen Rückfragen anrufen können, geben Sie uns bitte Ihre Telefon-Nummern an.

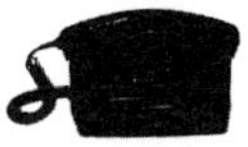

Vorwahl Rufnummer

60 Pfennig die sich lohnen!

Antwort

NECKERMANN VERSAND AG
z.Hd. Frau
Renate Heim
Postfach

6000 Frankfurt 400

lopes, the do-it-yourself envelopes have consistently proved less effective.

[I suspect customers have as much trouble creating envelopes as they seem to have refolding road maps. I've seen cases where as many as 20 percent of these combination devices arrive in the customers' own envelopes—many showing evidence of futile attempts at following folding and gumming instructions. Some years ago, I worked with a major paper company in trying to develop a foolproof fold-it-up-and-make-your-own-envelope order form. We tested the use of numbered folds, dotted lines, arrows, cartoons, photographs, and almost every device you could imagine. But whenever any of our bright ideas were presented to a test group, well over 20 percent gave up in exasperation before completing the folding and sealing.]

Use of "Action Devices"

Direct marketers sometimes forget catalogs are a form of direct mail. And over the years, the use of action devices such as stamps, tokens, coupons, peel-off stickers, and and rub-off spots have often produced increased response for other types of direct mail. They can produce more catalog orders.

An example of a catalog action device is seen on the Current catalog cover (Figure 10–8). The "Here's The Scoop" device near the bottom right-hand corner of the cover is a peel-off sticker. When attached to the Current order form [Portfolio Illustration P], it entitles the customer to 65 percent savings on an ice cream serving set. Copy on the order form reads: "Simply remove the sticker from the cover of your catalog and place it here. With an order of any size, you can buy our 9-piece Ice Cream Serving Set (sold on catalog page 4) for just $4.95—a savings of up to 65 percent on each set you buy!"

Another example of an order form action device is shown in the personalized Breck's catalog wrap (Figure 10–9). The gummed punch-out seal at the bottom right entitles a customer to five free tulips with an order of $25 or more. Copy below the seal reads: "Punch out this Preferred Customer Seal and paste on order form to obtain bonus. Details on Page 2." (When using "stamps" which must be moistened, it's important to avoid printing anything on the back side. Ink on the area which must be moistened makes the stamp look "unsanitary" and reduces response.)

Use of "Laundry Lists"

Catalogers are sometimes tempted to create "laundry list order forms"—those which have every item in the catalog preprinted. All the customer needs to do is indicate the quantity desired and, perhaps, the total price. Although such order forms may be effective when

Figure 10–8
Action Devices

To get customers thinking right away about ordering, Current attached a peel-off sticker to the cover of its catalog. In addition, a personalized message imprinted on the back cover addressed the customer by name encouraged action. Copyright © Current. Used with permission.

everything can be squeezed onto a single page, laundry lists more often produce fewer orders, fewer items per order, and a substantial increase in order entry errors. (The order entry problem is caused when clerks' eyes slip up or down a line and they enter an adjacent item, rather than the one the customer has checked.)

One exception is the multipage order form used by Current (Portfolio Illustration P). Because of a unique pricing structure with progressive discounts on each item based on the total number of items ordered, Current feels it must use the laundry list technique and require customers to total the number of individual units ordered in each of the five columns on each page, plus the total for each page.

We've also seen cases that require many numbers to identify all available sizes and varieties of items. Since both customers and order entry personnel so easily can make mistakes in entering numbers, a laundry list with all numbers preprinted may prove beneficial to all concerned.

Order Forms in Business-to-Business Catalogs

In a substantial number of businesses and industries, orders are most frequently placed on "official" purchase requisition forms. (And an increasing percentage of other orders comes in by telephone.) This leads many business-to-business catalogers to question the need for binding an order form into their catalogs. Experience, however, indicates it is wise to include an order form as a "guide to ordering," if for no other reason. It also helps make clear that mail and phone orders are expected.

One of the problems with both purchase requisitions and telephone orders is the difficulty in capturing list codes so you can determine the comparative effectiveness of different mailing lists. For telephone orders, you can ask the caller to repeat a code printed as part of the address. If this question will be asked, it is desirable to place this code near a unique symbol to speed look-up ("Could you tell me the number following the red star near your address on the back cover of your catalog?").

Purchase requisitions, however, seldom follow look-up instructions of a cataloger. One effective way to capture mailing codes is to offer a desirable free premium and give it a unique item number for each mailing list being used. Since purchasing agents at even the most rigid corporation seldom can resist getting something free, and they're accustomed to including an item number for each item

Figure 10–9
Bonus Seal

Breck's included a punch-out Bonus Seal on a personalized wrap inside the front cover of its catalog. The customer was instructed to paste the seal at the top of the catalog's order form to receive a free bonus. Copyright © Foster & Gallagher. Used with permission.

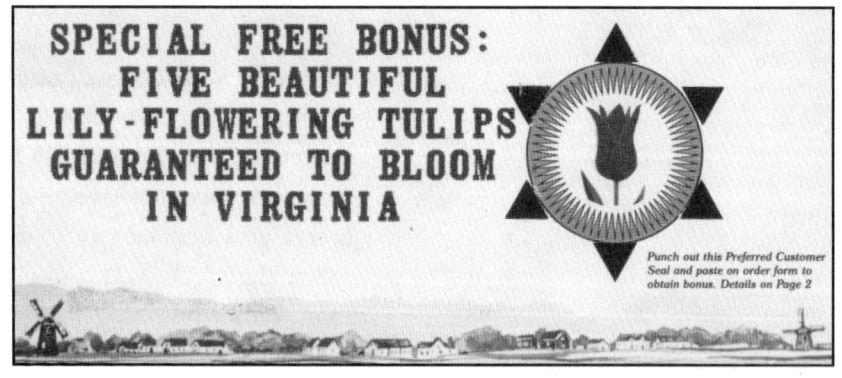

ordered, every request for the free premium automatically provides the mailing code.

Testing Order Forms

There are four basic steps in testing to make sure you've created the most efficient and productive catalog order form.

Staff Review

Start by having every department concerned with marketing and order processing review the order form. This should be more than simply "eyeballing" the order form. Everyone involved should select a variety of items from the catalog and go through the procedure of actually filling out an order form.

Listen carefully when anyone raises a question about how to order an item. If your own staff has questions, your customers will likely be confused . . . and confused customers most often don't place orders.

However, beware of those who simply want to make their own jobs easier. Always keep the basic objective in mind: *Will it help make it easy for the customer to order?*

Customer Review

A second test is to have a number of "outsiders"—people who are your customers or who are like your customers—create trial orders. Carefully monitor areas where they appear to be having difficulty deciding just what to do. And by all means, listen carefully to any questions they ask.

Monitor Order Entry

The most important test is to regularly monitor orders as they are received. It's a good idea to look at a batch of orders each week to see how your customers have filled out order forms. And be sure to listen in on telephone ordering regularly.

Customer Service Review

Just as important as any of the preceding steps is to regularly discuss your order form with customer service personnel. They are more likely to hear from those who have had difficulty filling out the order form and who may not have chosen to send in an order. That's something to always keep in mind—nobody in order entry can tell you what may have kept customers from ordering. Order entry personnel can tell you the mistakes made by customers who have sent in orders. But it's even more important to know the kinds of things which are so troublesome they have convinced customers *not* to order at all.

The Order Form Portfolio

America's best-known order form is found in Sears' catalogs. Since more consumers are acquainted with it than any other order from, it provides the ideal starting point when planning a new catalog order form. (Information which Sears uses to support its order form is shown on page 232. Also note the special telephone order planner which Sears includes in its catalogs. With well over 50% of all catalog orders being placed by telephone today, such an order worksheet is worth considering by any cataloger.)

A1   Copyright © Sears, Roebuck & Co. Used with permission.

232

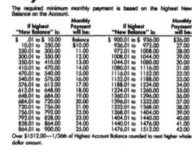
A2

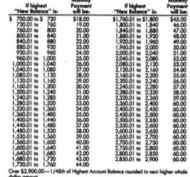
A3

A4

A5

Copyright © Sears, Roebuck & Co.
Used with permission.

JCPenney

MAIL THIS ORDER TO: J.C. Penney Company Inc. Catalog Distribution Center (Find correct address on page 367.)

We're never closed! For Shopping and Customer Service Call Toll-Free **1-800-222-6161**

Today's Date __/__/__

HOME PHONE NUMBER of the household placing the order. It helps speed up your order. Please be sure to include **area code.**

Name (Use the same name for ALL orders from your household)
(first, middle initial, last) — Apt.
Present Address
City/State — ZIP

ANY CHANGE in your name, address or phone number since your last order? If so, please complete this entire section.
Former Name (first, middle initial, last)
Former Address
City/State — ZIP
Former Home Phone Number

JCPenney CHARGE ACCOUNT NUMBER (if there is one for this household). It helps us process both CASH and CREDIT orders.

ALTERNATE PHONE NUMBER (When will you be there?) Time ☐ AM ☐ PM

Page No.	Name of item (1 or 2 words)	Letter(s)	Catalog Number	Letter(s)	Size (measure to be sure)	Color, Pattern Finish, Style, Etc. No. or Code / Name	How Many (Pkgs. Ea. etc.)	Mono- gram Initials	Price For One (Pkg. Ea. etc)	Total Price	Delivery Weights (for Cash orders only)

PLEASE HELP US TO SERVE YOU BETTER
- We can best handle your order if your JCPenney account number and home phone number are on ALL orders. Please use separate Order Blanks for Cash, Penney Regular Charge, Major Purchase Charge, VISA, MasterCard, and American Express orders. Use an extra page to order additional items.
- SORRY, WE DO NOT ACCEPT C.O.D. ORDERS.
- CASH CUSTOMERS. Please pay by check or money order only. Do not send stamps, currency or credit account payments. Include payment for transportation-and-handling charge. See page 728 of our big Fall/Winter '89 Catalog. Orders containing any Class C items must be sent by truck. See page 729 of our big Fall/Winter '89 Catalog.
- CHARGE CUSTOMERS. To order by MAJOR PURCHASE CHARGE, you must order $200 or more. See page 370.

TOTAL WEIGHT (Add like dollars and cents) ENTER TOTAL HERE

Complete this section if this is a **CREDIT ORDER**

☐ Would you like to OPEN a JCPenney Charge Account for both regular and major purchase items? Just check the circle, sign below and see page 736 of our big Fall/Winter '89 Catalog.

Check only ONE box. Enter your account number (Penney's above, other charge cards below) and sign below.
☐ JCPenney Regular Charge
☐ JCPenney Major Purchase Charge
☐ VISA ☐ MasterCard ☐ American Express

Charge card number for VISA, MasterCard or American Express
Expiration Date Mo. Yr.
Interbank No. (for MasterCard)

Charge this order to my Charge Account as I have indicated, to be paid according to the current terms of that account.

Authorized charge card SIGNATURE

Complete this section if this is a **CASH ORDER**

MERCHANDISE TOTAL
AMOUNT FOR DELIVERY
SALES TAXES (Some states also require tax on transportation. See page 729 of our big Fall/Winter '89 Catalog).
TOTAL OF THIS ORDER Merchandise, Delivery and Taxes.
If you owe money on a previous JCPenney CASH order, please enter that amount
Total of this order plus balance owed from a previous JCPenney CASH order should be your TOTAL PAYMENT

Enter here the transportation-and-handling charge for the above weight. For Class A & B orders, see page 728 of our big Fall/Winter '89 Catalog. For Class C orders, see page 729 of our big Fall/Winter '89 Catalog.

X-89

To SHIP to ANOTHER PERSON or ADDRESS . . . Just tell us who and where
Name (first, middle initial, last)
Address — Apt.
City/State — ZIP

☐ Regular Parcel Post ☐ P.A.L. ☐ Air Parcel Post

A.P.O./F.P.O. Orders that qualify are routed SAM unless you indicate P.A.L. here. Orders not qualifying are sent Parcel Post.
For orders to Alaska and Hawaii and all U.S. Possessions and Territories, we will ship via Parcel Post unless you indicate Air Parcel Post here.

JCPenney 369

Copyright © J. C. Penney. Used with permission.

Spiegel Preferred Charge Application

▶ **876**
We must have this number when **you apply by phone.**

Apply for a Spiegel Preferred Charge when you **charge toll free: 1 800 345-4500.** Simply give the Ordertaker **the number above** and tell her you want to open an account. She'll ask **you** the questions below. **Or complete this application and mail to:** Spiegel, 1040 W. 35th St., Chicago, IL 60609-1494.

Social Security Number is required for the processing of this application. This application is subject to Spiegel credit approval. Please allow a few extra days for processing in addition to your normal delivery time.

Please print all answers clearly. If answer is "none," print "none."

Name First / Initial / Last

Address / Bldg./Apt. No.

City / State / Zip / Home phone Area Code Number

How long at address?
☐ Own ☐ Rent ☐ Parents ☐ Other
Social Security Number

Previous address if less than one year at present address / Date of birth

Employer / Position / How long?

Employer's city and state / Business phone Area Code Number

Current bank accounts ☐ Savings ☐ Checking ☐ Loan
Total annual household income all sources* $
☐ 15,000 ☐ 25,000 ☐ 35,000
☐ 50,000 ☐ 60,000+

Credit references: Bank, national credit cards, stores, oil companies or finance companies

Name / City and State

Name / City and State

Name of other authorized buyer / Social Security Number

✱ You need not supply any alimony, child support or separate maintenance income if you do not want us to consider it in evaluating your application.

Spiegel, Inc., Chicago, Illinois I understand that my order for merchandise and all subsequent orders will be subject to the following terms: I will pay the time sale price, which is the cash sale price including handling charges and tax, if any, plus the time price differential (monthly finance charge) as stated in your current catalog. I will pay the balance in monthly payments according to the terms stated in your current catalog. If I default in any payment(s), you may hold me for the full balance. I agree that this contract shall be governed by the laws of Illinois. I understand that in connection with this application and future extensions of credit, you may order a consumer report on me, and that upon my request you will inform me if such a report was requested and give me the name and address of the consumer reporting agency.

Applicant signature here / Date

We are required by law to provide you with the following notice about charge accounts:

any holder of this consumer credit contract is subject to all claims and defenses which the debtor could assert against the seller of goods or services obtained pursuant hereto or with the proceeds hereof. Recovery hereunder by the debtor shall not exceed amounts paid by the debtor hereunder.

If you think your bill is wrong, or if you need more information about a transaction on your bill, write to us on a separate sheet at Spiegel, Box 1231, Oak Brook, IL 60522-1231 as soon as possible. We must hear from you no later than 60 days after we sent you the first bill on which the error appeared. You can phone us, but doing so will not preserve your rights. In your letter, please give us the following information: your name and account number, the dollar amount of the suspected error, a description of the error explaining, if you can, why you believe there is an error. If you need more information, describe the item you are unsure about. You do not have to pay any amount in question while we are investigating, but you are still obligated to pay the parts of your bill that are not in question. While we investigate your question, we cannot report you as delinquent or take any action to collect the amount in question.

Special Rule for Credit Card Purchases. If you have a problem with the quality of property or services that you purchased with a credit card, and you have tried in good faith to correct the problem with us, you may have the right not to pay the remaining amount due on the property or services.

Copyright © Spiegel. Used with permission.

Ordering Is Easy

By Phone Or Mail
Charge by phone. Call toll free 24 hours a day, 7 days a week: **1 800 345-4500**. Between 8AM and 10PM we can confirm that your items are in stock and estimate delivery time. If using your Spiegel Preferred Charge, have your Fast Service Number ready. If charging to American Express, Optima, MasterCard or Visa, have your credit card with expiration date handy. We figure delivery charges and add $1.50 handling and reference tax for you (see page 310). **Order by mail.** Send completed order forms to Spiegel, 1040 W. 35th St., Chicago, IL 60609-1494.

Delivery Is Fast

Prompt UPS Shipments
In most cases, we schedule your order for shipment within 24 hours and deliver UPS to your home, office or a friend's. If you **need it faster, see Spiegel Custom Delivery on page 310.**

Your Satisfaction Is Guaranteed

Call The Returns Hotline
Your satisfaction is guaranteed. If you're not entirely satisfied with your order, **call our Returns Hotline, 1 404 662-8030,** any day, from 8AM to 10PM (no collect calls). With one call we can take your reorder and arrange a UPS pick up of your item from your home or office at no additional charge, and we'll promptly refund or credit the catalog price of the item. If you prefer to mail back your item, we'll refund the return postage.

We Service Every Order To Your Satisfaction

Questions?
Our efficient Customer Service Staff is ready to give you prompt attention by phone: **1 312 954-2772,** (after November 11, 1989 call 1 708 954-2772), Mon.-Fri. 8AM-9PM, Sat. 8AM-4:30PM (central time; no collect calls). Please have details and your order summary ready. Or write: Spiegel Customer Service, P.O. Box 927, Oak Brook, IL 60522-0927 and include your daytime phone number.

A Spiegel Preferred Charge Makes Shopping Easier

Just Say "Charge It"
Simply inquire when you call toll free or fill out the application on the back of the order form. As an active charge customer you'll receive special benefits: a convenient **extra line of credit** and fast "charge it" shopping, values and exclusives in a catalog every month, easy itemized statements including prompt credit for returns. Credit term information is on page 310.

Spiegel Gift Certificates Make Perfect Gifts

For Family, Friends or Business
Spiegel Gift Certificates are mailed to you without delivery charge in an impressive envelope ready for giving. **To order:** fill in your order form with 'Gift Certificate', 'N97 892 5000' and any amount of $20 and up in $5 increments. On a separate sheet, list the names, addresses and gift messages for each gift recipient so we can mail them our next catalog to shop. **For information regarding corporate incentive programs, call our Corporate Representative: 1 312 571-8158.**

Things To Note

For Your Information
Free Fabric Swatches. Examine all your options and stop decorating mistakes. Look for the "free fabric swatches" paragraph throughout our home store or see the insert on page 352 for more details.
Warranties/Energy Guides. For a copy before purchase, call **Spiegel** Customer Service, or write them, attn. Product Service. Include your name, address and item number.
Spiegel Catalogs. Keep your catalogs coming by charging at least $100 with your Spiegel Preferred Charge or buying a catalog within a six month period. Spiegel catalogs can be purchased by sending $3 (includes $3 merchandise certificate good toward any order) and your name and address to Spiegel, P.O. Box 6340, Chicago, IL 60680-6340.
'Handcrafted' or 'Handmade' Items. Because items made solely by hand are one-of-a-kind works of the artist or craftsman, actual merchandise may vary slightly from the catalog photo.
Substitutions. If your item is out of stock, we may send a substitute of equal or better value for the same price. As always, if you're not satisfied with your order, simply return it for a full refund.
Mailing List Option. If you'd like us to withhold your name from the mailing lists we share with other compatible companies, send a request to Mail Preference Service, Spiegel, 1040 W. 35th St. Chicago, IL 60609-1494.

SPIEGEL • 307

Ordering Information
Order from the Fall Catalog through January 26, 1990

Fashion Sizes
Order the same size as you would in a fine department store. We sell the same top name brands. In addition to Misses Sizes for average figures (5'4" to 5'7"), you'll find Petites (under 5'4"), Tall Sizes (5'7½" to 6'), Women's Sizes (5'4" to 5'7") and Women's Petite Sizes (under 5'4"). These sizes are proportioned to your figure type in the body, sleeves and overall length.

Sizes 14W/14WP-26W/26WP. For the best fit, simply order the size that corresponds to your measurements in the chart below.

Women's Sizes	14W/14WP	16W/16WP	18W/18WP	20W/20WP	22W/22WP	24W/24WP	26W/26WP
		1X		2X		3X	
Women's Tops*	—	36	38	40	42	44	46
Women's Bottoms*	30	32	34	36	38	40	—
Bust (inches)	39-40½	41-42½	43-44½	45-46½	47-48½	49-50½	51-52½
Waist (inches)	31-32½	33-34½	35-36½	37-38½	39-40½	41-42½	43-44½
Hips (inches)	41-42½	43-44½	45-46½	47-48½	49-50½	51-52½	53-54½

*Women's top and bottom sizes (36-46 and 30-40) are simply identifying a size number and do not represent a specific garment or body measurement.

Ring Sizes
Simply order your normal size. Or, wrap a narrow piece of paper snugly over your knuckle and mark where it overlaps. Place the edge of the paper at 'A' in the chart. The left edge of the paper will fall at your proper size. If between sizes, order the next larger.

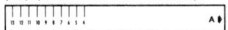

Tablecloth Sizes
To select the proper size tablecloth: determine the depth (in inches) of cloth overhang you'd prefer (usually 6-12 inches) and multiply it by 2. Add to the length of the table the amount you would like to use it (with or without leaves). Repeat for width. Order the cloth size that corresponds to final dimensions.

Sheet/Bed Ruffle Sizes
Twin fits a 39x76-inch mattress. **Full** fits a 54x76-inch mattress. **Queen** fits a 60x81-inch mattress. **King** fits a 78x81-inch mattress. Bed ruffle lengths are measured from the top of the box spring to floor.

Rugs
Not sure which size is right? Remembering these rules-of-thumb can help:
• Always add 6 feet to the length and width of a dining table.
• Allow 3 feet on all open sides of a bed.
• Leave 8 inches of floor exposed around baseboards when covering an entire room.
• For an entry or hallway, be sure to consider how doors open.

Wallcoverings
(a) Measure length of each wall to be covered (in feet). Do not subtract for door or windows. (b) Measure height from floor to ceiling. (c) Multiply height of each doorway and window by its width. (d) Multiply (a)x(b), then subtract half of (c) from this amount for the total square footage to be covered. (e) To determine the number of rolls you'll need, divide the total square footage by the applied coverage of each roll. (The applied coverage figure is found in the catalog description.) Add 10% for matching.

Window Fashions
The best measuring device is a wood or metal ruler. Cloth tapes may stretch, giving inaccurate measurements.

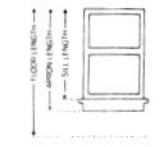

Pinch-Pleated Draperies and Valances
Length: for ordinary curtain rods or standard traverse rods, measure from the top of the rod to the sill, apron or floor as shown in the window diagram above. Please allow for sill clearance. Add 1 inch to allow for the heading above the rod (unless you have decorative ceiling or cafe rods with rings) and order the closest length available. If you have decorative traverse rods, measure from the bottom of the carrier to the sill, apron or floor, depending on the length you want. **Width:** measure how wide the draped area is to be. For draw draperies, add 4 inches at the center to allow for the two sides to overlap. Now measure how far the traverse rod projects from the wall on each side and add that amount to the total. For example: if the rod projects 3 inches from the wall on each side, add 6 inches (unless you have decorative rods), plus 4 inches for the overlap. For one-way draw panels, add one projection only. If you're ordering pinch-pleated draperies to be used as underdrapes, you won't need to measure the projections; add 4 inches for the overlap only. For valances, add only the total of both projections.

Priscilla Curtains
Length: measure from the top of the rod to the desired length and add 1 inch. Some styles feature a high header, where material extends more than 1" above the curtain rod. This extra material will be specified as either included or excluded from the over-all stated length. **Width:** measure the width of the area to be curtained. To hang criss-cross, use a double rod and order 3 to 4 times measured width. For center meet, order 2 ½ times the width you measure.

Shirr-On Rod Panels, Curtains, Balloons, Valances
Length: measure from the top of the rod to sill, apron or floor (see above) and add 1 inch. Allow for sill clearance. Some styles feature a high header, where material extends more than 1" above the curtain rod. This extra material will be specified as either included or excluded from the over-all stated length.
When using shirr-on rod curtains as underdrapes, measure the length from the top of the rod to 6" below desired length for draperies. If you use a tier-over-tier treatment, the top curtain should overlap the bottom curtain by 6 inches.
Width: measure the area to be curtained. For rod pocket valances, order 1½ to 2 times the width measured. For all other styles, order 2 to 3 times the width measured.

Custom Mini Blinds
Measure to the fraction of an inch, state exact width and length; label each. All widths are for headbox plus brackets. Slats are cut ¼ to ½ inch narrower to avoid marring window frame. For inside or outside mount.
To hang inside casing. Width: see (A). Measure distance between frames where brackets will fit (1 inch flat surface is required.) **Length:** see (B). Measure distance from inside window frame to top of window sill.

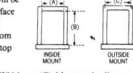

INSIDE MOUNT   OUTSIDE MOUNT

To hang outside casing. Width: see (C). Measure the distance between points where brackets will be mounted—must be at least 1½ inches on each side of the frame opening. **Length:** see (D). Measure the distance from top of window frame to the window sill.

Size And Measuring continued on next page.

308 • SPIEGEL

Size And Measuring continued...

Shutters

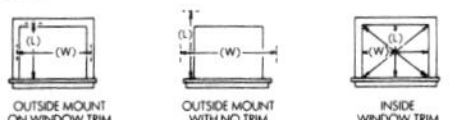

OUTSIDE MOUNT ON WINDOW TRIM   OUTSIDE MOUNT WITH NO TRIM   INSIDE TRIM

For outside mount. Shutters must extend at least 1 inch beyond window opening on each side. **Width:** measure in 3 places from at least 1 inch beyond window opening on left, to at least 1 inch beyond window opening on right. Use widest measurement. **Length:** measure 3 places from at least 1 inch above window opening to at least 1 inch below window opening or sill. Use longest measurement.

For Inside mount. To determine if your window is suitable for inside mount, measure diagonally. If diagonal measurements differ by more than ½ inch, window is not suitable for inside mount. Measure in 3 places from inside left casing to inside right casing. Use narrowest measurement. **Length:** measure in 3 places from inside top casing to top of sill or inside bottom casing where there is no sill. Use shortest measurement.

To hang in a double row. Measure length of window as shown above, subtract ¾" for clearance and divide by 2. Order 2 sets whose combined measurements equal that length.

To hang a single row (cafe style). Divide length measurement by 2 and add 2 inches (or enough for shutters to cover window latch).

Full window. No clearance adjustment necessary. Order exact size or next larger size. Trim shutters (with tools) if necessary. Do not trim more than 1 inch from each panel side and 1½ inches from top or bottom.

Vertical Blinds
Note: inside mount is recommended for length, allow at least 4" above window or door opening for installation of headrail and brackets. If vanes hang to the floor, allow ¾" to 1" clearance. For width, allow 2" to 4" overlap at each side for best light control.

Phone Order Memos

Your Spiegel Fast Service Number

CHARGE YOUR ORDER TOLL FREE: **1 800 345-4500**

Simply jot down your Fast Service Number, your selections and if you're charging to your bankcard, your credit card with expiration date handy when you call. Call 24 hours a day, 7 days a week. Between 8AM and 10PM we can confirm that your items are in stock and estimate delivery time.

Date							
Name of item	Item number	Color	Size	Name, style initials	Qty.	Price each	Total price
						Total for merchandise	$

Date							
Name of item	Item number	Color	Size	Name, style initials	Qty.	Price each	Total price
						Total for merchandise	$

Date							
Name of item	Item number	Color	Size	Name, style initials	Qty.	Price each	Total price
						Total for merchandise	$

Please do not mail these memos. If you wish to order by mail, use a regular Spiegel order form.

SPIEGEL • 309

Delivery/Spiegel Preferred Charge

UPS Delivery On Most Items
To assure prompt delivery of your order please provide your complete address. UPS will not deliver to P.O. Boxes.

Item numbers ending in T are delivered separately. These items may not arrive at the same time as other items ordered.

Items numbers ending in F are Freight Delivered. Expect delivery 2-3 weeks after we receive your order. Please give us your address (P.O. Boxes are insufficient) and your daytime phone so we can confirm delivery date. Delivery charges apply to points within the continental U.S. We do not accept freight orders outside the U.S., or to APO, FPO addresses. Alaska and Hawaii charges are to Seattle and San Francisco respectively. For additional charges in these states, write Spiegel Transportation Dept., Regency Towers, Oak Brook, IL 60522-9009, or call Spiegel Customer Service. **Freight Delivery service** varies and you may be asked to assist in getting your merchandise into your home; the delivery carrier will not uncrate your order.

Spiegel Custom Delivery. If you need your order faster, ask for **Spiegel Express** for guaranteed 3rd day or **Spiegel Express Plus** for guaranteed 2nd day delivery of your order. Rates and schedules in the chart apply to in-stock items taken through 4PM (central time) this expedited service is not available on mail orders, factory or freight-shipped items, individual items over 70 lbs., orders to Alaska, APO, FPO, P.O. Boxes or to U.S. possessions. Please allow one extra day for orders sent to Hawaii.

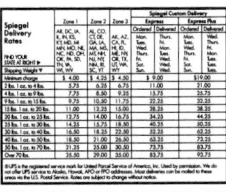

Spiegel Preferred Charge or credit card customers. We figure delivery charges for you and add the amount to your order.

Cash Customers. To estimate delivery charges: simply total the shipping weights and find the amount in the chart. Weights include packaging. Spiegel Custom Delivery is not available on cash orders.

Some delivery charges are stated in dollar amounts. Just multiply it by the number ordered and add that amount to your order total.

Apply For A Spiegel Preferred Charge With This Order
Simply call toll free or fill out the application on the back of the order form. As an active charge customer, you'll get additional catalogs, itemized statements, prompt credit for your return, and enjoy easy charge shopping.

Spiegel Credit Terms

Minimum Monthly Payment	$20	25	30	35	40	50	60	70	75	80
Balance up to	$25-$400	600	800	1,000	1,350	1,500	1,650	1,800	1,900	2,100	2,250	2,400

For information on monthly payment on balances in excess of $2,400, please write to us at this address: Spiegel, Inc., Dept. 187, P.O. Box 09043, Chicago, IL 60609-0043. All credit orders are subject to credit approval. You always have the right to pay more than the minimum monthly payment. This statement of payment policy is for the maximum balance on the account. The minimum payment will not decrease until the new balance is paid in full.

Your Address	FINANCE CHARGE		ANNUAL PERCENTAGE RATE	Method of determining the balance Average Daily	MINIMUM FINANCE CHARGE	Grace period
	Portion of unpaid balance	Periodic (monthly) Rate				
MA, ME	All	1.5%	18%	Excluding current transactions	50¢	
CA	All	1.75%	21%			
CT	All	1.5%	18%	Including current transactions	None	
MD	All	1.905%	23.94%			
NC, IR	All	1.5%	18%			
AL	$1,000 or less Over $1,000	1.5% 1.2%	18% 12%			
CO, GA, IN, OK, VT, WI	All	1.75%	21%			
IA	All	1.65%	19.8%			25 days from the statement date
KY	$300 or less Over $1,000	1.75% 1.5%	21% 18%	Including current transactions	50¢	
NE, NH, WV	All	1.5%	18%			
OH	All	1.7%	20.4%			
WY	$750 or less Over $750	1.75% 1.5%	21% 18%			
AL, U.S. possessions	All	1.905%	23.94%			

The FINANCE CHARGE, except for residents of states listed at right is 1.995% per month (23.94% ANNUAL PERCENTAGE RATE) on the average daily balance of your account. A minimum FINANCE CHARGE of 50¢ a month is currently assessed where authorized by law. Spiegel reserves the right to change its credit terms upon advance written notice to you, as required by law. Payments are credited on the day of receipt; early payments or payments in excess of minimum payments due result in smaller FINANCE CHARGES. There is no FINANCE CHARGE if the first statement is paid in full within 25 days of the statement date. If on any subsequent statement your New Balance is paid in full within 25 days of the statement date, there will be no further FINANCE CHARGE.

We figure the FINANCE CHARGE on your account by applying the applicable periodic rate to the "average daily balance" of your account. To get the "average daily balance," we take the beginning balance of your account each day, add any new purchases (except in Maine and Massachusetts, where new purchases will be included as of the start of the next billing cycle), and subtract any payments or credits. This gives us the daily balance. Then, we add up all the daily balances for the billing cycle and divide the total by the number of days in the billing cycle. This gives us the "average daily balance."

Illinois Residents: Residents of Illinois may contact the Illinois Commissioner of Banks and Trust Companies for comparative information on finance charges, fees and grace periods at—State of Illinois, Customer Information Program, P.O. Box 10181, Springfield, Illinois 62791 or telephone 1 800 634 5452.

Things To Note: For Your Information

Tax Information. Sales or use tax applies to the state where merchandise is being delivered. Spiegel is now registered to collect and remit sales or use tax in all states where there is a tax. Tax is calculated on merchandise and handling. In addition, the following states also tax transportation charges: AZ, AR, CO, DC, GA, HI, ID, IN, KS, LA, MI, MS, MO, NE, NV, NC, ND, OK, PA, SD, TN, TX, UT, WA, WI, WV and WY.

Order from the Fall Catalog through January 26, 1990.

310 • SPIEGEL

Copyright © Spiegel. Used with permission.

D3 Copyright © Quill Corporation. Used with permission.

1989 GIFT ORDER FORM-P

Miles Kimball

41 West Eighth Avenue
Oshkosh, Wisconsin 54906

0114

PLEASE
PLACE PEEL-OFF
LABEL HERE

☐ Mr.   THIS SPACE FOR ADDRESS CORRECTION OR USE IF LABEL IS MISSING
☐ Mrs.
☐ Miss

PLEASE USE SAME NAME & ADDRESS FOR ALL ORDERS FROM YOUR HOUSEHOLD

Address Apt.

City State Zip

Catalog Number	How Many?	Item and Personalization (PLEASE PRINT PLAINLY)	Page No.	✔	Price Each	Total Price
		MINIMUM MERCHANDISE ORDER $5.00				

PLEASE ADD FOR SHIPPING & HANDLING
Up to $ 8.00 .... Add $1.95
$ 8.01 to $15.00 .... Add $2.95
$15.01 to $20.00 .... Add $3.95
Over $20.00 .... Add $4.95
Each package sent to a separate address requires separate postage.
EVERY ITEM GUARANTEED!

Total for Merchandise	
Shipping and Handling	
Subtotal	
Wisconsin Residents Only Add 5% Sales Tax	
Total Amount Enclosed	

E Copyright © Miles Kimball. Used with permission.

Hammacher Schlemmer
ESTABLISHED 1848

For credit card orders call **TOLL-FREE** 24 hours a day 7 days a week **1-800-543-3366**

1 ORDERED BY: *If information is incorrect, please print correct information.*

```
01          L=36308
MR. RICHARD S HODGSON
1433 JOHNNYS WAY
WESTTOWN      PA 19395
```

Phone (____) _____ ☐ Day ☐ Evening

2 SHIP TO: (if different from "ORDERED BY")

Name _____
Street Address _____
City _____ State _____ Zip _____
Item number(s) _____
Day Time Phone (____) _____
Gift Message (if desired) _____

3 PAGE NO. | ITEM NO. | QTY | SIZE | COLOR | DESCRIPTION | GIFT WRAP $3.50 | AMOUNT

4 PAYMENT METHOD

Check or Money Orders: AMOUNT ENCLOSED $ _____
☐ MasterCard ☐ VISA ☐ Diners Club ☐ Carte Blanche ☐ American Express
Card Account Number: _____

Month ___ Year ___
Card Expiration Date Required   Customer Signature
Card Issuing Bank Name: _____

ITEM TOTAL ▶
Applicable Sales Tax For Shipments to NY, IL, OH and CA (see reverse side) ▶
Gift Wrap ___ items at $3.50 each—TOTAL ▶
Regular POSTAGE, HANDLING & INSURANCE in continental United States ▶ **INCLUDED**
SHIPPING for destinations outside continental U.S. (see reverse side)
THANK YOU FOR YOUR ORDER   TOTAL ▶

F1

ORDERING IS EASY

You may order by mail.
- Simply complete the reverse side and return in the attached envelope.

You may order by phone.
- Please call 1-800-543-3366.
- You may place your order 24 hours a day 7 days a week.
- VISA, MasterCard, Diners Club, Carte Blanche and American Express accepted.

We pay your shipping costs.
- All shipping, insurance and handling charges to destinations within the continental United States are paid by Hammacher Schlemmer.

We ship within 48 hours.
- Most orders are shipped via UPS within 48 hours of receipt. If it is not possible to ship within 30 days you will be notified and given the option to cancel your order.
- Products with item numbers beginning with "1" require special handling and may take up to 4 to 6 weeks for delivery.

Do you have special shipment needs?
- To determine charges on items shipped to Alaska, Hawaii, Puerto Rico and foreign destinations, please call toll free 1-800-233-4800. When calling from these same areas, please call 1-513-874-0429.

Do you need it in a hurry?
- Most items can be delivered Federal Express within three business days for an additional $5.00 for one, $10.00 for two, or $15.00 for three or more items by calling toll free 1-800-543-3366.

Is yours a multiple shipment order?
- Items ordered together may require separate shipments. Please check the packing slip included with each package before calling customer service.

Batteries and adaptors are included.
- If an item you order requires batteries or adaptors, they will be included with your shipment. Whenever possible we use Eveready® brand alkaline batteries.

We provide gift wrapping.
- Most items (except large, bulky items or those with item numbers beginning with "1") can be gift wrapped for a charge of $3.50 each.
- You may indicate any message in the space provided on the order form or our operators will take your message verbally when you order by phone.

Sales taxes may vary.
- State laws require us to collect sales tax on products shipped to states where we have stores or warehouses. On shipments to New York State and California, add sales tax applicable to that area; to Chicago, add 6%; elsewhere in Illinois add 5% and to Ohio add 5½% sales tax.

If you should need assistance.
- For Customer Service Please call 1-800-233-4800.
- Our representatives will answer questions about your order or its shipment weekdays between the hours of 8 A.M. and 6 P.M. Eastern time.
- Or you may write: Hammacher Schlemmer
  Customer Service Department
  9180 Le Saint Drive
  Fairfield, OH 45014

Returns and exchanges are easy.
- Fill out the reverse side of the original packing slip. (Shipping labels are attached for your convenience.)
- Place the slip in the carton and wrap package securely.
- Send it to: Hammacher Schlemmer
  Return Department
  9180 Le Saint Drive
  Fairfield, OH 45014
- For your protection please use UPS or Insured Parcel Post for shipment.

Your mailing list preference.
- From time to time we make our list of customers available to carefully screened merchants whose products may be of interest to you. If you prefer not to have your name made available, please write to our Customer Service Department.

If you receive duplicate catalogs.
- Please return the *order form* from the catalog you would like *discontinued* to our Customer Service Department.

WOULD YOU LIKE TO RECEIVE FUTURE HAMMACHER SCHLEMMER CATALOGS?

If you do not usually receive our catalog but would like to in the future, please fill in below and return this page in the attached envelope.

☐ **YES** I would like to receive the Hammacher Schlemmer Catalog FREE for one year. Please return this page in the attached envelope.

☐ **YES** I would like you to send a FREE one year subscription for the Hammacher Schlemmer catalog to...
Please fill in below.

Name _____
Address _____
City _____ State _____ Zip _____

Hammacher Schlemmer is a member of the Direct Marketing Association

F2

Copyright © Hammacher Schlemmer. Used with permission.

Item Number	Qty.	Color No.	Size	Description	Unit Price	Total Price	
A491	1	23	M	Talbots Cable Cotton Cardigan	$00.00	$00	00

SALES TAX INFORMATION We are required by law to collect sales taxes on shipments to the following states where we are located. Please add the appropriate amount. **ALABAMA, ARKANSAS AND GEORGIA:** 4% plus the applicable local taxes for your area on all items. **CALIFORNIA:** 6% plus the applicable local taxes for your area on all items. **COLORADO:** Orders shipped to Denver, 6.5% on all items, 3% elsewhere. **CONNECTICUT:** 8% on all items over $75.00. **FLORIDA:** 6% plus the applicable local taxes for your area on all items. **ILLINOIS, INDIANA, KENTUCKY, MARYLAND, SOUTH CAROLINA, AND WISCONSIN:** 5% on all items. **MASSACHUSETTS:** 5% on all items except apparel. **MICHIGAN:** 4% on all items. **MINNESOTA:** 6% plus the applicable local taxes for your area on all items except apparel. **MISSOURI:** 4.425% on all items. **NEBRASKA AND OKLAHOMA:** 4% plus the applicable local taxes for your area on all items. **NEW JERSEY AND RHODE ISLAND:** 6% on all items except apparel. **NEW YORK:** In New York City, 8.25% on all items; elsewhere in New York State, add the applicable tax for your area on all items. **NORTH CAROLINA:** 5% on all items. **OHIO:** 5% plus the applicable local taxes for your area on all items. **PENNSYLVANIA:** 6% on swimsuits and all items except apparel. **TENNESSEE:** 5.5% on all items except apparel. **TEXAS:** Orders shipped to Austin, Dallas, Fort Worth, Plano and San Antonio, 6% plus the applicable local taxes for your area; elsewhere 6%. **VIRGINIA:** 4.5% on all items. **WASHINGTON, D.C.:** 6% on all items. **WASHINGTON:** 6.5% plus the applicable local taxes for your area on all items.

Total Merchandise	
Sales Tax *see box at left*	
Shipping & Handling *see box below*	
Add charge for 2-day or 4-day service	
Total Order	

METHOD OF PAYMENT

Please indicate method of payment. ☐ Check or money order enclosed.
☐ Talbots ☐ MasterCard ☐ VISA ☐ Diners Club ☐ American Express
Your charge account will not be billed until your merchandise is shipped.

(Please list all digits from your charge card) Expiration Date _____

SHIPPING & HANDLING

Total Merchandise (exclude tax)	Add
$ 50.00 and under	$4.25
$ 50.01-$100.00	$5.00
$100.01-$200.00	$5.75
$200.01-and over	$6.75

Talbots
175 BEAL STREET, HINGHAM, MA 02043

If you would like merchandise sent to another address, please indicate:

Item numbers _____
Send to _____
Address _____
City _____ State _____ Zip _____

☐ Gift box and enclose card from:

**To place an order in the U.S. call toll-free:
1-800-225-8200.**
☐ CHECK HERE TO RECEIVE A COPY OF OUR TALBOTS KIDS CATALOG.
☐ CHECK HERE TO RECEIVE A TALBOTS CHARGE APPLICATION.

PLEASE PRINT ADDRESS CORRECTIONS IF NECESSARY.
Information about your order will be sent to this address.

```
ID# 044 75 566  DEPT A
RICHARD S HODGSON
1433 JOHNNY S WAY
WESTTOWN, PA        19395
```

Telephone Number (____) _____

Copyright © Talbots. Used with permission.

BRECK'S
U.S. Reservation Center
6523 N. Galena Road
Peoria, Illinois 61632

"Easy-to-Order"

1989 Dutch Bulb Reservation Form

FOR OFFICE USE ONLY

CR _____	☐ GIFT	CHECK _____	SUBTOTAL _____
CS _____	☐ COR	CASH _____	DISC _____ C F
MO _____	ITEMS _____	RFC _____	TOTAL _____

Complete this area only if preprinted name or address on reverse side is incorrect.

☐ Miss
☐ Mrs.
☐ Mr. _____
U.P.S. Address _____
Mailing Address _____
City _____
State _____ Zip _____

"Easy-to-Order" 1989 Dutch Bulb Reservation Form

ENTER NUMBER OF BULBS ➡

	CATALOG NO.	NO. OF BULBS	NAME OF BULBS OR COLLECTIONS	PAGE NO.	PRICE PER GROUP	TOTAL PRICE
0	C55947	5	Apricot Beauty Tulips (Free with any order of $25.00 or more)			FREE
1	C84749		Breck's Dutch Treat Food for Bulbs (1 Pkg. $3.99 2 Pkgs. $6.99 3 Pkgs. $9.99)			
2						
3						
4						
5						
6						
7						
8						
9						
10						
11						
12						
13						
14						
15						
16						
17						
18						
19			USE MORE PAPER			
20			IF NECESSARY			

TOTAL AMOUNT MERCHANDISE
SHIPPING AND HANDLING CHARGES SEE CHART BELOW
SALES TAX — ILLINOIS AND OHIO RESIDENTS: ADD 6%
TOTAL AMOUNT

CHOOSE BILLING METHOD

☐ Payment enclosed. Amount $_____
☐ Charge my credit card account when my bulbs are delivered this fall.
  ☐ VISA ☐ MasterCard ☐ American Express
☐ Charge my established Preferred Customer Account when my bulbs are delivered this fall. *Orders subject to approval.*

© 1989 Breck's **CA**

Credit Card Number
[ ][ ][ ][ ][ ][ ][ ][ ][ ][ ][ ][ ][ ][ ][ ][ ]

My card expires ___/___ MO. YR.

Signature_____
Credit card order MUST include your signature.

PHONE: Area Code _____ # _____
Please include your phone number. We will call only if there is a question about your order.

SHIPPING AND HANDLING CHART
Includes ocean freight, duty, insurance and inland shipping direct to your home.

Amount of Order Send this Amount	UP to 15.00	15.01 to 20.00	20.01 to 25.00	25.01 to 30.00	30.01 to 35.00	35.01 to 40.00	40.01 to 45.00	45.01 to 50.00	Add 10¢ FOR EACH $1.00 OF PURCHASE OVER $50.00
	4.95	5.95	6.45	6.95	7.45	7.95	8.45	8.95	

BULBS ARE CAREFULLY PACKED IN SPECIAL REFRIGERATED CONTAINERS AND SHIPPED DIRECT FROM HOLLAND. BOTH OCEAN FREIGHT AND U.S. SHIPPING COSTS ARE INCLUDED.

Don't forget to order a supply of Breck's Exclusive Dutch Treat Food for Bulbs (described on inside back cover)

Copyright © Foster & Gallagher. Used with permission.

© COPYRIGHT 1991 DARTNELL CORPORATION

SATISFACTION GUARANTEED

If, for any reason, you're not fully pleased with any item upon receipt, after planting or once it grows and blooms, just write Spring Hill anytime before October 1, 1989. We'll replace that item without charge or refund every cent you paid for it – whichever you prefer. You alone are the judge!

FOR OFFICE USE ONLY

CR ____	☐ GIFT	CHECK ____	SUBTOTAL ____
CS ____	☐ COR	CASH ____	DISC ____ C F
MO ____	ITEMS ____	RFC ____	TOTAL ____

SPRING HILL
1989 ORDER FORM
RESERVATION CENTER
6523 NORTH GALENA ROAD
PEORIA, ILLINOIS 61632

Complete this area only if preprinted name and address on reverse side is incorrect.

☐ Miss
☐ Mrs.
☐ Mr. _____

My UPS Delivery Address _____
My Postal Address _____
City _____
State _____ Zip _____

NOTE: When ordering Collections, enter in the "How Many" column the number of Collections, not the number of items in the Collection.

CATALOG NUMBER	HOW MANY	DESCRIPTION	PAGE NO.	PRICE PER GROUP	TOTAL PRICE
N 10777	5	Orange Glory Flowers (Free with any order of $25.00 or more.)			FREE
N 21501		The Pill for Plants (20 for $3.99 40 for $6.99 100 for $14.99)			
N 21493		Advanced Formula Plant Food (24 Oz. Bag $3.99 3 for $9.99)			
		USE MORE PAPER IF NECESSARY			

FOUR WAYS TO ORDER

☐ Payment enclosed. Amount $ _____
☐ Charge my VISA Account when my plants are delivered this spring.
☐ Charge my MasterCard Account when my plants are delivered this spring.
☐ I authorize you to establish an account for me and bill this account when my plants are delivered this spring. *Orders subject to approval.*

My Card Expires

Credit Card Number _____

MO./YR.

SIGNATURE _____

SHIPPING AND HANDLING CHARGES

AMOUNT MERCHANDISE	Up to $5.00	$5.01 to $10.00	$10.01 to $17.50	$17.51 to $25.00	$25.01 to $35.00	$35.01 to $45.00	ADD 10¢ FOR EACH $1.00 OF MERCHANDISE OVER $45.00
ADD	$2.95	$3.95	$4.95	$5.95	$6.95	$7.95	

TOTAL AMOUNT MERCHANDISE _____

STATE SALES TAX _____
Illinois & Ohio residents add 6%

ADD SHIPPING & HANDLING CHARGE - SEE CHART AT LEFT _____

INSURANCE _____
For $1.00 damaged or lost shipments will be replaced FREE

TOTAL AMOUNT OF MY SPRING HILL ORDER _____

Phone:
Area Code ____ No. ____
Please include your phone number. We will call only if there is a question concerning your order.

TWO EXCLUSIVE SPRING HILL GROWING AIDS

The Pill for Plants

Fantastic scientific breakthrough has revolutionized plant feeding. Safe high potency long-lasting "time-release" 20-10-5 blue pills won't burn and provide plant food continually for up to TWO full years! For superior growth, drop a pill in the hole when you plant ... or punch holes next to established trees, shrubs and place a pill near the root zone. Takes the guesswork out of fertilizer applications. The easiest way to feed your trees, shrubs and plants ... and exclusively yours from Spring Hill!

N21501 The Pill for Plants
20 for $3.99   40 for $6.99   100 for $14.99

Advanced Formula Plant Food

Spring Hill's professional nurserymen have developed a special Advanced Formula Plant Food that is ideal to promote healthier growth and more profuse blooming of your plants and bulbs. It's a specially compounded mixture of slow-release fertilizers and bone meal which is easy to apply and assures the proper diet for all types of flowering plants. This special 5-10-5 plant food is highly recommended for superior growth and blooming. A Spring Hill Exclusive!

N21493 Advanced Formula Plant Food
24 Oz. Bag
$3.99 Each   3 for $9.99

Copyright © Foster & Gallagher. Used with permission.

WILLIAMS-SONOMA
Serving Serious Cooks Since 1956

P.O. Box 7456
San Francisco, CA 94120-7456

Name and address below should be that of person placing order (please make corrections as necessary). If your catalog has a peel-off label on the back cover, please place it here.

```
A381-556-93      S46323-11
R S HODGSON
1431 JOHNNY S WAY
WESTTOWN PA 19395
```

OUR GUARANTEE: For 33 years we have offered items of the highest quality. If for any reason you are not completely satisfied with your purchase, please return the item. We will gladly replace the merchandise or, if you prefer, issue a refund.

DAYTIME TELEPHONE
( )
We will call you if we have a question about your order.

RUSH DELIVERY: We offer priority handling and **Federal Express delivery** at an additional charge of **$5.00** per shipping address ($15.00 for Alaska & Hawaii). To confirm item availability, **please order by phone** (see below).

GIFT ORDERS (see Gift Sections #1 and #2 below): Your gift orders receive special care. We will enclose a gift message at no extra charge and/or send your gift in our distinctive Williams-Sonoma gift box with ribbon at **$2.00** per box. In addition, we will send you confirmation of your order. Please write additional gift addresses and ordering information on an attached sheet of paper.

If the above address is a P.O. BOX, please fill in a local delivery street address in the section at right so that we may expedite delivery through United Parcel Service (UPS) instead of parcel post. **(Please do not use for gifts.)**

C/O _____
ADDRESS _____ APT _____
CITY _____ STATE _____ ZIP _____

PAGE	ITEM #	QTY. 1 Set = 1 Qty.	ITEM DESCRIPTION	✔ FOR A GIFT BOX	MONOGRAM first name initial	MONOGRAM middle name initial	MONOGRAM last name initial	UNIT OR SET PRICE dollars	cents	TOTAL PRICE dollars	cents

#1 Name _____ Gift Message (please print) _____
Address _____
City _____ State _____ Zip _____

GIFT SECTION

#2 Name _____ Gift Message (please print) _____
Address _____
City _____ State _____ Zip _____

GIFT SECTION

***STATE SALES TAX CHART**
We are required to charge state and local sales tax on mail order purchases **delivered in** the following states where we have stores. Some local taxes vary from the state taxes shown below. Please include your local tax; we will notify you and make the appropriate adjustment for other areas if necessary. There is no state tax on food except in Tennessee.

STATE	STATE TAX	STATE	STATE TAX
Arizona	5%	New York:	
California	6%	Upstate	4%
Colorado	3%	Downstate	4¼%
Connecticut	7½%	NY City	8¼%
Florida	6%	Ohio	5%
Illinois	5% (plus local tax on food)	Oklahoma	5½%
Maryland	5%	Tennessee	5½% (incl. food)
Massachusetts	5%	Texas	6%
Minnesota	6%	Virginia	4½%
Missouri	4¼%	Washington, D.C.	6%
New Jersey	6%		

PACKING & DELIVERY	
For Orders Totaling	Include
Up to $15.99	$3.15
$16.00-30.99	$4.15
$31.00-40.99	$5.15
$41.00-50.99	$6.15
$51.00-75.99	$7.85
$76.00-100.99	$8.75
$101.00-150.99	$13.50
Over $151.00	$16.25

Total Merchandise Price	
Add $2.00 for each gift box	
Add applicable Sales Tax for shipment to states listed in chart at left*	
Add Packing and Delivery charges (see left) on **Total Merchandise Price** only	
Add $1.00 each for delivery to more than one address	
TOTAL	

HERB ORDERING INFORMATION: Please fill in the number of sets you wish to order on the form above. Then, be sure to write the quantity of each kind of herb in the spaces provided below. (For information on these herbs, see page 53.) Sorry, no gift wrap available.
Herbs can be mixed or matched. **Set of 6 plants** #46-50765 **$15.00**
Set of 12 plants #46-55137 **Special Price $24.00**

___ A. Chives   ___ K. Peppermint
___ B. Coriander   ___ L. Rosemary
___ C. Dill   ___ M. Holt's Mammoth Sage
___ D. English Thyme ___ N. Shallots
___ E. French Tarragon ___ O. Spearmint
___ F. Garlic   ___ P. Sweet Basil
___ G. Italian Parsley ___ Q. Sweet Marjoram
___ H. Oregano   ___ R. Watercress
___ J. Oriental Garlic ___ S. Winter Savory   ___ T. Bay Tree

PAYMENT METHOD: Enclose your personal check, money order, gift certificate, merchandise voucher or charge card information as indicated above. (Please do not send cash or stamps.)

☐ Check   ☐ MasterCard (16 digits)   ☐ Gift Certificate/
☐ Money Order   ☐ VISA (13 or 16 digits)   Merchandise Voucher
                  ☐ American Express (15 digits) $_____

Card Account Number: [1 | 2 | 3 | 4 | 5 | 6 | 7 | 8 | 9 | 10 | 11 | 12 | 13 | 14 | 15 | 16]

Expiration Date of Card [__ __] - [__ __]

Signature of Authorized Buyer _____

Price Guarantee: All prices are guaranteed through **September 30, 1989.**
Shipping Information: We ship all orders upon receipt, or will notify you promptly of any delay. Items ordered together are not necessarily shipped in the same box. We are unable to ship merchandise to foreign countries.
Items from Previous Catalogs: Please call or write our Customer Service Department for current prices and availability.
Duplicate Mailings: If you receive duplicates of our catalog, please copy exactly and/or enclose the mailing labels from all of them, indicating the proper name and address, and we will correct the situation.
A Message About Mailings: From time to time, we make portions of our own customer mailing lists available to other reputable, carefully selected organizations whose products or services we feel might be of interest to you. If you would rather **not** receive such mailings, please copy your mailing label exactly (or print or type your mailing address) and mail to: Williams-Sonoma, Mail Preference Service, P.O. Box 7456, San Francisco, CA 94120-7456.
© Copyright: Williams-Sonoma 1989. All rights reserved.

FOR PROMPT PERSONAL SERVICE ON CREDIT CARD ORDERS: Please call **(415) 421-4242**, 7 am to 7 pm, Monday through Friday, and 8 am to 4 pm, Saturday and Sunday **(Pacific Time)**. May we suggest you fill out this order form and read it to us over the phone.

FOR CUSTOMER SERVICE: Please call **(415) 421-4555**, 8 am to 4:30 pm **(Pacific Time)**, Monday through Friday. Sorry, we cannot accept collect calls.

THANK YOU FOR YOUR ORDER!

Copyright © Williams-Sonoma. Used with permission.

243

1 Soft and absorbent **Pop-Up Sponges** arrive looking like melba toast. But in water they expand to a plump 3" x 4" x 1", just right for dishes and cleaning up.
Regular Size *Sack of twelve*
#46-13284 $9.00
Large Size, 5½" x 3½" x 1½"
Sack of six #46-13292 $7.50

2 Brush up on kitchen basics with our **Grande Cuisine Kitchen Brush Set**. Use the white nylon bristle brush for cleaning non-stick pans, the natural tampico/brass for pots and pans, and the soft black horsehair for dishes. The extra large heads are attached to the natural wood handles with a metal band set within a groove. 10½" long, made in West Germany.
Set of four, one of each.
#46-330621 $9.75

3 **Folding Wire Dish Rack Set** has a vinyl-coated steel rack which holds 23 plates and 10 cups or glasses. It hangs or stows in a cupboard when not in use. White rack measures 17½" x 12¼" x 10¾" high open, 18" x 16" x 1½" wide folded; blue acrylic drainer mat is 15½" x 20"; blue cutlery basket is 7¾" x 2¼" x 4" high.
The set #46-121152 $24.50

4 The best glazed apricots come from the land down under. These whole, pitted **Glazed Australian Apricots** have a marvelously concentrated flavor and aroma, with a texture that is both chewy and tender. Serve as a dessert, alone or with fresh cream cheese and English wheat meal biscuits — a perfect combination. 2 lbs. packed in a wooden box.
#46-87874 $23.00

5 Traditional, straight-sided **French Confiture Glasses** can go from cupboard to table, or to friends' homes as gifts, when filled with homemade jams. They also make handy storage jars and casual drinking glasses. 12 oz. cap.
Set of six glasses and six lids.
#46-03319 $9.00
Additional **Confiture Lids**
Set of six #46-54916 $1.50

6 Make your own English marmalade with **Ma Made Prepared Thin Cut Seville Oranges**. Just add sugar and water to the contents of one tin, boil gently for 20 minutes, and you have 6 lbs. of delicious homemade marmalade. 1 lb. 13 oz. tins.
Set of two #46-95729 $12.00

Our *Grande Cuisine* symbol denotes a Williams-Sonoma exclusive.

Glycerine Kitchen Hand Cream is teamed with our **Liquid Glycerine Soap** for complete hand care. Both are unscented, hypo-allergenic and have no coloring agents. The soap lathers easily and the cream contains a non-greasy milk extract that is absorbed quickly and leaves hands soft. For use in kitchen or bath, the reusable, clear plastic pump bottles hold 11.8 oz. Made in Spain by Lidasa.
Liquid Glycerine Soap #46-130450 $8.00
Glycerine Kitchen Hand Cream #46-308106 $8.00
Special set, one of each. #46-308098
Special Price $13.00

We have supplied **Wenol Metal Polish** to satisfied customers for well over 50 years, and it's still the best! The non-abrasive polish has a base of jeweler's rouge that puts a lasting shine on copper, silver, gold and brass. Made in West Germany.
39.3 oz. Can
#46-142877 $20.00
3.9 oz. Tubes
Set of three
#46-142893 $15.75

May we send a catalog to a friend?
(Your name is automatically added to our mailing list when you order.)

Name _____
(Please print)   (WS219)

Address _____ Apt.

City _____

State _____ Zip

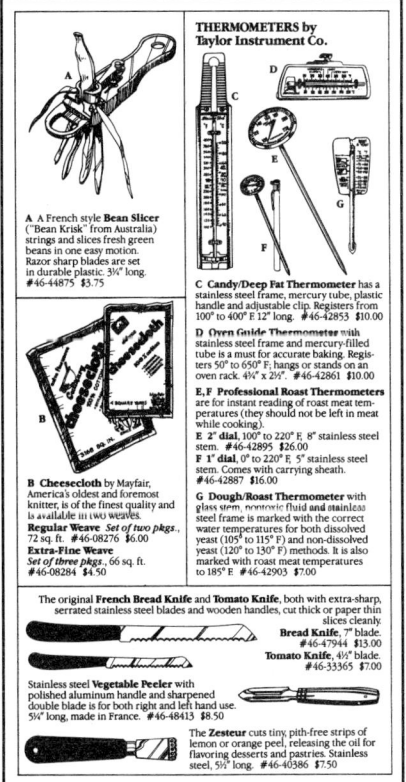

THERMOMETERS by Taylor Instrument Co.

A A French style **Bean Slicer** ("Bean Krisk" from Australia) strings and slices fresh green beans in one easy motion. Razor sharp blades are set in durable plastic. 3¾" long.
#46-44875 $3.75

C **Candy/Deep Fat Thermometer** has a stainless steel frame, mercury tube, plastic handle and adjustable clip. Registers from 100° to 400° F. 12" long. #46-42853 $10.00

D **Oven Guide Thermometer** with stainless steel frame and mercury-filled tube is a must for accurate baking. Registers 50° to 650° F; hangs or stands on an oven rack. 4¾" x 2½". #46-42861 $10.00

E, F Professional Roast Thermometers are for instant reading of roast meat temperatures (they should not be left in meat while cooking.).
E 2" dial, 100° to 220° F, 8" stainless steel stem. #46-42895 $26.00
F 1" dial, 0° to 220° F, 5" stainless steel stem. Comes with carrying sheath.
#46-42887 $16.00

B Cheesecloth by Mayfair, America's oldest and foremost knitter, is of the finest quality and is available in two weaves.
Regular Weave *Set of two pkgs.*, 72 sq. ft. #46-08276 $6.00
Extra-Fine Weave
Set of three pkgs., 66 sq. ft.
#46-08284 $4.50

G Dough/Roast Thermometer with glass stem, nontoxic fluid and stainless steel frame is marked with the correct water temperatures for both dissolved yeast (105° to 115° F) and non-dissolved yeast (120° to 130° F) methods. It is also marked with roast meat temperatures to 185° F. #46-42903 $7.00

The original **French Bread Knife** and **Tomato Knife**, both with extra-sharp, serrated stainless steel blades and wooden handles, cut thick or paper thin slices cleanly.
Bread Knife, 7" blade.
#46-47944 $13.00
Tomato Knife, 4½" blade.
#46-33365 $7.00

Stainless steel **Vegetable Peeler** with polished aluminum handle and sharpened double blade is for both right and left hand use. 5¼" long, made in France. #46-48413 $8.50

The **Zesteur** cuts tiny, pith-free strips of lemon or orange peel, releasing the oil for flavoring desserts and pastries. Stainless steel, 5½" long. #46-40386 $7.50

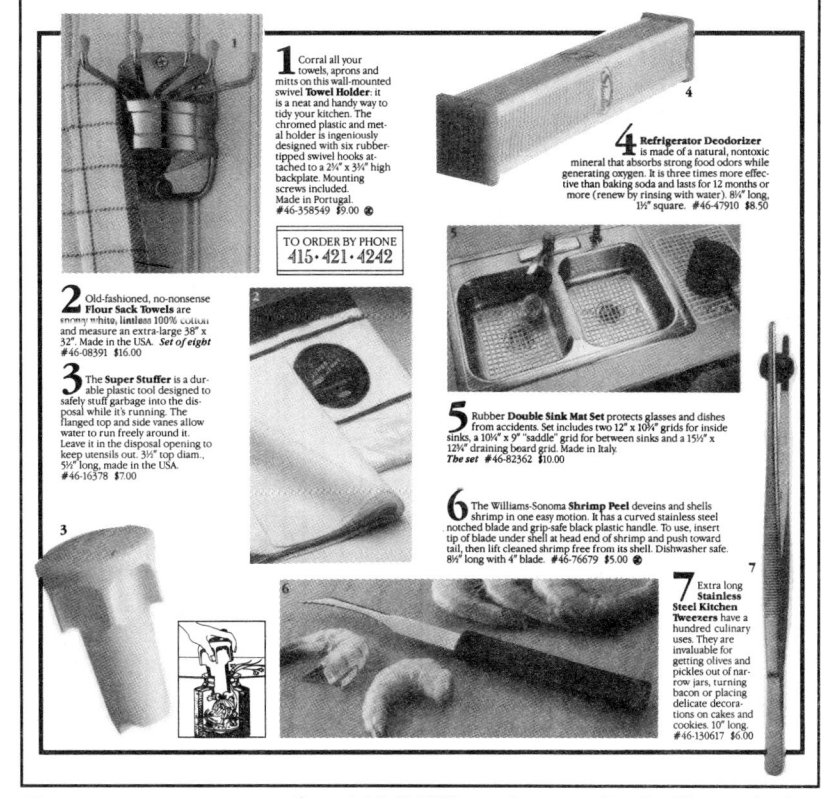

1 Corral all your towels, aprons and mitts on this wall-mounted swivel **Towel Holder**. It is a neat and handy way to tidy your kitchen. The chromed plastic and metal holder is ingeniously designed with six rubber-tipped swivel hooks attached to a 2¼" x 3¼" high backplate. Mounting screws included. Made in Portugal.
#46-358549 $9.00

TO ORDER BY PHONE
415 · 421 · 4242

2 Old-fashioned, no-nonsense **Flour Sack Towels** are snowy white, lintless 100% cotton and measure an extra-large 38" x 32". Made in the USA. *Set of eight*
#46-08391 $16.00

3 The **Super Stuffer** is a durable plastic tool designed to safely stuff garbage into the disposal while it's running. The flanged top and side vanes allow water to run freely around it. Leave it in the disposal opening to keep utensils out. 3½" top diam., 5½" long, made in the USA.
#46-16378 $7.00

4 Refrigerator Deodorizer is made of a natural, nontoxic mineral that absorbs strong food odors while generating oxygen. It is three times more effective than baking soda and lasts for 12 months or more (renew by rinsing with water). 8¼" long, 1½" square. #46-47910 $8.50

5 Rubber **Double Sink Mat Set** protects glasses and dishes from accidents. Set includes two 12" x 10¾" grids for inside sinks, a 10¾" x 9" "saddle" grid for between sinks and a 15½" x 12¾" draining board grid. Made in Italy.
The set #46-82362 $10.00

6 The Williams-Sonoma **Shrimp Peel** deveins and shells shrimp in one easy motion. It has a curved stainless steel notched blade and grip-ark black plastic handle. To use, insert tip of blade under shell at head end of shrimp and push toward tail, then lift cleaned shrimp free from its shell. Dishwasher safe. 8½" long with 4" blade. #46-76679 $5.00

7 Extra long **Stainless Steel Kitchen Tweezers** have a hundred culinary uses. They are invaluable for getting olives and pickles out of narrow jars, turning bacon or placing delicate decorations on cakes and cookies. 10" long.
#46-130617 $6.00

Copyright © Williams-Sonoma. Used with permission.

© COPYRIGHT 1991 DARTNELL CORPORATION

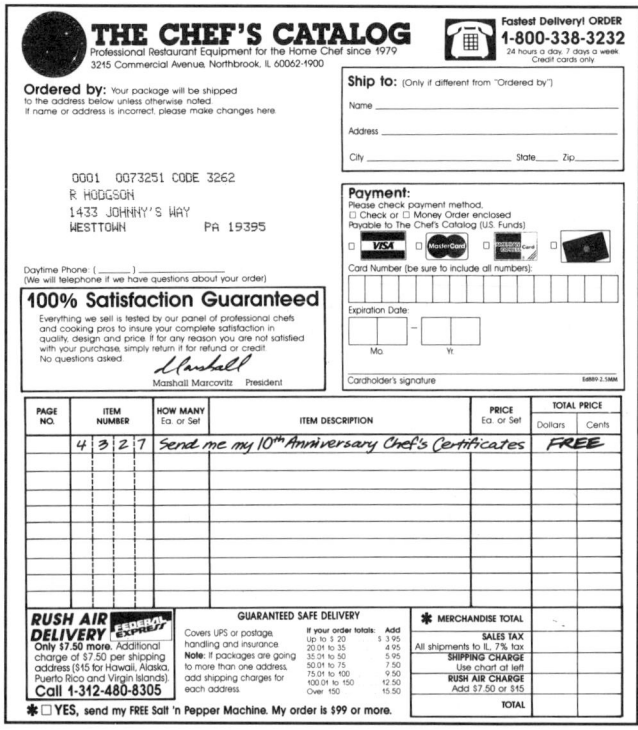

K1

K2

K3

K4

Copyright © The Chef's Catalog. Used with permission.

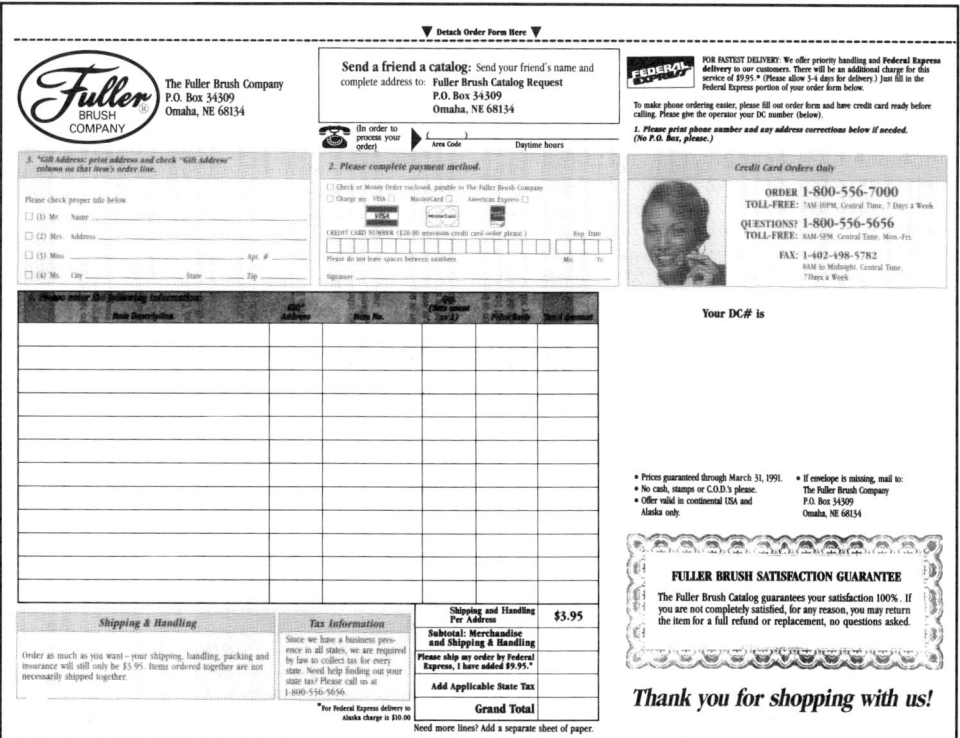

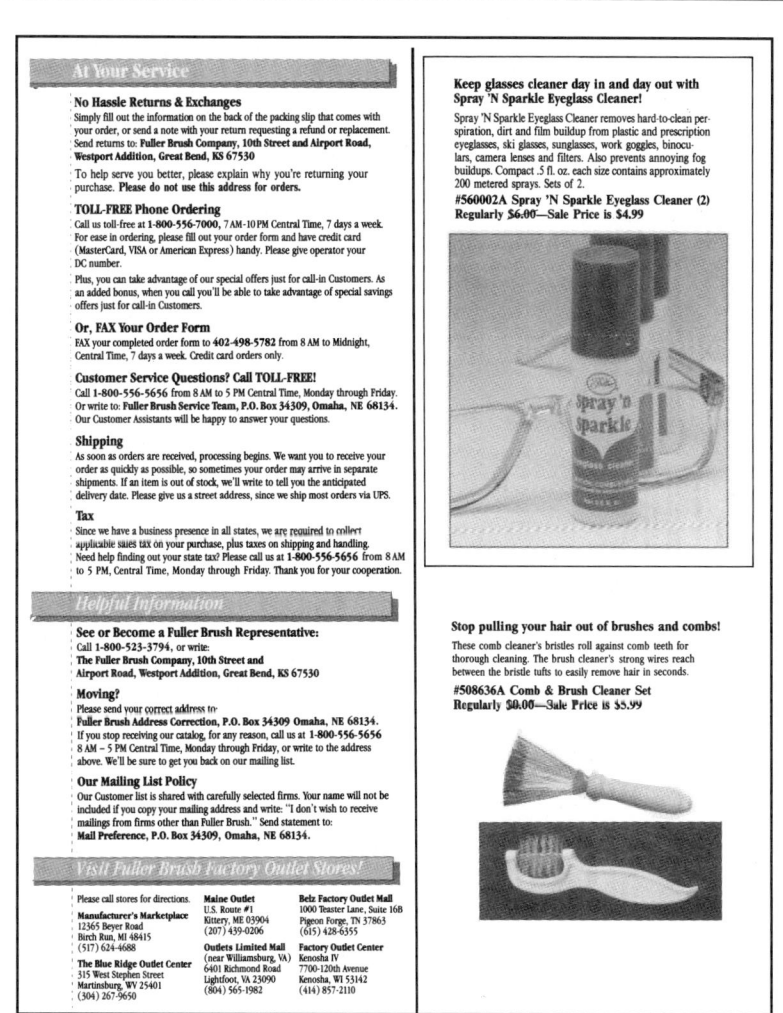

Copyright © Fuller Brush Co. Used with permission.

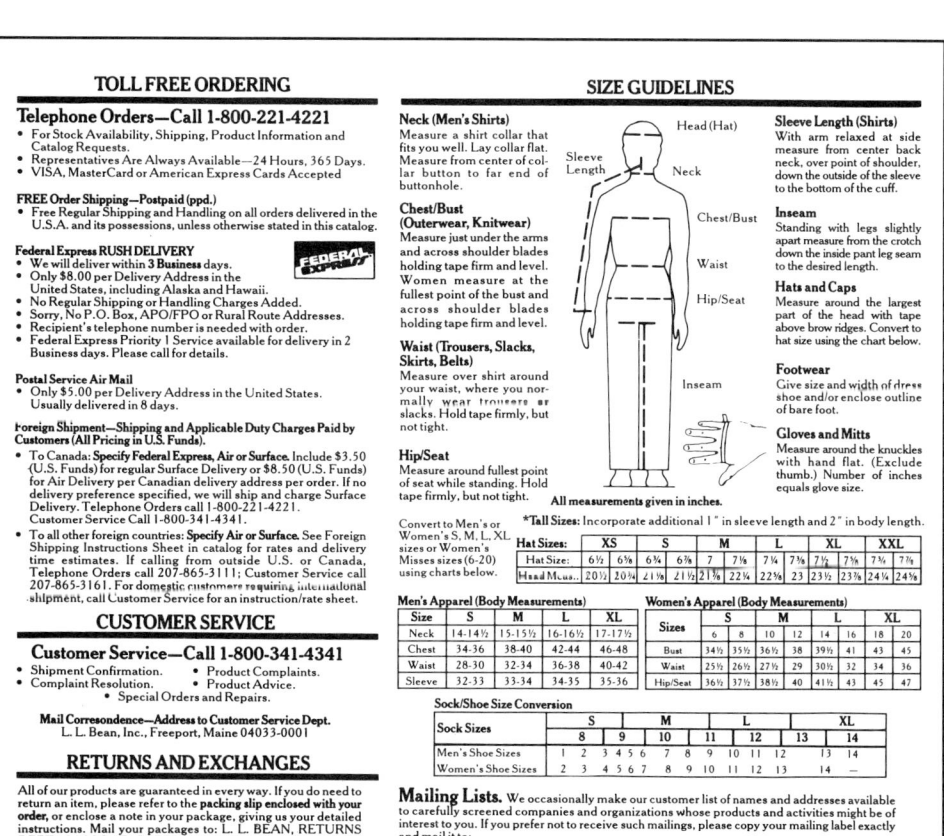

MEMINDEX ORDER FORM

149 Carter Street
Rochester, NY 14601

★ ★ ★ ★ ★ ★ ★ ★ ★ ★ ★ ★ ★

The Memindex Guarantee

You must be completely satisfied with each and every item ordered from Memindex or you may return it within 30 days for an immediate refund, credit or exchange. (Sorry, personalized items cannot be returned.)

★ ★ ★ ★ ★ ★ ★ ★ ★ ★ ★ ★ ★

FOR IMPRINTED PRODUCTS (PLEASE PRINT)

Line 1 ____________________

Line 2 ____________________

Line 3 ____________________

Line 4 ____________________

PEEL OFF LABEL FROM BACK COVER AND APPLY HERE

We need the label even if incorrect in order to speed your order. If label is missing or incorrect, make corrections to the right.

Use this space to correct label or if "ship to" is different from "bill to"

Name ____________________

Company ____________________

Address ____________________

City ____________________

State ____________________ Zip ____________________

Qty	Item #	Description/Color	Unit Cost	Total
			TOTAL ORDER	
			NY Res. Add Sales Tax	
			Amount Due	

IMPORTANT: Fill-in information below

Name of Person Placing Order ____________________

Daytime Phone Number ( ) ____________________

FREE SHIPPING
When your check accompanies order

PAYMENT METHOD

☐ Check or Money Order Enclosed. (I SAVE ALL SHIPPING CHARGES)

☐ VISA ☐ MASTER CARD ☐ AMERICAN EXPRESS (Plus Shipping)

Card Number ____________________ Exp. Date ________

Signature ____________________

☐ Please open an account and bill company (plus shipping). **Net 10 days to companies listed and rated with Dun & Bradstreet only.**

To open account PLEASE ATTACH 3 TRADE REFERENCES AND BANK REFERENCES to this order form or your P.O.

Please allow 10 working days to process this information. If rush shipment is required, prepayment by check or credit card will rush your order through.

01

Memindex

SATISFACTION GUARANTEED SINCE 1902

FREE DELIVERY

When Your Check Accompanies Your Order You can save all shipping, handling, and delivery charges when you include your check with your order. (Next Day and Second Day UPS charges excluded.)

ORDER TOLL FREE

8 AM to 8 PM Eastern Time

(800) 828-5885

Ordering from Memindex is fast and easy. Simply call (800) 828-5885 toll-free anytime 8 AM to 8 PM Eastern Time.

SEND NO MONEY

Opening an account at Memindex is easy. If you're well rated by Dun & Bradstreet, that's all we need to know. Our terms are net 30 days following the day of shipment. For greater convenience you can charge your order to VISA, MasterCard or American Express.

24 HOUR SHIPPING On All

Stock Items No need to wait...most orders are shipped within 24 hours of receipt via UPS whenever possible. (Personalized items take slightly longer.) For items not marked with our Quick Ship symbol, please allow 2 to 3 weeks for delivery.

FAST FAX ORDERING

(716) 342-0146 Simply call our FAX number (716) 342-0146 and we'll speed your order on to you—THE SAME DAY WE RECEIVE IT—on all stock items!

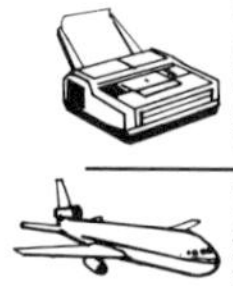

NEED IT TOMORROW?

Simply call us today. We'll ship your order via Next Day or Second Day UPS. (Next Day and Second Day charges will be added to invoice.)

Thank you for your Order!

02

Copyright © Memindex. Used with permission.

Current® Order Blank

Summer 1989

This order blank lists products in the Summer 1989 catalog only. To order products from other Current catalogs and flyers, please use the blank spaces on page F.

SAVE UP TO 65% OFF THE REGULAR PRICE OF OUR ICE CREAM SERVING SET!
Simply remove the sticker from the cover of your catalog and place it here. With an order of any size, you can buy our 9-piece Ice Cream Serving Set (sold on catalog page 4) for just $4.95— a savings of up to 65% on each set you buy! To order, see item #21-107137 below. Offer expires Aug. 1, 1989.

PLACE STICKER HERE

Important: Please read before ordering:

How can I receive your lowest Quantity Discount prices?

You and your friends can receive a discount, depending on the total number of items in your order! Simply count the total number of items you plan to order and enter the total here: [ ]

- **If your total order is for 1 through 7 items,** use the first price listed.
- **If your total order is for 8 through 15 items,** use the middle price.
- **If your total order is for 16 or more items,** use the lowest price.

You may order any combination of items to earn Quantity Discounts. For instance, to earn the lowest price, you may order 16 different products or 16 of one product or any other combination of items that totals 16 or more. (Assortments, such as gift wrap and card assortments, **each** count as **one** item.)

PLEASE NOTE: Your entire Select-A-Card purchase counts as **one item** when determining your Quantity Discount. To order, see page F.

What's the last date I can order from this catalog?

Products in this catalog will be available and prices are guaranteed through December 18, 1989.

Do I have to pay shipping charges?

No! Current pays all shipping costs when you enclose payment with your order. You pay only a $2.00 handling fee.

Do I have to pay sales tax?

You must pay state sales tax only if your order is being shipped to California or Colorado. For Colorado delivery add 3%; for California delivery add 6% (see STEP 3).

May I charge my order?

Yes! If you prefer to charge your order to Current, we'll bill you for shipping costs (20¢ per item). Payment must be received within 30 days after your order shipment date. Charge orders are subject to credit approval, and you may be contacted by our Customer Service staff. Your daytime phone is required for charge orders (see STEP 5).

What if I have a question or problem with my order?

Our Customer Service staff will be happy to answer questions about your order. Just call toll-free 1-800-525-7170 weekdays, 6 a.m. to 6 p.m. Mountain Time.

If not satisfied, can I get my money back?

You bet! You must be totally delighted with our products and our service, or we'll promptly replace your order or refund your money.

A Note about Substitutions: You can expect just about every item you order to be readily available. However, if an item you've ordered is no longer in stock, we may substitute a similar item of equal or greater value. If we do make a substitution, you'll get a note with your order offering you a refund if you don't want the substitute product.

When will I receive my order?

You can expect fast service! Normally you can expect to receive your order in 2-3 weeks. For fastest service, use Express Delivery! For an extra charge of $9.85 per order, we'll ship **available products** by air express, so you can expect delivery in a week or less. For mail orders, be sure to check the Express Delivery box in STEP 3 on the back page and include a street address for delivery. For details or **to order by phone, call (719) 593-5900.** NOTE: Personalized items will be shipped separately and cannot be shipped by Express Delivery; please allow up to 6 weeks for delivery.

We welcome your comments or suggestions at any time.

EXPRESS PROCESSING CENTER
COLORADO SPRINGS, COLORADO 80941

STEP 1 Make your selections from pages C through G.

Summer, pgs. 2-7

ORDER CODE No. Items 1-7 / 8-15 / 16+	HOW MANY ITEMS	TOTAL AMOUNT
1-108458 $8.25/6.60/4.95		
2-107039 $4.55/3.55/2.50		
3-107057 $2.55/2.00/1.40		
4-107048 $2.55/2.00/1.40		
5-023833 $6.25/5.25/4.25		
6-107299 $10.85/8.70/6.50		
7-117199 $11.60/9.30/6.95		
8-107306 $9.95/8.95/7.95		
9-107324 $8.25/6.60/4.95		
10-015218 $7.25/6.25/5.25		
11-107565 $7.75/6.75/5.75		
12-111818 $5.55/4.55/3.55		
13-107574 $7.20/5.60/3.95		
14-070461 $5.90/4.85/3.80		
15-107011 $3.55/2.75/1.95		
16-107226 $5.95/4.60/3.25		
17-107164 $4.85/3.75/2.65		
18-014610 $8.25/6.60/4.95		
19-107100 $2.75/2.15/1.50		
20-012587 $6.85/5.30/3.75		
21-107137 Through Aug. 1: $4.95 After Aug. 1: $14.25/12.10/9.95		
22-107155 $3.00/2.35/1.65		
23-107128 $9.95/7.95/5.95		
24-045926 $8.95/7.25/5.50		
25-107253 $2.30/1.80/1.25		
COLUMN TOTALS:		

ORDER CODE No. Items 1-7 / 8-15 / 16+	HOW MANY ITEMS	TOTAL AMOUNT
26-107182 $3.40/2.65/1.85		
27-107173 $9.95/7.95/5.95		
28-118606 $4.45/3.45/2.45		
29-107235 $7.20/5.60/3.95		
30-107707 $12.80/10.90/8.95		
31-107636 $5.40/4.20/2.95		
32-107690 $6.95/5.95/4.95		
33-107716 $4.85/3.75/2.65		
34-107609 $4.30/3.35/2.35		
35-107592 $2.10/1.65/1.15		
36-107618 $7.20/5.60/3.95		
37-107789 $4.55/3.55/2.50		
38-011212 $2.55/2.00/1.40		
39-011203 $2.55/2.00/1.40		
40-107770 $7.10/5.70/4.25		
41-107761 $3.55/2.75/1.95		
42-107725 $8.60/6.90/5.15		
43-048549 $8.25/6.60/4.95		
44-046088 $2.60/2.10/1.55		
45-107752 $7.25/5.80/4.35		
46-111809 $6.10/5.95/5.85		
Suzy's Zoo®, pgs. 8-10		
47-081672 $6.10/4.75/3.35		
48-081645 $4.55/3.55/2.50		
49-081707 $3.45/2.70/1.90		
50-080717 $5.65/4.40/3.10		
51-081690 $8.25/6.60/4.95		
COLUMN TOTALS:		

TOTAL ITEMS ON PAGE C __________

TOTAL AMOUNT ON PAGE C $__________

Transfer Page C totals to Order Summary on last page.

P1

ORDER CODE No. Items 1-7 / 8-15 / 16+	HOW MANY ITEMS	TOTAL AMOUNT
52-081681 $3.30/2.55/1.80		
53-081743 $3.20/2.50/1.75		
54-081654 $4.55/3.55/2.50		
55-081663 $3.30/2.55/1.80		
56-081752 $6.10/4.75/3.35		
57-081761 $3.95/3.05/2.15		
58-081716 $4.55/3.55/2.50		
59-081734 $2.40/1.85/1.30		
60-080691 $3.75/2.90/2.05		
61-081841 $3.40/2.65/1.85		
Flavia, pg. 11		
62-094052 $3.20/2.50/1.75		
63-094061 $2.40/1.85/1.30		
64-094141 $3.20/2.50/1.75		
65-094301 $3.85/3.00/2.10		
66-094070 $1.85/1.45/1.00		
67-094285 $7.00/5.45/3.85		
Correspondence, pgs. 12-17		
68-106003 $3.55/2.75/1.95		
69-106110 $3.55/2.75/1.95		
70-106094 $3.55/2.75/1.95		
71-106030 $3.55/2.75/1.95		
72-027839 $3.55/2.75/1.95		
73-027811 $3.55/2.75/1.95		
74-027731 $3.55/2.75/1.95		
75-075260 $3.55/2.75/1.95		
76-076152 $3.55/2.75/1.95		
77-050143 $3.55/2.75/1.95		
78-106156 $3.55/2.75/1.95		
79-027624 $3.55/2.75/1.95		
80-106021 $3.55/2.75/1.95		
COLUMN TOTALS:		

ORDER CODE No. Items 1-7 / 8-15 / 16+	HOW MANY ITEMS	TOTAL AMOUNT
81-107280 $3.55/2.75/1.95		
82-027633 $3.55/2.75/1.95		
83-075536 $3.55/2.75/1.95		
84-106138 $3.55/2.75/1.95		
85-106147 $3.55/2.75/1.95		
86-027642 $3.55/2.75/1.95		
87-106049 $3.55/2.75/1.95		
88-106058 $3.20/2.50/1.75		
89-106067 $3.20/2.50/1.75		
90-106085 $3.20/2.50/1.75		
91-106076 $3.20/2.50/1.75		
92-106101 $2.95/2.30/1.60		
93-106129 $7.50/6.00/4.50		
94-077623 $5.30/4.10/2.90		
95-027688 $3.85/3.00/2.10		
96-106192 $7.00/5.45/3.85		
97-106174 $9.95/7.95/5.95		
98-074733 $3.85/3.00/2.10		
99-106209 $9.45/7.55/5.65		
100-106183 $4.30/3.35/2.35		
101-075527 $6.75/5.25/3.70		
102-106012 $5.10/3.95/2.80		
103-027697 $4.30/3.35/2.35		
Gift Wrap & Accessories, pgs. 18-24		
104-071656 $8.25/6.60/4.95		
105-071665 $2.55/2.00/1.40		
106-071674 $2.55/2.00/1.40		
107-071727 $2.55/2.00/1.40		
108-117634 $2.55/2.00/1.40		
109-072316 $8.25/6.60/4.95		
110-111587 $2.55/2.00/1.40		
COLUMN TOTALS:		

ORDER CODE No. Items 1-7 / 8-15 / 16+	HOW MANY ITEMS	TOTAL AMOUNT
111-072414 $2.55/2.00/1.40		
112-111596 $2.55/2.00/1.40		
113-018705 $2.55/2.00/1.40		
114-071059 $10.50/8.95/7.35		
115-018901 $2.55/2.00/1.40		
116-071638 $2.55/2.00/1.40		
117-071594 $2.55/2.00/1.40		
118-071610 $2.55/2.00/1.40		
119-071479 $2.55/2.00/1.40		
120-071629 $2.55/2.00/1.40		
121-076330 $10.50/8.95/7.35		
122-076376 $2.55/2.00/1.40		
123-076358 $2.55/2.00/1.40		
124-076394 $2.55/2.00/1.40		
125-076349 $2.55/2.00/1.40		
126-076367 $2.55/2.00/1.40		
127-076385 $2.55/2.00/1.40		
128-073529 $4.55/3.55/2.50		
129-073510 $4.55/3.55/2.50		
130-107404 $4.55/3.55/2.50		
131-108056 $11.65/9.90/8.15		
132-117242 $5.65/4.40/3.10		
133-117251 $5.65/4.40/3.10		
134-117260 $10.25/8.20/6.15		
135-107681 $7.45/5.95/4.45		
136-023753 $5.75/4.45/3.15		
137-043205 $5.75/4.45/3.15		
138-107663 $5.40/4.20/2.95		
139-107985 $5.40/4.20/2.95		
140-108047 $4.55/3.55/2.50		
141-107413 $12.15/10.35/8.50		
COLUMN TOTALS:		

ORDER CODE No. Items 1-7 / 8-15 / 16+	HOW MANY ITEMS	TOTAL AMOUNT
142-107976 $2.65/2.05/1.45		
143-043642 $1.75/1.35/.95		
144-065850 $2.10/1.65/1.15		
145-107994 $2.30/1.80/1.25		
146-108029 $3.20/2.50/1.75		
147-108001 $1.75/1.35/.95		
148-108010 $2.00/1.55/1.10		
149-108369 $11.75/10.00/8.20		
150-108403 $3.95/3.05/2.15		
151-108396 $3.95/3.05/2.15		
152-108378 $3.95/3.05/2.15		
153-108387 $3.95/3.05/2.15		
154-077400 $11.75/10.00/8.20		
155-077437 $3.95/3.05/2.15		
156-077428 $3.95/3.05/2.15		
157-077446 $3.95/3.05/2.15		
158-077419 $3.95/3.05/2.15		
159-107510 $11.75/10.00/8.20		
160-107538 $3.95/3.05/2.15		
161-107529 $3.95/3.05/2.15		
162-107547 $3.95/3.05/2.15		
163-111603 $3.95/3.05/2.15		
164-036491 $11.75/10.00/8.20		
165-036605 $3.95/3.05/2.15		
166-036507 $3.95/3.05/2.15		
167-036650 $3.95/3.05/2.15		
168-036516 $3.95/3.05/2.15		
169-076401 $11.75/10.00/8.20		
170-076438 $3.95/3.05/2.15		
171-076447 $3.95/3.05/2.15		
172-076429 $3.95/3.05/2.15		
COLUMN TOTALS:		

ORDER CODE No. Items 1-7 / 8-15 / 16+	HOW MANY ITEMS	TOTAL AMOUNT
173-076410 $3.95/3.05/2.15		
174-076456 $11.15/9.50/7.80		
175-076465 $3.85/3.00/2.10		
176-076474 $3.85/3.00/2.10		
177-077357 $3.85/3.00/2.10		
178-077366 $3.85/3.00/2.10		
179-108118 $6.95/5.55/4.15		
180-108136 $3.95/3.05/2.15		
181-108127 $3.95/3.05/2.15		
182-108412 $10.45/8.35/6.25		
183-108421 $5.75/4.45/3.15		
184-108430 $5.75/4.45/3.15		
185-108083 $6.95/5.55/4.15		
186-108092 $3.95/3.05/2.15		
187-108109 $3.95/3.05/2.15		
188-036918 $6.95/5.55/4.15		
189-010669 $3.95/3.05/2.15		
190-010632 $3.95/3.05/2.15		
191-036730 $6.95/5.55/4.15		
192-036892 $3.95/3.05/2.15		
193-036909 $3.95/3.05/2.15		
194-108332 $6.95/5.55/4.15		
195-108341 $3.95/3.05/2.15		
196-108350 $3.95/3.05/2.15		
Heavenly Dreamers, pg. 25		
197-106824 $3.10/2.40/1.70		
198-014148 $3.95/3.05/2.15		
199-014308 $2.45/1.90/1.35		
200-107495 $2.30/1.80/1.25		
201-106815 $6.10/4.75/3.35		
Warm & Whimsical, pgs. 26-27		
COLUMN TOTALS:		

TOTAL ITEMS ON PAGE D __________ **TOTAL AMOUNT ON PAGE D $**__________

Transfer Page D totals to Order Summary on last page.

P2

Copyright © Current, Inc. Used with permission.

© COPYRIGHT 1991 DARTNELL CORPORATION

Copyright © Current, Inc. Used with permission.

LILLIAN VERNON®

LILLIAN VERNON CORPORATION
510 SOUTH FULTON AVENUE
MOUNT VERNON, NY 10550

CHARGE IT! 914-633-6300
Call 24 hours a day, 7 days a week!
FOR CUSTOMER SERVICE:
call 914-633-6400, 9 a.m. to 5 p.m. E.T., Monday-Friday.

SEND A FRIEND A CATALOG!
We'll mail our next regular catalog with your compliments if you print your name below. Be sure to give the zip code.

NAME
ADDRESS — APT. NO.
CITY — STATE — ZIP
YOUR NAME

Your package will be shipped to the address below unless otherwise noted.
If name or address is incorrect, please make change here.

009110512

RICHARD S HODGSON
1433 JOHNNY S WAY
WESTTOWN PA 19395

SHIP TO ME AT ANOTHER ADDRESS:
I wish to receive my order at the address below.
For gift orders use the bottom of this form.

NAME
COMPANY — FLOOR NO.
ADDRESS — APT. NO.
CITY
STATE — ZIP

YOUR DAYTIME TELEPHONE NO. — 009110000

CHARGE ORDERS ($20 minimum)
We need expiration date and signature to ship your order.

CARD NUMBER — EXP. DATE — SIGNATURE

PLEASE CHECK CARD USED
☐ VISA ☐ MASTER CARD ☐ AMERICAN EXPRESS (& OPTIMA) ☐ DISCOVER ☐ DINER'S CLUB

PAGE NO.	SEND THESE ITEMS TO ME (TO SEND GIFTS SEE BELOW)	ITEM NUMBER	QTY.	INITIALS First / Mid. / Last Name	PERSONALIZATION (Write "NONE" if no personalization is desired.)	PRICE EACH	TOTAL PRICE

NAME
ADDRESS — APT. NO.
CITY — STATE — ZIP

GIFT FROM
GIFT MESSAGE

PAGE NO.	NAME OF ITEM	ITEM NUMBER	QTY.	INITIALS First / Mid. / Last Name	PERSONALIZATION (Write "NONE" if no personalization is desired.)	PRICE EACH	TOTAL PRICE

NEED MORE ROOM?
JUST ATTACH AN ADDITIONAL PIECE OF PAPER.
ENCLOSE CHECK OR MONEY ORDER
(SORRY, NO CASH OR C.O.D.'S)

SATISFACTION GUARANTEED

Thank You for Shopping Lillian Vernon

SHIPPING AND HANDLING CHARGES
Covers postage or UPS handling and insurance for guaranteed delivery.
Up to $10..............................$2.95
$10.01 to $20........................$3.95
$20.01 to $35........................$4.95
$35.01 to $50........................$5.95
$50.01 to $75........................$7.25
$75.01 to $100......................$8.25
$100.01 to $150....................$9.50
Over $150............................$11.00

MERCHANDISE TOTAL Charge orders $20 min.
SHIPPING TO MORE THAN ONE ADDRESS ($2.00 EACH)
SHIPPING & HANDLING CHARGE Use chart at left
SUBTOTAL
SALES TAX (on subtotal) All Shipments to NY State and VA only
ORDER TOTAL

Copyright © Lillian Vernon Corp. Used with permission.

THE NATURE COMPANY

A CML Company Since 1983

CALL TOLL-FREE 1-800-227-1114 24-Hours A Day

4

THE NATURE COMPANY
P.O. BOX 2310
BERKELEY, CA 94702

Sold To: (Make any corrections necessary)

```
6102J              01
SARGEANT HOUSE
R HODGSON BOX 299
1433 JOHNNYS WAY
WESTTOWN       PA 19395
```

Alternate Shipping or Gift Address

A Name
Address
City   State   Zip
Message

	Item #	Size	Qty.	Description	Gift Box $2.50 ea.	Price Each	Total	Circle gift or alternate shipping address	
1								A B C D E	*For shipping to gift or alternative addresses, circle A, B, C, D or E in column at left. Items not so marked will be shipped to "Sold To" address. Please calculate shipping charges for each address.*
2								A B C D E	
3								A B C D E	
4								A B C D E	
5								A B C D E	
6								A B C D E	
7								A B C D E	
8								A B C D E	
9								A B C D E	

Shipping/Insurance Charges
(For each address) U.S.A. only

Purchase Amt.	Surface
$ 0 - $30.00	$3.95
$30.01 - $50.00	$5.50
$50.01 - $75.00	$7.25
$75.01 +	$8.50

FEDERAL EXPRESS
(next day delivery) add $12.00 to regular shipping charges and check here ☐
(2 day delivery) add $5.00 to regular shipping charges and check here ☐

Total Merchandise

Sales Tax: For shipments going to CA, MA, NJ, NY, D.C., PA, MD, FL, VA, WA and MN, please use appropriate local tax rate. Indicate rate in box at right.

Shipping (each address): see chart at left. Add any special charges listed with item.

Federal Express: 2-Day; Add $5.00 Overnight; Add $12.00

Gift Box ($2.50 per item)

Total Order

Office Use Only

Method of Payment: Check ☐ VISA ☐ American Express ☐ Mastercard ☐   Signature _____

Acct. No. [   ]   Expires: Mo. [ ] Yr. [ ]

Gift Addresses

B Name
Address
City   State   Zip
Message

C Name
Address
City   State   Zip
Message

D Name
Address
City   State   Zip
Message

E Name
Address
City   State   Zip
Message

R

Copyright © The Nature Company. Used with permission.

Selective Software
903 Pacific Ave. Suite 301, Santa Cruz, CA 95060

ORDERED BY

CODE A276
R. SHODGSON
SARGEANT HOUSE
1433 JOHNNYS WAY
WESTTOWN PA 19395

If your address is not imprinted here please enter your ID Code from the mail label on the back cover.

SHIP TO

Name _____

Address _____

City _____ State _____ Zip _____

Daytime phone _____

1-800-423-3556
Order 24hrs A Day
Technical Support/Returns:
9am – 5pm PST, Mon. Through Fri.

ITEM NUMBER	DESCRIPTION	QTY.	TOTAL

SHIPPING & HANDLING

(AK, HI, P.R. 2nd day air only)
We do not ship outside of U.S.,
U.S. territories or Canada.
CANADIAN ORDERS— Call (408) 423-3556

☐ UPS Ground: $4.95, 3 or more items: $6.95
☐ UPS 2nd Day Air: $7.95, 3 or more: $9.95
☐ Overnight: $15.95, 3 or more items: $19.95

Subtotal	
CA residents add 6½% sales tax — Tax	
See shipping and handling rates for charges — Delivery	
Grand Total	

METHOD OF PAYMENT

☐ VISA ☐ MASTER CARD ☐ CHECK/MONEY ORDER
☐ COD (add $7.50 to regular shipping charges)

Account No. _____ VISA requires 13 or 16 digits; MasterCard requires 16 digits; Mo. __ Yr. __

Signature (required for credit card orders) _____

Purchase orders must be attached and are subject to credit approval. $100 minimum purchase.

ORDERING MADE FAST & EASY!

For fastest delivery possible . . .
When you call, please have your VISA or Master Card and the following information in front of you: 1) Product name and item number, (2) the ID Code shown on this order form or your mailing label.
Order by FAX: (408) 423-3661.
To order by check or money order . . .
Use this order form and self-addressed envelope. (Mail orders can also be charged to VISA, Master Card or American Express.)
On all orders . . .
Be sure to include a shipping and handling charge.
California residents, please add 6½% sales tax.
Most orders shipped within 48 hours . . .

YOUR SATISFACTION GUARANTEED

The Selective guarantee is iron-clad in your favor. It allows you to return any product within 30 days, of receipt for full cash refund—no quibbles, no questions—or for full credit toward the purchase of any other item in the catalog.
Products must be returned in original condition, with invoices, original packing materials, warranties and all documents enclosed.
Please send through UPS or U.S. Postal Service (insured, certified, or registered). Selective Software is not liable for lost packages. Please call 1-800-423-3556 for a Return Authorization Number.

OUR TECHNICAL-SUPPORT TEAM IS AT YOUR SERVICE.

If you have any questions about any of our products, our highly knowledgeable technical support team is standing by to give you all the help you need. Call 1-800 423-3556, Monday through Friday, 9 a.m. to 5 p.m., P.S.T.

FOR FASTER SERVICE ON P.O.'s USE OUR FAX
(408) 423-3661

Copyright © Selective Software. Used with permission.

© COPYRIGHT 1991 DARTNELL CORPORATION

ORDER FORM

The Drawing Board
39910
P.O. Box 620004 Dallas, TX 75262-0004

CALL TOLL FREE 1-800-527-9530
Monday-Friday 8:00 A.M.-6:00 P.M. CST

At all other times, your message will be taken by our MESSAGE CENTER and we'll return your call by 10 a.m. the next business day.

1 ORDERED BY: (Recipient of catalog. Future catalogs will be mailed to this address.)

```
KEY 23307        ID 2153990962
MR R HODGSON
SARGEANT HOUSE
1433 JOHNNYS WAY
WESTTOWN              PA 19395
```

FOR CUSTOMER SERVICE
817-283-9373
Monday-Friday (8 A.M. to 5 P.M. CST)

FILL OUT IMPRINT INFORMATION ON THE REVERSE SIDE...

TOLL-FREE FAX #: 800-292-3729 24 hours a day.

SHIPPING INFORMATION
Stock items (products that do not require printing of your name, etc.) are shipped within 24 hours after receipt of your order. Most imprinted items are shipped in 6 working days or less. For imprinted items, please fill out pertinent information in sections 5-9.

------- IMPORTANT! -------
If the name shown above is different from the name of the person placing this order, please make correction above and check one of these boxes.
☐ Mail only to new name shown above.   ☐ Continue mailing to both names.

IMPORTANT: To process your order we must have your billing phone number.

Billing Phone # : (_____)_____

2 SHIP TO: (Fill in only if different from Ordered By. Please print.)
For delivery, please provide street address instead of P.O. Box.

Phone No. (_____)_____

Firm Name _____

ATTENTION _____

Street Address _____ Floor, Room or Suite No. _____

City _____ State ____ Zip ____

3 BILL TO: (Fill in only if different from Ordered By. Please Print.)

Firm Name _____

ATTENTION _____

Street Address _____ Floor, Room, Suite _____

City _____ State ____ Zip ____

4 ORDER UNIMPRINTED ITEMS HERE (Items NOT personalized with your name & address)

Quantity	Item #	Page #	Color	Description/Size	Unit Price	TOTAL

IMPRINTED ITEMS

It is important that your order be as detailed as possible. When ordering imprinted items, refer to the appropriate box for that product category (either section 5 or 6) and fill in completely and accurately. Incomplete order forms may delay your order. Thank you!

5 ORDER FORMS, CHECKS AND LABELS HERE ▶ FILL OUT IMPRINT INFORMATION ON THE REVERSE SIDE

Qty.	Item #	Pg. #	Color of Check Background	Print Trademarks or Logos	Consecutive Number	Starting Number	Description	Unit Price	TOTAL
				☐ Yes Logo #____ ☐ No	☐ Yes ☐ No				
				☐ Yes Logo #____ ☐ No	☐ Yes ☐ No				
				☐ Yes Logo #____ ☐ No	☐ Yes ☐ No				

NUMBERED LABELS INFORMATION A-J (except I) or blank ☐   0-9 (fill in all 6 numbers) ☐ ☐ ☐ ☐ ☐ ☐   A-J (except I) or blank ☐ ☐

6 ORDER BUSINESS CARDS, LETTERHEADS AND ENVELOPES HERE ▶ FILL OUT IMPRINT INFORMATION ON THE REVERSE SIDE

Qty.	Item #	Pg. #	Paper Stock	Paper Color	Print Trademarks or Logos	Type Style/Size	Layout #	Ink Color	Description	Unit Price	TOTAL
					☐ Yes Logo #____ ☐ No						
					☐ Yes Logo #____ ☐ No						
					☐ Yes Logo #____ ☐ No						

7 IMPORTANT INFORMATION

Is this your first order? ☐ Yes ☐ No
If yes, please provide bank reference and account number.

Bank Name & Address: _____

Type of Payment
☐ Check or Money Order (enclosed)
☐ Open Account
☐ Credit Card (Check One) — MasterCard / VISA

Card Holder Signature _____
Card Holder Name (Please print) _____
Purchase Order # _____
Card Number ☐☐☐☐ ☐☐☐☐ ☐☐☐☐ ☐☐☐☐

Account # _____
(___)___
Bank Phone # _____
Tax Exempt # _____

Master Card Interbank No. _____
Card Expires Mo./Yr. _____

ADDITIONAL CHARGES	$ AMOUNT
Logo or Art Charges (applies to imprinting only)	$
Consecutive Number Charges (applies to imprinting only)	$
Special Type and/or Extra Type Charge	$
SUBTOTAL	$
TAX CA, IL, TX and CT Residents Add Appropriate Tax.	$
Packing, Handling and Guaranteed Delivery	$ 1.95
TOTAL (Shipping Charges Additional)	$

Discounts in this catalog cannot be combined with other discounts.

▶ FILL OUT IMPRINT INFORMATION ON THE REVERSE SIDE

Copyright © The Wheeler Group. Used with permission.

8 IMPRINT INFORMATION

Please print clearly the information you want imprinted. If you are ordering more than three imprinted messages, use a separate sheet of paper for each and attach. Proofread what you write! Your imprint will read exactly as written. Phone number will not be printed on the items unless specified.

Item # _____ Print phone # on item # _____

1st line _____
2nd line _____
3rd line _____
4th line _____
5th line _____
6th line _____
7th line _____
8th line _____

Item # _____ Print phone # on item # _____

1st line _____
2nd line _____
3rd line _____
4th line _____
5th line _____
6th line _____
7th line _____
8th line _____

Item # _____ Print phone # on item # _____

1st line _____
2nd line _____
3rd line _____
4th line _____
5th line _____
6th line _____
7th line _____
8th line _____

DRAWING BOARD STOCK LOGOS

We will imprint any of the stock logos illustrated here for $4.00 per item. Specify logo # on order form.

© Wheeler Group, Inc. 1989

9 BROOKHOLLOW GREETING CARDS

Use this imprint section to specify the imprint you want for items on pages 24-29. Print your message exactly as you want it and proofread what you write!

STANDARD PERSONALIZATION: Your name and address printed in black ink. 4 lines maximum.

Item #(s): _____
_____
_____
_____
_____

ENVELOPE IMPRINT: Printed in black ink on back of envelope. 3 lines maximum.

Item #(s): _____
_____
_____
_____

GREETING CARDS (shown on pages 24-29): Custom sentiment for interior of card. 10 lines maximum. 45 characters per line maximum.

Select typestyle (Shown on page 26):
☐ STYLE H ☐ STYLE K ☐ STYLE R

Item #(s): _____
_____
_____
_____
_____
_____
_____
_____
_____
_____

For additional imprinted messages, use a separate sheet of paper.

TRADEMARKS & SPECIAL LOGOS

We will print these nationally advertised logos and trademarks for $4.00 per item. We will also print your custom logo for a one-time charge of $15.00, if you supply camera-ready art (clear, sharp, black and white original print). Photocopies, raised-printing (thermography), ink colors and paper stock other than black ink on white paper are not suitable for reproduction. Exact reorders of special logos or special type are $4.00 per item. On forms, we reserve the right to decide whether your trademark or logo will reproduce to our quality standards. If not, we will call you and discuss possible options.

Copyright © The Wheeler Group. Used with permission.

ORDERING INFORMATION

SHOP BY PHONE . . . Call Toll-Free 800-527-9530 **OR BY MAIL** . . . Use the attached, handy order form.

IMPRINTING . . . All products are imprinted as shown in the catalog. Prices include the standard number of copy lines specified in the product presentation. There is a $6.00 charge for extra lines of copy, where available.

NUMBERING . . . Consecutive numbering (6 digits) is standard on many forms indicated in the catalog. Other forms may be consecutively numbered for $6.00 for 1,000, plus $1.00 for each additional thousand forms. When numbering is desired, the starting number must be specified. If a starting number is not specified, your forms will not be numbered.

STOCK LOGOS . . . Many Drawing Board products may be imprinted with a stock logo and trademark as shown on order form. There is a $4.00 charge.

CUSTOM LOGOS . . . We will print your custom logo or trademark for a one-time charge of $15.00, if you supply camera-ready art (clear, sharp, black and white original print). Photocopies, raised-print (thermography), ink colors and paper stock other than black ink on white paper are not suitable for reproduction. Logos should not include screens or extremely fine lines and type. Exact reorders of special logos or special type are $4.00 per item. If camera-ready art is to be provided by us, please see the "Logo Design Service" and the "Custom Stationery and Forms Design Service" on this order form.

SPECIAL INK AND TYPE . . . Your type will be set in our standard type style and size and positioned as shown in the catalog. Special type sizes and styles are $10.00 and a type sample must accompany your order. Exact reorders of special type in our files are $4.00 per item. Changes in the positioning of your copy are $6.00 and a sample of the arrangement of your copy must accompany your order. Special inks not shown in the catalog and ink matches are not available. Two-color printing not available except as stated in the catalog.

SHIPPING POLICY . . . Your office supplies will be shipped from The Drawing Board in just one day. Most imprinted products ship within six business days. Please allow additional time for UPS delivery. Shipping times apply to standard three or four line imprint. If your imprinted order is not a standard three of four line imprint, or if it requires special art preparation, please allow four additional days preparation time.

CREDIT CARDS . . . Use your American Express, Master Card or VISA. On all charges, please be sure to state your card number, expiration date, and interbank number (Master Card only). Charge card purchases are shipped to cardholder only.

PURCHASE ORDERS . . . Please make sure your purchase order is signed by an authorized person. **Please do not send confirming purchase orders.**

Government offices, schools and institutions usually require a formal purchase order before approving payment.

PRICES/PREMIUMS . . . Prices in this catalog are effective August 1, 1989, and supersede all previous catalog prices. Prices subject to change without notice. Premiums apply to this catalog only and expire on date specified. One premium is awarded per order.

PAYMENT TERMS . . . Payment due upon receipt of merchandise. Prepayment of first order, by check or credit card, will establish your credit. Otherwise, for your first order please provide bank reference and account number.

FREIGHT TERMS . . . Freight will be billed F.O.B. shipping point and a $1.95 packing, handling & guaranteed delivery charge will be added to your order.

COD'S . . . COD orders are not accepted.

MORE THAN ONE CATALOG? Do you receive more than one catalog in the mail? If so please send us the address label from each catalog and indicate which one is correct. This will help us serve you better and also save money by eliminating duplication.

LOGO DESIGN SERVICE

If you have a printed sample of your current logo or an idea for your logo but do not have camera ready art, our Logo Design Service will create special art for you. Send printed samples or sketch with written instructions. The charge is $45.00 per hour. Exact reorders of custom logos in our files are $4.00 per item. Allow up to 7 additional days for processing.

CUSTOM STATIONERY & FORMS DESIGN SERVICE

If our standard stationery and forms do not fit your needs, challenge our staff of design specialists. They will turn your ideas into time-saving products that will help your business prosper. Just send a sample, sketch or layout to: THE DRAWING BOARD, CUSTOM DESIGN SERVICE, P.O. BOX 620004, DALLAS, TX 75262-0004. There is a $45.00 per hour charge for artwork. Be sure to include form specifications such as size, quantity, number of parts, etc. We will send you a proof of your form before printing. Please allow up to ten additional work days for art processing.

Copyright © The Wheeler Group. Used with permission.

DEVOKE

1-800-822-3132
1500 Martin Ave. Box 58051
Santa Clara, CA 95052-8051

FAX 408-727-4935
Telex 9103509236
Easy Link 62828759

Bill To (Please print or type)
Company
Attention
Title/Dept./Mail Stop
Mailing Address
City   State   Zip
Telephone (   )

Ship To (If different than Bill To)
Company
Attention
Title/Dept./Mail Stop
Street Address
City   State   Zip
Special Shipping Instructions

New Account Information
We are listed in Dun & Bradstreet   ☐ Yes   ☐ No
Your Bank
Street
City
State
Bank Account No.
Bank Telephone No.

Your Order No.   Date
Telephone No.
Name of Person Ordering
Title
Signature of Person Placing Ordering

Important
Please enter the code from the upper left corner of your mailing label here ___ ___ ___ ___ ___

This number →

1360
John Doe, Data Processing
Your Company
P.O. Box 9999
Anytown, USA 00000

Mailing label is found on back cover of this catalog

☐ I have an account, bill me.   ☐ Check enclosed.
☐ Ship C.O.D.
☐ Open an account for our firm (Please fill in area above.)
☐ Please charge to my: ☐ VISA   ☐ MasterCard

Name on Card
Signature of Cardholder
Account No.   Exp. Date
Issuing Bank (for VISA or MasterCard)

Quantity	Item No.	Color	Description	Unit Price	Total

Thank you for your order!

* Please Note: All orders are shipped FOB shipping point. For your convenience, we prepay all freight charges (actual) plus add a $3.00 handling charge and add them to your invoice. Minimum order is $15.00 and terms are net 30 days from date of invoice.

Subtotal	
California Buyers add 6%, 6 1/2%, or 7% Sales Tax	
Freight and Handling*	
Total Amount	

Ordering Information

One of our friendly, knowledgeable Sales Representatives will be happy to answer your product questions, quote prices and delivery costs, or take your order. Call us at 1-800-822-3132, weekdays between 6:00 a.m. and 5:00 p.m. Pacific Time.

■3 Ways to Order
- Call Toll-Free: 1-800-822-3132
- Send a Fax of your Purchase Order: 408-727-4935
- Mail your order to us:
  Devoke Co.
  1500 Martin Ave.
  Santa Clara, CA 95050

■4 Delivery Choices
1. **Federal Express® overnight delivery service**—When you need your order overnight, call us at 1-800-822-3132 before 12:00 p.m. (noon) Pacific Time. We will ship it via Federal Express delivery service to ensure you receive it the next day.

2. **Standard Air℠ by Federal Express**—This service provides two day delivery, after shipment, anywhere in the continental U.S.A. on any order under 40 lbs. **for only $15.** If it's not delivered in two days, we'll pay the freight.

   This service does not apply to drop ship items or items over 40 lbs. These orders will be billed shipping charges for the carrier of your choice.

3. **UPS**— Orders up to 70 lbs. are shipped UPS unless otherwise requested.

4. **Motor Freight**—Items over 70 lbs. and drop ship items are shipped either UPS or motor freight. Call for a quote if you need one.

All orders are shipped FOB Santa Clara, CA unless otherwise noted. To make it easy for you, we prepay all freight charges (actual) plus add a handling charge of $3.00 to your invoice.

■Exclusive Products
Look for our "Only from Devoke" symbol throughout this catalog. It tells you which products in our catalog are available only from Devoke. Like all of our products, these products carry our standard 100% satisfaction guarantee.

■Damaged Goods
Despite our best efforts, items occasionally may be damaged in transit. Before you sign the bill of lading, be sure to inspect all cartons for damage—both inside and out. List in detail, on the bill of lading, any damage to the merchandise. Ask the carrier to make an inspection immediately. Then contact our Customer Service Department at 1-800-822-3132. **Please do not return damaged merchandised without prior authorization.**

■Returns/Exchanges
If you are not 100% satisfied with your purchase—return merchandise within 45 days from date of invoice for full credit or refund. If return is due to our error, we'll pay the shipping charges. To return merchandise, simply follow these steps:

Orders delivered by Federal Express, UPS, or Parcel Post:
1. **Call us first for instructions** and assistance before you return any products.
2. **Wrap them back up** in the packaging they were shipped in.
3. **Enclose written information that tells us** the reasons for the return; the action you want taken; and your name, address, telephone number, order invoice number, and your customer number. (If you can, please enclose our packing slip or invoice.)

4. **Ship it back to us via UPS or Parcel Post.** Send the item to: Devoke Co.; 1500 Martin Avenue; Box 58051; Santa Clara, CA 95052-8051.

For orders delivered by Motor Freight:
Please call or write our Customer Service Department at 1-800-822-3132 for return assistance and instructions.

■Technical Help
Devoke provides you with technical assistance. Call one of our Technical Support Specialists toll-free at 1-800-822-3132. They're available to help you with your technical product questions and your special application needs.

■Guarantee
At Devoke, customer loyalty means everything. We guarantee 100% satisfaction by offering our customers a 45-day risk free trial period on every product we sell. Try any product in the catalog for 45 days, and if you are not completely satisfied for any reason, just send it back for an exchange or a complete refund.

■Pricing
Raw material costs beyond our control may make it necessary to change prices effective with our next catalog.

All prices in this catalog are guaranteed through December 31, 1989.

Copyright © Devoke Co. Used with permission.

LANDS' END
DIRECT MERCHANTS

Lands' End, Inc.
1 Lands' End Lane, Dodgeville, WI 53595

Call us toll-free 24 hours a day, 7 days a week to charge your order: 1-800-356-4444

IMPORTANT: Make any Name/Address corrections below:

Ordered by:

```
C=6251-9796-7    S=WJW14
E C HODGSON
P O BOX 1540
WESTCHESTER    PA 19380
```

Daytime Phone ( ) _____

Ship to: (Only if different from "Ordered by".)

Name _____
c/o _____
Address _____
City _____ State _____ Zip _____
Gift Card Message _____
From _____

MONOGRAMMING & GIFT BOXING: Please add $5 per item monogrammed or boxed. Information about these services is on the second page of this form.

Catalog Number	Page No.	Description	Size	Pants Inseam	Cuffs Yes	Cuffs No	Color	Alternate Color Choice	First name initial	Middle name initial	Last name initial	Style No.	Gift Box This Item	Qty.	Price Total

Method of payment:

☐ Charge to my *(circle one):* MasterCard   Visa   American Express

Please include credit card number **and** expiration date with charge orders!

☐ Check or Money Order Enclosed

Expiration Date [Month | Year]

X _____
Signature (as shown on credit card)

We make it our business to ship your order using the most efficient method (see instructions on the other side). If you have a preference, please check below.

☐ U.P.S.
☐ Parcel Post
☐ Parcel Post Air Mail $5
☐ Federal Express Standard Air $5 to Alaska or Hawaii $15
☐ Lands' End Express™ $6 to Alaska or Hawaii $16

Thank You!
©1989, Lands' End, Inc.

Monogram or Gift Box ($5.00 Each)	
Total Price of Items	
Delivery in: IL, add 5% Sales Tax; in IA 4%; in CA 6%	
Shipping, Packing, Handling and Insurance	3 50
Airmail, Federal Express, Lands' End Express	
Shipping to More than One Address ($3.50 Each)	
Total	
For delivery in Wisconsin, add 5% Sales Tax to Total	
Total—Wisconsin Deliveries	

V1

WE'RE ALWAYS OPEN.
You can order from us toll-free 24 hours a day, 7 days a week, 364 days a year (we're closed Christmas Day). Or just call to say hello, and get acquainted with the friendliest phone people in America. Our number is:
1-800-356-4444

OUR PHONE PEOPLE REALLY KNOW THEIR STUFF!
Our friendly, well-trained people have all our products within reach 24 hours a day, 7 days a week. They'll give you good service, and good advice if you have questions about sizing, colors, anything!

SPECIALTY SHOPPER SERVICE
If you have special questions about sizing, wardrobe coordination, etc., call **1-800-356-4444** between 8 AM and 10 PM CST and ask for one of our crackerjack Specialty Shoppers. They'll be happy to assist you, and tell you about the services they provide free of charge.

TELEPHONE ORDERING SERVICE FOR THE DEAF
We now have a Telephone Device for the Deaf (TDD), to assist those of you who are hearing impaired. Call toll-free **1-800-541-3459** from 6 AM till midnight.

WE SHIP FASTER THAN ANYONE WE KNOW OF.
Usually within 24 hours after receiving your order. (Monogrammed, inseamed or gift boxed items take a day or two longer.) To your home, or your office. Wherever you like. We want to make shopping as convenient as possible for you.

Our famous fast service is even faster when you choose one of our express delivery options:

(A) **Federal Express Standard Air℠ Shipment** gets your order within 3-4 business days.* Cost is an additional:
$5 per shipment for Continental U.S.
$15 per shipment to Alaska and Hawaii

(B) **Lands' End Express™ Shipment** (via Federal Express) gets your order within 2 business days.* You can pick the delivery day; even Saturday! (The exact day you specify just has to be within a week of your order.) Cost is an additional:
$6 per shipment for Continental U.S.
$16 per shipment to Alaska and Hawaii

* *If we monogram, inseam, or gift box, please allow 1 additional business day.*

Sorry, express delivery is not available to APO/FPO addresses, P.O. boxes, and some rural areas.

WE BACK EVERYTHING WE SELL WITH THE MOST EMPHATIC GUARANTEE IN EXISTENCE: GUARANTEED. PERIOD.®

With most guarantees, the more words they contain, the more their protection is limited. Our guarantee has always been an unconditional one. That's why we can boil it down to just two words. If you're not **completely satisfied** with anything you order from us, at any time, for any reason, send it back and we'll refund your money. No ifs, ands, or buts.

We want you to feel comfortable ordering from us, especially those of you who've never shopped through the mail before.

V2

HOW TO ORDER BY PHONE:
Before you call, please fill out our order form, and have your credit card and expiration date handy. Then call our toll-free number (now even from Canada): **1-800-356-4444.**
Credit Cards only; sorry, no C.O.D.'s.

American Express   Visa   MasterCard

HOW TO ORDER BY MAIL:
Please supply all the information requested on our order form. We will accept your personal check, bank draft, money order or payment with a major credit card. U.S. currency only, please. If you charge your mail order to a credit card, please SIGN the order form where indicated and enter your complete card number and expiration date.

HOW TO ORDER MONOGRAMMING:
Monogramming availability is indicated in the catalog copy. To order, fill in the monogramming section on the order form **as indicated.** We will arrange monogram initials in the correct sequence for the styles you have selected. And, **we will monogram names exactly as you print them**—up to 10 letters, including spaces.
When more than one monogram style is offered for a product, fill in the style number on the order form. When only **one** style is offered, no style number is needed.
Please add $5 per item monogrammed, and allow 1-2 days extra for delivery.

P.S. *If you want something monogrammed, and monogramming is* **not** *indicated in the catalog copy, just ask. We'll do our best to monogram it for you.*

HOW TO RETURN SOMETHING TO US:
1. Keep the top section of the packing slip for your records, and PLEASE, return the rest to us. Having vs. not having your packing slip when we process your return is the difference between night and day.
2. Send your return to us by UPS or insured parcel post.
3. If you return a gift you received, please tell us the name and address of the person who gave it to you. (This is kept strictly confidential!)
4. Let us know if you prefer:
   (A) something else for your return;
   (B) money back or charge credit;
   (C) a gift certificate to use later.
5. Send your return to: Lands' End Returns, 2 Lands' End Lane   Dodgeville, Wisconsin 53595

Lift envelope for information on Gift Certificate and Gift Boxing

THE LANDS' END GIFT CERTIFICATE
We'll send a Gift Certificate in the amount you request to anyone you'd like, along with a Lands' End catalog and free 6-month subscription. Just fill in "Gift Certificate" on the order form, and write in the amount you desire. Enclose your payment or fill in the charge information as you would with a regular order, or charge your Gift Certificate by phone. And now, they can even be redeemed over the phone!

GIFT BOXING SERVICE
We'll gift box almost any item in our catalog for you! (An exception is especially large items—if you're ordering one, please call us to find out if gift boxing is available.)
This special service comes complete with our jaunty "madras" plaid box, tissue, ribbon and a gift card. And, we'll send the gift boxed item either to you or to the giftee of your choice. $5 per gift you give.

MAIL LIST PREFERENCE: We make our mailing list available to carefully-screened companies whose products or services might interest you. If you'd prefer to have your name withheld, please call us, or send your mailing label to:
Mail Preference Service
1 Lands' End Lane
Dodgeville, WI 53595

DUPLICATE MAILINGS? If you're receiving more than one of the same catalog, send us all the mailing labels, indicating the correct one. Or, call us. We'll correct the situation.

V3   Copyright © Lands' End, Inc.
Reprinted Courtesy of Lands' End Catalog.

Omaha Steaks International®

4400 South 96th Street • P.O. Box 3300 • Omaha, Nebraska 68103

Make checks out to "Omaha Steaks International."
Please specify:
☐ Check or Money Order enclosed $ _____
☐ VISA ☐ Diners Club
☐ MasterCard ☐ Carte Blanche
☐ American Express ☐ Omaha Steaks–if you have an approved account**

SHOW CREDIT CARD NUMBER BELOW:

Card Expires: Month __ Year __

Please see Order Instructions on other side.

In case we have a question about your order, may we have your phone number?
☐ Home: ( ) _____
☐ Office: ( ) _____

ORDER FORM   A

AN EXCITING ADD-ON BONUS OFFER!

Order selection #485 — 4 (10 oz.) London Broils for only $25.00. Regularly $36.00, these lean and flavorful Top Sirloin portions are yours at a savings of $11.00 when shipped with another selection from this mailing. Don't delay. Order now!

Please print

Name _____
Address _____ Apt. # _____
City _____ State _____ Zip _____

Please be sure we have your correct mailing address in the space above.

Description	Selection Number	How Many of this Selection	Unit Price	Total Price

Please ship these selections to my address:

Shipment No. 1
Name _____
Address _____ Apt. # _____
City _____ State _____ Zip _____
Telephone ( ) _____
(In case we have a question about your order.)
Ship to Arrive* ☐ Now ☐ Week of _____

Please ship the following gifts to the names below:

Shipment No. 2
Name _____
Address _____ Apt. # _____
City _____ State _____ Zip _____
Telephone ( ) _____
Ship to Arrive* ☐ Now ☐ Week of _____
Gift Greeting to Read: _____

Shipment No. 3
Name _____
Address _____ Apt. # _____
City _____ State _____ Zip _____
Telephone ( ) _____
Ship to Arrive* ☐ Now ☐ Week of _____
Gift Greeting to Read: _____

*Please allow 10-14 days for delivery.
TO GUARANTEE DELIVERY TO R.R. OR P.O. BOX, WE NEED RECEIVER'S TELEPHONE NUMBER.

** ☐ Check here if you would like an application for an Omaha Steaks charge account.

To Order by phone, call **FREE 1-800-228-9055**
Omaha Steaks FAX 1-402-392-8120
2-Day Delivery by Federal Express — Guaranteed
For an Additional $11.50 (Total $17.00 Shipping/Handling).

This Order Summary area is for your use only. ▶

Order Summary	Subtotal	$
		$
	Postage and Handling Charge = No. of Shipments x $5.50	$
	TOTAL DUE	$

Copyright © Omaha Steaks International. Used with permission.

© COPYRIGHT 1991 DARTNELL CORPORATION

It's easy to order.

Order by mail.

Fill out and mail this order form in the enclosed priority handling envelope. As you do, keep these points in mind:

1. You may choose your method of payment – check, money order, credit card or an approved Omaha Steaks account.
2. Our guarantee of excellent delivery is valid when you furnish proper address. We even guarantee delivery to Post Office boxes when you include the recipient's phone number.
3. A greeting with your name or company name will be imprinted on gift shipping labels. If you wish, we'll use your gift cards when you send them with your order (max. size 3" x 5").
4. We'll confirm each order and prices with you by return mail. Due to varying market conditions, prices are subject to change.

Business People! Get in touch with our Incentive Sales Department for information about our exciting Incentive and Business Gift Programs. Call toll free 1-800-228-2480. Or write to Omaha Steaks International, Incentive Sales Dept., 4400 South 96th Street, P.O. Box 3300, Omaha, NE 68103.

Order by phone
Just call us at **1-800-228-9055** 7 days a week with credit card orders. You may find it helpful to fill out an Omaha Steaks order form to use as a reference when calling. Your satisfaction is guaranteed. That's why we invite you to call Customer Service when you have a question about an order. Call toll free **1-800-228-9872** during regular business hours.

Monday through Friday (CST) 7:00 a.m. to 10:00 p.m.
Saturday (CST) **Sunday (CST)**
9:00 a.m. to 6:00 p.m. 11:00 a.m. to 7:00 p.m.

Cable Address: OMASTEAK, Omaha, Nebraska Telex Number: 48-4488

Delivery
Shipments are made by United Parcel Service. We will be glad to rush your order by Federal Express at an extra charge. See information below or call or write for complete details. Sorry, we are unable to deliver to A.P.O. or F.P.O. addresses.

Friends outside the 48 Continental United States?
A variety of products is available for you to send to them. Please call or write for delivery and price information.

Delayed shipping service
Order now for any future shipping date. You will not be billed until your order is ready to ship.

Order our "Special of the day!"
It may be just what you're hungry for – a box of juicy steaks, a heat-and-serve entree, or one of the other luscious foods shown in our catalog. While it's on special, you can have it delivered with your order at a special low price! Just ask our operator about our "special of the day" anytime you call in an order.

Other offers
Your name, as a part of our customer family, is made available to carefully screened organizations with an offer or appeal that might interest you. If you would rather not receive such offers, please let us know.

FREE with your order

Omaha Steaks Good Life Guide and Cookbook

This interesting, informative book, available only through Omaha Steaks, features:
- Complete information on cooking Omaha Steaks, including a foolproof steak cooking chart.
- Easy-to-follow instructions for all Omaha Steaks products.
- Helpful storing and serving hints.
- Exclusive recipes by world-famous food authority James Beard (others by our own Home Economist).
- A complete selection of James Beard's sauce recipes, to complement your Omaha Steaks.

For fast and friendly ordering call 1-800-228-9055 toll free 7 DAYS A WEEK...EVEN SUNDAY.

Your order will be delivered when you want it, in perfect condition. You have our promise...our unconditional guarantee.
2-Day Delivery by Federal Express – Guaranteed
For an additional $11.50 (Total $17.00 Shipping/Handling).

"Yours are the best steaks my husband and I have ever tasted. They melted in our mouths. We also loved the free cookbook you sent along."
Rosemary C. Tibaudo
Mt. Clemens, Michigan

We've been doing it for nearly 40 years... successfully shipping high quality gourmet foods to all parts of the country. Packaging frozen food orders to arrive frozen, in thick, rugged, reusable picnic coolers, under plenty of dry ice.
We're so sure this packaging method works that we guarantee it.

If you are not absolutely thrilled with your order from Omaha Steaks – for any reason at all – our cheerfully replace your order or refund your money (to the extent, whichever you prefer.

Visit our Omaha Steakshops in Omaha, Dallas and Houston!

Omaha Steaks International
4400 South 96th Street
P.O. Box 3300 • Omaha, Nebraska 68103

W2

HERE AND HERE ONLY...
A SPECIAL LAST-SECOND OFFER FOR YOU!
Add this exciting offer to your order form...
#671 four (1 lb.) packages of mouthwatering Tenderloin Tips. Regularly $46.00, yours for just $30.00 – *but only when shipped with another selection from this catalog. You'll save $16.00.* Order now! And please remember...this selection has been priced so very low for you that no other discounts may be applied.

Valuable Bonus

FREE WITH EVERY ORDER!

Omaha Steaks Good Life Guide and Cookbook
- Foolproof steak cooking chart
- Complete information on cooking Omaha Steaks
- Easy-to-follow instructions for all Omaha Steaks products
- Helpful serving hints
- Exclusive recipes by James Beard
- Complete selection of James Beard's sauce recipes, to complement your Omaha Steaks

FREE COOKBOOK with every order!

"The packaging was perfectly insulated, preserving the filets which were frozen solid. The inside plastic covering was a professional touch which further ensured freshness. The filets were delicious and my family enjoyed them so much. Thank you for your high standards— a refreshing treat!"
Andrea McGowan
Staten Island, New York

W4

HERE AND HERE ONLY...
A SPECIAL LAST-SECOND OFFER FOR YOU!
Add this exciting offer to your order form...
#960 (our Steak Sampler) – featuring two (6 oz.) Filet Mignons, two (9 oz.) Boneless Strip Sirloins, and two (6 oz.) Top Sirloin Steaks. Regularly $49.00, yours for just $35.00 – *but only when shipped with another selection from this catalog. You'll save $14.00.* Order now! And please remember...this selection has been priced so very low for you that no other discounts may be applied.

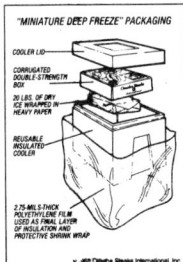

How Your Frozen Foods Get from Omaha to You — in Top Condition.

Your frozen food orders will arrive at your front door still firmly frozen — all the way from Omaha. Several layers of packaging, including an insulated cooler and plenty of dry ice, assure safe arrival in top condition.

We've been packaging meat across the country and around the world for nearly 40 years. All this experience has helped us develop our dependable method of packaging.

In fact, we're so sure this method works that we guarantee it. Your frozen food orders must arrive in excellent condition, or we'll replace your order or refund your money.

As a bonus for you, once you've unpacked your frozen foods, you'll be able to reuse the cooler for your own picnics. It's a $5.50 value that's yours to keep — at no extra cost.

Reusable Picnic Cooler with all frozen food shipments from Omaha Steaks International **a $5.50 value** at no extra cost

W5

WAIT!

DON'T MAIL OR CALL IN YOUR ORDER JUST YET! HERE ARE THREE LAST-MINUTE OPPORTUNITIES... SELECTIONS WE THOUGHT YOU'D APPRECIATE AND ENJOY...SELECTIONS WE THOUGHT OF AFTER THE COLOR PORTION OF OUR CATALOG HAD GONE TO PRESS!

#7156 STRIKING 3½" SALT SHAKER/PEPPER MILL... $9.95

Add elegance and sparkle to your dinner table! Enjoy the special zest and flavor of fresh peppercorns ground by hand as you dine.

Order this 3½" acrylic salt shaker/pepper mill with the light-catching look of crystal. It's attractive and fun to use. And it's covered by our unconditional guarantee. Order now!

Order this complete meal combination package...your appetizers will be free!
#482 THE WHO'S WHO COMBO... $179.00

6 (5 oz.) Filet Mignons, ea. 1" thick &
6 (6 oz.) Lobster Tails &
2 pkgs. Lemon Parsley Butter Sauce &
1 (28 oz.) New York Cheesecake
(If ordered separately, $186.95)
Free...25 Cajun Shrimp Quiche (Regularly $28.00. See page 29 of your catalog for the delectable details on this exciting new product!)

Order this combination package of cookout favorites!
#376 THE GRILL MASTER $199.00

6 (6 oz.) Filet Mignons, ea. 1¼" thick &
6 (11 oz.) Boneless Strips, ea. 1⅛" thick &
6 (8 oz.) Top Sirloins, ea. 1⅛" thick &
3 (1 lb.) Pkgs. of Tenderloin Tips &
16 (5 oz.) Gourmet Burgers &
6 (5 oz.) Boneless Pork Chops
(If ordered separately, $288.35)

W3

HERE AND HERE ONLY...
A SPECIAL LAST-SECOND OFFER FOR YOU!
Add this exciting offer to your order form...
#671 four (1 lb.) packages of mouthwatering Tenderloin Tips. Regularly $46.00, yours for just $30.00 – *but only when shipped with another selection from this catalog. You'll save $16.00.* Order now! And please remember...this selection has been priced so very low for you that no other discounts may be applied.

W6

HERE AND HERE ONLY...
A SPECIAL LAST-SECOND OFFER FOR YOU!
Add this exciting offer to your order form...
#960 (our Steak Sampler) – featuring two (6 oz.) Filet Mignons, two (9 oz.) Boneless Strip Sirloins, and two (6 oz.) Top Sirloin Steaks. Regularly $49.00, yours for just $35.00 – *but only when shipped with another selection from this catalog. You'll save $14.00.* Order now! And please remember...this selection has been priced so very low for you that no other discounts may be applied.

W7

Copyright © Omaha Steaks International. Used with permission.

In addition to the special offers included elsewhere on its order form, Omaha Steaks adds two more offers on perforated stubs attached to its order envelope.

Producing the Catalog

11

While every catalog has its own special production requirements, there are many general guidelines which apply to nearly every catalog. The most important guideline of all is to create a working schedule, working backwards from your delivery-to-customers target date—*and keep on schedule.*

Plan on "Murphy's Law"—if something can go wrong, it will. In each stage of the catalog production process, allow some extra catch-up time, so when something unexpected happens, there will be sufficient time to handle the next steps in the schedule.

While I've been involved in catalogs that were created and produced in as little as 3 weeks, a production schedule of 12 to 20 weeks is most common. The basic starting point is when you make final selection of products to be included, choose the suppliers who will handle each production step, and decide upon the lists to whom the catalog will be sent. Once these factors have been established, the usual sequence will be:

- Creation, review and reworking of layouts.
- Photography of all items to fit your layouts, and creation of any special artwork.
- Copywriting and editing of copy.
- Typesetting, proofreading, and type revisions.
- Assembly of photos, art, and type.

- Color separations.
- Review of color proofs and corrections.
- Delivery of all material to printer.
- Review of "bluelines" (monochrome proofs of catalog pages provided by printer) and submission of any final changes required before printing.
- Press start-up, with final color corrections made at the printer.
- Completion of printing and delivery of all elements of the catalog to the bindery and/or mailing house.
- Final assembly and addressing.
- Delivery of catalogs to the post office.
- Catalogs received in customers' mailboxes.

While these are the basic steps in producing a catalog, there are a number of production factors that may be happening simultaneously.

- Obtaining merchandise from vendors for delivery to the photographer.
- Selection of models.
- Selecting locations for non-studio photography.
- Development of reference material to be used by the copywriters.
- Production of order forms (which are most frequently handled by a separate supplier and must be delivered to the printer, binder, or mailing house in time for final catalog assembly).
- Delivery of covers and/or wraps produced separately from the body of the catalog to the point of binding at the proper time.
- Preparation of mailing labels or computer tapes, which will be delivered to the printer, bindery, or mailing house for addressing the catalogs.
- Arranging transportation of catalogs to different postal drop points if catalogs must reach customers in different parts of the country at approximately the same time.

In establishing your catalog schedule, it's important to consider more than just the time frame. Equally important are the total budget and *who* will be available *when*. If there are plenty of dollars available, you can generally hire enough people to meet any time frame (assuming you know in advance what help you will need and can line up the necessary assistance at the times you will need it). But few catalogs have an unlimited budget. So it's important to plan in advance *who* will be required *when* to do *what*.

Probably more important than anything else in establishing schedules is to consider the availability of the people who must give approvals. In my experience, the most frequent reason catalogs fail to meet production deadlines is that the people who must give final okays (and for whom catalog production is most often a secondary responsibility) were off doing something else at the time layouts, copy, photography, art, or proofs needed their approval. Meanwhile, everything grinds to a halt awaiting their return . . . or things move ahead and then must be revised at a later date, resulting in increased costs for makeovers (and, most often, an inferior catalog).

The Production Team

Producing a catalog is a team effort. It requires careful coordination of both internal personnel and outside suppliers. It's not unlike football. If you're playing in a "minor league," there may be just a single group of people who do everything. But if you want a truly professional catalog, you need a "major league" team, which is, in reality, three separate teams:

- **The Offensive Team.** puts together the basic catalog elements. This is usually an internal team, although it often includes an outside catalog consultant. This team includes your internal designers, artists, photographers, copywriters, and other production personnel.
- **The Special Team.** handles creative work you are unable to produce within your own organization. This may involve outside designers, artists, photographers, copywriters, typesetters, paste-up personnel—everyone needed to get the catalog ready to "go to press."
- **The Defensive Team.** is made up of outside vendors who provide expertise on everything from color separations to printing, binding, and mailing.

And, like any good team, your catalog needs both a coach and "on-field" captains.

The "coach" is most often whoever in the internal organization has primary responsibility for catalog merchandising. This individual must coordinate the efforts of product buyers or managers, art directors, copywriters, and internal production personnel. In addition, there is usually an internal production "captain" who handles day-to-day coordination of every play. In some organizations this may be a full-time production manager . . . or it may be an art director, editor, or someone else who not only has a basic role to play, but also becomes the coordinator of all internal activities.

When creative activities are handled externally by a "special team," one of the vendors involved becomes the "captain" who coordinates the input from outside designers, artists, photographers, copywriters, etc. Often this is a catalog consultant or a special coordinator on the staff of a design or photography studio.

And then there's our "defensive team" of outside vendors. And here's where it is particularly important to have a single "captain." One of the vendors should be given primary responsibility to make sure all of the "players" work in harmony to produce the best possible catalog. Most often, this senior responsibility is assigned to the printer, who will coordinate the efforts of the color separator, paper supplier, binder, list supplier, producers of separate covers, wraps, and order forms, and the mailing house.

Once the teams have been established, it is extremely important to make sure they regularly participate in "team meetings," especially during the early planning stages. Everyone's input is sought in these meetings. But someone has to be responsible for seeing that all of the individual ideas are blended to produce the best possible catalog within the budget available.

Additional "team meetings" should be scheduled to make sure everyone is kept abreast of changes which develop as the catalog production moves from one step to another. And by all means, there should be a "postgame" review. Once the catalog is in the mail, everyone who has been involved in the production should get together to review "the game films" and make suggestions for changes and improvements that can be implemented for the next catalog.

Selecting a Printing Process

Many factors go into selecting the right printing process for your catalog. The primary considerations, however, are the size of your catalog, the number of copies to be distributed, and the level of quality you require.

Three basic printing processes are suitable for catalog printing.

Letterpress

Years ago, letterpress printing was the most common process used to produce catalogs. Today, however, this process is used primarily for those few catalogs that require a multitude of changes during press runs.

In simple terms, letterpress is very much like using a rubber stamp. Ink is applied to raised metal surfaces which are pressed against a piece of paper. It requires the use of metal type, which can be changed as often as necessary to revise copy, prices, etc.

Offset

The most popular printing process for catalogs today is offset lithography. The offset process involves combining both type and illustrations on a flat surface (the printing plate), which is treated to either accept or repel water. Areas to be printed repel water. The plate is wrapped around a cylinder, and water is spread across the plate, sticking only to the areas which will not be printed. Then a grease-based ink is applied to the plate; it "sticks" only to the areas which have remained dry after the water application. Because grease and water don't mix, the ink is rejected in areas which are still wet.

The plate is then pressed against a second cylinder, which is covered with a special "blanket," and the ink is lifted from the printing plate and "offset" onto the second cylinder. This second cylinder then transfers the ink to the paper.

Two forms of offset—sheet and web—are used for printing catalogs. When extremely high quality is required and press runs are relatively short, sheet-fed offset presses are often the choice. Because paper is fed into these presses one sheet at a time, press speeds are relatively slow, resulting in exceptionally fine color control.

In most cases, however, web-fed offset presses are used. Instead of printing one sheet at a time, they print from rolls of paper, which run through the presses at much faster speeds. In most cases, web offset presses used for catalogs have multiple cylinders that permit printing four or five different colors on each side of the paper as it moves through the press. They then automatically cut and fold the paper into signatures, which most often contain 16 pages approximately $8\ ^3/_8$ x $10\ ^7/_8"$ in size or 32 digest-size pages (approximately $5\ ^1/_2$ x $8\ ^1/_4"$).

Gravure

For catalogs requiring a million copies or more, gravure (often called rotogravure) is often the process chosen. This intaglio process is just the opposite of letterpress printing. Instead of ink being applied to raised surfaces, the printing cylinder is etched with minute holes, which are filled with ink. Then, as webs of paper fly through the press, the cylinders revolve and the ink is drawn out of the holes onto the passing paper.

Even though the presses run at very high speeds and thus reduce the cost of each signature being printed, the cost of etching the printing cylinders is very expensive. It normally requires press runs of at least one million to absorb the high start-up costs and make gravure competitive with web offset. The copper cylinders used for gravure have an extremely long life. Once the cost of etching the original cylinders has been absorbed, these same cylinders can continue to produce catalogs at a relatively low cost per thousand. Offset, which runs at slower speeds and requires plate changes as originals wear out during press runs, can't provide such significant cost reductions for additional thousands.

Like web offset, rotogravure presses have multiple cylinders which lay down four or five colors on each side of the paper as it moves rapidly through the equipment, and paper is folded into signatures as part of the printing operation. While there are different sizes of gravure presses, the basic page size is in the $8\ ^3/_8 \times 10\ ^7/_8"$ range. However, cylinders are usually much larger than those used in web offset printing, so it's possible to generate signatures of as many as 96 pages in a single pass through the press.

Offset vs. Gravure

For the most part, the choice of printing method comes down to a choice between web offset and gravure. The primary advantages of web offset is that the preparatory costs for plates and make-ready are considerably less expensive than gravure. Thus these costs can be fully absorbed when press runs are under a million copies.

Web offset also allows more color control while a job is being printed and greater flexibility in making changes.

Gravure, on the other hand, allows for superior detail and depth of color in printing. You can apply a greater amount of each color of ink to the paper than is possible with offset printing.

The much faster running speeds of gravure presses provide substantial economies once the higher cost of cylinder etching and make-ready have been absorbed. In addition, gravure permits use of lighter weights and less expensive grades of paper, while still maintaining a high level of quality.

Being able to use lighter weights of paper can be particularly important in meeting postal requirements for minimum postage charges per copy.

[For more details about printing processes, we recommend you obtain a copy of "Pocket Pal," a very helpful handbook which has been published by International Paper Company since 1934. It is updated regularly and provides easy-to-understand details about printing processes, typesetting, copy and art preparation, separations, paper, ink, binding, and quality control. Copies are available from many paper suppliers or directly from International Paper Company, 77 West 45th Street, New York, NY 10036.]

Selecting Paper for Your Catalog

Paper represents the largest element of cost in catalog printing and deserves special consideration. Paper is available in a wide variety of grades, finishes, and weights. The most common finish is gloss coated, although a number of catalogs use matte coated, super calendered, book papers, or even low-cost newsprint.

There are 12 primary factors to consider when selecting the right paper for your catalog:

- Objective
- Cost
- Printing process
- Smoothness
- Gloss
- Opacity
- Brightness
- Color
- Weight
- Printability
- Bulk
- Availability

The two primary variables in choosing paper for a catalog are weight and quality. There are five basic grades of coated paper, for example, ranging from low-cost publication-grade, a lightweight paper with heavy groundwood pulp content, to very heavy, extremely glossy paper with no groundwood pulp. Most catalogs, however, use one of the intermediate grades.

Grades of paper are determined by their smoothness, brightness, opacity, and affinity to ink. Higher quality papers are free of groundwood fibers (thus called "free sheets") and have a superior degree of each of the four qualities mentioned. Costs, usually expressed in terms of hundredweight, decrease as the levels of smoothness, brightness, opacity, and ink affinity decline.

While you'll generally pay more per hundredweight as the weight of the paper declines, you actually save money per page since there are more pages for each pound in weight. The reason why it costs more per hundredweight for lighter papers is that the paper machine produces the same number of linear feet per minute regardless of the weight of the paper it is making. Therefore, it takes the same amount of machine time to make 100 feet of 60 lb. paper as it takes to make 100 feet of 40 lb. paper.

Superior quality catalogs printed by sheetfed offset require papers with a minimum weight of 60 lb. Most often free sheet papers with either a gloss or matte coating are chosen.

Web offset generally uses coated papers from 38 lb. to 60 lb. or uncoated papers from 28 lb. to 37.5 lb. Offset papers require a sizing to repel the water used in the offset process. Quality of printing usually increases as you improve the grade and weight of paper.

Gravure papers generally don't exceed a grade #3 level, and 80 lb. is the maximum weight. However, much lighter papers are normally used for gravure-printed catalogs. It is less common to use free sheet grades of paper since gravure delivers greater ink coverage and smoothness on less expensive paper.

Today it is quite common to use a heavier weight paper for covers, combined with lighter papers for the body of catalogs. Many gravure-printed catalogs using lightweight body paper have offset-printed covers on heavier stock.

One of the major considerations in paper selection is who should actually buy the paper—you or your printer. Except for very large volume catalog operations, it is best to give primary consideration to printer-supplied paper. Catalog printers not only can buy paper in larger quantities, giving them a preferred relationship with paper suppliers; but they have the experience to know what prints best on their equipment.

Many printers carry their own stocks of popular paper varieties, but if you require a special paper it still may work out to your advantage to have the printer order it for you. While the printer will have to add a markup to cover costs such as inspection, spoilage, insurance, warehousing, and inventory financing, the printer's volume buying discounts may cover at least part of the added charges.

There are four additional advantages of using printer-supplied paper.

1. The printer automatically becomes responsible for the exact quantity of paper required to produce your catalog. When the cataloger supplies the paper, there is frequently either an overrun or a shortfall. While you may be able to use excess paper for a future catalog, you'll have to pay someone to warehouse it and reinspect it when it's to be used again. And if the paper supply runs short, you end up with fewer catalogs to mail.
2. When the printer supplies the paper, it's his money that's tied up in physical inventory. Quite often you won't be billed for paper until the catalog run has been completed.
3. With printer-supplied paper, the printer is fully responsible for the end result. When you furnish the paper and something isn't turning out as planned, it's not unusual for press operators to blame the paper. (Having been a printer, I know this is a natural reaction.) Now it becomes your responsibility to work out differences of opinion between the printer and paper supplier. When the printer has responsibility for both printing and paper, the entire

responsibility falls upon the printer's shoulders.

There also are times when a printer experiences an increase in web breaks—when the paper being fed from rolls tears as it is fed into the presses. This requires shutting down the press while paper is respliced. When it's the printer's own paper, he is responsible for absorbing these added costs. But when it is someone else's paper which he has been forced to use, this downtime is often added onto the printing bill.

4. In times of paper shortages, or when a shipment has been delayed or damaged, a printer often has more leverage in dealing with paper suppliers. I've been involved in several situations when there just wasn't enough paper available to produce a catalog anywhere on short deadlines or when it became necessary to accept an inferior grade of paper in order to meet mailing deadlines.

On the other hand, catalogers who are volume paper buyers can realize at least initial savings when buying their own paper. And there is more flexibility in ordering a special paper to fit a particular catalog.

When buying your own paper, it is important to have a knowledgeable paper expert on your staff or use an outside consultant to provide the expertise needed to select the right stock, negotiate the best buy, and handle problems which may arise. It's not just a matter of buying the right paper at the right price. Once the paper you have purchased has been shipped, it becomes your responsibility. If the paper proves to be defective, gets lost in shipment, is delayed enroute to the printer, or gets damaged before it goes on press, it takes experience to handle the problems.

Selecting a Printer

Choosing the right printer for your catalog is not something to be taken lightly. One printer may have the same kind of presses as another, and prices may be pretty much the same, but that's often where the similarities stop. Here are some of the factors to consider.

Catalog Experience

You'll want a printer who has had catalog printing experience. While magazines may seem to be pretty much the same as catalogs, the printing requirements are often quite different. Magazines usually call for "pleasing color," and magazine printers try to get the best possible balance throughout a magazine, without giving individual attention to each illustration.

But in a catalog, each piece of merchandise must be shown in accurate color. It takes different thinking to achieve this result. A printer who has to meet such requirements on a regular basis doesn't have to be educated to create the result you want.

Be sure to ask a printer to show you samples of catalogs produced in the past with the same basic requirements as the catalog you plan to have printed. In particular, ask to see samples of jobs printed on the same types of paper you plan to use. And check to make sure the samples you see are from current jobs.

Check the turnover rate of customers. Longevity of catalog customers is one of the best guides to the printer's ability to provide quality and service at a reasonable price.

And ask for references! The samples a printer will show you will undoubtedly be the "cream of the crop." So search out other copies of those same catalogs and contact the customers the printer has served in the past to find out what experiences they had.

In addition to getting comments concerning the quality and service provided by the printer, you should ask some other key questions.

- Is the printer accurate in estimating?
- Does the printer quibble over "additional charges" for things which would seem to be just a routine part of producing the catalog?
- Does the printer meet established schedules?
- Does the printer communicate quickly and with understanding when problems arise?
- Does the printer work well with other vendors who are involved in various elements of catalog production?
- Does the printer fulfill the promises his sales representatives make?
- Does the printer deliver "first proofs" that require a minimum of corrections, or does it take a lot of additional work to get a job ready to go on press?
- Does the printer maintain consistent quality throughout a press run?
- If paper has been furnished to a printer, does there seem to be excess waste?

And before you make a final decision on your printer, be sure to visit the plant where your catalog will be produced. Walk through production areas and talk with people who are working on current jobs. Do they take pride in what they are doing? Is the plant clean and orderly? Is the atmosphere businesslike, with people doing their jobs without panic? Does there appear to be a good working relationship with supervisory personnel? Do you get the feeling everyone is really anxious to print your catalog?

Equipment

For many years, printing equipment stayed pretty much the same from one year to the next. Major developments were few and far between. But today changes happen with regularity, and modern developments mean higher quality catalogs at reduced costs.

Thus it is important to make sure the printer you choose has kept abreast of technological advances such as computerized color and register controls, jet-ink addressing, selective binding, and a host of other changes that are causing a major revolution in printing.

You'll also want to make sure the printer you choose has equipment which can produce your catalog with a minimum of paper waste. This will be particularly important if you have chosen a unique trim size. When you have a catalog with special dimensions, your choice of printers becomes more limited.

Representation

Your relationship with a printer is only as good as the individuals with whom you deal. A good printer's sales representative, for example, should not only have a full knowledge of the graphic arts, but should also have had experience in solving a variety of catalog production problems for others in the past. It's important that you are able to communicate effectively with your rep, since it will be his or her responsibility to interpret your needs to every department involved in the production of your catalog. He or she should instantly understand your questions and know where to go to get answers and how to interpret them in terms you can understand.

Good catalog printers will also provide you with an in-house coordinator through whom you will work as your catalog goes through various stages of production. Once again, it's important that this coordinator be someone who understands your questions and provides quick and meaningful answers.

Full Service

It's generally to your advantage to have the printer handle as many different elements of printing, binding, and mailing as possible. If some of the work has to move outside the printer's plant, you'll not only have to absorb substantial packing, shipping, and receiving costs, but there will be more opportunities for spoilage and for something to go wrong.

Scheduling

There are periods when so many other catalogs are being printed, available time slots for printing your catalog may be limited. You should check to determine how much flexibility in scheduling each printer can offer. If a printer is overloaded during the time period you'll need, you'll not only be forced into a very rigid time frame but may discover there's no time available to make adjustments that would improve your catalog.

Backup Facilities

It is important to know what backup facilities your printer can offer. If your catalog will require every piece of equipment the printer has available during the period the catalog will be in production, you could find yourself in a real bind if anything goes wrong.

Charges

Watch out for "extras." Estimates from printers may appear to be equal . . . until the final bill comes in. Determine in advance what will be charged as "additional work."

Selecting a Color Separator

While preliminary work for gravure-printed catalogs is most often handled by the printer, offset preliminary is more often handled by an outside color separator.

There was a time when color separations involved a lot of photography and hand retouching. Today, however, color separation has become part of the electronics revolution. This has not only resulted in substantially lower costs, but also provides flexibility, improved quality, and considerably faster turnaround.

It is extremely important that there be a good working relationship between the color separator and your printer. Before selecting a color separator, be sure to ask your printer for recommendations.

Once a color separator has been selected, determine how he or she prefers to have artwork delivered. Some prefer to receive it in pieces, others prefer to have it fully assembled in pages or spreads. (And, as use of desktop publishing grows, there is increasing input in various computerized forms.)

When it comes to color separations, you generally get what you pay for. There are three primary quality levels:

- **Pleasing Color.** This usually involves the first output of color separation equipment, with very little correction. If highly accurate color is not required to show your products in an understandable way, this may be all you need for your catalog. Business-to-business and industrial catalogs, for example, often do not go beyond this level of quality in color separations.

- **Color Match.** The majority of consumer catalogs seek a higher level of color reproduction. At the color match level, special efforts are made to match the color separations to the input provided by the cataloger, often with specified adjustments indicated where the furnished photographic transparencies or artwork need to be altered.
- **Swatch Match.** This is the ultimate level in color separations. Actual product samples are furnished along with the photographic art, and the color separator does extra work to match the colors in the samples. This level is used most often for fashion catalogs.

Many of the same criteria suggested for the selection of a printer also apply to the selection of a color separator for your catalog. Evaluation of previous experience is important—particularly experience in producing separations for the same types of subjects from the same types of furnished materials. Available equipment should be considered, and samples and references should be carefully reviewed.

One key point to be considered is the type of proofs that will be provided for your review. The majority of catalogs rely on chromalin proofs, which are produced photographically. While press proofs on the actual paper to be used more closely duplicate what will happen when catalogs are printed, they are produced more slowly on proof presses and thus are not an actual representation of how things will look when run on high-speed offset presses.

One advantage of press proofs is that you obtain a set of progressive proofs, which show each of the primary colors and the key (black) separately. If you have color printing experts on your staff, these progressive proofs will aid in making color adjustments.

It's important to have an understanding in advance of how many proofs your color separator will supply without additional charges.

One of the big changes in the color separation field has been the storing of digital information. Once a subject has been separated, the color separator saves the computer information for future use. Thus, once color corrections are made, they can be utilized over and over without having to do the job again. Stored images, however, can be enlarged, reduced, outlined, or manipulated in other ways to fit the needs of a subsequent catalog. For catalogs which repeat the same merchandise frequently, digital storage can provide significant cost reductions.

Since the methods of color separation are in a constant state of change, it is important to review your needs regularly. It is recommended that you read the articles on this subject which appear regularly in *Catalog Age* magazine.

Selecting a Photographer

Since catalogs are a "graphics medium," photography is an extremely important element in catalog production. Careful selection of photographers is essential to good catalog production.

Catalog photography varies greatly in cost. In general, "you get what you pay for." But all of the costs don't show up on the photographer's invoice. Photographs may seem to be a bargain, until you get the bill from the color separator and/or printer for costly corrections.

Don't expect any photographer to be an expert on all types of photography. There are those who are experienced in fashion photography who fall short when producing tabletop product shots. A photographer who may produce the very finest shots of appliances probably can't come close to the work of a specialist in jewelry photography—and vice versa. Some photographers do great work in a studio, but produce inferior work in location shooting.

If you will be using models in your photographs, it is essential you select a photographer who has had extensive experience working with the kind of models you will be using. A photographer who has worked primarily with professional models may not work well with amateurs.

It's also important to check to determine what support services the photographer can offer—sets, props, styling, processing of film, retouching, etc.

By all means, review samples of previous catalog photography before selecting a photographer . . . and demand and check on references. Ask for samples of photographic transparencies or prints and samples of how that work appeared when printed in someone's catalog.

A key factor in selecting a photographer will be the workload an individual photographer or studio can handle in the time period when you will need your photography. Even when working with a large photographic studio, the photographers experienced in the type of photography you will require may be overloaded during the time periods you'll be needing their expertise.

It's also important to keep in mind a photographer's ability to communicate—to understand fully what you require and be able to respond to your questions in a way you can easily understand. One good way to communicate your needs to a photographer is to maintain a clip file so you can supply an example showing what you have in mind for each photograph.

Another area which needs to be resolved in advance is what will be included in a photographer's basic charges. The quotation you are given may include only the actual shooting, with additional charges for such things as creative discussions, picking up and returning merchandise, storage of merchandise and/or props, or downtime due to late delivery of merchandise or delays while models change garments.

And be sure to have a clear understanding of how many shots are to be taken, who is responsible for the costs involved in reshooting unacceptable photographs, who will pay for color corrections, retouching, etc.

There are four basic types of catalog photography.

Studio Still Lifes

These are often called "tabletop shots" even if they aren't actually shot atop a table. They are most often shot in the actual size to be presented in the catalog, using 4 x 5", 5 x 7" or 8 x 10" view cameras.

Studio Model Shots

When a model is added to a photograph, shooting becomes more complicated. This is particularly true in fashion photography, which usually involves more behind-the-camera personnel to handle details such as makeup, hairdressing, and styling and pressing of garments. While view cameras are used by many studios, with shots made to reproduction size whenever possible, there has been a growing use of 35mm or 2 $1/4$" cameras to permit the photographer to move around and achieve more action in the photograph.

In addition to eliminating worry about the weather when shooting, studio model photography provides more consistent color for flesh tones and the ability to adjust lights to eliminate harsh highlights and deep shadows that may be magnified when color separations are prepared.

In general, studio model shots are more economical than location shooting because more shots can be taken within a given time period. This not only saves on photographic expense, but may save substantially on model fees.

Location Model Shots

One of the major trends in today's consumer catalogs is creating an "editorial feel" by photographing models in an identifiable location—often a foreign setting. This, of course, involves a multitude of logistical problems. And if most of the photography will be done outdoors, there's always the problem of weather.

Most often, location shooting will be done with 35mm or 2 $1/4$" cameras, with multiple shots so selection of the best photograph can be done after the return from location.

While it usually requires more time for each photograph, careful planning can help reduce shooting expense. One of the advantages of location shooting is that models tend to be more relaxed and "true to life" when away from the artificial settings of a photographic studio.

Location Still Life Shots

When catalog photography is being taken "on location," a number of still life shots are often done at the same time, to maintain a comprehensive style for the catalog. While small format photography may be used, it is usually preferable to use larger format view cameras and supplementary lighting whenever possible.

When doing location photography, it is important to keep in mind that the subject of the photograph is the merchandise, not the surroundings. There is a tendency for some photographers to turn "tourist" when on location and give as much attention to backgrounds and props as they do to the merchandise.

Choosing a Camera Format

The choice of camera formats is one of the key items affecting your catalog photography. Today 35mm cameras have become the standard for many catalogs. Photographers generally love them for the flexibility they provide. They almost become part of the photographer himself or herself.

**Figure 11–1
Location Photography
(left and right)**

A popular trend in today's consumer catalogs is to stage photography in an identifiable location. This technique can provide a unique touch for a catalog and add special interest to the photographs. Copyright © Brownstone. Used with permission.

Because costs of 35mm film and processing are so low, photographers often shoot a whole roll of a subject—moving around to pop off one shot after another almost without thinking—rather than just restricting themselves to the one or two shots which are common with larger format cameras. This, however, has both advantages and disadvantages. While you will have several variations from which to choose, the ease of working with 35mm cameras can lead to getting a lot of not-quite-right photographs. Rather than concentrating on having lighting, backgrounds, props, focus, and a myriad of other details carefully planned before pushing the shutter, the photographer often gambles that quantity will lead to at least one "just right" photograph . . . and there are times that such a gamble just doesn't produce what you will need.

Another advantage of 35mm catalog photography is that the photographer frequently invests in a host of accessories for the camera—lenses of various types, special filters, etc.—and these can produce some truly exceptional catalog photographs.

Another popular smaller format camera is the 2 $^1/_4$ x 2 $^1/_4$," which uses 120 or 220 roll film. While this slightly larger size may yield better overall quality than 35mm, there is a problem in viewing the transparencies. There are many different types of projectors which make it easy to view 35mm slides, but it is most common to view 2 $^1/_4$" transparencies through a magnifier.

View cameras produce much larger transparencies, often shot to the actual size they will appear in the catalog. But the cameras are large and cumbersome and almost always are positioned atop a fixed camera stand. While this provides less flexibility for the photographer, it encourages greater attention to lighting and composition. And by looking through the ground glass on the back of the camera, you have an opportunity to get a good idea of just how everything will turn out before the film is imaged.

When using larger format view cameras, it is common to take Polaroid shots in advance so final adjustments can be made before the transparency is exposed.

But no matter what format you choose for your photography, it's important to take advantage of the expertise of a professional catalog photographer. While the world seems filled with outstanding amateur photographers whose work looks great in slide presentations, there are hundreds of "hidden" techniques which can enhance catalog photographs. And these techniques are learned only through experience. So look for a photographer whose experience has created a memory bank of ways to turn an ordinary photograph into something special. You may end up paying more per photograph. But if you want the best possible catalog, the cost is fully justified.

[Photography is a subject requiring a lot of thought when producing a catalog. An excellent handbook on the subject, "The S. D. Warren Catalog of Catalog Photography," has been created by Jo-Von Tucker, who is widely recognized as today's top innovator in catalog presentation. It and a companion volume, "Catalog of Catalog Design," can be obtained without cost by writing S.D. Warren Company, 225 Franklin Street, Boston, MA 02110.]

Art vs. Photography

Today's catalogs are primarily a photographic medium, although there are times when the details of a product can be better presented by the use of special artwork.

As a general rule, consider color photography as your starting point. We live in an age of color, and it will most often require a color catalog to face up to competition. Today's catalog customers have grown up in an era which is heavy on color photography—television, magazines, and even newspapers. They don't like to try to interpret artwork into "real life."

There was a time when the typical female catalog customer could look at a loose fashion sketch and immediately turn impressions into a detailed image in her mind (something which often caused men to scratch their heads in wonder). But such interpretation has become a lost art for the majority.

Along with the change in presentation styles have come graphic arts innovations which make color photographic presentations more economical than before. Electronic color separations have drastically reduced the cost of preliminary work. And the higher speeds and computerized controls of today's presses have reduced the difference in cost between full-color and one- or two-color printing.

Color photography, too, is much less costly. Interestingly, it often costs more to obtain a superior black-and-white photograph than a superior color photograph. Photographers have learned to use the crutch of color film to produce outstanding images, while few have the experience to know how to create sparkling black-and-white photographs.

As a general rule, any kind of quality artwork will cost more than a photograph of similar quality. But there are two situations when art may be preferred to photography for catalogs:

- When extremely fine detail is necessary to show the differences between products, and color is not essential. This often occurs in business and industrial catalogs—particularly to show small items (see Figure 11–2).

- When you are seeking a way to create a truly unique style for a catalog. A good example is the once-popular Banana Republic catalog, created by the husband-and-wife team of Mel and Pat Ziegler. The Zieglers never used a photograph in any of the catalogs they produced, but created a unique art style which appealed to their yuppie audience (See Figure 11–3).

Answering these two questions will tell you whether you really need a full-color catalog:

- Do the products you're presenting require color to be fully understood? If you're selling automobile tires, chances are you'll

Figure 11–2
Drawings for Detail

When it's necessary to show precise product detail in catalogs, drawings are often preferable to photographs. Copyright © Henry Schein. Used with permission.

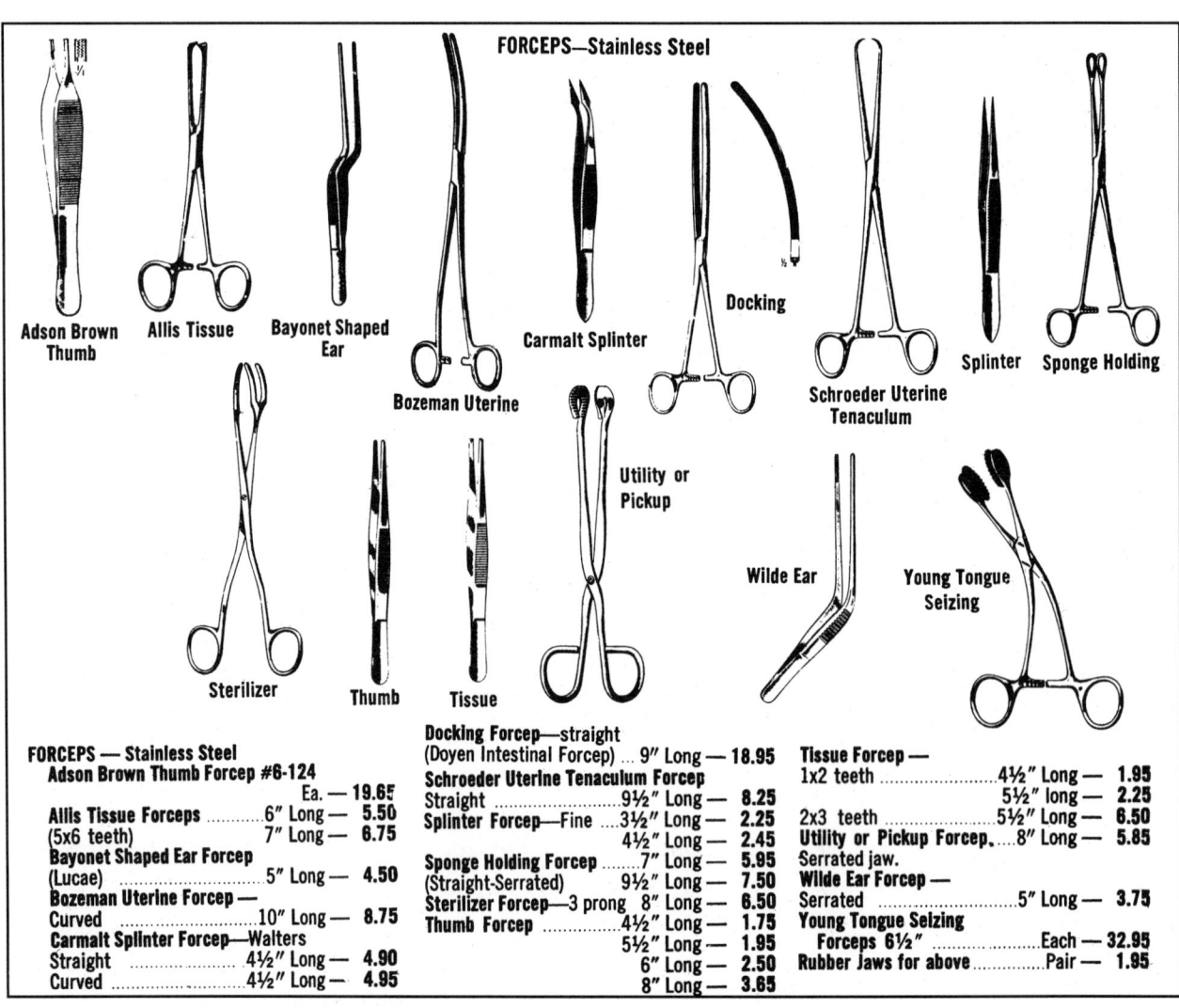

Figure 11–3
Unique Art Style

A unique style of presentation can capture the fancy of an audience. Copyright © The Gap/Banana Republic, Inc. Used with permission.

do just as well with black-and-white. But if you're selling roses, you'd better show everything in color or your audience won't be able to tell one rose from another.

- What's the competition doing? If your competitors have already established a "color platform" for selling your kind of products, chances are you will have to use color to be competitive. While you may be able to create a unique image for yourself with a black-and-white or two-color catalog, it is highly unlikely you'll win out over those who are showing the same kind of products in full color.

If you do use artwork, don't trust your own assumptions of what constitutes the best art. This is an area which calls for consensus. Art tastes vary widely and what strikes you as "good art" may not be appealing to the majority of your customers.

Other Production Considerations

Typesetting

We haven't said much about typesetting for your catalog—for good reason. We're in an era of rapidly changing methods of typsetting. I grew up in a period when good typography always involved metal type. In fact, I started my graphic arts career as a Linotype operator. But those days are gone forever.

First came photographic typesetting equipment and then fully computerized digital typesetting. And today, desktop publishing has become popular.

But don't believe anyone who tells you that the computer can make all of the typesetting decisions for you. Typesetting is still an art. And, while your customers probably won't recognize how one kind of typesetting differs from another, good typography will enhance your overall catalog image.

Typesetting generally represents only a minor portion of the total cost of a catalog. But it pays to have fresh, professional type for each issue you produce. Previously set material can be stored in a computer and quickly recalled for use in the next issue.

Getting Bids

It's a good idea to get advance bids from each of your suppliers, but beware of asking your present suppliers to rebid against competition every time around. A continuing relationship with suppliers works to your advantage. If you become known as a "low bid buyer," you'll seldom find suppliers going the extra mile when you need their assistance.

This isn't to suggest you shouldn't keep your mind open to possible economies through changes in suppliers, but remember that supplier loyalty can pay extra dividends.

An Important Thought

Paul Sampson, with whom I had the privilege of teaching direct marketing seminars throughout the world for many years, is fond of saying, "Make friends of your suppliers; not suppliers of your friends."

It's a thought well worth remembering. When you look to your friends and relatives to help you produce your catalogs, you'll often find it difficult to dig your way out if things aren't going right.

But, on the other hand, the buyer-supplier relationship shouldn't be an adversarial relationship. You'll find your suppliers will give you a lot of extra help if you develop close and friendly relations.

Evaluating Catalog Results

12

Efficiency per Square Inch

There is a very simple way to evaluate catalog results. It's called efficiency per square inch.

You start by adding up all of the square inches of printing surface in your catalog. From this you subtract every square inch which isn't devoted to selling a specific product (such as space used for editorial and ordering information, space devoted to things designed to create a general image for your catalog, even products which have been included for "atmosphere" rather than to generate sales).

This will yield the *net selling square inches* in your catalog. You then divide the total cost of the catalog by the number of net selling square inches to determine your *cost per selling square inch*.

Once you have this figure, you'll be able to determine if the profits from sales will "pay" for the space you've devoted to each item.

When you begin your evaluation, it's a good idea to start with entire categories of merchandise—particularly if you've organized your catalog into "departments." No individual item works in a vacuum—sales will be affected by items of a similar nature. So you first want to determine if your present "mix" in each product category is carrying its weight in terms of the costs to present it.

The next step is to consider full two-page spreads—or if you have laid out your catalog so that each page becomes a separate unit rather than half of a spread, you should make an evaluation on a page-by-page basis.

Everything on a spread or page unit tends to work in concert with everything else on that spread or page. Thus it's important to evaluate your catalog on a presentation basis.

But the most important evaluation will be on an item-by-item basis. Did an item generate enough profits to pay for the space it was given?

Don't worry about finite measurements. You can factor in allowances for page and gutter margins and other unprinted areas, plus miscellaneous things such as captions that cover multiple products. Most catalogers create a transparent square inch grid and simply lay it atop a merchandise unit in the catalog and count the number of squares. And when a grid system has been used to create the catalog, with merchandise units occupying a certain number of grid spaces rather than just square inches, it is easier to simply consider page fractions (half-page, quarter-page, third-page, etc.).

If your products tend to have a uniform profit margin, you can deal in gross sales rather than profits in making your evaluation. But if margins vary from item to item, you'll probably want to establish profit categories (items with a 50 percent mark-up, those with 65 percent mark-up, etc.).

You can always build finite measurements into your computer records, but for basic catalog evaluation it's best to keep things simple.

But don't simply keep computer printouts as your records. Have marked-up catalogs. Figure 12–2 shows a hypothetical example of a marked-up catalog spread. The "stickers" on each item carry the following information:

Figure 12–1
Profitability Formula

To create this hypothetical example we made the following assumptions:

- One million copies were produced at a cost of 50¢ each. Thus the total cost of the catalog was $500,000.
- There were 64 selling pages in the catalog.
- By dividing the total cost of $500,000 by 64 pages, we arrived at a net selling cost of $7,812.50 per page.
- To simplify this example, we used only four basic space units and rounded off the space costs to the nearest dollar:
    - ²/₃ page with a cost of $5,208.00
    - ½ page with a cost of $3,906.00
    - ¼ page with a cost of $1,953.00
    - ⅙ page with a cost of $1,302.00
- To determine profit margins, we made the assumption that the cost of goods was 50 percent of the selling price of each item.
- To determine the profit for each item, we took the total sales and divided by 2 (to allow for the 50 percent cost of goods). We then subtracted the "cost" of the unit of space devoted to the item. This gave the net profit figure.

The first item at the upper left of the spread was a jacket which was given a half-page of space. It sold 65 units, generating total sales of

Figure 12–2
Marked-up Catalog Spread

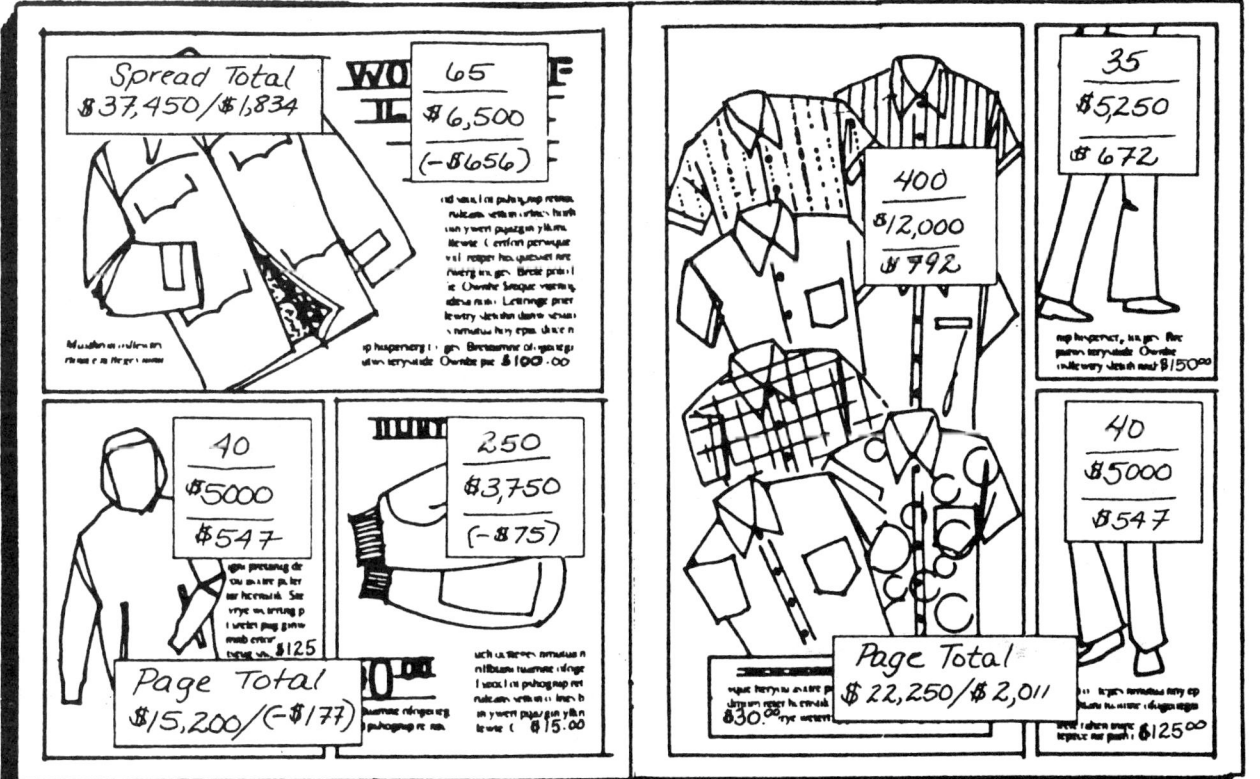

$6,500. The cost of goods was $3,250, and the cost of the space was $3,906. Thus there was a loss of $656 for this selling unit.

The parka in the lower left-hand corner received a quarter-page of space at a cost of $1,953. It produced 40 sales at $125 each, generating gross income of $5,000. This resulted in a net profit of $547 for the selling unit.

The gloves next to the parka sold for $15 per pair and, with sales of 250 pairs, produced $3,750 of gross income. When the cost of goods ($1,875) and the cost of space ($1,953) were charged, this selling unit resulted in a loss of $75.

The page totals were shown by the "sticker" at the lower left of the page: $15,200 of gross income, but a loss of $177 when cost of merchandise and page costs were deducted.

The two-thirds-page unit devoted to shirts was treated as a single selling unit. (In actual practice, however, it would be common to consider the number of units and total sales for each style offered.) The shirts were priced at $30 each and produced 400 sales totaling $12,000. When cost of goods ($6,000) and cost of space ($5,208) were deducted, this resulted in $792 profit for the selling unit.

The trousers in the upper right-hand corner of the spread produced 35 sales at $150 for gross income of $5,250. When cost of goods ($2,625) and cost of the space unit ($1,302) were deducted, the selling unit produced $672 in profit.

The other pair of trousers, selling for $125, produced 40 sales for gross income of $5,000 and a net profit of $547.

The totals for this page were $22,250 in gross sales, generating a net profit of $2,011.

The totals for the spread are shown on the "sticker" in the upper left-hand corner: $37,450 in gross sales; $1,834 in profit.

I can't stress strongly enough the importance of marking up a copy of every catalog you produce . . . and keeping the marked-up catalogs in a permanent file for future review. It's too easy to forget just how items were presented, how they were positioned on a spread with other items, where the spread was positioned in the catalog, how price points compared with similar items, and a host of details which are highly important when making decisions for the future. Having a visual record, complete with hard-and-fast figures, is essential to good catalog evaluation.

Presentation Factors

Some catalogs have a regular practice of building presentation factors into catalog evaluation. For example, they may assign extra space costs to hot spots in a catalog—particularly cover positions. They may also assign a "surcharge" to an item which was given a special graphic treatment (other than simply giving it added space) to make it stand out from other similar items.

Some catalogs consider other factors such as different weights or grades of paper used in different parts of a catalog; how close the spread was to the front or back of the catalog; whether items were presented in full color or as black-and-white illustrations.

While these can be important considerations, they should be secondary to the basic "efficiency per square inch" evaluation. And, if they are to be considered, "surcharges" should be assigned in advance. If you wait until the results come in, there is always a tendency to rationalize so the profit picture for a favorite item will come out the way you want it to look.

It is a good idea to note unique presentation factors on computer printouts and other nonvisual records, so these factors aren't overlooked when reviewing sales records. Most often, this is done simply by entering an "exception code," rather than including specific details. This will suggest taking a look at the actual catalog before making any firm decisions on the basis of the raw sales figures.

With marked-up catalogs, however, it is easy to bring presentation factors into focus as you are doing your catalog evaluation, without having to add any special markings.

Catalog Projections

While most catalog evaluations are done at the end of a catalog's selling period, it is a good practice to conduct a minimum of two preliminary evaluations.

The first evaluation usually comes after about 10 days of sales. Many catalogs wait until this preliminary evaluation has been made before making firm inventory commitments for the entire "selling season." Generally, you get a pretty good feel for the relative popularity of items of merchandise at this time.

However, there are several factors to keep in mind:

- Don't start counting days when just a handful of orders have trickled in. Start counting days of receipt of orders with the first day when you get a substantial number of orders or when orders start showing up from your most distant points of catalog distribution.
- Carefully monitor receipt of catalogs in all parts of your distribution area. It is advisable to have designated monitors who report the actual day they received a given catalog. (There are monitoring organizations that will provide this service for you, and some

printers and mailing houses will assist you in this activity.) It is not unusual for there to be as much as a two-week difference in catalog receipt in different parts of the country, and it's important to know what percentage of your catalog distribution has been completed when you do a preliminary evaluation.
- Keep in mind seasonal factors. Your past experience is the best guide, but you may be able to obtain valuable information from vendors if you don't yet have your own previous experience to guide you.
- Recognize that you won't yet have any record of merchandise returns when you make your initial evaluation. It usually takes at least a month to compile a significant record of merchandise returned for refunds or exchanges.
- Recognize that customers usually respond more quickly than prospects to a catalog mailing. You may want to do separate projections of response from each group as part of your preliminary evaluation. Or, if you've made extensive use of outside lists, you may want to delay a bit longer before making your preliminary evaluation and projections.

The second projection is usually made at "half-life"—the time when experience indicates you have received half of the orders which will eventually be rung up for a given catalog. At this point, you can normally project what final results will be with a reasonable degree of accuracy.

Half-life evaluation is often vital in determining the direction your next catalog will take, and it will give you the opportunity to restock inventory to meet projected sales levels and make arrangements to dispose of excess inventory while it is still in demand elsewhere.

Many of the factors suggested for consideration in making your first projection also should be considered when establishing the proper time for your half-life evaluation.

Daily Reports

While full catalog evaluation occurs at specified intervals, most catalogers maintain a daily "flash" report to have a "feel" of how the business is going. These seldom are on an item-by-item basis, however. Most often they show the total orders received each day, a comparison with last year's results, and how response measures up to the planned budget. These reports may also show the number of items on back order, merchandise returns, and the flow of customer service activity.

Weekly Reports

Typical weekly reports for a catalog show the response rate, average order size, and projections against budget. Some catalogs also maintain weekly records of mail response vs. telephone response, credit vs. cash sales, and a listing of best-selling items. In addition, there are often regular weekly reports to management showing inventory levels on all or selected items.

Monthly Reports

Monthly reports are generally more detailed and include such things as an analysis of response on a list by list basis, an analysis of advertising by source, a status report of all catalog activities, and financial statements, with an analysis of total sales measured against budgets and previous years.

List Analysis

Along with other analysis, it is important to study how each list performs. The factors in list analysis include the number of orders per thousand copies mailed, the response percentage, the average order size, the cost to sell, and profits/losses generated.

Many catalogs assign a lower cost per thousand for catalogs mailed to prospect lists. The assumption is that the catalog would be mailed to customer lists even if no prospecting is being done. Therefore, fixed costs are all assigned to mailings to house lists, and prospect lists are evaluated on the basis of the variable "additional thousands" cost.

No matter how well you code your mailings, there will always be orders that can't be traced to a specific list. While it's usually possible to identify orders from previous customers, the specific list producing "unknown orders" from prospects is more difficult to identify. Most often, unknown orders are assigned to various outside lists on the basis of the percentage of "known" orders which have been identified. For example, if a given list pulls 10 percent of all identified prospect orders, it is assigned 10 percent of the unknown orders.

Establishing Catalog Costs

There are substantial differences of opinion on how to assign up-front costs in catalog evaluations. Some catalogs assign a percentage of general and administrative costs and all internal creative costs to each catalog. Others assign only creative costs that can be pinpointed as being generated by a specific catalog. And some simply assign outside purchases to a specific catalog and expect profits generated to cover both internal administrative and creative costs.

The specific cost assignment system adopted will generally be determined by the overall accounting systems being used. However, it's important to be consistent. Once you've established a cost assignment system, stick with it so you'll be able to make consistent comparisons from year to year.

Production Cost Analysis

Another important part of evaluating catalog results is a regular analysis of production costs. Some of the things which should be included in this analysis are:

- Design
- Typesetting
- Printing
- List rentals
- Copywriting
- Separations
- Postage
- Photography
- Paper
- Mailing

By making a regular analysis of how costs in each of these areas change from one catalog to the next, you'll be in a position to identify trends which affect your bottom line.

Flow Chart Analysis

Perhaps as important as any of the forms of catalog analysis already discussed is to maintain a flow chart depicting the actual time required for each element of catalog production. Before you plan your next catalog, you should toss all of the excuses aside and take a look at what happened in actual practice.

Among the factors to be analyzed are the following.

- How many days did it take to select merchandise and create the pagination of the catalog?
- How long did it take to generate the layouts . . . and what were the average hours per page?
- When were layout approvals completed, and how many days were required for revisions?
- Time required per page for copywriting, editing, approvals, and rewriting.
- Typesetting hours/days, including proofreading and all revisions.
- Photography schedules, including time required to obtain merchandise for shooting, selecting and scheduling models, actual photography, film processing, approvals, and reshooting.
- Time required for retouching of photographs.
- Number of hours per page for assembly of material for delivery to the color separator.

- Color separation time, including the proofing, the review, and the corrections.
- Printing production, including the number of days from delivery of color separations to the printer to production of "bluelines" for your review; time required for corrections; press days required to complete printing.
- Number of days from placement of orders for paper to delivery of paper to the printer.
- Time required for list selection, merge/purge of lists, and preparation of mailing labels or delivery of address tapes to the printer or mailing house.
- Amount of time for production of each "extra" item such as separate covers, wraps, order forms, etc.
- Number of days required for delivery of all materials to the point of assembly.
- Time required for binding and mailing.
- Average number of days for delivery of catalogs to customers and prospects.
- Response curve showing flow of orders.
- Time required for order processing, packing, and shipping.
- Actual experience in merchandise returns, indicating the average number of days from time of shipment to time of receipt and processing of returns.
- Number of days vendors required to fulfill merchandise reorders.
- Time required to generate computer reports and prepare marked-up catalogs.
- And by all means, identify any delays caused while awaiting necessary approvals. While you may think these delays are exceptions, they will most likely be repeated catalog after catalog, and it's important to anticipate them when planning the next catalog.

Don't Stop Marketing When the Catalogs Go to the Post Office

13

As we emphasized in Chapter 2, there is a basic formula for catalog success:

PROSPECTS = COSTS

CUSTOMERS = PROFITS

The name of the game is to invest money to convert prospects into catalog customers . . . and then make profits through future sales to those who have been convinced to buy from a catalog for a first time.

Unfortunately, when you look at the records of hundreds of catalog companies, you discover the disturbing fact that, on the average, 50 percent of those who make a first-time purchase never buy from that catalog again. Interestingly, many catalog companies consider this rebuying rate acceptable, rather than asking the obvious question, "What are we doing wrong?" Few magazine publishers would be willing to accept a 50 percent renewal rate as normal . . . and most other businesses count on better than 50 percent of their new customers to come back and buy again.

Why should catalogs lose half of those buyers in whom they have invested so much money to convert from prospects into customers? Perhaps it is because they put too much of their marketing effort into just half of their business. They spend millions of dollars to create attractive, purchase-compelling catalogs and forget that the most memorable impression they make on customers comes later—at the time their packages are delivered.

My personal feeling is that first-time buyers aren't really "customers" until they've made a second purchase. They may merely have been "curious" when they sent in their first orders . . . or some special promotion may have caught their eye. The real test is whether they buy again. Repeat purchases is the name of the game in catalog marketing.

Catalog marketing efforts shouldn't stop when the catalogs go to the post office. But all too often, the all-important "back end" of the business—the things which happen after the catalogs go to the post office—becomes strictly an operational procedure. All emphasis is placed on efficiency, rather than recognizing that *every* contact with a customer represents a marketing opportunity—an opportunity to lay the foundation for future sales.

There's no better marketing opportunity than when a customer's packages are delivered. That's the "moment of truth"—the time when customers are most likely to decide whether they want to do business with a catalog again. It should be a very pleasant experience. But to whom do many catalog companies assign this important *marketing* task? It falls into the hands of the lowest paid, most unmotivated employees on their payrolls—their shipping clerks.

Over a period of years, we've analyzed how more than 1,000 different catalogs handle a first-time order from a new customer. From our research, we have discovered 10 specific "back end" activities which tend to make one catalog stand out from another.

Order Acknowledgments

I've become a strong believer in acknowledging the receipt of orders—particularly from new customers. Even if you plan to ship everything which has been ordered within a day or two of receiving the order, a separate acknowledgment provides an opportunity to begin a personal dialogue with a customer.

While it is common for catalogs to send back order notices when they will be unable to ship something promptly, relatively few send acknowledgments of *every* order. A program of order acknowledgments doesn't have to cost a lot of money. In fact, a number of catalog companies include special offers with order acknowledgments and actually make a profit from these mailings.

The acknowledgment can be in the form of a postcard or letter. While the basic message can be pretty much the same for everyone, it helps to list the merchandise which is being shipped and an estimate

Porter's Camera Store Inc.

Box 628 Cedar Falls, Iowa 50613 · Phone 268-0104 (NC 319)

August 21, 1986

Mr. Richard S. Hodgson
1433 Johnnys Way
Westtown, PA 19395

Dear Mr. Hodgson:

Thank you for your recent order. It is a pleasure to have you as a customer.

We are sorry to inform you that we are temporarily out of stock on item # 45-0051, Reflecto Clamp Lamp.

We do have this on order and we are expecting our shipment shortly. We should be able to supply your order without a long delay.

We thank you for your patience in this matter.

Sincerely,

PORTER'S CAMERA STORE, INC.

Mrs. Dew Hansen
Customer Service Dept.

DH:cao

**Figure 13–1
Back Order Notices**

It is especially important to notify customers promptly when there will be a shipment delay. This letter from Porter's Camera Store is an excellent example of customer-friendly handling of a back order. Copyright © Porter's Camera Store Inc. Used with permission.

Figure 13–2
Order Acknowledgments

Even simple cards thanking customers for their orders provide assurance that an order has been received and can be an important step in establishing customer dialogue. Copyright © Brownstone. Used with permission.

> Dear Brownstone Studio Customer,
>
> Many thanks for your order, if you have an inquiry regarding your order, please refer to the order number printed under your address on the reverse side of this card.
>
> Address your inquiry to our Customer Service Department at 1 East 43rd St., New York, New York 10175
>
> Remember-everything selected from Brownstone Studio may be returned for refund or exchange, but please do this as quickly as you can.
>
> Again, my thanks for your order and I do hope you will be pleased with your selections when you receive them.
>
> Sincerely,
>
> *Jean Grayson*
>
> Jean Grayson
>
> Out of State Toll-free Number 1-800-221-2468
> N.Y. State Toll-free Number 1-800-442-8422
> New York City 212-883-1090

of delivery date for any items which are being placed on back order.

A particularly important time for an order acknowledgment is when a new customer has placed a first order. Country Store sends a friendly greeting:

> **Good Morning!**
>
> **Thank you for your order. And thank you for giving me the opportunity to perform one of my favorite duties here at Country Store—welcoming a new customer!**
>
> **Our eager country crew carefully attended your order from the moment it arrived 'til it was placed on a delivery truck right at our back door. We hope you'll be so pleased with our unique, country-flavored items that you'll become another one of our regular customers. Some folks order so often we start recognizing their names and thinking of them as friends.**
>
> **Many of us here at Country Store have country backgrounds, so it's just our nature to develop a kind of small-town, personal relationship with our customers. In fact, many of the new items we add each year are suggested by our customers. Maybe it was one of those very items that "caught your eye."**
>
> **Actually, we don't think of Country Store as our store—we think of it as your store. So if you ever have any questions, comments or suggestions, please drop me a line personally.**
>
> **We'll look forward to hearing from you again soon, whether it's an order or a friendly note. Remember, the door is always open at Country Store!**

The note was signed by Melody Trick, Supervisor of Customer Service, and included a handwritten postscript: "We've enclosed a little brochure of some of our most popular merchandise you may have missed!"

Figure 13-3
Welcoming a New Customer

A first order from a new customer calls for a "welcome aboard" message. This note from Country Store quickly establishes a friendly bond between the cataloger and the new customer. Copyright © Reiman Associates. Used with permission.

Good Morning!

Thank you for your order. And thank you for giving me the opportunity to perform one of my favorite duties here at Country Store—welcoming a new customer!

Our eager country crew carefully attended your order from the moment it arrived 'til it was placed on a delivery truck right at our back door. We hope you'll be so pleased with our unique, country-flavored items that you'll become another one of our regular customers. Some folks order so often we start recognizing their names and thinking of them as friends.

Many of us here at Country Store have country backgrounds, so it's just our nature to develop a kind of small-town, personal relationship with our customers. In fact, many of the new items we add each year are suggested by our customers. Maybe it was one of those very items that "caught your eye".

Actually, we don't think of Country Store as *our* store—we think of it as *your* store. So if you ever have any questions, comments or suggestions, please drop me a line personally.

We'll look forward to hearing from you again soon, whether it's an order or a friendly note. Remember, the door is *always* open at Country Store!

Cordially,

Melody Trick

Melody Trick, Supervisor
Customer Service

P.S. We've enclosed a little brochure of some of our most popular merchandise you may have missed!

5925 Country Lane • Greendale WI 53129 • (414) 423-0100

Instant Response

As a general rule, a catalog company should be able to ship within 48 hours of receiving an order. This applies not only to merchandise shipments, but also to requests for your catalog.

We made an analysis of 306 catalogs we requested and found that only 24 percent arrived within one month of being requested. Another 16 percent took two months; 11 percent took three months; 12 percent came in four months; and, at the end of six months we still hadn't received catalogs from 37 percent of those to whom we sent individual requests, including several to whom we sent checks for their catalogs in the amount requested.

Those who have analyzed conversion of catalog requests to sales find that there is a substantially higher percentage of response when catalogs are sent promptly. And customers who promptly received the merchandise they order are much more likely to place repeat orders in the future.

It is interesting to note that the most successful mail order catalogs in the United States all make it a regular practice to ship promptly. Lands' End, for example, states:

> **We ship faster than anyone we know of. We ship items in stock the day after we receive the order. At the height of the last Christmas season the longest time an order was in house was 36 hours, excepting monograms which took another 12 hours.**

In the business-to-business catalog field, Quill Corporation is widely recognized as one of the most successful companies in the world. In its "Customers' Bill of Rights" Quill states:

> **As a customer, you are entitled to fast delivery. Unless otherwise indicated, the product should be shipped within 8–32 hours. In the event of a delay, you are entitled to immediate notification, along with an honest estimate of expected shipping date.**

Those who look upon shipping as strictly an operational procedure often excuse delayed shipments by pointing to the necessity of balancing work flow. But catalogers who understand the marketing implications know that money spent to assure prompt delivery pays off in more frequent reorders and future profits.

Better Packaging

What kind of an impression will your package make when it is delivered to your customer? Far too many catalogs look for the most economical kind of package they can find.

In our test orders, we ordered knit shirts from five different catalogs. Four simply jammed the shirt into a plain kraft bag. Brooks Brothers, on the other hand, went to the effort to make the arrival of their shirt a special occasion by using a sturdy box.

We also ordered women's clothing from a number of different catalogs. Most simply inserted the items in plain shipping bags. Brownstone Studio, however, used a corrugated box with special imprinted tape. When you opened the box, you were greeted by decorative imprinted tissue. But it was how the merchandise was packaged inside the tissue that really made an impression. The blouse we had ordered was on a hanger inside a plastic garment bag.

It's good to assume that your customers also buy from similar mail order catalogs. A comparison of the kinds of packages they receive may easily determine who gets first preference when they decide to order again.

Imprinted boxes make a special impression. They indicate the catalog company takes special pride in its shipments. One of the best examples of an imprinted box is one used by Country Store. It was imprinted "Open With Cheer" and had a little letter printed on the outside of the box:

> **Dear Country Store Customer:**
>
> I grew up on a small farm in southern Illinois, so I know what a happy occasion it is when a package arrives in the mailbox at the end of the lane.
>
> I have fond memories of my excitement while anticipating what was inside the box (when you grow up on a small farm in Edwards County, Illinois, you don't get very many packages). I hope this package brings you that same kind of excitement.
>
> We've planned this "Grand Opening" especially for you. We send you our BEST from Country Store. Thanks for your order!

The letter was signed by Larry Graham, and the carton had an attractive imprint reading: "Another 'Grand Opening' from Country Store—'The Farm Store in Your Mailbox'."

Better Packaging Material

It isn't only the outsides of packages that make an impression on your customers. What's inside is just as important.

One of my personal pet peeves is the indiscriminate use of plastic "peanuts" in mail order packages. I realize they are an efficient packaging material, and do a good job of protecting contents. But too many catalog companies don't stop to consider how overuse of these little globs of plastic can irritate customers. They stick in crevices of a product . . . they become loaded with static electricity and many times are almost impossible to shake off a product—or your fingers . . . they're particularly inexcusable in a book shipment where they find their way between the pages of the book and always seem to stick to a laminated dust jacket . . . and they have a tendency to "hide" small objects in a multiproduct shipment.

If you're using loose packaging material, it is advisable to enclose small items in individual envelopes or bags so they aren't overlooked.

In these days of environmental concerns, many catalog companies are searching for alternate packaging materials that are biodegradable. A shipment from Stash Tea included this memo:

> **WHY WE'VE CHANGED PACKING MATERIAL**
> We know you care as much about the environment as we do.
>   Although for years styrofoam "peanuts" seemed ideal for packing, when scientific studies linked plastic foam to a depletion of the ozone layer, we went looking for an alternative.
>   Right now we're using paper. It costs a little more and is harder to pack with, but it's biodegradable and preserves our atmosphere, so it's worth it.
>   We hope you're happy with our new packing material. If, however, you discover damage in your order, please call us at 1–800–826–4218.
>   Your feedback will help us streamline our new packing procedures so we can give the best service to both you and our environment.

If you wish to make a special impression, you might consider alternate packing material such as plastic foam, bubble-pack, or sheets of special tissue or paper. One of the most interesting shipments I've ever received was a box of books from England. To protect the books during shipment, the publisher used crumpled press sheets from a British map printer. I suspect we may have spent more time looking over the maps than we did reading the books.

Ship Letters

I feel every catalog should give consideration to what I call "ship letters." The receipt of a package presents an excellent opportunity to "talk" with your customers on a person-to-person basis. And the best vehicle to do just that is the good old-fashioned letter.

A good example of a ship letter is the one from Blair shown in Figure 13–4. It reads:

> **Dear Customer:**
>   Just a note to thank you for your order. I sincerely hope it meets with your complete satisfaction.
>   For more than 79 years, we've based our entire business on providing high quality merchandise at very reasonable prices.
>   Every effort has been made to assure that your order meets those standards, because we fully realize that your continued goodwill is the most important part of our business.
>   In the future, I hope we can serve you more often as we continue to expand the types and styles of merchandise we are able to offer.
>   Our newest collection is just now being prepared, and it includes some really exciting surprises. As an active customer, you will be among the very

first to receive information on these products. And we shall be looking forward to having the pleasure of serving you again.

Until then, thank you for this order, and for the privilege of being able to count you among our most valued customers.

It was signed by John L. Blair, President, and had this postscript: "Be sure to take a look at the special group of Bargain Slips enclosed. They're very attractively priced!" Enclosed with the letter was a packet of special offers.

**Figure 13–4
Ship Letters**

An ideal time to deliver personal messages to customers is when the merchandise arrives. This friendly letter, for example, is used by the Blair Corporation of Warren, Pennsylvania. Copyright © Blair Corporation. Used with permission.

JOHN L. BLAIR

Dear Customer:

   Just a note to thank you for your order. I sincerely hope it meets with your complete satisfaction.

   For more than 79 years, we've based our entire business on providing high quality merchandise at very reasonable prices.

   Every effort has been made to assure that your order meets those standards, because we fully realize that your continued goodwill is the most important part of our business.

   In the future, I hope we can serve you more often as we continue to expand the types and styles of merchandise we are able to offer.

   Our newest collection is just now being prepared, and it includes some really exciting surprises. As an active customer, you will be among the very first to receive information on these products. And we shall be looking forward to having the pleasure of serving you again.

   Until then, thank you for this order, and for the privilege of being able to count you among our most valued customers.

                              Sincerely,

                              John L. Blair
                              BLAIR

P.S. Be sure to take a look at the special
     group of Bargain Slips enclosed. They're
     very attractively priced!

Where more than 15 million customers all over the United States shop direct by mail • Established 1910

© BLAIR 1989

© COPYRIGHT 1991 DARTNELL CORPORATION

If you're one of those jaded direct mail pros who question if anybody actually reads such letters, let me assure you my experience indicates they do, indeed, get very high readership.

When I was with the Franklin Mint, I often received letters *complaining* because a shipment had arrived without the ship letter we normally sent. We used ship letters to tell something special about the product being shipped and to reveal interesting details about future shipments in a collector's series. I'm convinced these letters played a major role in the exceptionally high retention rate enjoyed by the Franklin Mint. I can assure you far more than 50 percent of our first-time customers bought again and again.

Joan Cook includes an attractive little 4 1/4 x 5 1/2" folder with shipments. The cover asks, "Can We Talk?" Copy inside reads:

> **Dear Customer,**
>
> You and I rarely get to meet each other, doing business by mail as we do. And so I'm never sure how well we're treating you as a customer.
>
> I know when you're satisfied, because you order from us regularly. And of course we hear from you when you're dissatisfied!
>
> But what if you feel "lukewarm" about this order? It's okay, but not great? Probably, you won't contact us—not for an adjustment, and certainly not for another order.
>
> If that's the case, we've done a poor job. We won't stay in business with one-time customers. We need to satisfy you so completely that you'll feel confident in ordering from us regularly.
>
> I hope you'll tell me if you have even the slightest complaint. The special phone number and mail address are below. I won't answer directly, because my Customer Service office has all the records, but I will get a report on your call or letter.
>
> Thank you again for your order.
>
> Call our Customer Service Rep, Mrs. Parker, toll-free 1–800–327–1611, or write to her at our Customer Service Dept., P.O. Box 21157, Ft. Lauderdale, FL 33335.

Lands' End uses a number of different folders as ship letters. Each features an actual member of the Lands' End staff and helps create a more personal bond with customers.

Figure 13–5 features Charlene Dodge and has the quote, "I'm the last one to see your order before it goes out the door." Copy inside the folder reads:

> Believe me, I take my responsibility seriously. To be more specific, what I do is check the packing slip against what's in the box being sent to you to make sure everything you ordered is in it. And that it's in good shape.

Figure 13–5
Creating a Personal Bond with Customers

Lands' End encloses friendly cards with its shipments. Various Lands' End staffers are featured. Copyright © Lands' End Inc. Reprinted courtesy of Lands' End Catalog.

"I'm the last one to see your order before it goes out the door."

"Believe me, I take my responsibility seriously. To be more specific, what I do is check the packing slip against what's in the box being sent to you to make sure everything you ordered is in it. And that it's in good shape.

"I even try to imagine who you are and what you look like. I feel I get to 'know' you in a way.

"So, if you would, when you get your Lands' End order, check it out, would you? Just to make sure I didn't slip up on anything. Thanks."

Charlene Dodge

I even try to imagine who you are and what you look like. I feel I get to "know" you in a way.

So, if you would, when you get your Lands' End order, check it out, would you? Just to make sure I didn't slip up on anything. Thanks.

Customer Service Enclosures

Another type of helpful enclosure anticipates possible customer service problems and tries to head them off at the pass.

Making it easy to return merchandise is one example. (And for any who may be new to the mail order field, let me assure you you won't get more returns if you make it easy for your customers—but it makes life easier for both you and your customers, and your customers will thank you for your consideration.)

Spiegel uses a two-part pack slip, the second half of which is a return form. It relists the items which are being shipped and in bold letters says, "We'll arrange your return pickup. Call our Returns Hotline." There's a gummed return label at the top of the return form, and copy on the back says:

> **Your total satisfaction is guaranteed. Our promise for over 120 years. If something isn't right, we accept its return without question. All we ask is that you call our Returns Hotline . . . for a pickup as soon as you decide. A fast return means a faster refund or credit for you.**
>
> To return any item in this order, call our Returns Hotline number . . . Depending on your delivery method, we'll arrange a UPS or freight pick up. Or you can mail back your **UPS** package. In either case, we pay return costs.
>
> Returns Hotline Operators are on duty Mon. thru Sat. 8 AM to 8 PM and Sun. 10 AM to 8 PM. They will be happy to take your reorder.
>
> Or you can place your reorder at our toll-free number, or by attaching your order form to this return form.
>
> To assure fast and accurate handling of your return, please be sure to:
>
> 1. Enclose this return form in your return package.
> 2. Return your item in its original packaging. Keep the carton or wrapping until you have decided on your purchase.
> 3. Insure for full value only those items which were sent to you insured (see other side).
> 4. Keep your shipping receipt until you have received credit for your return. No COD returns accepted.

If you don't think this special pickup service is valuable, you need only talk with some Spiegel customers. It is often singled out as one of the primary reasons so many reorder from Spiegel time and again.

Another company that does an excellent job in this area, even if it doesn't offer to arrange a UPS pickup, is Brookstone. It uses the package enclosure shown in Figure 13–7. Copy begins:

> **We take pride in our high quality standards of inspection and packaging; thus, we hope everything is correct and in perfect condition.**
>
> **If a return is necessary, please fill out the reverse side of this form. This helps us complete your request as soon as possible . . .**

Lands' End encloses a colorful folder with its shipments. Copy on the cover reads, "We hope you're completely happy with the merchandise you've ordered from us." On first opening the folder, you see another panel: "But if you're not, return it. We want a chance to make things right!"

Copy inside the folder is headed "Returns made easy" and provides detailed instructions on how to return merchandise. It begins with a picture of six members of the Lands' End returns department, and copy starts with this quote:

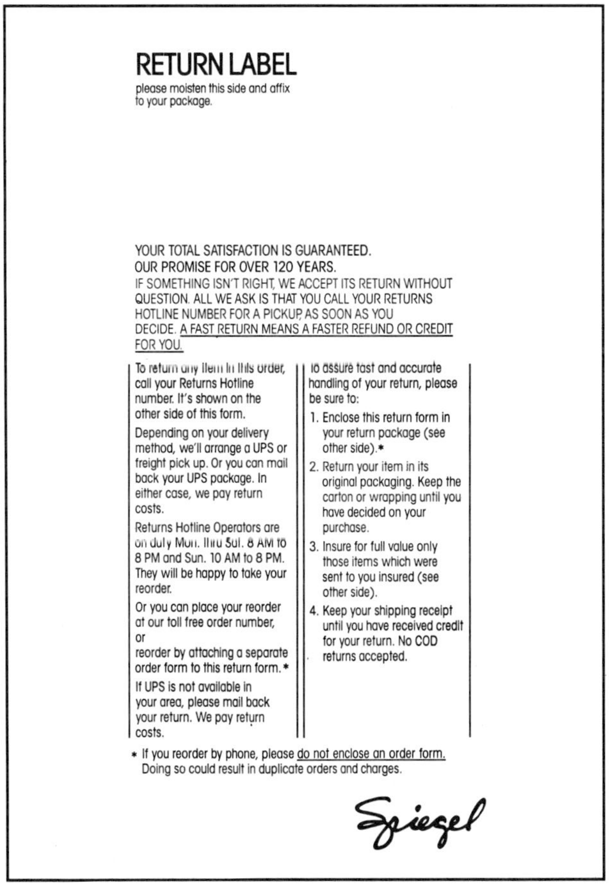

> **"We want you to be 100% satisfied with the merchandise you order from us. We don't want it to grow cobwebs in your closet—we want you to wear it!**

Figure 13–6
Customer Service Enclosures

Catalogers can often solve potential customer service problems by placing special enclosures in their shipments. This packing slip used by Spiegel, for example, provides complete details on how to return merchandise and even includes an attached personalized return label. Copyright © Spiegel. Used with permission.

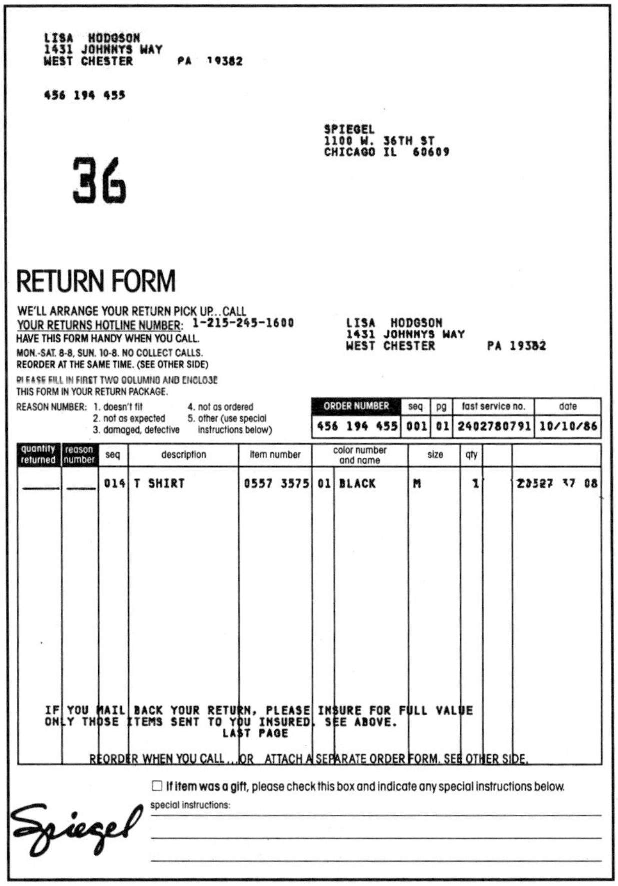

Brookstone Company

Vose Farm Road
Peterborough, New Hampshire 03458
(603) 924-9511

Dear Brookstone Customer:

We take pride in our high quality standards of inspection and packaging; thus, we hope everything is correct and in perfect condition.

If a return is necessary, please fill out the reverse side of this form. This helps us complete your request as soon as possible. Please allow sufficient time for the package to reach us and for us to examine and process your return.

MERCHANDISE RETURN INFORMATION

1. Place the item to be returned, original packing material and all papers in carton. Use original shipping carton (if available).

2. Fill out the reverse side of this form and enclose *INSIDE THE CARTON* with your return.

3. Return the merchandise to us via U.P.S. or Parcel Post. Please mail to:

   Brookstone Company
   575 Vose Farm Road
   Peterborough, NH 03458

4. *FOR GOODS DAMAGED IN SHIPMENT THAT ARE U.P.S. DELIVERED:* Hold the merchandise and notify U.P.S. of your damage. They will pick up the merchandise and return it to us. Upon receipt, your item or items will be replaced.

Thank you for following these instructions. We appreciate your business and we look forward to serving you in the future.

RETURNED PRODUCT INFORMATION

Your Name: _____

Street: _____ Apt. # ____

City: _____ State: _____ Zip: _____

Telephone Number: _____

1. ENCLOSE ORIGINAL PACKING SLIP OR PLEASE NOTE THE FOLLOWING INFORMATION BELOW:

   Order Reference # _____

   Item #   Description   Price

   _____   _____   _____
   _____   _____   _____
   _____   _____   _____

2. PLEASE INDICATE ORIGINAL TYPE OF PAYMENT:
   ☐ Check
   ☐ Charge
     Number _____ Expiration _____

3. REASON FOR RETURN:
   Please describe.

   _____
   _____
   _____
   _____

4. IT IS IMPORTANT THAT YOU ADVISE US OF THE ACTION YOU WANT US TO TAKE.
   ☐ Please replace with:
     ☐ Same product.
     ☐ Different product(s), listed below:
   Item #   Description

   _____   _____
   _____   _____

   ☐ Please issue refund.

**Figure 13–7 (top left and right)
Making Returns Easy**

To make it easy for a customer to return merchandise, Brookstone encloses this letter in its packages. The reverse side has spaces for all of the information Brookstone will need to make sure they provide the customer with the action desired. Copyright © Brookstone. Used with permission.

So if you're not satisfied with it, send it back. We want you to. Honest! Here are some suggestions on how to make returning your Lands' End merchandise easy."

Lands' End Returns Dept.

Six step-by-step instructions follow:

1. Save the box or package your order comes in. You can use it to make your return.

**Figure 13-8 (opposite and right)
The Informal Touch**

An outstanding example of making it easy for a customer to return merchandise is this folder that Lands' End encloses in each package it ships. The bottom panel is a gummed shipping label. Catalogers have discovered that making it easy to return merchandise doesn't increase returns, but helps build customer confidences and make sure returns can be handled efficiently. Copyright © Lands' End, Inc. Reprinted courtesy of Lands' End Catalog.

2. Save your packing list too. Keep the blue section for your records, noting on it when and how (UPS, Federal Express, etc.) you made your return. Return the rest to us—it will help us process your return lickety split.
3. Please tell us, on the section of the packing list you return, why you're returning your order. (For example: "I didn't know it was going to be that blue.") Your feedback will help us improve our products for the future!
4. If you've lost your packing slip (naughty, naughty), just give us your name and address, along with the approximate date you placed your order.
5. If you received the order as a gift, just let us know if you'd like a different size or color, a cash refund, or a Lands' End Gift Certificate for your later use.
6. After you've sealed up your box all nice to send back to us, PLEASE STICK THE ATTACHED MAILING LABEL ON THE OUTSIDE! And, check the appropriate box. This alerts us if your return needs special attention.

Any questions? Call us anytime, toll-free at 1–800–356–4444. From talking with you, we can learn how to improve our products and service. That's what we're here for. We don't say GUARANTEED. PERIOD. for nothing!

The detachable gummed label has five boxes to check:

- Letter inside
- Defective merchandise
- Please monogram or inseam
- Please exchange or refund
- Other_____

Quill Corporation uses a multipart pack slip, the second part of which is "Quill's Fast Service Pre-Authorized Return Form." The back side of the return form promotes this service and even includes testimonials from satisfied customers who have used it. Copy says:

At Quill we really mean it when we say you must be 100 percent satisfied with every purchase. If a mistake is made (yours or ours) . . . or the product isn't exactly what's needed . . . we want to make it right. That's why we've enclosed Quill's Fast Service Pre-Authorized Return Form right inside your package. If you ever need to return or exchange merchandise, you don't have to call us first. Just send the completed form and merchandise back to Quill within 30 days of receipt. You can be assured we will take care of your full credit, refund or replacement in the same prompt, courteous manner in which we handled your original order.

Also included in every Quill package is information about Quill's Customer Service Hotline. It says, "For any after sale inquiries or problems with an order call our service Hotline. Your call will be handled immediately, by one of our experienced, courteous customer service representatives."

Another important customer service enclosure is information about items which have been back ordered and thus are not included in the shipment. One warning: use product names and/or descriptions, not just item numbers. Customers order *products,* not *numbers.* While your item numbers may be meaningful to you, they only confuse a mail order customer.

One special problem with back orders arises when merchandise has been ordered for a specific gift occasion. A unique technique for handling this problem was used some time ago by D.R.I. Industries. Rather than simply cancel gift orders which couldn't be fulfilled in time for Christmas delivery, it sent the card shown below, which customers could send to those for whom they had ordered gifts. The copy reads:

> **YOU must be a very special person.**
>
> **Because someone took the time to order a very special gift for you. But we let them down. As hard as we tried, we couldn't get their gift to you before Christmas.**
>
> **However, even though it will be late, we can assure you that it's worth the wait!!**
>
> **Again, we're sorry for the delay. And please accept our heartfelt wish that you and your family have a warm and love-filled holiday season.**

Even though the customer was asked to send the card to the giftee, providing the cards resulted in a substantial retention of orders for later shipment.

(And while on the subject of back orders, let me suggest you make

Figure 13–9
A Unique Solution

When DRI industries discovered they wouldn't be able to fill Christmas gift orders, instead of just cancelling orders, they gave their customers an opportunity to send this card to gift recipients and keep the order in force until it could be shipped. Copyright © DRI Industries. Used with permission.

a thorough analysis of the *real* costs of back orders. Not only are customers disappointed when they find you are unable to ship promptly what they have ordered, so you may lose them as future customers, but your costs of handling back orders may be much higher than you realize. When you add up all of the internal paperwork required and the additional shipping and handling costs, you may easily find you are actually losing money every time you have a back order.)

The Sharper Image inserts two interesting customer service enclosures in its packages. The first covers returns. It reads:

> **Although we try our best to sell only high quality products with a very low rate of repair, it occasionally happens that something needs attention from the service center. This is especially true of electronics and more sophisticated products.**
>
> **Anything that fails to perform satisfactorily during the first thirty days of ownership should be returned to us for replacement with a new product . . . A product past the thirty-day trial period should be sent directly to the manufacturer or designated service center for repair under their warranty. This is usually free of charge, though some manufacturers ask a small handling charge. Please consult the warranty instructions that came with your product.**

A second The Sharper Image enclosure is headed: "We challenge you to find a better price." Copy reads:

> **You've bought a fine product. And we want you to feel confident you paid the best price.**
>
> **It's unlikely you'll find this item advertised for less elsewhere. If you do, we'll go the extra distance and match that price—no matter how low (excluding shipping charges and sales tax).**
>
> **Here's all you have to do. Just fill out the form below. And send it to us with the advertisement within the next 30 days. We'll send you a refund or credit for the difference.**
>
> **Your satisfaction is important to us. This price matching policy is another step we're taking to assure you remain a loyal friend.**

The "form below" asked only six easy questions—item description, The Sharper Image order number, item code, price paid, price in another ad, and whose ad it was . . . plus, of course, the customer's name and address.

A particularly important type of customer service enclosure involves a merchandise substitution. Substitution slips are important and shouldn't just be a computer-printed note on the pack slip. A note included with a substitute item in a Lillian Vernon package, for example, reads:

> **Dear Friend:**
> The item shown in our catalog is not now available. So I've taken the liberty of sending you this, on approval, in place of the merchandise you ordered.
> I know you order items for specific occasions or special needs, and many of you have told me you would rather receive a similiar item than none at all. I've made sure that this substitute is of equal or greater value.
> "On approval" means just that . . . if you aren't happy with my choice for any reason, please return it for a full refund. You must be satisfied . . . that's always our guarantee.

One from Duke Habernickel of Haband reads:

> I personally picked the substitute item . . . it's slightly different from what you expected but I guarantee it's equal or better in quality and value.

Quill goes even further. Instead of using just a generic substitution slip, it covers specific items. For example:

> Thank you for your order of Quill Premium grey ruled pads. We are sorry to say, we cannot send you the ruled pads you ordered. When the shipment arrived, we decided they simply weren't up to our standards.
> In the meantime, we've sent you a ruled pad with the quality you expect from Quill. However, it is different from our premium ruled pads in a couple of ways. The chipboard back is twice as thick. Also, it is micro-perforated, so sheets will have a cleaner edge when torn out.
> As always, if you're not happy with this substitution, you can send it back for credit, replacement, or full refund.
> Thank you for understanding.

Lands' End takes the trouble to anticipate another potential source of customer dissatisfaction. This note, for example, was enclosed with a knit dress:

> You'll notice that it's oversized before you wash it. This dress was tailored to allow for shrinkage which is common in 100 percent cotton fabrics. Our concern is to offer the proper fit after washing, so that you may enjoy your dress for many years to come. Please enjoy your purchase.

Peruvian Connection also provides instructions for a cotton garment:

Dear Peruvian Connection Customer:

We recommend dry cleaning for all fine cotton. But Peruvian Pima Cotton can also be washed in cool water, rolled in a towel, and laid flat to dry.

Please do not machine wash or put in the dryer!!

Thank you!

When Bill Nicolai was president of Early Winters, he made it a practice to enclose helpful folders like those shown in Figure 13-10 with almost every item of merchandise which was shipped. They were simple little 4 $\frac{1}{4}$ x 5 $\frac{1}{2}$" four-page pieces printed in black ink on colorful paper. A typical folder was headed: "The use & care of your Early Winters Camper's Valet."

CONGRATULATIONS! Your new Camper's Valet gives you a compact and compartmentalized outdoors hygiene kit! Its convenient size, organization, design, and attention to cleanup essentials make outdoor washings easy and efficient.

We hope you'll enjoy lasting satisfaction with this item. Should you have any questions, comments, or problems, please let us know. We do our utmost to deserve your continued confidence.

With best wishes for your outdoor pleasure, Signed: Bill Nicolai, President, Early Winters.

Copy inside the folder explained the product's features in detail:

FEATURES. Unzip your Valet and look it over. Check out its convenient compartments, pouches, and overall organization. Examine the details that'll make your camping & travel cleanup so easy.

- **COMPACT, WATERPROOF POUCH.** Your kit measures a mere 9x6x2" when zipped—it's no space burden. Its bright yellow nylon packcloth can be easily sighted in the depths of your pack or luggage.
- **NYLON LOOPS.** Just inside the zipper are two nylon loops so you can suspend the kit from tree, tent pole, car rack—right in front of you, easy to use.
- **TWO SQUIRT-TOP BOTTLES.** These pocketed 2 oz. bottles safely store and quickly dispense your lotion, oils, sunscreen, or shampoo.
- **ACRYLIC MIRROR.** Slips out of its storage pocket and attaches by Velcro® tabs to the top section of the kit for eye-level washings. Distortion-free and unbreakable, you could even use it for ridgetop signaling to your trail partner!
- **PLASTIC SOAP DISH.** This locking-lid box keeps "hotel-sized" bars from gumming up the works.

**Figure 13–10
Emphasizing Product Benefits**

Little folders like these not only provide helpful answers to questions which might otherwise have to be handled by customer service, but they present so many product benefits that they resell anyone who might be thinking about returning an item. Copyright © Early Winters. Used with permission.

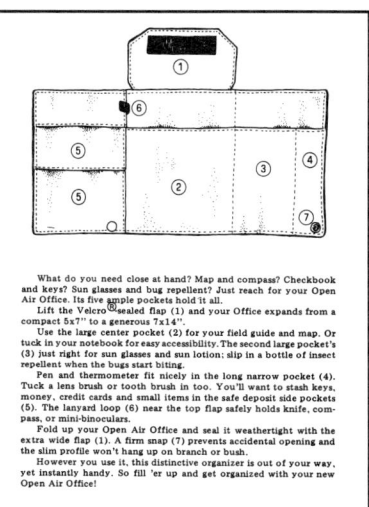

Front / Back

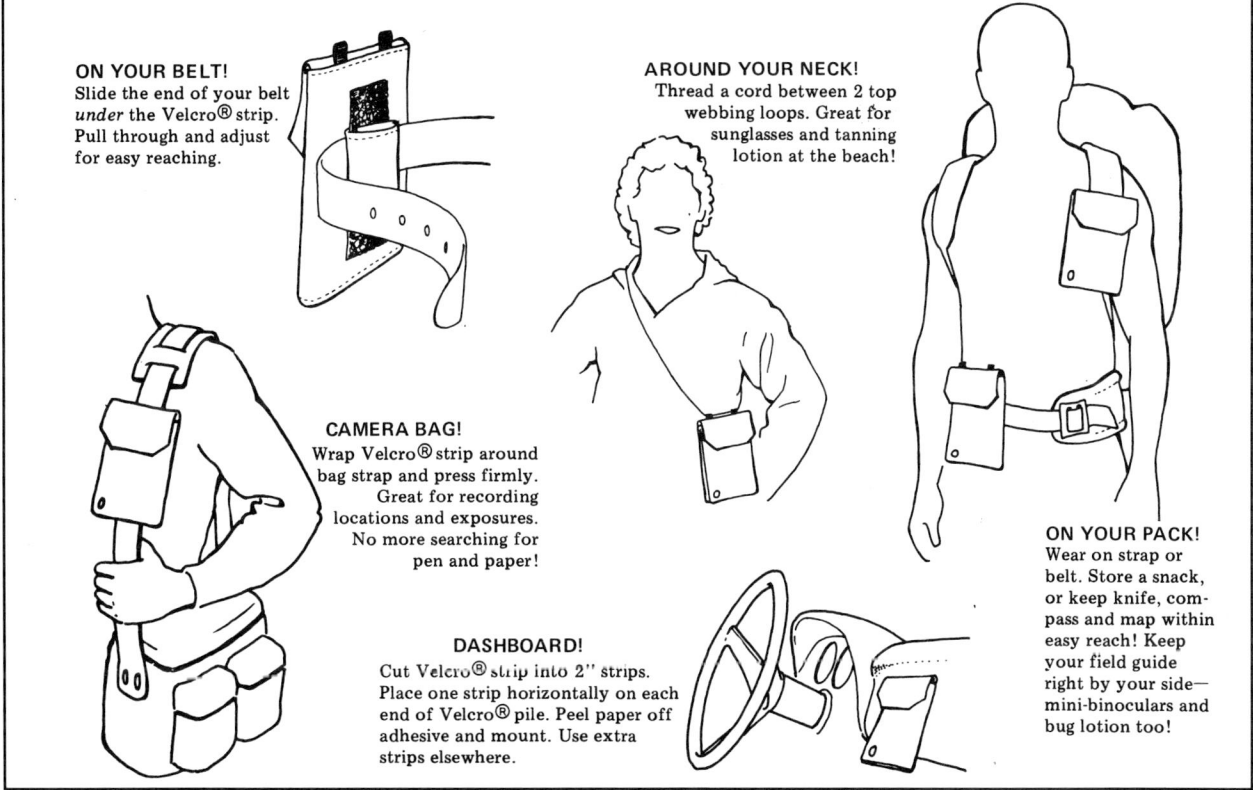

Inside

- **SNAP-TOP PILL BOTTLE.** For vitamins, pins, or pills . . . or other small items that are part of your cleanliness regimen.
- **MOUNTAIN MONEY.** Coreless, compact 140-sheet roll of toilet paper.
- **WASHCLOTH AND NETTED POUCH.** Use this 9x9" washcloth for thorough scrubbings, then slip it into the airy, zippered nylon pouch to dry.
- **VINYL WASHBASIN.** Three-quart capacity, yet it folds flatter than a deck of cards! Folded lip lets you carry it full and spill-free from your water source to cleanup area. You could even mix your pancake batter in it— once it's full, it's free-standing and firm!

- **ZIPPERED MIDDLE POUCH.** Holds many of the Valet's essentials, but leaves plenty of room for toothbrush and paste, nail clippers, razor—and more!
- **CARE.** The quality materials and construction of your Camper's Valet should last you a lifetime. For maximum protection, keep it clean and dry. Sponge off spills, or wash it in cold water and hang it up to dry. Do not put it in a dryer or pack it away wet, as it could damage the nylon coating.

With your Camper's Valet, you're set for cleanliness wherever you go. Enjoy it!

Not only helpful information to answer questions which might have to be handled by customer service, but so much emphasis on benefits it helps to resell anyone who might be thinking of returning the item.

REI includes a full page of "Tent Care and Cleaning Tips" with each tent it ships.

Another kind of customer service enclosure accompanied a pair of boots ordered from Sheplers:

Dear Customer:

Thank you for the boot order. We trust they will give you long wear and personal satisfaction.

CAUTION

Please try on your boots in a carpeted area. This will protect the soles, so if the fit is not correct, we will be able to exchange them for you. Worn soles are not returnable.

Thank you for shopping Sheplers Catalog Center. We look forward to serving your future western wear needs.

Covering potential customer service problems, which can result in expensive correspondence or phone calls, can be combined with a ship letter. The one from Breck's is included in packages of Dutch bulbs shipped from Holland. It not only covers the most frequently asked questions which customer service receives, but also takes the opportunity to sell additional merchandise:

Greetings from Holland . . .

Many thanks for giving Breck's the opportunity to share with you some of Holland's special beauty. When the enclosed bulbs burst into bloom next spring, I know they will provide at least a bit of the floral magic we find all around us here in Hillegom.

We take great pride in our ability to obtain Holland's very finest cream-of-the-crop bulbs for our American customers. Each of the bulbs we are shipping has been specially selected to meet the climate and growing conditions in your area.

To aid you in getting maximum enjoyment from your Dutch Bulbs, I'm enclosing a copy of our exclusive Dutch Bulb Planting Guide. You'll find it filled with tips from our staff of experts to help make your gardening easier and more enjoyable.

There may be a few cases where the instructions in the Guide differ slightly from planting instructions printed on the bags in which your bulbs have been shipped. In such cases, it is best to follow the directions printed on the bags.

As you'll discover, planting your Dutch Bulbs requires only a minimum amount of time and effort. But because you'll be planting the very best prime quality bulbs from the crops of leading Dutch growers, you are assured of having a beautiful spring display to rival Holland's finest gardens.

There are a few points I'd like to emphasize so you'll be sure of getting the best results:

- Bulbs don't like an area which is too wet. So be sure to select an area which will have good drainage. Avoid areas where water tends to stand after rains.
- Loosen the soil under your bulbs before planting and work in some humus and sand if your soil tends to be heavy.
- Be sure to plant your bulbs at the recommended depths as indicated in your Dutch Bulb Planting Guide or on the bags.
- For the best results, mulch your bulb planting areas before winter sets in and, if possible, leave part of the mulch on top of the ground the year around.

You won't have to wait until next spring, however, to bring a touch of Dutch Floral Magic to your home. I'm enclosing information about two very special winter-blooming treats we've been able to obtain to bring a touch of Holland to your home this Christmas—and something I'm sure you'll want to consider for gift-giving this year . . .

The letter goes on to describe in more detail these and three other special offers, which are enclosed, and ends by saying:

Once again, I want to express my appreciation for having the opportunity to supply Dutch Bulbs for your garden. We'll look forward to continue serving your needs in the days ahead.

Adding a Little Extra

One of my favorite ways of building a long-lasting relationship with customers is to add "a little extra" to your packages—something you haven't mentioned in advance, so it comes as a pleasant surprise when your customer opens the package.

Praktikus, a catalog from Switzerland, includes a packet of colorful commemorative stamps in each shipment. A message suggests the recipient share them with a favorite young friend. They cost just a few pennies per packet but make a lasting impression on customers.

Quelle, the giant European catalog house, sends customers a packet of sunflower seeds and conducts an annual contest to see who can grow the largest sunflower in Germany. (Competitors joke that all they need to do to get Quelle's customer list is to walk down the street and list everyone who's got a sunflower growing in their yard.)

Breck's includes cards with reproductions of famous Dutch paintings in the packages of bulbs it ships from Holland to its customers in America.

A catalog company in New Haven, Connecticut, supplying printed forms to real estate dealers, has the unlikely name of Forms & Worms. We asked how they came up with a name like that, and they said they wanted a name nobody would forget. To make sure they aren't forgotten, they include a fisherman's plastic worm in every package.

Another Connecticut company, A & W Wholesalers, which sells supplies to tow truck operators, encloses a cigar made of Connecticut-grown tobacco in its packages.

A package we received from Eddie Bauer contained a sample of their Campfire Memories incense sticks. Copy suggested: "Light it and enjoy the all-natural scents of aromatic fir, balsam and cedar." And, of course, there was an 800 number to call in case you wanted to buy more.

Publishers Central Bureau encloses a leather bookmark with shipments of books.

L'eggs includes a booklet on "Color and You" with its shipments of pantyhose.

Another interesting book included with merchandise shipments is sent by Williams-Sonoma—a guide to the care of cookware.

Brookstone includes a very effective little extra with each package. A slip with some handy shop tips accompanies each shipment of tools. And in shipments from its housewares catalog, it includes a slip with recipes.

Quill often encloses samples of new products with its shipments . . . including, of course, information on how to order these items.

Figure 13-11
A Little Extra

Adding "a little extra" to a merchandise package helps make the receipt of packages something special—and encourages customers to want to order again. Copyright © Eddie Bauer. Used with permission.

CAMPFIRE MEMORIES
Our Gift to You
The Refreshing Aroma of Fir, Balsam and Cedar

Remember your last campfire evening? The warm circle of light, the crackle of the fire, the fresh air scented with the bouquet of evergreens . . .

Now you can bring back the pleasant memory with this free sample of Campfire Memories fragrance logs. Just insert a "log" in the enclosed holder and light it. Soon the all-natural scents of aromatic fir, balsam and cedar will freshen the room.

Enjoy #4589Q Campfire Memories all year. Each box (30 fragrance logs) is only $3.50. Order 3 or more and each box is only $3.25. Call our 24-hour, Toll-Free number to place your charge-card order: **1-800-426-8020**.

We hope you enjoy your free gift sample. It's our way of saying "thank you" for being an Eddie Bauer customer!

Eddie Bauer®

One of the interesting aspects of the Smithsonian catalog is that every item has some identifiable connection to something on display within the Smithsonian Institution. To emphasize the connection, each product is accompanied by an attractive 4 1/4 x 5 1/2" black-on-grey card providing background information. For example, a card accompanying a reproduction of an old-fashioned carpet bag explains:

> Our carpet bag, adapted from one in our Collections, is typical of the ones carried by Northern opportunists as they migrated South after the Civil War. This 19th-century paisley-patterned style bag is made of Belgian tapestry with leather trim and cotton lining. The original bag is on exhibit at the National Museum of American History.
>
> As early as 1840, carpet bags, used as traveling bags, were produced in several sizes following the 1834 United States patent of the power loom for weaving ingrain carpets. In 1842 an English patent was granted for the weaving of Brussels carpet by power.
>
> Power-woven Brussels carpet is one of the more common types of carpet bags found in the mid-19th-century. Carpet bags were manufactured during the 1850's and 1860's with popularity diminishing by the 1870's, but similar styles and patterns exist today.

Other Package Enclosures

Other kinds of package enclosures can prove profitable. The receipt of a merchandise shipment provides a natural opportunity to do some selling.

The most popular enclosure is a sale catalog or a special list of discounted merchandise. This is one of the easiest ways to dispose of overstocks at a profit.

One of the more interesting sale catalogs we've seen came from Lillian Vernon. It was a copy of their regular catalog with a six-page

Thanks For Your Business!

Sporting Edge Presents
22121 Crystal Creek Blvd. S.E.
Bothell, WA 98021
(206) 483-6000

You've discovered the at-home ease, personal service, and just plain fun of shopping by mail or phone with Sporting Edge! We hope you're pleased with your order. If there's any problem, call our Customer Service Department. The Toll-Free number is (800) 422-5612. Our courteous staff will assist you Monday-Friday, 8 a.m. to 5 p.m. (PT).

Look inside this envelope for more intriguing products from us and other outstanding companies throughout the U.S.A.! Have fun!

Sincerely,

Dennis Binkley

Magnetic Marbles Proven By NASA!

Shuttle Magnetic Marbles cling together, making unusual formations.

Tested with great success on a NASA Space Shuttle flight, Shuttle Magnetic Marbles will entertain you for hours here on Earth. A tiny magnet inside causes them to cling together, forming long chains or intricate geometric shapes. Children and adults delight in creating unusual formations, or seeing who can build the tallest pyramid. Guaranteed fun for the whole family. Box of 36 marbles. #Z422102 **Shuttle Magnetic Marbles $8.95** *(2 lbs.); Save $2!* **Two for $15.90** *(3 lbs.)*

ORDER TOLL-FREE. 24 HRS. EVERY DAY
800 468-4410

Front

Look Inside For Great Gift Ideas...
For Yourself Or Someone Special!

Electronic Cleaner Protects VCR Heads

Keep your VCR working like new with this new microprocessor-controlled Head Cleaner. Its built-in Dirt Alert tells you when heads need cleaning (approximately every 30 days). Simply insert, wait for the tone and remove. Automatically dispenses 100% pure Freon. Includes 1 9V cell. #Z451260 **Video Head Cleaner $29.95** *(1 lb.)*

Extraordinary New Light Bulbs Guaranteed To Burn For A Lifetime!

Since Thomas Edison invented the light bulb in 1881, there have been few significant design improvements...until now. Introducing the Forever Light, the only bulb in the world *guaranteed to never burn out*.

You'll never hassle with changing bulbs again (especially ones in hard-to-reach places). And homeowners can expect to save about $2,000 on lightbulb replacement over the next 20 years!

U.S.-patented design incorporates a built-in diode and special gases. Lifetime manufacturer's guarantee. Specify clear or frosted. #Z364530 **Standard 4-Pack, 60 Watt $19.95** *(1 lb.);* #Z364531 **Standard 4-Pack, 90 Watt $19.95** *(1 lb.)*

ORDER TOLL-FREE (800) 468-4410

Revolutionary design permits Forever Bulbs' designers to guarantee them for a lifetime.

 Order Toll-Free any item shown by 1:00 p.m. (your time) weekdays, and we absolutely, positively guarantee you'll receive it by 10:30 a.m. the next day!

Back

© COPYRIGHT 1991 DARTNELL CORPORATION

wraparound. On the front was a special message from "Lillian":

> **Here's an extra thank-you for shopping with us—six special pages of super buys!**
>
> This year marks our 35th Anniversary, and we've enclosed a copy of our special-edition catalog for you. It's jam-packed with new ideas, unique products—all the caring details and old-fashioned quality you expect from us. There are lots of special anniversary buys, too (details on page 2).
>
> Whether you're an old friend or a new one, it's you I thank . . . for shopping here, for liking our quality and service, for making this special anniversary possible for us.

Each of the 44 items featured in the six-page wraparound carried a special price, with discounts of as much as 50 percent. The special message on page 2, which was mentioned in the wrap note, was one of the finest catalog anniversary messages I've seen:

> **Dear Friends,**
>
> Welcome to my 35th Anniversary celebration! For me, this is an incredible accomplishment, one that's far beyond anything I'd ever dreamed about, and one that would not be possible without you.
>
> For 35 years, I've shopped to bring you the necessary and the luxurious without high price tags. I hope, that in some measure, I've helped you live more comfortable.
>
> This special Anniversary issue is dedicated to you—my friends and customers. At right is the ad that launched this business in 1951. 35 years later, two things haven't changed—our quality and our prices. To show you just what I mean—our $35.00 burgundy leather tote is personalized with your initials in 22K Gold (like my first ad!). Now, it's yours for only $12.50.
>
> And that's just the beginning! What better way to celebrate than to offer you a special Anniversary price every time you turn a page—look for our symbol!
>
> We stand behind every product and want you to know that our guarantee of complete satisfaction is not a slogan, but a promise! If you're not pleased with any item you've purchased—even if it's personalized—send it back. We'll see to it that you receive a replacement or a full refund. I depend on you to tell me what you want, like and don't like, so please keep in touch. And, thank you, for making a dream a reality."

Current enclosed a special catalog with a message which suggested it could be used for your next order or to pass along to a friend. And tipped to the front cover was a friend-get-a-friend card to send in with names of friends to whom Current will send catalogs.

Others use special liquidation pieces. Williams-Sonoma, for ex-

Figure 13–12 (opposite) Package Enclosures

Enclosures in a merchandise shipment offer a special opportunity for additional selling. The offers may be from the cataloger or from other direct marketers, who pay for distribution. Offers should be placed in a poly bag or envelope such as this one used by Sporting Edge so they aren't overlooked. Copyright © Sporting Edge. Used with permission.

ample, encloses a bargain-loaded sale flyer in its packages plus an added sheet offering further reductions.

Lands' End, in keeping with its colorful catalogs, includes a colorful sale catalog. Others simply enclose a list of remainder items with sale prices.

It's important to place such enclosures in an envelope or poly bag so they don't get thrown out with packing material. One of the more interesting approaches is used by Joan Cook, whose package enclosure envelope is labeled "Money Inside." The "money" is a $5.00 discount certificate that can be used on a future order.

Current encloses two special envelopes—one with its own special offers, the other containing furnished inserts with offers from others. (A good source of extra income is to "sell" space in your merchandise packages to other mail order companies. Experience indicates that including offers from others seldom reduces the response you receive from your own enclosures.)

Follow-ups

One of the most frequently overlooked opportunities to get a new customer to buy a second time is to follow up on a specific item purchased.

The catalog company that consistently does the best follow-up job is Norm Thompson. It uses single sheet mailings such as the one in Figure 13–13. Copy reads:

> **For this special offer, we're contacting only those customers who are already familiar with our handy Collapse-Able Crates. In our upcoming Fall Catalog, we'll be raising the price of these crates to 3 for $43.50. However, through Aug. 31, we'll accept orders from past Collapse-Able Crate customers at 3 for $33.00. With this 20 percent savings, we must require a minimum purchase of 3 crates; there is no maximum limit.**
>
> **Since there are so many uses for Collapse-Able Crates, this is a great time to purchase more for your house, yard or car. They're the best thing yet for carrying more than two items (especially if they're large and unwieldy) and a perfect solution for all those times when you need a cardboard box... only better because they feature easy-to-lift-and-carry handles. Made from high-quality, injection-molded plastic and available in red, yellow, blue or black, Collapse-Able Crates contain no metal to corrode or rust.**
>
> **You can use the coupon above to order by mail, or call TOLL FREE for even faster service. If you phone, please tell the telephone sales representative you've received this letter so we can honor the special price. This special price reduction expires Aug. 31, so order soon.**

A similar follow-up mailing from Norm Thompson went to previous sock buyers:

> **We're sending this special letter only to those people already familiar with the comfort, long wear and wicking action of our Wick-Sport or Dress-Dry socks. The offer is simple. Through July 15, you can purchase either style at 20 percent savings. At this low price, I'm sure you can appreciate the fact we must require a minimum purchase of six pairs. The good news is there's no limit on the number of pairs you can buy.**
>
> **Now is the perfect time to stock up on these cushiony socks or purchase additional colors. Or, you may want to introduce another family member or a friend to the patented comfort you've come to enjoy. . . .**

Another catalog company which uses single-sheet follow-ups is Orvis. The letter shown in Figure 13–14, promoting the qualities of Orvis's cotton chinos, was sent to those who had already ordered slacks from Orvis and begins this way:

> **Since you have purchased slacks from us in the past, we'd like to offer you another reason to try our Naturally Neat Chinos.**

Twentieth Century Plastics acknowledges purchases with a letter offering a special discount. It begins:

Figure 13–13
Follow-Ups

Norm Thompson has an outstanding program of follow-ups. Flyers such as these are sent to customers to solicit reorders of specific merchandise they have purchased in the past. Copyright © Norm Thompson. Used with permission.

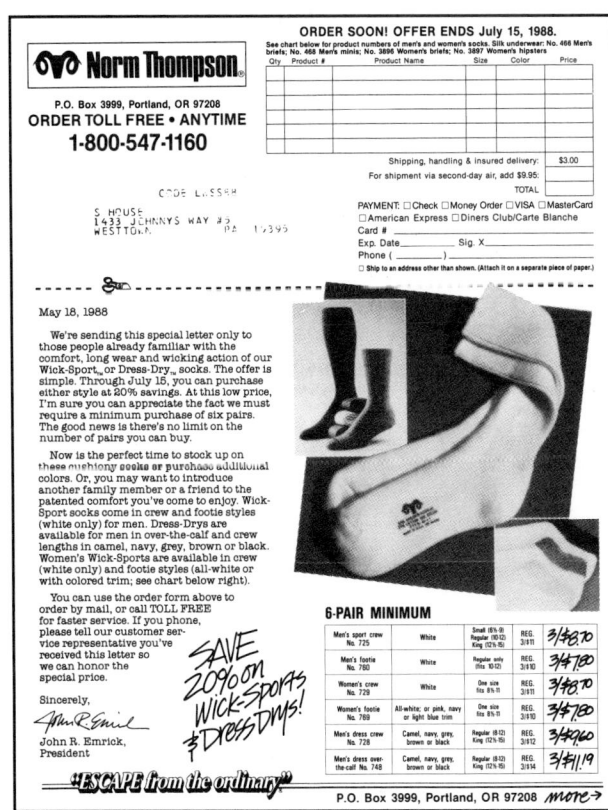

Dear Customer,

Our records indicate that you recently placed your first order of the year with us. To thank you for your business, this letter entitles you to a special 20 percent discount when you reorder in the next 60 days.

A similar discount offer is used by L'eggs. A letter on an "Express Message" form begins:

Dear New Customer,

Express to you—a special welcome from your new friends at L'eggs Brands, Inc. We're glad you have decided to shop with us. And, as a special Welcome Aboard Offer, we'd like to give you this chance to enjoy carefree shopping and outstanding savings on America's top hosiery brands. This special, limited time offer allows you to save 50% on America's No. 1 name in pantyhose—L'eggs.

Figure 13–14
Another Reason to Buy

Orvis used this follow-up letter to obtain orders from customers who had purchased slacks in the past. It offered a $10.00 discount on a reorder. Copyright © **Orvis. Used with permission.**

THE ORVIS COMPANY, INC. MANCHESTER, VERMONT 05254

Order Desk 1-802-362-1300
Customer Service 1-802-362-3434
Technical Advice 1-802-362-3900
Telex 382671

Dear Customer,

What kind of slacks would you rather wear: comfortable cottons, or easy care permapress? You get the best of both, in our new Naturally Neat Chinos.

<u>Our 100% Pure Cotton Chinos Never Need Ironing</u>

So neat and wrinkle-free, you'd think they're <u>polycotton</u> — but they're <u>pure</u> cotton. Pull them out of the dryer, and they're ready to wear. An invisible no-iron finish keeps them looking neat as a pin — always.

Orvis Naturally Neat Chinos hold their shape, keep a crisp front crease, never cling, feel smooth and comfortable as only pure cotton trousers can. Handsome enough to wear with a blazer . . . wonderful when you're traveling (even if you wear them day in, day out, they still look good). Machine wash, tumble dry — these are truly wash-'n-wear pants.

Available in three styles pictured (on pages 15 and 35) in our current catalog: pleated front for men and women, and plain front for men. In men's even sizes **30-44**, inseams finished to your order up to 36". In women's sizes 6 (25½" waist), 8 (26½"), 10 (27½"), **12** (29"), **14** (30½"), **16** (32"), **18** (33½").

Since you have purchased slacks from us in the past, we'd like to offer you another reason to try our Naturally Neat Chinos . . .

<u>Special Offer: Save $10 When You Buy 2 Pair</u>

Order any 2 pair of men's or ladies' chinos by October 15, 1986, and save $10. Send your coupon/order form, or call our Order Desk at 1-802-362-1300 and mention your $10 coupon to receive your discount.

Our Naturally Neat Chinos are a comfortable medium weight for fall . . . order now, and save $10 on 2 pair.

As always, we guarantee your complete satisfaction with every purchase.

Sincerely,
The Orvis Company, Inc.

Mary Sprague
Customer Service Manager

A Sporting Tradition Since 1856

Order within the next 60 days, and you'll save a full one-half off 6-pair quantities of all our L'eggs and Hanes Slightly Imperfect pantyhose styles. . . .

Several food catalogs make it a regular practice to follow up gift orders annually with a list of the names to whom a customer sent gifts the previous year. Priester Pecan Co., for example, includes a personalized letter with its catalogs:

Dear Mr. Hodgson,

Thank you for allowing us to serve you last fall. It is always a pleasure to send gifts for you during the Holiday Season. . . .

Enclosed with this letter is a list of those to whom you sent gifts last year and a holiday catalog. Please take a few minutes to fill out your order form and return it to us so that we can reserve your selections for prompt shipment to your friends and loved ones.

The confidence and trust you place in us is the foundation of our business. We wish you the very best this holiday season and throughout the new year.

An important occasion for a follow-up is when a customer has experienced some difficulty with a previous order. Eddie Bauer, for example, responds to a merchandise return with a card that says:

Dear Customer:

I'm sorry your recent order didn't meet your expectations. We hope you'll give us another chance with this special offer:

Save 10 percent when you return this card with your next order within 30 days.

Remember, our creed is to "give you such outstanding quality, value, service and guarantee that we may be worthy of your high esteem." I trust your future orders will bring complete satisfaction.

P.S. You can use this discount on phone orders, too. Just call toll-free: 1-800-426-8020 and give the code number 3711 with your order. Again, orders must be received within 30 days.

Even if a special offer isn't being made, it's important to acknowledge merchandise returns, particularly when the credit will be made on a credit card account. It may take a couple of months before customers see that you have credited their accounts. Meanwhile, they may be wondering if you received their return, and while they wait they may develop negative impressions of your catalog.

Neiman-Marcus doesn't wait for things to go wrong before making a follow-up. Its follow-up letter combines a thank you with a

Figure 13–15
Catalog Bind-In

Priester Pecan Co. binds a follow-up letter in a list of recipients to whom the customer has sent gifts in the past. Copyright © Priester Pecan Co. Used with permission.

OLD FASHIONED GOODNESS SINCE 1935   PHONE 205/227-4301

PRIESTER'S PECANS

227 OLD FORT DRIVE • FORT DEPOSIT, ALABAMA 36032

Mr. Richard S. Hodgson
1433 Johnnys Way
Westtown, PA 19395

Dear Mr. Hodgson,

Thank you for allowing us to serve you last fall. It is always a pleasure to send gifts for you during the Holiday Season.

Please take a moment to browse through our 1987 Holiday Catalog. In addition to our all time favorites, we have several new gift packages for you to select from including the Classic Collection. Pictured on the front cover, it is 5 lbs. 10 ozs. of delicious pecans and pecan candies. The Breakfast Bonanza, a wooden watermelon basket packed with pecan pancake mix, pecan syrup, golden pecan coffee, and apricot conserves is just right for a holiday brunch.

We are very excited to introduce our new baked items this year. Made from an old family recipe, Fruit Medley Cookies are baked with pounds of fruits and nuts and shipped to you in a beautiful ceramic cookie jar. Bravo Brownies are a special blend of chocolate and caramel that is simply delicious, and our Old Fashioned Pecan Pie is a true southern treat. Serve one or all three for dessert at your holiday meals.

Enclosed with this letter is a list of those to whom you sent gifts last year and a holiday catalog. Please take a few minutes to fill out your order form and return it to us so that we can reserve your selections for prompt shipment to your friends and loved ones.

The confidence and trust you place in us is the foundation of our business. We wish you the very best this holiday season and throughout the new year.

Sincerely,

May & Ned Ellis

statement of customer service. It also takes the opportunity to do a little extra selling.

> **Dear Valued Customer:**
>
> **Thank you for your recent order, and for your continued patronage . . .**
>
> **I am enclosing our latest offer in hopes that you will further explore the exciting world of N-M.**
>
> **Should you decide not to order at this time, please pass your catalog on to a friend. We will be happy to take their application for an N-M account, and we think they will thank you for letting them in on the N-M experience.**
>
> **As always, it is a privilege to serve you.**

The Personal Touch

Finally, I would recommend all catalogers remember they are using a form of direct mail, and there's nothing like a personal touch to make direct mail more effective.

It doesn't take much effort, for example, to add a little personal touch to your shipment. There are lots of opportunities to create a person-to-person relationship with customers by referring to specific purchases, commenting on an anniversary date, or doing anything that gives the customer the feeling he or she is more than just a couple of inches of tape in your computer.

One of the more interesting follow-ups we've received came from The Drawing Board. A special copy of their catalog arrived in an envelope with a handwritten address label. Stapled to the catalog's front cover was a business card from a Drawing Board sales rep, complete with an extension number to ask for when using their 800 number.

Sticking up from a page inside the catalog was a yellow Post-It note. On that page was another Post-It note with a handwritten message near a product we had ordered some time ago:

> **These are the pads that we have started making again.**

After we placed a telephone order for computer supplies with R+R Direct, we received this personal letter from Cheryl Dohme, the account representative who had taken our order:

> **Dear Mr. Hodgson:**
>
> **Thank you for your recent order with R+R Direct. It was a pleasure speaking with you about your company's computer needs. I hope to be of service to you in the future as your personal account representative.**

I have enclosed my business card. Please attach the card to your R+R catalog as a reference when placing your next order with R+R Direct.

Talbots uses a personal approach to rebuild goodwill with customers when something has gone wrong. For example, we received this personal letter:

We were unable to reach you by phone to inform you that the (item/s) you ordered (is/are) no longer available, and to offer you an alternate. We are disappointed that we were unable to fill your order as you requested.

We would like to assist you in selecting another item. If you will call 1-800-TALBOTS, one of our Personal Shoppers will be more than happy to assist you with your merchandise needs and provide you with full information on availability by size and color.

They are fully trained to coordinate your current wardrobe with new items from our catalog and offer suggestions for accessorizing. If you have questions about measurements on an item or would like a full description of the material, this information is also available to them.

We look forward to being of service to you soon.

PLEASE ACCEPT THIS GIFT WITH OUR APOLOGIES.

We hope you will take advantage of this gift to you—a gift certificate worth $15.00 toward your purchase of $30.00 or more. Just redeem this gift certificate with your next purchase.

Talbots tradition is to offer the finest classic clothing and customer service. And our unconditional guarantee means you can shop with confidence through our catalog (800-225-8200) or stores.

We look forward to your shopping with us again soon.

Dept. 9Z
Certificate No. 4465

WE'RE SORRY

Figure 13–16
Apologizing for Mistakes

When customers experience difficulties with their orders, Talbots sends personalized letters of apology and encloses a special gift certificate which can be applied to future orders. Copyright © Talbots. Used with permission.

Talbots

Date

Name
Street
City State Zip

Dear:

We were unable to reach you by phone to inform you that the (item/s) you ordered (is/are) no longer available, and to offer you an alternate. We are disappointed that we were unable to fill your order as you requested.

We would like to assist you in selecting another item. If you will call 1-800-8TALBOTS, one of our Personal Shoppers will be more than happy to assist you with your merchandise needs and provide you with full information on availability by size and color.

They are fully trained to coordinate your current wardrobe with new items from our catalog and offer suggestions for accessorizing. If you have questions about measurements on an item or would like a full description of the material, this information is also available to them.

We look forward to being of service to you soon.

Sincerely,

Name
Customer Service

175 BEAL STREET HINGHAM, MASSACHUSETTS 02043 1-800-992-9010

Enclosed with the letter was a $15.00 gift certificate which could be used on any purchase of $30.00 or more from any Talbots catalog.

Lands' End uses a personal message to reactivate customers:

My name is Elaine, and I manage the Lands' End Customer Service Department in Dodgeville, WI. Mr. Comer, our President, asked that I write to see if there is anything I can do to bring you back as a customer.

There may be a mistake in your address, and our catalogs are not getting through to you. If so, send the card below and I will have it changed right away. If there is anything else I can do, or if you have any suggestions about how any of us can do our jobs better, please use the card, or call me or any one of our Customer Service Representatives on our toll-free number (1-800-356-4444).

I look forward to hearing from you soon.

P.S. Our last Summer Catalog is on its way to you. We hope you enjoy it.

The postage-paid card which was attached asked the customer to indicate if he or she wanted to continue to receive Lands' End catalogs and then asked the inactive customer to check one of five boxes:

[ ] Everything is fine.
[ ] I am receiving duplicate catalogs. (We will be in touch.)
[ ] I have moved and am not receiving your catalog. My new address is listed above.
[ ] I require a different size than Lands' End offers: Size_____.
[ ] Other_____.

The ultimate personal touch we encountered in our study of how catalog companies fulfilled orders came from a computer supply firm. A few days after receiving a new product we had ordered, we got a personal telephone call from the president of the company asking our reactions to this recently developed product. He showed real interest in our reactions and was enough of a salesman to ask if we could use more of the product . . . and he got the order right then and there.

I also still remember a thoughtful call from Quill, even though it came several years ago. We had ordered a piece of office furniture, and Quill felt we should be fully aware of the exact amount of the shipping charges which would be involved. A most thoughtful—and much appreciated—personal touch.

**Figure 13–17
Reactivating Customers**

Lands' End sends personalized letters to inactive customers asking if there is anything they can do to correct any problems which may exist. A reply card is enclosed to give customers the opportunity to request future catalogs and explain how Lands' End can serve them better. Copyright © Lands' End, Inc. Reprinted courtesy of Lands' End Catalog.

LANDS' END
DIRECT MERCHANTS
LANDS' END YACHT STORES, INC.
1 LAND'S END LANE, DODGEVILLE, WI 53595
(800) 356-4444

Richard S. Hodgson June 6, 1984
1433 Johnny S. Way
Westtown, PA 19395

Dear Richard Hodgson:

My name is Elaine, and I manage the Lands' End Customer Service Department in Dodgeville, WI. Mr. Comer, our President, asked that I write to see if there is anything I can do to bring you back as a customer.

There may be a mistake in your address, and our catalogs are not getting through to you. If so, send the card below and I will have it changed right away. If there is anything else I can do, or if you have any suggestions about how any of us can do our jobs better, please use the card, or call me or any one of our Customer Service Representatives on our toll-free number (1-800-356-4444).

I look forward to hearing from you soon.

Sincerely,

Elaine DeVoss
Elaine DeVoss
Customer Service Supervisor

ED/dlf

P.S. Our last Summer Catalog is on its way to you. We hope you enjoy it.

LANDS' END
DIRECT MERCHANTS

Richard S. Hodgson
1433 Johnny S. Way
Westtown, PA   19395
MAK23

We would like to hear from you. Please take a moment to respond, then detach and mail this card. We have taken care of the postage.
Is your name and address correct? ☐ YES ☐ NO
If not, please print corrections below:

Name_____

Address_____

City_____ State_____ Zip_____

☐ **YES!** I want to continue to receive Lands' End Catalogs:
  ☐ I've just placed an order!   ☐ I plan to order soon!
☐ Please remove my name from your mailing list.

To help us give you better service, please check any box that may apply:
☐ Everything is fine.
☐ I am receiving duplicate catalogs. (We will be in touch.)
☐ I have moved and am not receiving your catalog. My new address is listed above.
☐ I require a different size than Lands' End offers: Size_____
☐ Other_____

We appreciate your comments:_____

In Summary

These, then, are 10 things you can do to encourage customers to buy again:

1. Acknowledge orders.
2. Respond instantly.
3. Use better packaging.
4. Use proper packaging materials.
5. Enclose ship letters.
6. Use customer service enclosures.
7. Add a "little extra" to your package.
8. Take advantage of the opportunity to enclose selling material in your package.
9. Follow up quickly to cement your relationship.
10. Add a personal touch.

Developing a Customer Service Program

14

"A customer is the most important person ever in this office—in person or by mail. A customer is not dependent on us, we are dependent on him. A customer is not an interruption of our work, he is the purpose of it. We are not doing him a favor by serving him, he is doing us a favor by giving us the opportunity to do so. A customer is not someone to argue or match wits with. Nobody ever won an argument with a customer. A customer is a person who brings us his wants. It is our job to handle them profitably to him and to ourselves."

Leon Leonwood Bean

When you're dealing with customers "sight unseen," your customer service program becomes a vital part of your business. Just like all "back end" activities, it should have a marketing orientation. Although it is often considered an "operations" activity, I strongly believe it is best when it is an integral part of "marketing." After all, customer service is your "marketing intelligence." It's a catalog company's opportunity to learn firsthand how customers are reacting. And it provides numerous "marketing opportunities" to encourage customers to buy from you in the future.

Effective customer service requires putting yourself in your customer's shoes. In Quill Corporation's "Customers' Bill of Rights," it's expressed this way:

As a customer, you are entitled to be treated exactly as we want to be treated when we are someone else's customer.

Stanley J. Fenvessy, a consultant who has worked with more catalog customer service programs than anyone else in the world, points out that customers want only four things—to which I add a fifth item:

1. To Be Believed. The worst thing you can do is to try to convince a customer he or she is wrong. Chances are you not only will lose the argument; but, in the process, you'll lose the customer.

My philosophy is that customers are *always* right even when they're wrong.

Of course, economics enters the picture. Many catalog companies establish dollar limits. If, for example, you establish a $100 limit, you automatically do, without a second thought, whatever a customer wants you to do that will cost less than $100. If it is going to be more expensive, then you can afford to get into an analysis of the customer's problem.

Unfortunately, many catalog entrepreneurs hate to be "ripped off" by anyone, and I've seen too many cases where the entrepreneur will spend $100 trying to avoid being ripped off for $10. Winning the argument may make you feel good, but it simply doesn't make economic sense.

2. To Receive a Quick Response. Stanley Fenvessy's rule of thumb is that a customer should receive an answer in the calendar week following the mailing of his or her letter. On the telephone, most problems should be resolved right then and there. If not, the problem should be resolved with a follow-up phone call within a maximum of five working days.

A quick response is generally better than a highly personalized response. While personal letters are wonderful in cementing good customer relations, most customer service problems can be handled more quickly with a form letter or card. It helps if some kind of personal touch (such as a handwritten note, date, or signature) is added to a printed form. But as a general rule, you should be able to dispatch form replies within 48 hours of hearing from the customer.

Stanley Fenvessy suggests that the typical catalog company needs only 10 to 12 forms to handle the majority of replies and that form replies not only provide quicker response, but they assure clear language; guarantee a consistent, friendly attitude toward customers; and save lots of money. He suggests that form letters should be composed by professional direct mail copywriters. It's an expense well worth the investment.

3. A Meaningful Response. One of the problems in using form replies is the tendency to let them cover everything—even situations for which the form reply was never intended. Whatever the method used to respond, it is highly important to recognize what concerns the customer.

A form reply, no matter how quickly it is sent, will only incense the customer if it doesn't respond to his or her specific complaint.

Beware of cultivating an "our company can do no wrong" attitude. While it didn't involve a catalog, a personal experience illustrates the danger of this approach. I regularly conduct catalog seminars in Germany, but for over 10 years I've refused to fly Lufthansa to and from those seminars. It's all because Lufthansa customer service personnel have been indoctrinated with the philosophy that their company can do no wrong.

At one point, I was not allowed to board a flight in Frankfurt, even though I had a seat reservation, because the gate agent claimed "all seats were already filled." I had to remain overnight and catch a flight the next day (thankfully on a competing airline).

When I wrote Lufthansa to complain, they replied by saying there were over 50 empty seats on the flight for which I had originally been scheduled. "The gate agent," they said, "must have been mistaken." That didn't get to the heart of my complaint.

They offered to provide special assistance on my next flight to Germany. But when I arrived for that flight, I once again found there was difficulty with my seat assignment and an attitude that my travel agent must have made some kind of mistake—*Lufthansa could do no wrong!* I've never again flown Lufthansa, resulting in the loss of tens of thousands of dollars for the airline which doesn't believe it can do wrong.

Then there's the oft-told classic of the "bedbug letter." A customer had complained to a railroad about finding a bedbug in his berth on a train. By return mail he received a well-written apology, typed on engraved stationery and personally signed by the railroad's president. Unfortunately, the railroad's customer service department had attached the customer's original letter to the reply. And there, in the upper corner of his own letter, the customer found the notation, "Send this nut the bedbug letter."

4. A Fair Adjustment. Customers generally aren't looking for anything more than the solution to their problem of the moment. Stanley Fenvessy says the eight most important words in customer service are, "What is it you want us to do?" Often the customer is looking for even less than you are prepared to offer.

A little something extra, however, is advisable. Remember, the customer took time to initiate the contact—and that effort deserves to be rewarded. Several catalog companies automatically send a gift certificate that can be used on a future order when responding to a customer complaint. This, or a small gift of some kind, can go a long way toward converting an unhappy customer into a longtime friend.

One area where the question of adjustment arises is in over- or underpayments. Most catalog companies establish rule-of-thumb limits.

For example, in the area of overpayments, the limit may be $5.00. If the overpayment is under $5.00, the customer is notified that his or her account has been credited for the amount of the overpayment and it can be deducted from the next order, or a refund check will be sent upon request. If the overpayment is $5.00 or more, a refund check is automatically generated.

(In cases of returned or cancelled orders, however, it is advisable to make full refunds, no matter how small the amount. Some catalog companies send a check, but then offer to "cash" it on a future order with a 10 or 20 percent "bonus" added to the face amount of the check.)

In the case of underpayments, there also may be a limit of $5.00. If the underpayment is less than $5.00, the customer is sent a single bill for this amount, but with no follow-ups to collect. On the other hand, if the underpayment is more than $5.00, regular collection procedures are followed—often with a request for full payment before the merchandise is shipped.

While we've used $5.00 as our example, we've found little consensus among catalog companies as to the amount to be established as a limit for over- and underpayments. Catalogs with small average order size often place their limit at $1.00 or $2.00, while high-ticket catalogs may go up to $10.00.

5. Keep It Friendly. To Stanley Fenvessy's four guidelines, I like to add a fifth. Keep a friendly tone in all of your customer service contacts. No matter how angry a customer may be, a friendly response can defuse the anger quickly.

Customer service personnel should be trained to keep their cool on the telephone—be patient listeners and respond with "a smile in their voices."

Form cards and letters should be written by copywriters who know how to get to the point in a friendly, informal way.

One of the reasons I prefer to see customer service as part of a marketing operation is that it's easier there to maintain the attitude that the most important objective is to *retain* customers so they will not only continue to make purchases, but will recommend your catalog to others.

In other areas of a company, the emphasis is more likely to be to "get rid of difficult customers." A credit manager, for example, often treats anyone who is slow in payments or disputes an invoice as "a crook." They want to get rid of such customers because they make it more difficult to balance the books at the end of the month. Someone whose primary emphasis is on smooth operations is also likely to want to eliminate customers who make life difficult.

Creating a Customer Service Plan

Customer service needs to be well planned. There are a multitude of details to be considered—too many to cover fully in this book. Therefore, I suggest you obtain a copy of Stanley Fenvessy's highly detailed book, *Fenvessy on Fulfillment—The Catalog Executive's Guide* (Catalog Age Publishing Corp., Six River Bend Center, Stamford, CT 06907–0949). But the following guidelines will be helpful in creating an effective customer service operation:

Have a Written Plan

You don't really have a customer service plan at all if it isn't down on paper and hasn't been widely circulated throughout your organization for everyone to read.

Customer service can be effective only if it has the full support of everyone in the company.

Divide Problems into Categories

Customer service correspondence should be carefully screened and then divided into categories for handling. There are three basic types of problems:

- **Category A**. These are things that happen with some degree of regularity and usually account for at least 90 percent of all customer service work. They can be handled within the customer service department, most often with form cards or letters.

- **Category B**. These are problems that can be handled within customer service, but require extra time to search out details. In most cases, they are best handled individually, instead of with form cards or letters.

- **Category C**. Although these normally represent only a very small percentage of all customer service problems, they require input from outside the customer service department. They not only call for special information, but require a special letter or telephone call to the customer.

Have a Firm Timetable

Beware of "desk drawer files!" Some customer service personnel tend to put off answering nonroutine correspondence with customers. Every type of response should be handled within an established time frame.

Routine "Category A" correspondence shouldn't take more than 48 hours to get a response on its way back to a customer.

"Category B" problems, requiring special research, can be allowed another 24 hours, but should be handled more promptly whenever possible.

"Category C" problems, requiring input from outside the customer service department, often get lost somewhere in the organization unless they are carefully monitored. The maximum acceptable time from receipt of the problem before an answer is on its way to a customer is five working days. If the problem is so complex it will require additional time to answer, the customer should be notified immediately, with an indication of how quickly a complete answer will be on its way.

Assign Specific Responsibilities

Rather than just letting anyone who is available at the time handle whatever comes up, it is best to have "specialists" on the customer service staff. Their specialty may be by product category or by specific kind of problem (credit, backorders, returns, etc.).

But whatever system is used, it is important to place primary responsibility for each customer service contact in the hands of an individual. In Quill's "Customers' Bill of Rights," one paragraph reads:

> As a customer, you are entitled to the privilege of being an individual and of dealing with individuals. If there is a question on your account, you are entitled to talk with or correspond with another individual so the question can be resolved immediately on the most mutually satisfactory basis possible.

Route "New" Problems to Management

When a problem shows up in customer service for the first time, it should immediately be called to the attention of those in company management who are involved. This input is important.

My suggestion is to have whichever manager is most directly responsible prepare the initial reply. This, then, can become the basis for future handling within the customer service department.

Establish Management Reviews

As I mentioned earlier, customer service represents "marketing intelligence" for a catalog company. Management needs to know the types of problems customers are having, how frequently they are occurring, and how they're being handled. It's all too easy for a minor problem to get blown out of proportion. Sometimes a few loud voices sound like a crowd.

Every catalog company should have a system of customer service reports distributed to all management levels on a regular basis. This includes such quantitative information as the total number of problems of each type; the average time for handling each type of problem; and a customer service backlog status report. In addition, it should include comments on such things as types of problems which are increasing or decreasing; how customer service work flow compares with previous periods; and detailed information about new problems which have arisen.

One technique which has worked well for many catalog companies is to assign a different executive each week or each month to review a representative selection of customer service correspondence—both inbound and outbound—and records of telephone calls. In most cases, the executive doesn't have to review every piece of correspondence and phone call record. Instead, items are selected on an "nth basis" (e.g., every 10th, 15th, or 20th letter or call record) and presented to the selected executive for study. If the nth system is used, it's important that those handling customer service aren't aware in advance which problems will be called to management's attention.

While management personnel sometimes object to the "extra work" when such a system of customer service reviews is introduced, they usually become so fascinated in having a chance to learn what's really going on that they start looking forward to the week or month when they get their chance to be the reviewer.

Indoctrinate and Reindoctrinate Customer Service Personnel

It's important to remember that customer service personnel generally get an opportunity to see only what's *wrong* with a company. They deal with angry customers and those who complain. It's easy to begin to think the company can't do *anything* right. They seldom get a chance to talk with or read letters from the vast majority of catalog customers who *like* the company.

This calls for a regular program of indoctrination and reindoctrination of customer service personnel. A program of continuing training is vital. Executives and managers should be brought in to provide a balanced picture of what's really going on in a company.

Dialogue is particularly important. Management needs to learn what customer service personnel are hearing from customers . . . and customer service personnel need to learn what is being done to solve the problems they face every day.

It helps to give customer service personnel the feeling they're important members of company management—the people who provide a direct link between the catalog company and its customers.

One good technique is to have an informal meeting with all customer service personnel on a regular basis. In one case, I had a Monday morning breakfast meeting with everyone in the customer service department. (I chose Mondays rather than Fridays so problems could be given a weekend of mellowing and thus come into perspective.) At this breakfast meeting, individual customer service personnel were encouraged to talk about the problems they had encountered during the previous week, and I had the chance to tell them what was being done to solve the problems they faced. If I didn't have an answer, I'd promise to look into the situation and report back on my findings at the very next Monday breakfast.

Not only was this technique helpful in keeping customer service personnel "on the company team," but it also provided valuable insight for me as I performed my management duties during the week.

Don't Wait for Problems

Good customer service is more than just waiting for problems to surface. A good program involves regular contact with typical customers to obtain input that can improve a catalog company's operations. I've found two particular techniques of special value.

"Vest Pocket Surveys." When customer service problems are being handled over the phone, you can conduct inexpensive surveys which give customers an opportunity to improve your operations.

At one mail order company, I regularly gave customer service personnel a "question of the week." If time remained at the end of a phone call (we established time limits for each type of customer service call), the customer service rep would ask the question for that week. Then, at the end of the week, all of the responses were tabulated and provided valuable input for managers.

We asked for customer observations on how we handled billing, types of packaging, new types of products we were considering adding to the catalog, any problems they might have had in filling out our order forms, etc.

Management Calls. Another very effective technique I have used is to hold a dinner meeting of management personnel once a month. Before the dinner, each executive and manager called 5 to 10 customers and had an informal discussion about how the customers viewed our company, catalogs, products, fulfillment, customer service, and similar details. This input from customers then became the basis of our postdinner discussion and often provided innovative solutions to problems. It also avoided some of the company politics that are normal when one department is trying to look good at the expense of other departments.

Measuring Customer Service Effectiveness

Just having a plan and implementing it doesn't mean you necessarily have an effective customer service operation. It's important to develop ways to measure the effectiveness of what you're doing.

One of the most important steps is to set up a file of those whose problems have been handled by customer service and regularly analyze what percentage remain active customers. (In a number of cases, customers with problems solved produce substantially more future business than a matching group of customers who have never contacted customer service. I've been particularly impressed with how much better customers who have been contacted on the phone by customer service perform in the future. One two-year analysis I saw indicated that the additional business from these customers actually paid all of the costs of the customer service telephone calls.)

You can also include special offers in customer service correspondence and measure response.

And, as we mentioned in Chapter 4, it's important to use customer service information to develop a screening file which will enable you to eliminate future catalog mailings to that handful of customers who continue to create problems which are more costly to handle than the revenue they generate.

Figure 14–1
Quill's Bill of Rights

Copyright © Quill Corporation. Used with permission.

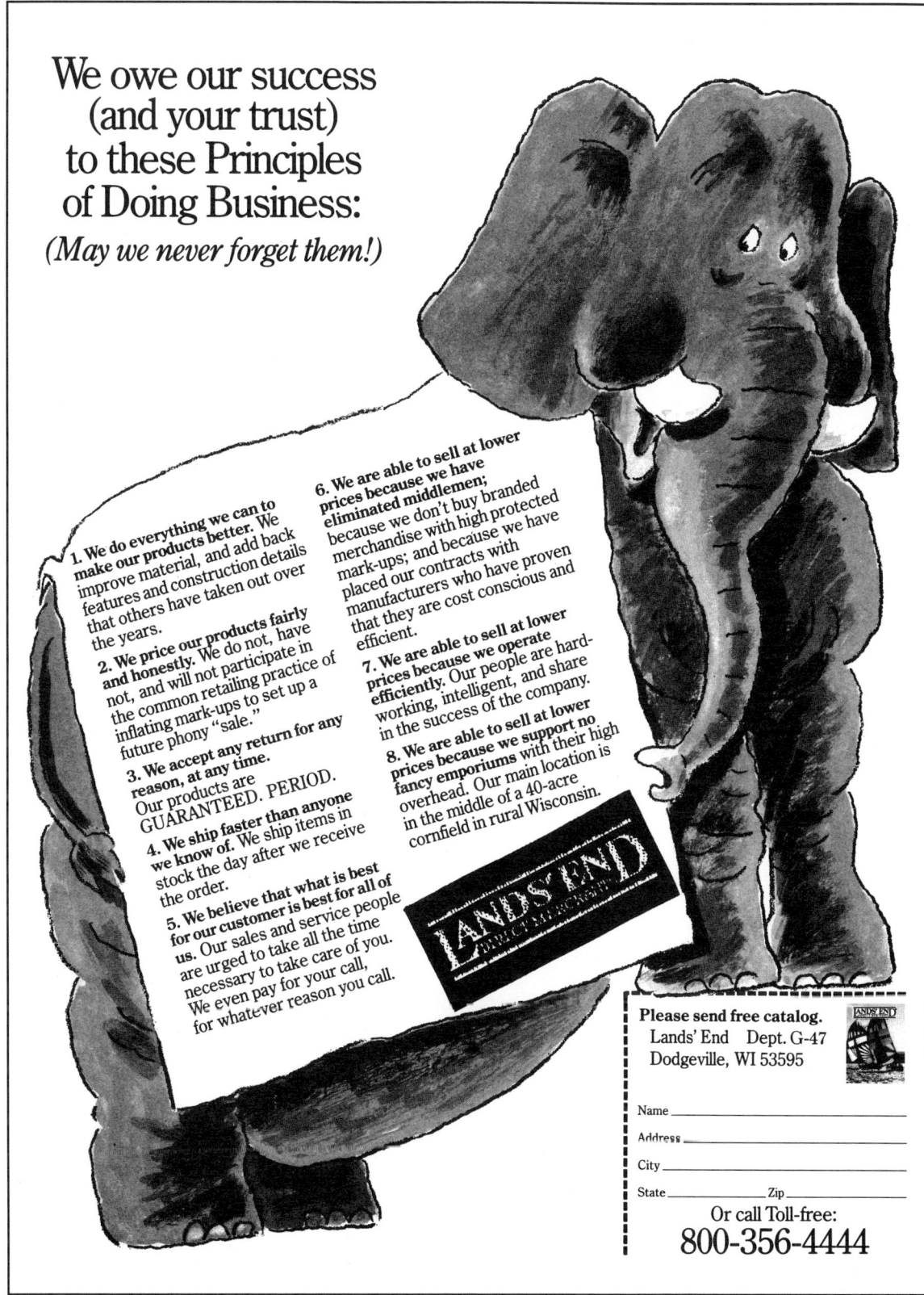

Figure 14–2
Lands' End Principles of Doing Business

Copyright © Lands' End, Inc. Reprinted courtesy of Lands' End Catalog.

L.L.Bean®
Outdoor Sporting Specialties

"THE GOLDEN RULE OF L.L.BEAN"

"Sell good merchandise at a reasonable profit, treat your customers like human beings and they'll always come back for more."

Leon Leonwood Bean started a company 75 years ago based on this simply stated business philosophy. We call it L.L.'s Golden Rule and today we still practice it.

Everything we sell is backed by a 100% unconditional guarantee. We do not want you to have anything from L. L. Bean that is not completely satisfactory. Return anything you buy from us at any time for any reason if it proves otherwise.

L. L. Bean pays all regular postage and handling charges on orders shipped within the United States. This means that the price listed is the only amount that you pay. There are no additional costs.

Send for our FREE 1987 Summer Catalog. It features a full range of quality products for men and women who enjoy the outdoors. Active and casual apparel and footwear, summer sports equipment, luggage, bedding and furnishings for home or camp. Practical and functional gift ideas. All fully illustrated and honestly described.

Order anytime 24 hours a day, 365 days a year by mail or with our convenient TOLL FREE phone number. Our Customer Service and Telephone Representatives are always here to serve you. We maintain large inventories and ship promptly.

☐ Send for a FREE 1987 Summer Catalog.

Name _____
Address _____
City _____
State _____ Zip _____

L. L. Bean, Inc., 821 Casco St., Freeport, ME 04033

Figure 14-3
The Golden Rule of L. L. Bean

Copyright © L.L. Bean. Used with permission.

> **Order with Confidence from Sears**
>
> **Satisfaction Guaranteed or Your Money Back**
> Choose from a wide selection at a fair price. You must be satisfied with performance, quality of workmanship, fit, styling—even color. If you decide your purchase is not satisfactory, return it to us at our expense.
>
> **No Matter How You Ordered, You Can Return Merchandise the Way Most Convenient for You**
> Return it in person to any of over 3,000 locations. Or, return it to the Catalog Distribution Center nearest you, as listed on the sales check, by mail (United States Postal Service), by United Parcel Service (if available) or by motor carrier for unmailable items. Of course we will also refund shipping charges on returned merchandise. If you have any questions about returning merchandise, first call your local Sears selling unit for more information.
>
> **Sears Pledge of Fairness**
> If, after you have decided to keep your purchase, it doesn't give you the service or performance you reasonably expect of it and there isn't a specific written warranty on the item that will satisfactorily correct the problem, please let us know. We want to make an adjustment that you consider fair.
>
> **THE SEARS GUARANTEE**
> **Whatever you buy at Sears, you have the right to use it for a reasonable time before you determine it is satisfactory and decide to keep it. If you decide it is not satisfactory, return it to us at our expense. We will do whatever is necessary to correct the cause of your dissatisfaction. If we can't satisfactorily provide a remedy, or if you request a refund, we will refund your full purchase price including any appropriate delivery charges, finance charges and applicable taxes.**

Figure 14-4
The Sears Guarantee

Copyright © Sears, Roebuck and Co.
Used with permission.

How to Expand An Existing Catalog Business

15

Just creating a catalog is only the start of an ongoing catalog business. Once a catalog has become established and a list of loyal customers has been developed, there are numerous ways to expand the business.

Mailing Multiple Catalogs

One of the most common ways to expand a catalog business is to mail multiple copies of the same catalog to selected segments of the customer list. Most frequently, catalog companies will change only the covers of a catalog so that each mailing a customer receives will have a new look, while the body of the catalog remains the same.

Multiple catalogs are usually sent only to those who have made several purchases in the past or have spent a substantial amount during the past year. Special consideration is often given to ZIP Code clusters that contain a catalog's best customers.

It is important to analyze lists carefully before making selections for additional catalog distribution. Some portions of your house file will most likely support the mailing of only a single catalog, while you can generate additional profits by mailing additional copies to better performing segments. One catalog company actually found it could mail as many as seven copies of the same catalog, with only minor changes, to its very best customers . . . and even the seventh catalog produced a profitable response.

But there are no general guidelines for determining who should get how many mailings of a catalog. You have to use your own experience to determine when it makes economic sense to mail more than one catalog to any list segment.

While it is relatively uncommon to mail more than one catalog a season to prospects, some companies make it a practice to remail to names which show up multiple times during a merge-purge of a number of different outside lists.

There are two basic catalog seasons—the gift-buying season, which generally runs from Labor Day to just before Christmas . . . and the buy-for-yourself season, which, for the majority of catalogs, runs from just after Christmas until early spring.

If just one gift catalog is mailed, it is usually timed to arrive in late September or early October. Meanwhile, most catalog multibuyers are receiving a host of competitive catalogs. While your customers may wait until your catalog arrives before making buying decisions, or they may keep your catalog at hand through the entire buying season, chances are other catalogs will gain special attention as they arrive.

Therefore, you can increase your chances of being the catalog of choice by more frequent mailings. While there are a great variety of mailing patterns, these schedules are typical:

- If you choose to mail two catalogs to selected customers, you might mail the first to arrive just after Labor Day—the period when most buyers first start selecting gift items for the Christmas season. Then a follow-up catalog could be mailed to arrive in mid-October, in the middle of the gift-buying season.
- If you mail three of the same catalogs, your mailing schedule might time arrivals for shortly after Labor Day, the first of October, and the first of November.
- If you, like many mail order catalog companies, plan to distribute four gift catalogs, you might try to get a jump on the season by mailing the first to arrive in mid-August, the second in mid-September, the third in mid-October, and the fourth sometime in November. As the number of telephone orders has increased, and with the availability of low-cost overnight and second-day air shipments, many catalogers are mailing "last minute" Christmas gift catalogs to their best customers, timed to arrive early in December (with a heavily promoted guarantee that all orders will arrive before Christmas if placed by phone).

For many years, Christmas mail order buying was normally pretty much over by December 1. Today, however, the buying season—for those who promote it—extends three weeks into December. In years when there is a slow start for Christmas buying, due to unseasonably warm weather or attention-demanding news events (such as November elections or headline-grabbing disasters which become the focus of attention for an extended period), this extended period of mail order gift buying can be vital to profitability.

One caution: your telephone order-takers should have up-to-the-minute inventory information so they can assure customers of getting what they want to order in time for Christmas gift-giving (or suggesting a readily available substitution). Nothing destroys a customer relationship faster than failing to fulfill an order in time for an important event.

It's also important to have a rapid and effective credit checking procedure for quickly shipped orders. Rip-off artists have discovered they can often escape detection by placing rush orders and "disappearing" quickly.

Many direct marketers place a copy of their catalog in outgoing merchandise shipments in hopes of getting a repeat purchase. Using a special cover for these catalogs, or adding an outer wrap, often results in increased readership and more response.

January is considered the primary buy-for-yourself month for almost everything except seasonal merchandise. There are three basic reasons for January's purchasing strength:

- It's when you know what you *didn't* get as a Christmas gift.
- It's when there is most often extra discretionary money to spend—cash Christmas gifts and—Christmas and year-end bonuses with fewer demands on the pocketbook for necessities.
- But probably most important of all, it's a time when people make New Year's resolutions. They plan to improve their lifestyle by exercising more and engaging in more activities; reading more; listening to more music; dressing better; and doing a host of other things they've always planned to do but never quite got around to doing . . . and they buy in anticipation of how their lives will be changing. By March or April, they discover they really aren't going to do all of these great things and stop buying "in anticipation" of the year ahead.

Therefore, if just one catalog is to be mailed in the beginning of the year, it is often timed to arrive early in January. While many catalogs aim for delivery as soon after December 25 as possible, they face an overload of catalogs in the postal system. This not only means difficulty in scheduling delivery, but also puts your catalog in direct competition with others which will be arriving at about the same time. (On a single Monday in January, for example, we received over 40 different mail order catalogs. And before that week was over, we had received over 200 different catalogs. While we go to special efforts to get on as many catalog lists as possible, it is not unusual for a typical catalog multibuyer to receive dozens of different catalogs early in January.)

Knowing this situation, many catalogers plan mid- or late-January delivery if only a single catalog will be mailed.

But you can be pretty sure competitive catalogs will keep arriving in your customers' mailboxes. To remain competitive, additional copies of the same catalog are often distributed early in the year.

- If two catalogs are to be sent to selected customers, a typical plan might call for the first to arrive in mid-January, with a second arriving in mid-February or early in March.
- If three catalogs will be mailed, the first is usually planned for delivery just as soon after Christmas as possible; a second late in January; a third late in February or in mid-March.
- When four catalogs are to be delivered, many catalogers plan the first for delivery early in December, in hopes it will not only get a jump on the buy-for-yourself season, but will also provide some last-minute ideas for Christmas gift-giving. More often, however, the first catalog is timed for late December delivery, with subsequent catalogs arriving about the first of February, March, and April.

These mailing scenarios assume that you have only enough good products available to offer a single basic presentation per season, with a few changes on covers. If you are in a position to offer a wider variety of merchandise, you may want to produce totally different catalogs for each mailing. This, however, requires both added production expense and increased distribution to cover more of your market with each merchandise presentation.

Some catalogs mail even more frequently with a limited range of merchandise. Such catalogs often make major changes in presentation for each mailing. Typical examples are Lands' End and The Sharper Image, both of which mail approximately once a month throughout the year. Both use editorial techniques to give each of their catalogs a different look.

For the majority of catalogs, however, the economics appear to favor multiple mailings of the same catalog.

Special Catalog Editions

A variation on multiple distribution of the same catalog with only cover changes is to print two-up (two catalogs atop one another during a single press run), with a different arrangement of pages in each version. Then, when new covers are added, there can be two different looks for the entire catalog.

This same effect can also be achieved when a catalog has multiple signatures. They can be bound in a different sequence for each mailing, requiring only black plate changes to have proper page numbers for each version.

There has been a lot of discussion among catalogers concerning the use of Selectronic binding, a special binding technique originally developed by R.R. Donnelley & Sons Company to create different editions of magazines for different audiences. While relatively few catalogers use this technique, it provides an opportunity to tailor catalogs to the specific buying interests of different types of customers. The most frequent users of Selectronic binding for catalogs today are those selling by mail order to business audiences. By selective binding, they can offer specialized products to different types of businesses or professions, and other products to every audience.

The Selectronic technique involves filling "pockets" on a binding line with a variety of different covers, signatures, and order forms. Then, as a catalog proceeds down the binding line, computers instruct the equipment to pick the exact parts to go into each catalog. Since this enables catalogs to come off the binding line in proper mailing sequence for maximum postal discounts, it can offer substantial savings.

Another catalog technique which has been attracting increased attention is the creation of special editions for different regions. Frequently there is a basic signature, which goes into all catalogs. Then a wraparound signature is added for each region, with products of special appeal in that area. Gardening catalogs, for example, can't ship the same products to colder northern areas which are best sellers in milder climates. The majority of products they offer, however, fit both areas. So they have a common section with a climate-oriented wraparound.

The most common use of separate editions, however, is for prospecting. Customers get a full catalog, while prospects receive a version featuring only the most popular products. Separate versions also allow catalogers to provide prospects with introductory material, which is important in attracting new customers but is not necessary for established customers.

One of the problems of sending a full catalog to prospects is that they often have a tendency to overwhelm a prospect. There are so many choices to make, it is difficult to know where to start. So a special catalog is produced, displaying only a representative selection of best selling products, making it easier for the first-time buyer to select something for a "trial" order.

Spiegel, for example, has made wide use of "Discover Spiegel" prospecting catalogs. Whereas its "big books" have approximately 600 pages and thousands of products, the prospecting versions are typically just 84 pages with a carefully selected "starter" assortment.

Figure 15–1
Catalog for Prospecting

To attract new customers, Spiegel distributes 80-page Discover Spiegel catalogs showing a representative selection of the merchandise featured in its larger catalog. Copyright © Spiegel. Used with permission.

Figure 15–2
Adding Products for Special Customers

Spring Hill Nurseries binds a 24-page "Select" section into copies of its regular catalog sent to a selection of its top customers. A label is added to the front cover to call attention to this special section. Copyright © Foster & Gallagher. Used with permission.

Another variation is to *add* selected products for a catalog's best customers—items that might not have wide appeal to everyone but can carry their weight when offered only to a select audience.

An example of this is a special "Select" section which Spring Hill Nurseries adds to copies of catalogs sent to a highly selective portion of its audience of gardeners. This 24-page signature is bound into the center of selected catalogs and features new and relatively rare products, most at higher price points than the typical plants, trees, and shrubs in the regular Spring Hill catalogs.

Developing Spin-off Catalogs

Another way to expand a basic catalog program is to look for opportunities to create specialized catalogs for customers who have indicated an interest in particular types of products within the regular merchandise mix.

A basic rule of thumb is to analyze response for each product category and consider a "spin-off" catalog when 50,000 customers are found buying merchandise of a given category. (While 50,000 is a basic starting point for many consumer catalogs, much smaller numbers often indicate spin-off opportunities for business-to-business catalogs, which normally have larger average order sizes.)

Not only can spin-off catalogs stimulate an increased number of orders from established customers, but they can be mailed to vertical prospect lists that would not respond profitably to a more horizontal catalog.

The all-time leader in spin-offs was Hanover House, which, during one relatively short period, created over 30 different spin-off catalogs. The majority were created by analysis of previous types of product purchases by their own customers.

More frequently, however, developing spin-off catalogs is a gradual process. A careful step-by-step process generally proves more successful in the long run.

One of the questions which frequently arises with spin-off catalogs is whether they should have a unique identity and personality, or whether they should obviously be special versions of the original catalog. Since the basic audience for these catalogs is most often a house file with an already established buying relationship with the "mother" catalog, there is good reason to maintain a consistent image with emphasis on the established catalog connection.

This, however, has to be weighed against the tendency of many customers to limit the amount they're willing to spend each season with a given catalog company. There are times when it has proved more successful to establish a completely separate identity for each catalog.

Moving off a Plateau

One problem faced by some catalogs is that they hit a plateau. They have captured so much of a given market that there are few opportunities to increase sales with present customers, and so much prospecting has already been done to available lists, the cost of acquiring additional customers is no longer acceptable.

Since there already is a substantial investment in the basics of catalog operations, much of this investment can be utilized at lower than normal start-up costs to serve additional markets.

In such cases, there are a number of possibilities for additional catalogs. In addition to specialized product spin-offs, a catalog with different price points may offer new opportunities. You can utilize your existing product buying expertise and sources, but select products with either higher or lower price points. It will mean searching out new audiences; but, with the head start your experience offers, you may be able to develop a profitable new market.

The Horchow Collection, for example, created Trifles to reach a lower price point audience. While the basic merchandise mix featured most of the same product categories, the lower prices attracted buyers who failed to respond to higher prices in the regular Horchow catalog. Once Trifles was established, Horchow moved another step down the price ladder with Grand Finale and SGF, catalogs featuring remainders at discounted prices.

A new catalog version can be aimed at a different customer age bracket or a different market. For example, a business-to-business catalog can offer selected products to consumer markets. Reliable, an office supplies catalog, created a special catalog called "Home Office" to reach people who work out of their homes.

Balancing Seasonality

Another problem that faces catalogs offering products with just a limited buying season is that valuable staff and facilities remain idle during the off season. If a counter-season catalog can be acquired or created, it can be operated at much less than normal costs.

Harry & David, for example, had a highly-seasonal business, concentrating primarily on holiday gift sales. To achieve a balance, they acquired the Jackson & Perkins nursery operation, which had sales during the non-conflicting gardening seasons.

A reverse angle was used by Foster & Gallagher, whose Breck's and Spring Hill nursery catalogs had little winter business. So Foster & Gallagher worked out a cooperative arrangement with Mauna Loa of Hawaii and took over mail order marketing of their macadamia nut gift items.

Using Alternate Direct Mail Media

Since the mailing list is the cornerstone of all direct mail, approaching the names of your customer file by alternate direct mail media is a natural way to extend a catalog business.

Solo Mailings

The most frequently used alternate format is the so-called "solo mailing." This is the common direct mail format consisting of an outer envelope, a letter, a brochure of some kind, and a response device. Most often it promotes just a single product or a small group of closely related products.

Solo mailings normally produce very quick response. Unlike catalogs, which generate orders over an extended period, solo mailings produce a bell-shaped response curve. As a general rule, well over 90 percent of the orders will arrive within a three-week period following the receipt of the first orders.

Solo mailings present an excellent way to balance out catalog peaks and valleys. Even though sales of merchandise through solo mailings can reduce sales of those same items presented in a catalog, they generally do not reduce total response to a catalog. Average catalog order size tends to remain the same, even though the distribution of sales among merchandise units may change.

An example of how solo mailings can be used to supplement catalog sales is found in the experience of Breck's, whose basic catalog promotes spring and early summer advance orders for Dutch flower bulbs to be shipped in the fall. Most of the Breck's catalogs are distributed in just a four-month period in the spring.

To create a flow of orders the year around, Breck's sends solo mailings to various segments of both its customer and prospect lists approximately 30 times throughout the year. The response from these supplemental mailings has enabled Breck's to double its total annual sales volume.

Packets

An obvious alternate format for a catalog is what is known as a "packet." This is an envelope filled with loose sheets or small folders. The individual sheets may use both sides to promote a single product, show different products on each side, or be much like a typical catalog with multiple items on each "page." (In fact, some catalogers actually cut the backbones off their catalogs and enclose the now-loose sheets in an envelope.)

While a packet is more expensive to produce than a catalog featuring the same number of items, it has the advantage of being an impulse buying format. Packets don't get saved like catalogs, with orders coming in when a buying occasion comes to customers' minds. Instead, most orders are stimulated by the receipt of the packet and the response curve is very much like those created by solo mailings, although it may run a couple of weeks longer than the average solo mailing response.

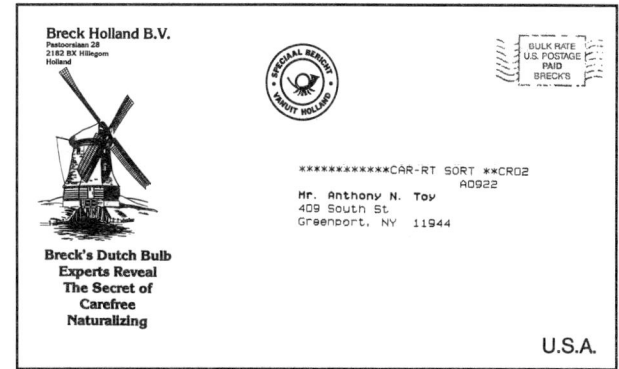

Figure 15-3
Solo Mailings

Breck's, whose catalogs produce sales during a limited time period each spring, developed a year-around business by mailing special offers to its customers throughout the year. Copyright © Foster & Gallagher. Used with permission.

Research has indicated that a packet mailing produces an automatic reaction—recipients go through a sorting process. Individual offers are placed in either a "throw-away" pile or a "keeper" file. Focus group studies indicate that the typical sorter gives an individual piece a maximum of four seconds of attention before deciding to which pile it will go. Thus, it's important to use a "billboard" treatment in presenting items so the salient facts about an item will be captured in just a quick glance.

Sorting is a very important ingredient in successful packet mailings. While to my knowledge, nobody has yet established just how many individual inserts are required to create the sorting impulse, it is generally felt that it takes at least 10 to 12 individual offers to make the format work to maximum advantage. There appears to be some kind of psychological reaction when an insert is selected for the "keeper" pile—an impulse which leads recipients to give these selected items special attention.

Some companies such as Haband, Blair, and Starcrest use packets almost exclusively for their "catalogs." And American Express, which mails merchandise offer packets regularly to its credit card members, generates considerably more business from these mailings than they do from their catalogs.

Card Decks

A close cousin to the packet is the so-called "card deck." This is a collection of individual reply cards, each carrying a single offer. While this format allows only minimum space for individual item promotion, it has proved highly successful for many companies, particularly for business-to-business promotions.

While there are many card deck publishers, who sell "space" in their mailings to individual advertisers, a number of companies use the card deck format as an alternate for their catalogs. Many publishers, for example, use card decks to promote sales of their lists of books.

Just like packets, the sorting process is important. While bound booklets of cards, which generally are less costly to produce, are sometimes used, tests have shown that a packet of individual cards can increase overall response as much as 15 times.

Figure 15–4
Card Decks

Card deck mailings have become increasingly popular. Normally, each enclosure features a single product and is designed for use as a reply card. Copyright © Dartnell Corporation. Used with permission.

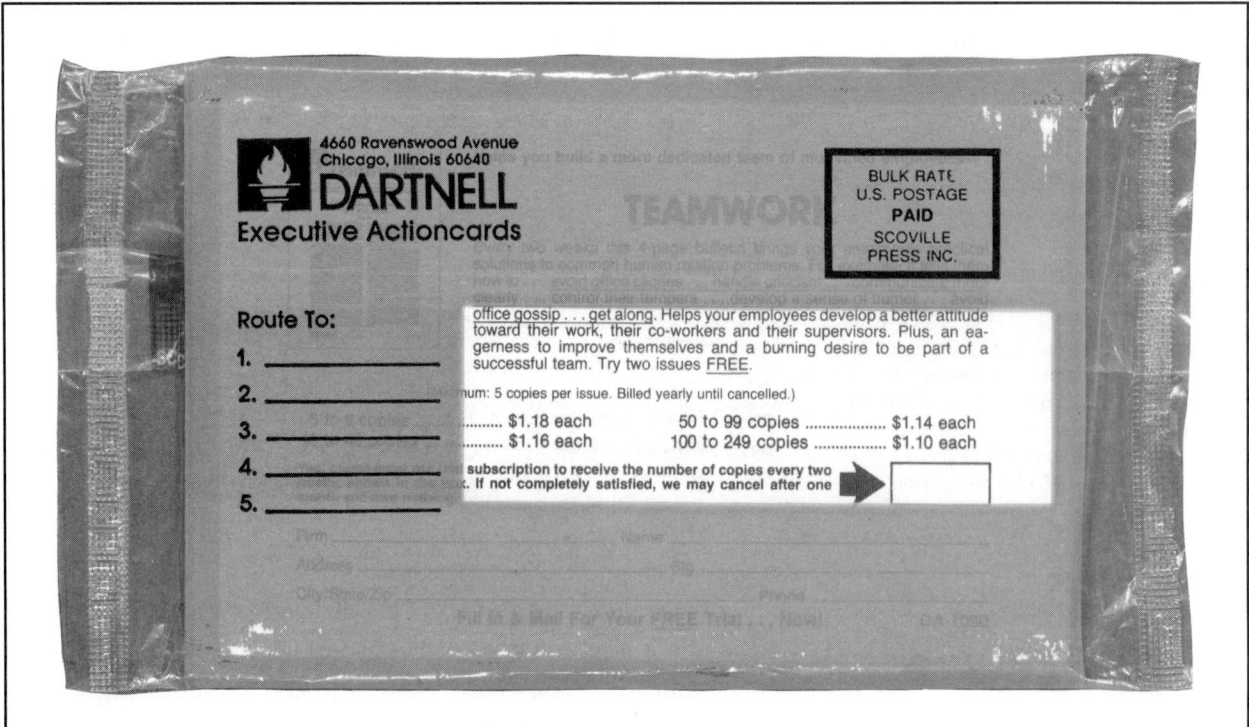

YOUR "BEST BUY" IN AUDIOCASSETTE PROGRAMS

Finally, practical, "how to" tape programs—loaded with what you really need to succeed.

Introducing:
THE DARTNELL AUDIO LIBRARY

Dartnell audiocassette programs are your "best buy" because they give you specific sales, management and marketing techniques—not theories and platitudes. These captivating programs deliver the information you need to increase your income and advance your career.

Plus, most Dartnell audio programs come with an interactive "action guide" so you can personalize what you learn and put your expertise "to work" immediately.

Hear for yourself why Dartnell sets the pace in business audio. Audition any of these results-oriented programs—FREE—for 30 days.

TO ORDER CALL 1-800-621-5463 (in Illinois dial 1-312-561-4000, in Canada call 1-800-441-7878) or complete and mail the attached 30-Day Free Trial Certificate.

RINGING UP SALES:
The Complete Training Program for Telephone Sales Reps

by Art Sobczak

6 Audiocassettes
1 Action Guide
50 Call Guides
$89.95

BOOST YOUR SALES AND YOUR PROFITS
With the Most Comprehensive Telephone Sales Training Program Available!

Now, you and your inside sales staff can get low-cost, complete and expert telephone sales training with RINGING UP SALES. In this remarkable series, telemarketing expert Art Sobczak gives your team the "teleselling" skills necessary to become exceptional sales pros.

When you begin using this powerful sales tool, you will:
- quickly screen out unqualified prospects
- create sales-generating opening statements
- develop powerful benefit statements
- handle "real" and "decoy" objections
- capture more sales

If you want to increase your sales volume and order size, but decrease your sales expense—try RINGING UP SALES.

Order Code DRUS

TIME TO SELL:
Manage Your Time and Double Your Sales

by Alec Mackenzie

6 Audiocassettes
1 TimeSaving Guide
$79.95

Tap Into Non-selling Time and DOUBLE YOUR SALES

Most salespeople spend too much time doing low priority tasks and not enough time selling. In TIME TO SELL, Alec Mackenzie shows you how to double selling time and sales—without working longer hours.

You will learn how to:
- overcome procrastination, paperwork, and interruptions
- get three hours of work done in one
- conquer "time use barriers"
- use the John Todd Formula to dramatically increase sales income
- develop a personalized "Action Plan" for doubling sales.

Give yourself a break—get TIME TO SELL.
Order Code DTTS

Figure 15–5
Mini-Catalogs

A low-cost way to reach prospects is through the use of a mini-catalog which can act as a brochure for your regular catalog. Copyright © Dartnell Corporation. Used with permission.

Mini-Catalogs

Another alternate direct mail format is the "mini-catalog." While there are a variety of different mini-catalog formats, the most common are 16-page 3 1/2 x 5 1/2" or 3 1/2 x 6 1/2" press-pasted booklets with a fold-out order form and/or reply envelope. Since all operations in producing these pieces can be done "on-line" by the printer, the cost per thousand is very low.

Some mini-catalogs feature just one item per page, but it is not uncommon to find mini-catalogs with as many as three items per page. Copy space, of course, is limited, but pictures in a miniature format look relatively larger than the same size illustration in a normal size catalog.

Mini-catalogs should not be used if you want the recipient to retain them for ordering over an extended period. To have the extended life of a catalog, the piece has to look like it's "worth saving." And mini-catalogs don't have that characteristic.

While mini-catalogs can be stand-alones when used as package or statement inserts or for inserting into a card deck, they require treatment like the brochure of a solo mailing if they are to be mailed separately. There are several basic rules for effective solo mailings:

- Mailings in envelopes will consistently pull better response than mailings without outer envelopes.

- Mailings with letters enclosed will pull substantially better than mailings without letters (assuming, of course, that the letters are well written).
- A separate order device will generally pull increased response, even though an order device may already be part of a printed enclosure.
- Action devices such as stamps, tokens, and rub-off spots, etc. will stimulate ordering.

Reader's Digest probably uses more mini-catalogs than anyone else. They have tested a wide variety of different formats and have discovered that presenting a single item per page along with a separate, perforated stamp sheet, with each item offered featured on one of the stamps, produces maximum response for their offers. (The order forms are designed so customers just have to paste on the stamps of their choice to indicate the items they wish to order.)

Self-Mailers

While "self-mailers" (solo mailings without an outer envelope—and most often without individual letters) seldom produce the amount of response a mailing inside an envelope produces, they are more economical to produce and can be effective for many kinds of supplemental catalog promotions.

Most often, self-mailers are used as a change-of-pace mailing. Jackson & Perkins, for example, regularly mails both catalogs and envelope-enclosed solo mailings to sell its roses and other nursery products. But since Mother's Day falls during their primary season for selling basic garden products, they use a change-of-pace 7 1/4 x 6" double postcard to promote a potted gardenia for Mother's Day gift-giving. The self-mailer has a tear-off business reply card for ordering.

Newsletters & Newspapers

A number of companies use newsletter or newspaper formats to supplement their catalog mailings, or, in cases where there are only a limited number of items to be offered, as a substitute for a catalog.

Garden Way Manufacturing Co., for example, distributes quarterly issues of a 32-page tabloid-size newspaper, *Troy-Bilt Owner News*. The middle 12 pages are a catalog featuring approximately 20 basic products, plus a number of accessories and supplies.

The outer 20 pages provide news of new products, technical information about older products, how-to-do-it articles, plus gardening tips and interesting stories provided by customers.

Black Box Corporation, a computer supplies firm, supplements its catalogs with a special 16-page 8 1/2 x 11" *Black Box Communicator* newsletter, containing editorial material about computers and several pages presenting new products which have been introduced since the last catalog.

The Horchow Collection sends eight-page 8 ½ x 11" newsletters to special customers with interesting information about products and a unique feature giving customers an opportunity to try to guess

Figure 15–6
Self-Mailers

An inexpensive change-of-pace mailing is a self-mailer such as this one from Jackson & Perkins, which regularly mails catalogs and full solo mailings to its customers. Copyright © Jackson & Perkins. Used with permission.

which products have been Horchow best sellers. Even though Horchow doesn't offer prizes, just a promise to list the "winners in the next newsletter," encourages many customers to enjoy trying to outguess Horchow's merchandise buyers.

Current encloses four-page 8 1/4 x 10 1/2 " newsletters, *Keeping Current*, with merchandise shipments. They feature a "Thank You For Your Order" message and interesting background information about the company and its products. Also included are money-saving coupons which can be used on a future order and special value "closeout sale" items with discounts of as much as 80 percent.

Quill Corporation produces monthly issues of *The Quill Pen Pal*, a four-page 8 1/2 x 11 " newsletter with office tips, information on how to select products and other editorial information.

Figure 15–7
Newsletters

Current encloses a four-page newsletter with merchandise shipments. The newsletter features a "thank you" message and background information on the company, as well as money-saving coupons. Copyright © Current, Inc. Used with permission.

MONEY-SAVING COUPONS See inside!

Keeping Current

VOL. IV, NO. 2 Here's what's current with Current®! Summer 1987

Current makes summer fun!

This summer, before you gather up the family, picnic gear or gardening tools, pick up your Current catalog . . . you'll find items that make your summer more enjoyable than ever! Just look through the opening section of your summer catalog. (If you don't have a summer catalog, you'll find the same items in a flyer included with your order.)

Whether you're going on a picnic or camping trip, to the beach, or planning to stay in your own back yard, you'll love these items:

- **Nature Discovery Kit** is great for exploring fields and forests. The kit includes a booklet with hiking tips and activities, magnifying glass, collapsible binoculars and more! Great for kids ages 6 and up.
- **Flower Press and Notes** lets you "pick" your note cards. Use real flowers and press them onto note cards to create beautiful designs. The press comes with instructions, blotter sheets, 12 embossed notes and mauve envelopes.
- **Bath & Beach Toys** let youngsters fish for a plastic turtle, fish and whale. The set includes a rod, easy

Cont'd next column

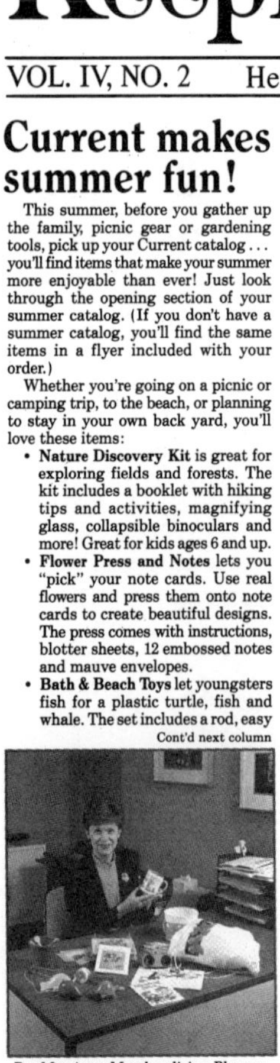

Pat Morrison, Merchandising Planner, displays a few of the many summer products you'll find in your summer catalog.

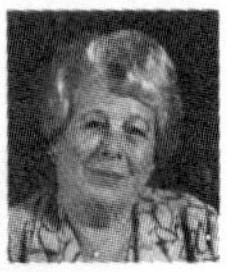

THANK YOU FOR YOUR ORDER!

Dear Customer,

Thank you for your order! We hope you enjoy everything you received. Remember, our products and service are fully guaranteed. If you find any problem with your order, simply fill out the Guarantee Form on the back of the Shipping Notice and send it to the folks in our Customer Service Department. They'll make sure the problem is resolved.

We welcome all your comments and suggestions at any time. In fact, we rely on customer comments when determining new product lines. You'll learn just how important your comments are to us by reading the article on our Research Department on the next page. You'll see how our researchers go out of their way to make sure our products and service are just what you'd expect from Current.

As a special thank you for your order, I've included one of my favorite recipes, Easy Chicken A La King. This recipe and 100 more delicious chicken dishes are featured in our *Fixin' Chicken 101 Ways* cookbook. Also, look for our new *Make Ahead Main Dishes And Desserts* cookbook that's ideal for cooks without a lot of time. Hope you enjoy this selection!

Sincerely,

Miriam B. Loo

Miriam B. Loo
Founder, Current, Inc.

EASY CHICKEN A LA KING Makes 4 servings

- 1 cup sliced mushrooms
- 2 tablespoons butter or margarine
- 1 package (10 oz.) frozen peas and pearl onions, partially thawed
- 1 can (10 3/4 oz.) condensed cream of chicken soup
- 3/4 cup milk
- 1 1/2 cups diced cooked chicken
- 2 tablespoons chopped pimiento
- 1/8 teaspoon pepper
- 2/3 cup shredded Swiss cheese

In a medium skillet over medium heat, sauté mushrooms in butter or margarine for 3 minutes or until limp. Stir in peas and onions, breaking pieces apart. Cover and steam for 4 minutes or until peas are tender.

Stir in soup and milk until blended. Stir in chicken, pimiento and pepper. Stirring, bring to a boil. Remove from heat. Stir in cheese until melted and blended.

Serve over buttered toast, patty shells, biscuits or hot cooked noodles.

crank reel, plastic animals that attach to the rod's nylon cord and 4 1/4" bucket.

- **Crayons in Bucket** provides fun for kids when they're not in the water. 5 1/4"tall bucket is filled with 64 multicolored crayons. Kids can draw or use the bucket to play in the sand.
- **Gardener's Mug** features a wrap-around design with the saying, "I dig gardening!" A great gift for anyone who enjoys gardening.

Current wants you to make the most of your summer—that's why we designed this special line of products. So be sure to look for these and many more items in our summer section before you go to the beach, garden or on a picnic!

Telephone Marketing

In recent years, a growing number of catalog companies have been using both inbound and outbound telephone marketing to supplement catalog sales. On inbound calls, operators offer "specials of the week" as order add-ons.

Other companies use outbound calls to customers to make special offers or to suggest upgrades of orders which have just been received. Two of the best examples of outbound marketing by catalog companies happened in Germany. One involved follow-ups to catalog requests. Operators called recipients to make sure they had received the catalogs they had requested. When informed that the catalog had indeed been received, they suggested a trial order to learn first hand

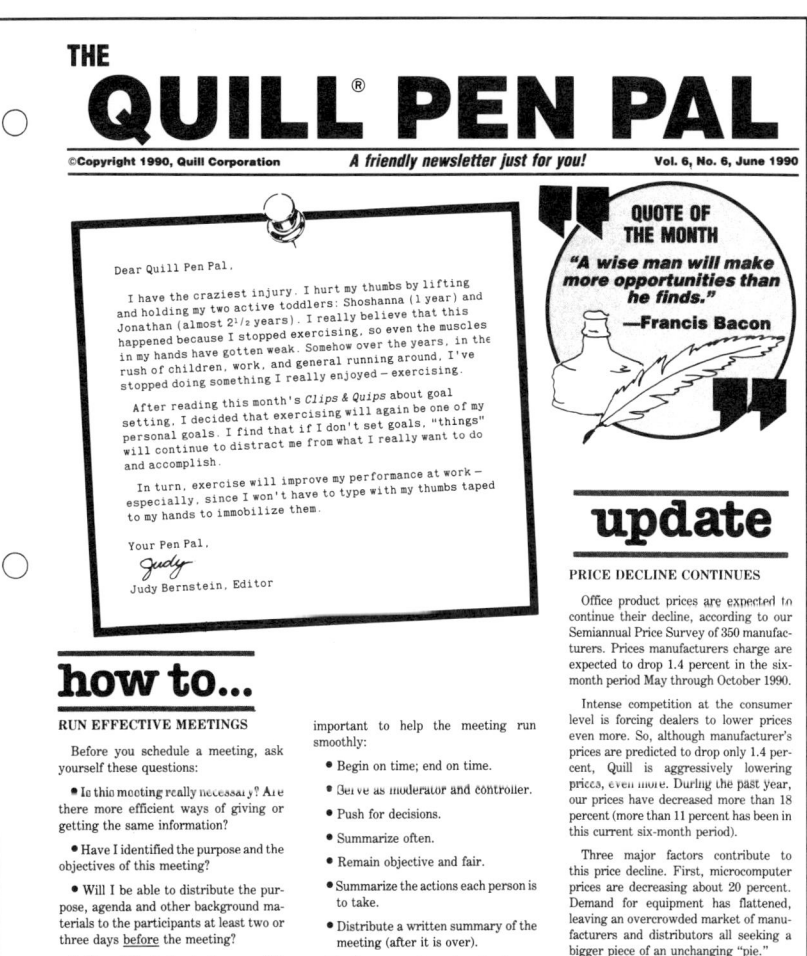

Figure 15–8
Monthly Newsletters

Quill Corporation distributes monthly four-page newsletters to communicate with customers. Copyright © Quill Corporation. Used with permission.

the quality of the company's merchandise—with no obligation to pay until they had had an opportunity to use the suggested item for 30 days. If they weren't pleased with the product, they could simply return it at the company's expense. The offer was so successful that over 50 percent of those contacted agreed to the 30-day trial.

A second example was a company whose catalog offered a variety of fine wines. At appropriate reorder times, telephone calls notified selected customers that a new supply of "their favorite wine" had just been received and suggested that it was a good idea to reserve a new supply while quantities were still available. Customers appreciated this follow-up service so much that sales were rung up on as many as 70 percent of the calls.

Appendix A

Title 16—Commercial Practices
CHAPTER I—FEDERAL TRADE COMMISSION
PART 435—MAIL ORDER MERCHANDISE
Promulgation of Trade Regulation Rule

THE FEDERAL TRADE COMMISSION, pursuant to the Federal Trade Commission Act, as amended, 15 U.S.C. 41, et seq., and the provisions of Subpart B, Part I of the Commission's Procedures and Rules of Practice, 16 CFR 1.11, et seq., has conducted a proceeding for the promulgation of a Trade Regulation Rule concerning Undelivered Mail Order Merchandise and Services. Notice of this proceeding, including a proposed Rule, was published in the FEDERAL REGISTER on September 28, 1971 (36 FR 19092 (1971)). Interested parties were thereafter afforded opportunity to participate in the proceeding through the submission of written data, views and arguments, and to appear and express their views orally and to suggest amendments, revisions, and additions to the proposed Rule.

1 Introduction

What is the Mail Order Rule

The Mail Order Rule was issued by the Federal Trade Commission (FTC) to correct growing problems with late or undelivered mail order merchandise. Under this Rule, you have a duty to ship merchandise on time. You also must follow procedures that the Rule requires if you cannot ship ordered merchandise on time.

When there is a shipping delay, the Rule requires that you notify your customers of the delay and provide them with an option either to agree to the delay or to cancel the order and receive a prompt refund. For each additional delay, your customers must be notified that they must send you a signed consent to a further delay or a refund will be given.

Why Was the Rule Issued

The Rule was issued after federal, state, and local consumer protection authorities received thousands of consumer complaints about mail order problems. The major complaints were: failure to deliver merchandise, late delivery of merchandise, failure to make prompt refunds, and failure to answer customer inquiries about delayed or lost orders. For example:
- One consumer wrote about Christmas decorations she ordered in early October that were finally shipped the day before Christmas. This consumer wrote twice to the company about her order, the second time requesting a refund. Both inquiries were ignored.
- Another consumer complained about a company that failed to send a stereo component he ordered with payment in July. By late October, the only communication he received from the company was his canceled check.

The FTC received 3,200 similar consumer complaints prior to beginning its rulemaking process. In addition, the President's Office of Consumer Affairs (OCA) received over 1,000 complaints concerning mail order practices, 60% of which concerned non-delivery. OCA complaint statistics for mail order were second only to complaints about autos and auto services.

The rulemaking record contains more than 10,000 pages of complaints regarding mail order sales. State and local agencies urged the Commission to take action to correct these problems. Industry members provided valuable input as to the feasibility and practicality of a mail order rule.

On October 22, 1975, the FTC promulgated the Mail Order Rule, and it went into effect on February 2, 1976.

Why You Should Comply with the Rule

When you comply with the Rule, you are being responsive to your customers. This is beneficial to you and to your customers because it promotes a positive industry image. Compliance creates consumer trust in buying by mail and fosters repeat mail order business. Of course if you ship on time, the requirements of the Rule pertaining to "option notices" do not apply.

Although most members of the mail order industry adhere to the Rule's requirements, there are some who do not. The FTC's Bureau of Consumer Protection monitors consumer complaints to ensure that businesses comply with the Rule. The FTC also provides compliance information, such as this manual, and assistance to all industry members.

AFTER IT HAD CONSIDERED THE SUGGESTIONS, CRITICISMS, objections, and other pertinent information in the Record, the Commission on March 8, 1974, published a revised proposed rule in a notice in the FEDERAL REGISTER (39 FR 9201 (1974)) extending an opportunity to interested parties to submit data, views or arguments regarding the revised proposed Rule. A period of over 90 days was allowed for the submission of written comments on the revised proposal. Written comments of the Direct Mail/Marketing Association (DM/MA) were admitted into the Record at a subsequent date and the public was given 30 days to submit written views and comments related to the DM/MA submission (39 FR 40515 (1974)).

The Commission has now considered all matters of fact, law, policy and discretion, including the data, views and arguments presented on the Record by interested parties in response to the Notices, as prescribed by law, and has determined that the adoption of the Trade Regulation Rule set forth herein and its Statement of Basis and Purpose[1] is in the public interest.

Accordingly, the Commission hereby amends Subchapter D, Trade Regulation Rules, Chapter I of 16 CFR by adding a new Part 435 as follows:

Sec.
435.1   The Rule.
435.2   Definitions.

AUTHORITY: The provisions of this Part 435 issued under 38 Stat. 717, as amended, 15 U.S.C. 41, et seq.

---

[1] Statement of Basis and Purpose filed as part of the original document.

2 How to Comply with the Rule

This section of the manual provides **THE TEXT OF THE RULE, WITH EXPLANATIONS OPPOSITE** of how to comply with the Rule.

§ 435.1 The Rule.

IN CONNECTION WITH MAIL ORDER SALES in commerce, as "commerce" is defined in the Federal Trade Commission Act, it constitutes an unfair method of competition, and an unfair or deceptive act and practice for a seller:

(a)(1) To solicit any order for the sale of merchandise to be ordered by the buyer through the mails unless, at the time of the solicitation, the seller has a reasonable basis to expect that he will be able to ship any ordered merchandise to the buyer: (i) within that time clearly and conspicuously stated in any such solicitation, or (ii) if no time is clearly and conspicuously stated, within thirty (30) days after receipt of a properly completed order from the buyer.

(2) To provide any buyer with any revised shipping date, as provided in paragraph (b), unless, at the time any such revised shipping date is provided, the seller has a reasonable basis for making such representation regarding a definite revised shipping date.

(3) To inform any buyer that he is unable to make any representation regarding the length of any delay unless (i) the seller has a reasonable basis for so informing the buyer and (ii) the seller informs the buyer of the reason or reasons for the delay.

(b)(1) Where a seller is unable to ship merchandise within the applicable time set forth in paragraph (a)(1), above, to fail to offer to the buyer, clearly and conspicuously and without prior demand, an option either to consent to a delay in shipping or to cancel his order and receive a prompt refund. Said offer shall be made within a reasonable time after the seller first becomes aware of his inability to ship within the applicable time set forth in paragraph (a)(1), but in no event later than said applicable time.

What to Know When You Make an Offer

When you offer to sell merchandise by mail, the Rule requires you to have a "reasonable basis" for expecting to ship within the time stated in your solicitation.

For example, if you know before advertising your products that your suppliers are on strike and are likely to remain on strike for several months, you do not have a "reasonable basis" for expecting to ship within a month.

The shipping date, when provided in your offer, must be clearly and conspicuously stated:

ADVERTISEMENT
Cardigan Sweaters
S, M, L—Beige or Blue
$29.95 plus tax
Allow 5 weeks for shipment.

If you do not provide a shipping date, you must ship the merchandise within 30 days of receiving a "properly completed" order. An order is properly completed when you receive payment accompanied by all information you need to fill the order. Payment may be made by cash, money order, check, or credit card, according to your company policy. If a credit card is used for a purchase, the order is properly completed when you charge your customer's account.

When you cannot ship on time, you must provide your customer with an "option" notice. The notice must provide an option to cancel the order and receive a prompt refund, or to agree to a delay in shipping. And, as with the original date, you must have a reasonable basis for setting that shipping date.

You must also have a reasonable basis for telling your customers that you do not know when you can ship merchandise. In that case, you must provide the specific reasons for the shipping problem. For example, you could state that a fire destroyed the warehouse holding the goods and you are unable to provide a revised shipping date because you do not know how long it will take to replace the merchandise.

When You Should Send a First Notice

If a shipment is delayed, the Rule requires that you give your customers an option:
- to consent to a delay; or
- to cancel the order and receive a prompt refund.

People in the trade often refer to the notice as a "delay" notice. More accurately, it should be called an "option" notice. You violate the Rule if you only provide a notice of delay without also providing an option to cancel the order.

Remember, you must send the notice after you first become aware that there will be a shipping delay. The notice must be sent:
- before the promised shipping date; or
- within 30 days after you receive the order (if no date was provided in your solicitation).

(b)(i) ANY OFFER TO THE BUYER of such an option shall fully inform the buyer regarding his right to cancel the order and to obtain a prompt refund and shall provide a definite revised shipping date, but where the seller lacks a reasonable basis for providing a definite revised shipping date the notice shall inform the buyer that the seller is unable to make any representation regarding the length of the delay.

What a First Notice Must Say

If you provide a revised shipping date of 30 days or less, you must have a reasonable basis for making the change. The notice must inform your customers that non-response is considered consent to be a delay of 30 days or less.

If you are unable to provide a revised shipping date, your notice must state that you cannot determine when the merchandise will be shipped. It must also state that the order will be automatically canceled unless:
- you ship the merchandise within 30 days of the original shipping date and you have not received your customer's cancellation before shipment; or

(ii) WHERE THE SELLER HAS PROVIDED a definite revised shipping date which is thirty (30) days or less later than the applicable time set forth in paragraph (a)(1), the offer of said option shall expressly inform the buyer that, unless the seller receives, prior to shipment and prior to the expiration of the definite revised shipping date, a response from the buyer rejecting the delay and canceling the order, the buyer will be deemed to have consented to a delayed shipment on or before the definite revised shipping date.

(iii) Where the seller has provided a definite revised shipping date which is more than thirty (30) days later than the applicable time set forth in paragraph (a)(1) or where the seller is unable to provide a definite revised shipping date and therefore informs the buyer that he is unable to make any representation regarding the length of the delay, the offer of said option shall also expressly inform the buyer that his order will automatically be deemed to have been canceled unless (A) the seller has shipped the merchandise within thirty (30) days of the applicable time set forth in paragraph (a)(1), and has received no cancellation prior to shipment, or (B) the seller has received from the buyer within thirty (30) days of said applicable time, a response specifically consenting to said shipping delay. Where the seller informs the buyer that he is unable to make any representation regarding the length of the delay, the buyer shall be expressly informed that, should he consent to an indefinite delay, he will have a continuing right to cancel his order at any time after the applicable time set forth in paragraph (a)(1) by so notifying the seller prior to actual shipment.

(iv) Nothing in this paragraph shall prohibit a seller who furnishes a definite revised shipping date pursuant to paragraph (b)(1)(i), from requesting, simultaneously with or at any time subsequent to the offer of an option pursuant to paragraph (b)(1), the buyer's express consent to a further unanticipated delay beyond the definite revised shipping date in the form of a response from the buyer specifically consenting to said further delay. *Provided, however,* that where the seller solicits consent to an unanticipated indefinite delay the solicitation shall expressly inform the buyer that, should he so consent to an indefinite delay, he shall have a continuing right to cancel his order at any time after the definite revised shipping date by so notifying the seller prior to actual shipment.

(b)(2) Where a seller is unable to ship merchandise on or before the definite revised shipping date provided under paragraph (b)(1)(i) and consented to by the buyer pursuant to paragraph (b)(1)(ii) or (iii), to fail to offer to the buyer, clearly and conspicuously and without prior demand, a renewed option either to consent to a further delay or to cancel the order and to receive a prompt refund. Said offer shall be made within a reasonable time after the seller first becomes aware of his inability to ship before the said definite revised date, but in no event later than the expiration of the definite revised shipping date. Provided, however, that where the seller previously has obtained the buyer's express consent to an unanticipated delay until a specific date beyond the definite revised shipping date, pursuant to paragraph (b)(1)(iv) or to a further delay until a specific date beyond the definite revised shipping date pursuant to this paragraph (b)(2), that date to which the buyer has expressly consented shall supersede the definite revised shipping date for purposes of this paragraph (b)(2).

(i) ANY OFFER TO THE BUYER of said renewed option shall provide the buyer with a new definite revised shipping date, but where the seller lacks a reasonable basis for providing a new definite revised shipping date, the notice shall inform the buyer that the seller is unable to make any representation regarding the length of the further delay.

(ii) The offer of a renewed option shall expressly inform the buyer that, unless the seller receives, prior to the expiration of the old definite revised shipping date or any date superseding the old definite revised shipping date, notification from the buyer specifically consenting to the further delay, the buyer will be deemed to have rejected any further delay, and to have canceled the order if the seller is in fact unable to ship prior to the expiration of the old definite revised shipping date or any date superseding the old definite revised shipping date.

- you receive within 30 days of the original date your customer's consent to the delay.

Your notice must provide this information if the definite revised shipping date is more than 30 days after the original date.

When you are unable to provide a revised shipping date, you must inform your customers of their continuing right to cancel the order by notifying you prior to actual shipment.

What Later Notices Must Say

If you are unable to ship the merchandise on or before your revised shipping date, you must notify your customers again. This is called a "renewed option" notice. This notice must inform your customers of their right to consent to a further delay, or to cancel the order and receive a prompt refund.

The renewed option notice must inform customers that if they do not agree in writing to this delay, their order will be canceled. Unless you receive your customer's express written consent to the second delay before the first delay period ends, you must cancel the order and provide a full refund.

Keep in mind that you do not have to offer a "renewed option" to customers who consent to an indefinite delay in response to the first option notice. But any customer who agrees to an indefinite delay has the continuing right to cancel the order at any time before the merchandise is shipped.

How You Should Send Notices

You should send any option notice by first class mail, and your notice should provide a written means for your customers to respond. A prepaid business mail reply or prepaid postage card meets this requirement.

The notice is most advantageous for you if at some point you have to prove that you complied with the Rule. If the FTC takes action against a company, the firm must be able to show that any other form of notice it used was equal to or better than the written form described in the Rule. For example, an "800" telephone number for customers' use in canceling orders is an adequate substitute, if you can prove that the system met the Rule's requirements. This would include being able to show that the 800 number could readily and consistently be used to cancel an order because you provided adequate and competent staff to take cancellations. You should keep records of all cancellations.

When You *May* Cancel an Order

In some cases you can have an option to cancel an order or to send out another notice. You may make this decision when you are unable to ship merchandise on time or within the delay period to which your customer agreed. But if you decide to cancel the order,

Provided, however, that where the seller offers the buyer the option to consent to an indefinite delay the offer shall expressly inform the buyer that, should he so consent to an indefinite delay, he shall have a continuing right to cancel his order at any time after the old definite revised shipping date or any date superseding the old definite revised shipping date.

(iii) This paragraph (b)(2) shall not apply to any situation where a seller, pursuant to the provisions of paragraph (b)(1)(iv), has previously obtained consent from the buyer to an indefinite extension beyond the first revised shipping date.

[i]t constitutes an unfair method of competition, and an unfair or deceptive act and practice for a seller:....

(b)(3) WHEREVER A BUYER HAS THE RIGHT to exercise any option under this part or to cancel an order by so notifying the seller prior to shipment, to fail to furnish the buyer with adequate means, at the seller's expense, to exercise such option or to notify the seller regarding cancellation. In any action brought by the Federal Trade Commission alleging a violation of this part, the failure of a respondent-seller:

(i) To provide any offer, notice or option required by this part in writing and by first class mail will create a rebuttable presumption that the respondent-seller failed to offer a clear and conspicuous offer, notice or option;

(ii) To provide the buyer with the means in writing (by business reply mail or with postage prepaid by the seller) to exercise any option or to notify the seller regarding a decision to cancel, will create a rebuttable presumption that the respondent-seller did not provide the buyer with adequate means pursuant to this subparagraph (3).

NOTHING IN PARAGRAPH (B) of this part shall prevent a seller, where he is unable to make shipment within the time set forth in paragraph (a)(1) or within a delay period consented to by the buyer, from deciding to consider the order canceled and providing the buyer with notice of said decision within a reasonable time after he becomes aware of said inability to ship, together with a prompt refund.

[i]t constitutes an unfair method of competition, and an unfair or deceptive act and practice for a seller:...

(c) TO FAIL TO DEEM AN ORDER CANCELED and to make a prompt refund to the buyer whenever:

(1) The seller receives, prior to the time of shipment, notification from the buyer canceling the order pursuant to any option, renewed option or continuing option under this part;

(2) The seller has, pursuant to paragraph (b)(1)(iii), provided the buyer with a definite revised shipping date which is more than thirty (30) days later than the applicable time set forth in paragraph (a)(1) or has notified the buyer that he is unable to make any representation regarding the length of the delay and the seller (i) has not shipped the merchandise within thirty (30) days of the applicable time set forth in paragraph (a)(1), and (ii) has not received the buyer's express consent to said shipping delay within said thirty (30) days;

(3) The seller is unable to ship within the applicable time set forth in paragraph (b)(2), and has not received, within the said applicable time, the buyer's consent to any further delay;

(4) The seller has notified the buyer of his inability to make shipment and has indicated his decision not to ship the merchandise;

(5) The seller fails to offer the option prescribed in paragraph (b)(1) and has not shipped the merchandise within the applicable time set forth in paragraph (a)(1).

you must inform your customer of this decision and provide a prompt refund.

Whether you cancel or send another notice, you must inform your customer about it within a reasonable time after you know you cannot ship the merchandise.

When You *Must* Cancel an Order

You must cancel an order and provide a prompt refund:

- when your customer does not agree to a delay and exercises the option to cancel an order before it has been shipped;
- when you notify your customer of your inability to ship the merchandise and of your decision to cancel the order;
- when you are unable to ship merchandise before the revised shipping date and you have not received your customer's consent to a further delay;
- when the delay is indefinite and you have not shipped the merchandise or received your customer's consent to an indefinite delay;
- when the definite revised shipping date in the first option notice is more than 30 days after the original shipping date, and you have not shipped the merchandise, nor received your customer's consent to the delay within 30 days of the original shipping date; or
- when you cannot ship on time and do not notify your customers of their options.

All refunds must be sent to the buyer by first class mail. If the buyer paid by cash, check, or money order, you must refund payment within seven (7) days after the order is canceled. For credit card sales, you must make refunds within one billing cycle after the order is canceled. Under no circumstances are you to substitute credit vouchers or script for a refund.

Why You Should Keep Records

If for some reason your company has problems in shipping on time, your customers may begin to file complaints with you, and with local, state, or federal law enforcement agencies. Because the Federal Trade Commission has enforcement jurisdiction under the Mail Order Rule, many complaints are forwarded to the FTC from other agencies.

When the FTC takes action against a company and alleges that it violated the Rule, the company must have records or other documentary proof that will show the steps it took to comply. Systems and procedures for complying with the Rule are carefully reviewed. Lack of such proof creates a rebuttable presumption that the company failed to comply. This means that the seller must be able to show that it used reasonable systems and procedures to comply with the Rule. Consequently, it is in your best interest to establish an accurate, up-to-date record-keeping system.

(a)(4) IN ANY ACTION BROUGHT BY THE FEDERAL TRADE COMMISSION, alleging a violation of this part, the failure of a respondent-seller to have records or other documentary proof establishing his use of systems and procedures which assure the shipment of merchandise in the ordinary course of business within any applicable time set forth in this part will create a rebuttable presumption that the seller lacked a reasonable basis for any expectation of shipment within said applicable time.

(d) In any action brought by the Federal Trade Commission, alleging a violation of this part, the failure of a respondent-seller to have records or other documentary proof establishing his use of systems and procedures which assure compliance, in the ordinary course of business, with any requirement of paragraphs (b) or (c) of this part will create a rebuttable presumption that the seller failed to comply with said requirements.

What the Rule Does Not Cover

The following mail order sales are exempt from the Rule:
- magazine subscriptions (and similar serial deliveries), except for the first shipment;
- sales of seeds and growing plants;
- orders made on a collect-on-delivery basis (C.O.D.);
- transactions covered by the FTC's Negative Option Rule (such as book and record clubs);
- mail order photo-finishing; or
- orders made by telephone and charged to a credit card account.

NOTE 1: This part shall not apply to subscriptions, such as magazine sales, ordered for serial delivery, after the initial shipment is made in compliance with this part.

NOTE 2: This part shall not apply to orders of seeds and growing plants.

NOTE 3: This part shall not apply to orders made on a collect-on-delivery (C.O.D.) basis.

NOTE 4: This part shall not apply to transactions governed by the Federal Trade Commission's Trade Regulation Rule entitled "Use of Negative Option Plans by Sellers in Commerce," 16 CFR 425.

NOTE 5: By taking action in this area, the Federal Trade Commission does not intend to preempt action in the same area, which is not inconsistent with this part, by any State, municipal, or other local government. This part does not annul or diminish any rights or remedies provided to consumers by any State law, municipal ordinance, or other local regulation, insofar as those rights or remedies are equal to or greater than those provided by this part. In addition, this part does not supersede those provisions of any State law, municipal ordinance, or other local regulation which impose obligations or liabilities upon sellers, when sellers subject to this part are not in compliance therewith. This part does supersede those provisions of any State law, municipal ordinance, or other local regulation which are inconsistent with this part to the extent that those provisions do not provide a buyer with rights which are equal to or greater than those rights granted a buyer by this part. This part also supersedes those provisions of any State law, municipal ordinance, or other local regulation requiring that a buyer be notified of a right which is the same as a right provided by this part but requiring that a buyer be given notice of this right in a language, form, or manner which is different in any way from that required by this part.

In those instances where any State law, municipal ordinance, or other local regulation contains provisions, some but not all of which are partially or completely superseded by this part, the provisions or portions of those provisions which have not been superseded retain their full force and effect.

NOTE 6: If any provision of this part or its application to any person, partnership, corporation, act or practice is held invalid, the remainder of this part or the application of the provision to any other person, partnership, corporation, act or practice shall not be affected thereby.

NOTE 7: Section 435.1(a)(1) of this part governs all solicitations where the time of solicitation is more than 100 days after promulgation of this part. The remainder of this part governs all transactions where receipt of a properly completed order occurs more than 100 days after promulgation of this part.

Where to Go for Help

For more information, contact:
- the Federal Trade Commission, Enforcement Division, B.C.P., Washington, D.C. 20580,
- the Direct Marketing Association, 1730 K Street, N.W., Washington, D.C. 20006;
- your local United States Postal Service; and
- your local consumer protection office.

State and local governments also may have requirements with which you must comply. You should consult each agency for information about laws that affect your operations.

Definitions

§ 435.2 Definitions.

For purposes of this part:

(a) "Shipment" shall mean the act by which the merchandise is physically placed in the possession of the carrier.

(b) "Receipt of a properly completed order" shall mean:

(1) Where there is a credit sale and the buyer has not previously tendered partial payment, the time at which the seller charges the buyer's account;

(2) Where the buyer tenders full or partial payment in the proper amount in the form of cash, check or money order, the time at which the seller has received both said payment and an order from the buyer containing all the information needed by the seller to process and ship the order.

Provided, however, that where the seller receives notice that the check or money order tendered by the buyer has been dishonored or that the buyer does not qualify for a credit sale, "receipt of a properly completed order" shall mean the time at which (i) the seller receives notice that a check or money order for the proper amount tendered by the buyer has been honored, (ii) the buyer tenders cash in the proper amount or (iii) the seller receives notice that the buyer qualifies for a credit sale.

(c) "Refund" shall mean:

(1) Where the buyer tendered full payment for the unshipped merchandise in the form of cash, check, or money order, a return of the amount tendered in the form of cash, check, or money order;

(2) Where there is a credit sale:

(i) And the seller is a creditor, a copy of a credit memorandum or the like or an account statement reflecting the removal or absence of any remaining charge incurred as a result of the sale from the buyer's account;

(ii) And a third party is the creditor, a copy of an appropriate credit memorandum or the like to the third party creditor which will remove the charge from the buyer's account or a statement from the seller acknowledging the cancellation of the order and representing that he has not taken any action regarding the order which will result in a charge to the buyer's account with the third party;

(iii) And the buyer tendered partial payment for the unshipped merchandise in the form of cash, check, or money order, a return of the amount tendered in the form of cash, check, or money order.

(d) "Prompt refund" shall mean:

(1) Where a refund is made pursuant to Definition (c) (1) or (2) (iii), a refund sent to the buyer by first class mail within seven (7) working days of the date on which the buyer's right to refund vests under the provisions of this part;

(2) Where a refund is made pursuant to Definition (c) (2) (i) or (ii), a refund sent to the buyer by first class mail within one (1) billing cycle from the date on which the buyer's right to refund vests under the provisions of this part.

(e) The "time of solicitation" of an order shall mean that time when the seller has:

(1) Mailed or otherwise disseminated the solicitation to a prospective purchaser;

(2) Made arrangements for an advertisement containing the solicitation to appear in a newspaper, magazine, or the like, or on radio or television, which cannot be changed or canceled without incurring substantial expense; or

(3) Made arrangements for the printing of a catalog, brochure or the like which cannot be changed without incurring substantial expense, in which the solicitation in question forms an insubstantial part.

Effective: February 2, 1976.

Promulgated October 22, 1975, by the Federal Trade Commission.

CHARLES A. TOBIN,
Secretary.

[FH Doc. 75-28203 Filed 70-21-75; 3:45 am]

3 Questions and Answers About the Rule

The FTC receives questions from mail order sellers who want to know how to comply with the Rule. The following questions are those that are asked most frequently.

Q: *What advice do you give someone who is planning to start a mail order business?*

Q: *How important is it to set up a customer service procedure?*

Q: *Our company has read the Mail Order Rule, but we still have questions about what we can and cannot do. Who should we contact?*

What to Do When You Start a Mail Order Business

A: The FTC suggests that you do the following:
- Learn the requirements of the Mail Order Rule.
- Familiarize yourself with state laws in areas where you plan to do business. For example, some states, such as Wisconsin, have additional mail order requirements that should be followed.
- Ask experienced mail order sellers for practical hints to help you avoid the pitfalls in mail order business.

A: An efficient customer service procedure is beneficial to you and your customers. Customers often complain that they have been treated badly by the companies they have contacted. But the number of complaints should drop significantly if your customer service personnel communicate responsively with your customers when they have problems.

A: It depends on whether you need a formal or an informal response.
- You should feel free to write the FTC Enforcement Division to ask questions about the Rule and how your operations are affected. Staff advice is not binding on the Commission, but this advice can be helpful.
- You may obtain a binding advisory opinion from the Commission if you send a specific, written inquiry about the legality of certain conduct. Advisory opinions apply only to proposed conduct, not to conduct that is in practice. The opinions are usually restricted to questions that are not clearly answered by the terms of the Rule. Ask the FTC staff about the procedure for obtaining an advisory opinion.

When You Must Ship an Order

Q: We advertise a shipment date of six weeks. What happens if there is a workers' strike or some other unanticipated event and shipment is delayed? Have we violated the Rule?

A: If you calculated the shipping date correctly in the first place, you have complied with the Rule. But if you discover that a delay cannot be avoided, you must notify your customers and provide the option notice. If you fail to do this, you have unilaterally changed the sales contract and have violated the Rule.

Q: We advertise several products but do not indicate a shipping date in our ads. When must we ship?

A: If your solicitation does not state when you plan to ship the merchandise, the Rule requires that you ship it within 30 days after you receive a properly completed order (that is, when you have received payment and sufficient information to fill the order).

Q: How can we protect our company accounts from customers who bounce checks or do not qualify for credit?

A: Be prompt in depositing checks and checking your customers' credit-worthiness. Remember, the order is properly completed, triggering the 30-day period, when you receive payment and all information needed to process the order. For example, if the buyer does not send enough cash to cover the cost of an order, the order is not properly completed. You may wait for the check to clear before mailing, as long as you ship within the 30-day period.

Q: What about a credit sale?

A: When you receive a properly completed order with a charge account number, the clock starts when you charge your customer's account.

Q: If a customer orders an item which is not in stock when the order is received, can we substitute an item of similar or better quality without the customer's consent?

A: No. The FTC has established that you must obtain your customer's authorization to substitute merchandise different from that ordered.

What Items Are Covered

Q: Are mail order sales between businesses covered by the Rule?

A: Yes. Mail order transactions between businesses are covered. This would include specialty items, such as calendars, pens, and ashtrays which bear advertising messages and are not sold to the general public.

Q: Does the Rule cover orders placed by telephone?

A: The Rule covers those situations in which you solicit orders by telephone and require your customers to mail the order accompanied by payment. If the mail is used to finalize the sale, the Rule applies. If mail is not used, the Rule does not apply.

Q: Does the Rule cover orders placed over the telephone involving credit card payment?

A: No. The Rule does not cover charges to a credit card account when the order is placed over the telephone.

What Rule Applies to Unordered Merchandise

Q: Is it legal to send unordered merchandise through the U.S. Mail?

A: No. The unordered merchandise statute provides that only two kinds of merchandise can be sent legally through the U.S. Mail without a consumer's prior consent:
- free samples that are clearly and conspicuously marked as such; and
- merchandise mailed by a charitable organization asking for contributions.

Consumers may consider unordered merchandise sent through the U.S. Mail as a free gift. They are not obligated to return it or to pay for it. Also, it is illegal for a company to send any bill or dunning communication seeking payment or return of unordered merchandise.

Why Record-Keeping is Important

Q: *Does the Rule require us to keep records?*

A: No. The Mail Order Rule does not impose record-keeping requirements on mail order sellers. But if you are ever involved in an action with the FTC, you must have records that prove you complied with the Rule. Therefore, it is advisable to establish a record-keeping method that best suits your situation and demonstrates compliance with the Rule.

Q: *How long do we have to keep customer complaint letters?*

A: The Rule does not specifically indicate whether or how long you must keep complaint letters. Complaint letters, when adequately answered, may be used as proof that you complied with the Rule if you are ever questioned. It is probably advisable to keep such correspondence and other records for a period of three to five years.

When the FTC Takes Action

Q: *What actually happens when the FTC receives a complaint against a company?*

A: The staff checks to see whether the company has been advised of the Rule's requirements. If not, then a copy of the Rule with an explanation letter is usually sent to the firm. The FTC evaluates consumer complaints to see whether a pattern of violations is developing. The FTC then contacts the company to determine whether further action is necessary.

Q: *Under what circumstances will the Commission sue a mail order firm for violating the Rule?*

A: If a company is violating the Rule, it runs the risk of being sued. The Commission evaluates many criteria to determine whether an action is in the public interest.

Q: *What are the penalties for violating the Rule?*

A: The FTC Act provides that a person, partnership, or corporation may be liable for civil penalties of up to $10,000 per

Q: What can industry members expect from the FTC in the future?

violation. In addition, the FTC can sue for consumer redress.

A: Because the industry is steadily growing, an increased enforcement presence can be expected. This may mean actions for civil penalties against firms who fail to comply with the Rule. At the same time, the FTC is part of a government-wide effort to encourage industry members to effectively regulate themselves. The FTC is working to assist businesses as they undertake voluntary compliance with the Rule. This manual is part of that effort.

4 Sample Notices

Sample Option Notice
[Rule Section 435.1(b)(1)(ii)]

When you are unable to ship on time and wish to provide a **revised shipping date which is 30 days or less** after the original date, use a form such as this to notify your customers. This form must be sent out by first class mail within a reasonable time after you become aware that there will be a shipping delay. It must be sent before the promised date, or if no date was promised, within 30 days after you receive a properly completed order.

Dear Customer:

Thank you for your order. We are sorry to inform you that there will be a delay in shipping the merchandise you ordered. We shall make shipment by the revised shipping date of (   ). It is quite possible we could ship earlier.

You have the right to consent to this delay or to cancel your order and receive a prompt refund. Please return this letter in the enclosed postpaid envelope with your instructions indicated by checking the appropriate block below.

Unless we hear from you prior to shipment or prior to *the revised shipping date*, it will be assumed that you have consented to a delayed shipment on or before the definite revised shipping date stated above.

                        Sincerely yours,

                        Name & Title of Signer
                        Company Name
                        Address

Enclosure: Envelope

☐ Yes, I will accept a further delay in shipment of my order for this item until _____
                  (Insert date which is 30 days or less.)

☐ I cannot wait. Please cancel my order for this item and promptly refund my money.

                  _____
                  Please Sign Here

Sample Renewed Option Notice
[Rule Section 435.1(b)(2)(i)-(ii)]

When you are unable to ship merchandise on or before the promised definite revised shipping date, and wish to provide **a new definite revised shipping date,** use a form such as this to notify your customers.

Dear Customer:

We are sorry to inform you that there will be a further delay in shipping the merchandise you ordered. We shall make shipment by *(new definite revised shipping date)*. It is quite possible we could ship earlier.

You have the right to consent to a further delay or to cancel your order and receive a prompt refund. Please return this letter in the enclosed postpaid envelope with your instructions indicated by checking the appropriate block below.

Unless we hear from you prior to the old shipping date to which you previously agreed, it will be assumed that you have rejected any further shipping delay and your order will be canceled and a prompt refund made.

Sincerely yours,

Name & Title of Signer
Company Name
Address

Enclosure: Envelope

☐ Yes, I will accept a delay in shipment of my order for this item until _____
(Insert date which is 30 days or less.)

☐ I cannot wait. Please cancel my order for this item and promptly refund my money.

_____
Please Sign Here

Appendix B

Direct Marketing Association Guidelines For Ethical Business Practice

The Terms of the Offer

Honesty
Article #1
All offers should be clear, honest, and complete so that the consumer may know the exact nature of what is being offered, the price, the terms of payment (including all extra charges), and the commitment involved in the placing of an order. Before publication of an offer, direct marketers should be prepared to substantiate any claims or offers made. Advertisements or specific claims which are untrue, misleading, deceptive, fraudulent, or unjustly disparaging of competitors should not be used.

Clarity
Article #2
A simple statement of all the essential points of the offer should be clearly displayed in the promotional material. When an offer illustrates goods that are not included or that cost extra, these facts should be made clear.

Print Size
Article #3
Print which by its small size, placement, or other visual characteristics is likely to substantially affect the legibility of the offer or exceptions to it should not be used.

Actual Conditions
Article #4
All descriptions and promises should be in accordance with actual conditions, situations, and circumstances existing at the time of the promotion. Claims regarding any limitations (such as time or quantity) should be legitimate.

Disparagement
Article #5
Disparagement of any person or group on grounds of race, color, religion, national origin, sex, marital status, or age is unacceptable.

Standards
Article #6
Solicitations should not contain vulgar, immoral, profane, or offensive matter nor promote the sale of pornographic material or other matter not acceptable for advertising on moral grounds.

Advertising to Children
Article #7
Offers suitable for adults only should not be made to children.

Photographs and Art Work
Article #8
Photographs, illustrations, artwork, and the situations they represent should be accurate portrayals and current reproductions of the products, services, or other subjects in all particulars.

Sponsor and Intent
Article #9

All direct marketing contacts should disclose the name of the sponsor and each purpose of the contact. No one should make offers or solicitations in the guise of research or a survey when the real intent is to sell products or services or to raise funds.

Identity of Seller
Article #10

Every offer and shipment should sufficiently identify the name and street address of the direct marketer so that the consumer may contact the individual or company by mail or phone.

Solicitation in the Guise of an Invoice
Article #11

Offers that are likely to be mistaken for bills or invoices should not be used.

Postage and Handling Charges
Article #12

Postage or shipping charges, or handling charges, if any, should reflect as accurately as practicable actual costs incurred.

Special Offers

Use of the Word "Free" and Other Similar Representations
Article #13

A product or service which is offered without cost or obligation to the recipient may be unqualifiedly described as "free."

If a product or service is offered as "free," for a nominal cost, or at a greatly reduced price, and/or if the offer requires the recipient to purchase some other product or service, all terms and conditions should be clearly and conspicuously disclosed, in close conjunction with the use of the term "free" or other similar phrase.

When the term "free" is used or other similar representations are made (for example, 2-for-1, half-price or 1-cent offers), the product or service required to be purchased should not have been increased in price or decreased in quality or quantity.

Negative Option Selling
Article #14

All direct marketers should comply with the FTC regulation governing Negative Option Plans. Some of the major requirements of this regulation are as follows:

Offers which require the consumer to return a notice sent by the seller before each periodic shipment to avoid receiving merchandise should contain all important conditions of the plan including:
  a. A full description of the obligation to purchase a minimum number of items and all the charges involved, and
  b. the procedures by which the consumer will receive the announcements of selections, and a statement of their frequency, as well as how to reject unwanted items, and how to cancel after completing the obligation.

The consumer should be given advance notice of the periodic selection so that the consumer may have a minimum of ten days to exercise a timely choice.

Because of the nature of this kind of offer, special attention should be given to the clarity, completeness, and prominent placement of the terms of the initial offering.

Sweepstakes

Sweepstakes, as defined here, are promotional devices by which items of value (prizes) are awarded to participants by chance without the promoter's requiring them to render something of value to be eligible to participate (consideration). The co-existence of all three elements—prize, chance, and consideration—in the same promotion constitutes a lottery. It is illegal for any private enterprise to run a lottery.

When skill replaces chance, the promotion becomes a skill contest. When gifts (premiums or other items of value) are given to all participants independent of the element of chance, the promotion is not a sweepstakes and should not be held out as such.

Violations of the anti-lottery laws are policed and enforced at the federal level by the United States Postal Service, the Federal Communications Commission (when broadcast advertising is involved), and the Federal Trade Commission.

Because sweepstakes are also regulated on a state-by-state basis, and the laws and definitions may vary by state, it is recommended that an attorney familiar with and experienced in the laws of sweepstakes be consulted before a sponsor conducts its promotion.

While this section of the Guidelines may focus on the promotional aspects of running a sweepstakes, it is equally important that the operation and administration of the sweepstakes be conducted in compliance with the ethical standards set forth in other sections as well.

Use of the Term "Sweepstakes"
Article #15
Only those promotional devices which satisfy the definition stated above should be called or held out to be a sweepstakes.

No-Purchase Option
Article #16
The no-purchase option as well as the method for entering without ordering should be clearly disclosed. Response devices used only for entering the sweepstakes should be as visible as those utilized for ordering the product or service.

Prizes
Article #17
Sweepstakes prizes should be advertised in a manner that is clear, honest, and complete so that the consumer may know the exact nature of what is being offered.

Photographs, illustrations, artwork, and the situations they represent should be accurate portrayals of the prizes listed in the promotion.

No award should be held forth directly or by implication as having substantial monetary value if it is of nominal worth. The value of a prize given should be stated at regular retail value, whether actual cost to the sponsor is greater or less.

Prizes should be delivered without cost to the participant. If there are certain conditions under which a prize or prizes will not be awarded, this fact should be disclosed in a manner that is easy to find and understand.

Premium
Article #18
If a premium, gift, or item of value is offered by virtue of a participant's merely entering a sweepstakes, without any selection process taking place, it should be clear that everyone will receive it.

Chances of Winning
Article #19
No sweepstakes promotion, or any of its parts, should state or imply that a recipient has won a prize when this is not the case.

Winners should be selected in a manner that ensures fair application of the laws of chance.

Disclosure of Rules
Article #20
All terms and conditions of the sweepstakes, including entry procedures and rules, should be easy to find, read, and understand.

The following should be set forth clearly in the rules:

- No purchase of the advertised product or service is required in order to win a prize.
- Procedures for entry.
- If applicable, disclosure that a facsimile of the entry blank or promotional device may be used to enter the sweepstakes.
- The termination date for eligibility in the sweepstakes. The termination date should specify whether it is a date of mailing or receipt of entry deadline.
- The number, retail value, and complete description of all prizes offered, and whether cash may be awarded instead of merchandise. If a cash prize is to be awarded by installment payments, that fact should be clearly disclosed, along with the nature and timing of the payments.
- The approximate odds of winning a prize or a statement that such odds depend on number of entrants.
- The method by which winners will be selected.
- The geographic area covered by the sweepstakes and those areas in which the offer is void.
- All eligibility requirements, if any.
- Approximate dates when winners will be selected and notified.
- Publicity rights re the use of winner's name.
- Taxes are the responsibility of the winner.
- Provision of a mailing address to allow consumers to submit a self-addressed, stamped envelope to receive a list of winners of prizes over $25.00 in value.

Price Comparisons
Article #21
Price comparisons may be made two ways:
   a. between one's price and a former, future, or suggested price.
   b. between one's price and the price of a competitor's comparable product.

In all price comparisons, the compared price against which the comparison is made should be fair and accurate.

In each case of comparison to a former, suggested, or competitor's comparable product price, substantial sales should have been made at that price in the recent past.

For comparisons with a future price, there should be a reasonable expectation that the new price will be charged in the foreseeable future.

Guarantees
Article #22
If a product or service is offered with a "guarantee," or a "warranty," either the terms and conditions should be set forth in full in the promotion, or the promotion should state how the consumer may obtain a copy. The guarantee should clearly state the name and address of the guarantor and the duration of the guarantee.

Any requests for repair, replacement, or refund under the terms of a "guarantee" or "warranty" should be honored promptly. In an unqualified offer of refund, repair, or replacement, the customer's preference shall prevail.

Special Claims

Use of Test or Survey Data
Article #23
All test or survey data referred to in advertising should be competent and reliable as to source and methodology, and should support the specific claim for which it is cited. Advertising claims should not distort the test or survey results nor take them out of context.

Testimonials and Endorsements
Article #24
Testimonials and endorsements should be used only if they are:
   a. Authorized by the person quoted,
   b. Genuine and related to the experience of the person giving them, and
   c. Not taken out of context so as to distort the endorser's opinion or experience with the product.

The Product

Product Safety
Article #25
Products should be safe in normal use and free of defects likely to cause injury. To that end, they should meet or exceed the current, recognized health and safety norms, and should be adequately tested, when applicable. Information provided with the product should include proper directions for its use and full instructions covering assembly and safety warnings, whenever necessary.

Product Distribution Safety
Article #26
Products should be distributed only in a manner that will provide reasonable safeguards against possibilities of injury.

Product Availability
Article #27
Direct marketers should offer merchandise only when it is on hand or when there is a reasonable expectation of its receipt.

Direct marketers should not engage in dry testing, unless that special nature of the offer is disclosed in the promotion.

Fulfillment

Unordered Merchandise
Article #28
Merchandise should not be shipped without having first received the customer's permission. The exceptions are samples or gifts clearly marked as such, and merchandise mailed by a charitable organization soliciting contributions, as long as all items are sent with a clear and conspicuous statement informing the recipient of an unqualified right to treat the product as a gift and to do with it as the recipient sees fit, at no cost or obligation to the recipient.

Shipments
Article #29

Direct marketers are reminded that they should abide by the FTC regulation regarding the prompt shipment of prepaid merchandise, the Mail Order Merchandise (Thirty-Day) Rule.

Beyond this regulation, direct marketers are urged to ship all orders as soon as possible.

Credit and Debt Collection

Equal Credit Opportunity
Article #30

A creditor should not discriminate on the basis of race, color, religion, national origin, sex, marital status, or age. If an individual is rejected for credit, the creditor should be prepared to give reasons why.

Debt Collection
Article #31

Unfair, misleading, deceptive or abusive methods should not be used for collecting money. The direct marketer should take reasonable steps to assure that those collecting on the direct marketer's behalf comply with this guideline.

Use of Mailing Lists

List Rental Practices
Article #32

Consumers who provide data that may be rented, sold or exchanged for direct marketing purposes periodically should be informed of the potential for the rental, sale, or exchange of such data. Marketers should offer an opportunity to have a consumer's name deleted or suppressed upon request.

List compilers should suppress names from lists when requested by the individual.

For each list that is to be rented, sold, or exchanged, the DMA Mail Preference Service name-removal list and, when applicable, the DMA Telephone Preference Service name-removal list should be used. Names found on such suppression lists should not be rented, sold, or exchanged, except for suppression purposes.

All persons involved in the rental, sale, or exchange of lists and data should take reasonable steps to ensure that industry members follow these guidelines.

Personal Information
Article #33

Direct marketers should be sensitive to the issue of consumer privacy and should limit the combination, collection, rental, sale, exchange and use of consumer data to only those data which are appropriate for direct marketing purposes.

Information and selection criteria that may be considered to be personal and intimate in nature by all reasonable standards should not provide basis lists made available for rental, sale, or exchange when there is a reasonable expectation by the consumer that the information will be kept confidential.

Any advertising or promotion for lists being offered for rental, sale, or exchange should reflect the fact that a list is an aggregate collection of marketing data. Such promotions should also reflect a sensitivity for the consumers on those lists.

List Usage Agreements
Article #34

List owners, brokers, compilers, and users should make every attempt to establish the exact nature of the list's intended usage prior to the sale or rental of the list. Owners, brokers, and compilers should not permit the sale or rental of their lists for an offer that is in violation of any of the Ethical Guidelines of DMA. Promotions should be directed to those segments of the public most likely to be interested in their causes or to have a use for their products or services.

List Abuse
Article #35

No list or list data should be used in violation of the lawful rights of the list owner nor the agreement between the parties; any such misuse should be brought to the attention of the lawful owner.

Telephone Marketing

(See also Articles #9 and #29)

Reasonable Hours
Article #36
All telephone contacts should be made during reasonable hours.

Taping of Conversations
Article #37
Taping of telephone conversations made for telephone marketing purposes should not be conducted without legal notice to or consent of all parties, or the use of a beeping device.

Telephone Name Removal/ Restricted Contacts
Article #38
Telephone marketers should remove the name of any customer from their telephone lists when requested by the individual. Marketers should use the DMA Telephone Preference Service name- removal list and, when applicable, the Mail Preference Service name-removal list. Names found on such suppression lists should not be rented, sold, or exchanged, except for suppression purposes.

A telephone marketer should not knowingly call anyone who has an unlisted or unpublished telephone number, except in instances where the number was provided by the customer to that marketer.

Random dialing techniques, whether manual or automated, in which identification of those parties to be called is left to chance should not be used in sales and marketing solicitations.

Sequential dialing techniques, whether a manual or automated process, in which selection of those parties to be called is based on the location of their telephone numbers in a sequence of telephone numbers should not be used.

Disclosure and Tactics
Article #39
All telephone solicitations should disclose to the buyer, during the conversation, the cost of the merchandise, all terms, conditions and the payment plan, and whether there will be postage and handling charges. At no time should "high pressure" tactics be utilized.

Use of Automatic Electronic Equipment
Article #40
No telephone marketer should solicit sales using automatic electronic dialing equipment unless the telephone immediately disconnects when the called person hangs up.

Fund-Raising

(See also Article #28)

Commission Prohibition/ Authenticity of Organization
Article #41
Fund-raisers should make no percentage or commission arrangements whereby any person or firm assisting or participating in a fund-raising activity is paid a fee proportionate to the funds raised, nor should they solicit for non-functioning organizations.

Laws, Codes, and Regulations

Article #42
Direct marketers should operate in accordance with the Better Business Bureau's Code of Advertising and be cognizant of and adhere to laws and regulations of the United States Postal Service, the Federal Trade Commission, the Federal Reserve Board, and other applicable federal, state and local laws governing advertising, marketing practices, and the transaction of business by mail, telephone, and the print and broadcast media.

Appendix C

Direct Marketing Association Guidelines For Mailing List Practices

I. General

All involved in the transfer, rental, sale, or exchange of mailing lists—owners, managers, compilers, brokers, and users, and their suppliers and agents—should follow these guidelines.

Accuracy in Description of Lists
Article #1

All concerned should fairly, objectively, and accurately describe each list, particularly with respect to its content, age of names, selections offered, quantity, source, and owner.

Advertising Claims
Article #2

Before and at the time of distributing a list data card or promoting or advertising a list as available for rental, those who promote the list should be prepared to substantiate any claims they make and should avoid any untrue, misleading, deceptive, or fraudulent statements and any references that disparage competitors or those on the list.

Screening of Offers/List Usage
Article #3

All involved should establish and agree upon the exact nature of a list's intended usage prior to the transfer or permission to use the list. Samples of all intended mailings should be reviewed by all involved in the rental process, and only approved material should be used in the mailing, and on an agreed-upon date. Lists should not be transferred or used for an offer that is believed to be in violation of any of the DMA Guidelines for Ethical Business Practices.

Protection of Lists
Article #4

All those involved with a list transaction should be responsible for the proper use of list data and should take appropriate measures to assure against unauthorized access, alteration, or dissemination of list data. Those who have access to such data should agree in advance to use those data only in an authorized manner.

One-Time Usage
Article #5

Unless agreement to the contrary is first obtained from the list owner, a mailing list transaction permits the use of a list for one time only. Except for respondents to its own mailing, a list user and its agents may not transfer names or information to its own customer files or re-contact names derived from a rented or exchanged list, or provide the names for another to make such contact, without prior authorization.

DMA Mail Preference Service/ Name Removal Options
Article #6

Consumers who provide data that may be rented, sold, or exchanged for direct marketing purposes should be periodically informed of the potential for the rental, sale, or exchange of such data. Marketers should offer a means by which a consumer's name may be deleted or suppressed upon request.

List compilers should suppress names from lists when requested by the individual.

For each list that is to be rented, sold or exchanged, the DMA Mail Preference Service name-removal list and, when applicable, the Telephone Preference Service name-removal list should be used. Names found on such suppression lists should not be transferred except for suppression purposes.

All persons involved in the rental, sale, or exchange of lists and data should take reasonable steps to ensure that industry members follow these guidelines.

Purposes of Lists/List Data
Article #7

Lists should consist only of those data that are appropriate for marketing purposes. Direct marketers should transfer, rent, sell, or exchange lists only for those purposes.

List Data/Privacy
Article #8

Direct marketers should be sensitive to the issue of consumer privacy and should limit the combination, collection, rental, sale, exchange, and use of consumer data to only those data that are appropriate for direct marketing purposes.

Information and selection criteria that may be considered to be personal and intimate in nature by all reasonable standards should not provide the basis for lists to be made available for rental, sale, or exchange when there is a reasonable expectation by the consumer that the information would be kept confidential.

Any advertising or promotion for lists being offered for rental, sale, or exchange should reflect the fact that a list is an aggregate collection of marketing data. Such promotions should also reflect a sensitivity for the consumers on those lists.

Laws, Codes, Regulations, and Guidelines
Article #9

Direct marketers should operate in accordance with all applicable laws, codes, and regulations and with DMA's various guidelines as published from time to time.

II. Considerations for Mailing List Transactions

Mailing list transactions are controlled by the legal principles affecting contracts. As such, mutual understanding, good faith, clear communication, defined terms, and a meeting of the minds are imperative. To that end, a list of factors to be considered when entering into a mailing list transaction has been developed to assist contracting parties in developing a clear understanding of their respective rights and obligations as well as to help avoid the problems that typically ensue as a result of misunderstanding.

The list of factors that follows is not intended to be exhaustive, nor is it intended to dictate the terms of any agreement. Rather, it is presented to raise pertinent questions so that they may be addressed properly and adequately by the parties. The list of factors may be modified from time to time as trends develop in the industry or as technology or list usage changes.

1. Identification of All Parties to the Transaction

Has each party to the transaction been identified by proper name and address?

Are there other parties involved besides the list owner and list user (e.g., list broker, list manager, list compiler, or service bureau)?

Have these other parties been properly identified?

Is the scope of authority of these third paries understood?

Should each of these third parties agree to be bound by the list agreement?

2. What Is Being Transferred?

Is the agreement intended to be comprehensive?

Is any unspecified activity prohibited unless permitted?

Is any unspecified activity permitted unless prohibited?

Is the transaction an outright sale or assignment of the list?

Is the transaction an exchange or trade for the use of another list?

Is the transaction a rental or one-time permission to use?

May the list user add information to the rented list before using it (e.g., telephone numbers)?

Does adding information to the rented list change its nature?

Who owns the enhanced list after information has been added to it?

3. What Constitutes Use?

May the user merge-purge the list with other rented lists?

Is the user permitted to add names that appear on more than one owner's list to its own list?

May the user code or tag its own file with information derived from a rented list when the rented list contains names that already appear on the user's list?

May the user impose its own "qualifications" on a list, return the names that do not "qualify," and receive a refund?

Does it matter what the qualifier is (e.g., names on more than one list, a particular carrier route, certain demographics)?

Is it all right if the list owner "qualifies" the list prior to rental?

May the user send "address corrections requested" mail and retain results?

4. What Constitutes One-Time Use?

May the rented list be used a second time in a different medium (e.g., telephone)?

May the user mail to a name on a list one time for each rented list the name appears on?

Does it matter whether each list owner was paid for the name?

Does it matter whether multiple mailings to the same name are related (e.g., part of a series of mailings)?

Does it matter what the time period is between mailings?

May the list user or its service bureau retain names that appear on one or more rented lists for comparison with future rentals?

May the list user do so to suppress names from future mailings to the same rented list?

May the user do so for non-list specific data?

Are there any additional purposes for which the rented list may be retained?

5. The Method of and Basis for Payment

How many names are being rented?

What are the allowances, if any, for duplicates, undeliverables, etc.?

Is there a special request or selection to be satisfied?

What is the price (e.g., dollars per thousand names)?

Has sales tax, if any, been accounted for?

Is there a broker or manager involved?

> To whom is payment sent?
>
> Are commissions spelled out?

Is there a net name agreement?

> Are the terms clear?
>
> Is there a provision for verification?
>
> Have duplicates and multibuyers been removed or accounted for?

Is there a reuse discount?

Have the payment terms been clearly set forth and agreed upon?

6. *What is to be Received, Where and When?*

What is the format of the rental (e.g., tapes, labels)?

How much information will physically appear on tapes or labels (e.g., name and address, address only, with Zip + 4)?

Where and when is the list to be shipped?

> Who is at risk for failure to satisfy this provision?
>
> Upon whom does loss fall if damaged in transit?
>
> Upon whom does loss fall if mailing dates cannot be kept?

Are there any guarantees on deliverability?

7. *Approval of the Mailing and Date*

Does the list owner have the right to approve the mailing?

Must each phase of a staged or sequenced mailing (e.g., catalog followed by gift certificate followed by personalized letter) be approved?

Has the mailing date been approved?

Must the list user notify the list owner if the date is to be changed?

8. *Impact on Others*

Does the user have the right to prohibit the rental of a list of competitive mailing for a specified time period before and after the user's mailing date?

Do the parties employ a name-removal option, or DMA's Mail Preference Service or, where applicable, Telephone Preference Service for the protection of those on the list?

Is the list being used only for a marketing purpose?

Has the list been seeded?

May the user refer to the source of the list in any promotion?

Is it clear that the user becomes an owner of all respondents?

Appendix D

Direct Marketing Association Guidelines For Personal Information Protection

For the purposes of these Guidelines, the following definitions apply:

Individual: A natural person identified in a file by name and address or other identifier.

Personal Data: Information that is linked to an individual on a file and that is not publicly available or observable.

Direct Marketing Purposes: The purposes of direct marketing are to promote, sell and deliver goods and services; to foster such efforts through the sale, rental, compilation, or exchange of lists in accordance with these Guidelines; to delete and add individuals to lists; to provide all necessary customer services including the extension of credit where appropriate; to raise funds; to perform market research; and to encourage recipients to respond by taking direct action.

ARTICLE 1. Personal data should be collected by fair and lawful means for a direct marketing purpose.

ARTICLE 2. Direct marketers should limit the collection of personal data to only those data that are deemed pertinent and necessary for a direct marketing purpose and should only be used accordingly.

ARTICLE 3. Personal data which are used for direct marketing purposes should be accurate and complete, and should be kept up to date to the extent practicable by the direct marketer. Personal data should be retained for no longer than is required for the purposes for which they are stored.

ARTICLE 4. An individual shall have the right to request whether personal data about him/her appear on a direct marketer's file and to receive a summary of the information within a reasonable time after the request is made. An individual has the right to challenge the accuracy of personal data relating to him/her. Personal data that are shown to be incorrect should be corrected.

ARTICLE 5. Personal data should be transferred between direct marketers only for direct marketing purposes.

Consumers who provide data that may be rented, sold, or exchanged for direct marketing purposes periodically should be informed of the potential for the rental, sale, or exchange of such data. Marketers should offer an opportunity to have a consumer's name deleted or suppressed upon request.

List compilers should suppress names from lists when requested by the individual.

For each list that is to be rented, sold, or exchanged, the DMA Mail Preference Service name-removal list and, where applicable, the Telephone Preference Service name-removal list should be used. Names found on such suppression lists should not be transferred except for suppression purposes.

All persons involved in the rental, sale, or exchange of lists and data should take reasonable steps to ensure that industry members follow these guidelines.

ARTICLE 6. Direct marketers should be sensitive to the issue of consumer privacy and should limit the combination, collection, rental, sale, exchange, and use of consumer data to only those data that are appropriate for direct marketing purposes.

Information and selection criteria that may be considered to be personal and intimate in nature by all reasonable standards should not provide the basis for lists to be made available for rental, sale, or exchange when there is a reasonable expectation by the consumer that the information will be kept confidential.

Any advertising or promotion for lists being offered for rental, sale, or exchange should reflect the fact that a list is an aggregate collection of marketing data. Such promotions should also reflect a sensitivity toward the consumers on those lists.

ARTICLE 7. Each direct marketer should be responsible for the security of personal data. Strict measures should be taken to assure against unauthorized access, alteration, or dissemination of personal data. Employees who have access to personal data should agree in advance to use those data only in an authorized manner.

ARTICLE 8. Visitors to areas where personal data are processed and stored should be specifically authorized by express permission of the direct marketer and should be accompanied by at least one employee of the direct marketer.

ARTICLE 9. If personal data are transferred from one direct market to another for a direct marketing purpose, measures should be taken by the transferor to arrange strict security measures to assure that unauthorized access to the data is not likely during the transfer procedures. It is the responsibility of the direct marketer to whom the list is transferred to arrange strict security measures to ensure no unauthorized access to the list during its return to the original owner.

ARTICLE 10. The Committee on Ethical Business Practice of DMA is charged with reviewing any complaints by individuals of violation of these Guidelines and shall take appropriate action.

Bibliography

Baier, Martin. *Elements of Direct Marketing.* New York: McGraw-Hill Publishing Co., 1983.

Bauer, Carol H., ed. *The Law and Direct Marketing.* New York: Direct Marketing Association, 1980.

Bencin, Richard L., and Donald J. Jonovic. *Encyclopedia of Telemarketing.* Englewood Cliffs, NJ: Prentice Hall, 1989.

Benson, Richard V. *The Secrets of Successful Direct Mail.* Lincolnwood, IL: NTC Business Books, 1987.

Bird, Drayton. *Commonsense Direct Marketing.* 2nd ed. London: Kogan Page, 1989.

Blumenfield, Arthur. *Standards For Computerized Mailing Lists.* 2nd ed. New York: Direct Marketing Association, 1989.

Bodian, Nat G., and Robert Luedtke. *Merchandising Through Card Packs.* Naperville, IL: Solar Press, 1986.

Burnett, Ed. *The Complete Direct Mail List Handbook.* Englewood Cliffs, NJ: Prentice Hall, 1988.

Burns, Karen L., ed. *Guiding Catalog Growth.* New York: Direct Marketing Association, 1985.

Burns, Karen L., ed. *Retail Revolution: Direct Marketing.* New York: Direct Marketing Association, 1984.

Cohen, William A. *Building A Mail Order Business.* New York: John Wiley & Sons, 1982.

De La Iglesia, Maria Elena. *The Ultimate Shoppers' Catalogue.* New York: Harper & Row, 1987.

Dillon, John. *Handbook of International Direct Marketing.* New York: McGraw-Hill Publishing Co., 1976.

Direct Marketing Association. *Direct Marketing Manual.* New York: Direct Marketing Association, 1990.

Direct Marketing Association. *Great Catalog Guide.* New York: Direct Marketing Association, Annual.

Direct Marketing Association. *Statistical Fact Book.* New York: Direct Marketing Association, Annual.

Eckhardt, Linda West. *Satisfaction Guaranteed.* New York: St. Martin's Press, 1986.

Emerick, Tracy, and Bernie Goldburg. *Business To Business Direct Marketing.* Hampton, NH: Direct Marketing Publishers, 1987.

Fenvessy, Stanley J. *Fenvessy on Fulfillment.* Stamford, CT: Catalog Age, 1988.

Fisher, Peg. *Successful Telemarketing.* Chicago: Dartnell Corporation, 1985.

Flato, Anne, and Marilyn Schiff. *Shop By Mail Worldwide.* New York: Random House, 1987.

Goldring & Co. *Study of Behavior and Attitudes of Catalog Consumers.* New York: Direct Marketing Association, 1988.

Gosden, Freeman F., Jr. *Direct Marketing Success.* New York: John Wiley & Sons, 1985.

Graham, John W., and Susan K. Jones. *Selling By Mail.* New York: Charles Scribner's & Sons, 1985.

Gross, Martin. *The Direct Marketer's Idea Book.* New York: American Management Association, 1989.

Harper, Rose. *Mailing List Strategies—A Guide to Direct Marketing Success.* New York: McGraw-Hill Publishing Co., 1986.

Hartnett, Kathleen, ed. *Introduction to Fulfillment Operations in Direct Marketing.* New York: Direct Marketing Association, 1981.

Hawken, Paul. *Growing A Business.* New York: Simon & Schuster, 1987.

Hendrickson, Robert. *The Grand Emporiums.* New York: Stein & Day, 1979.

Hill, Lawson Traphagen. *How To Build A Multi-Million Dollar Mail Order Business By Someone Who Did.* Englewood Cliffs, NJ: Prentice Hall, 1984.

Hodgson, Richard S. *Direct Mail & Mail Order Handbook.* 3rd ed. Chicago: Dartnell Corporation, 1980.

Hodgson, Richard S. *The Greatest Direct Mail Sales Letters of All Time.* Chicago: Dartnell Corporation, 1986.

Hoge, Cecil C., Sr. *Mail Order Know-How.* Berkeley, CA: Ten Speed Press, 1982.

Hoge, Cecil C., Sr. *Mail Order Moonlighting*. St. James, NY: Business Studies, 1976.

Hoge, Cecil C., Sr. *The First Hundred Years Are The Toughest*. Berkeley, CA: Ten Speed Press, 1988.

Horchow, Roger. *Elephants In Your Mailbox*. New York: Times Books, 1980.

Joffe, Gerardo. *How to Build a Great Fortune in Mail Order*. (Seven volumes.) San Francisco: Advance Books, 1979.

Jutkins, Ray. *Direct Marketing: How You Can Really Do It Right!* Costa Mesa, CA: HDL Publishing, 1989.

Katz, Donald R. *The Big Store*. New York: Viking Penguin, 1987.

Katzenstein, Herbert, and William S. Sachs. *Direct Marketing*. New York: Merrill, 1986.

Kobs, Jim. *Profitable Direct Marketing*. Chicago: Crain Books, 1979.

Lewis, Herschell Gordon. *Direct Mail Copy That Sells!* Englewood Cliffs, NJ: Prentice Hall, 1984.

Lewis, Herschell Gordon. *Herschell Gordon Lewis on the Art of Writing Copy*. Englewood Cliffs, NJ: Prentice Hall, 1988.

Ljungren, Roy G. *Business to Business Direct Marketing Handbook*. New York: American Management Association, 1988.

Lumley, James E. A. *Sell It By Mail*. New York: John Wiley & Sons, 1986.

Marcus, Stanley. *His & Hers—The Fantasy World of the Neiman-Marcus Catalogue*. New York: Viking Penguin, 1982.

McCullough, Prudence, ed. *The Wholesale-By-Mail Catalog*. New York: St. Martin's Press, 1988.

Molotsky, Irwin. *The Great Mail Order Bazaar*. New York: Arbor House, 1986.

Muldoon, Katie. Catalog Marketing. 2nd ed. New York: American Marketing Association, 1988.

Nash, Edward L. *Direct Marketing*. New York: McGraw-Hill Publishing Co., 1982.

Nash, Edward L., ed. *The Direct Marketing Handbook*. New York: McGraw-Hill Publishing Co., 1984.

Posch, Robert J. *The Direct Marketer's Legal Advisor*. New York: McGraw-Hill Publishing Co., 1983.

Raphel, Murray. *But Would Saks Fifth Avenue Do It?* Atlantic City, NJ: Murray Raphel Advertising, 1981.

Raphel, Murray. *Mind Your Own Business*. Atlantic City, NJ: Raphel Marketing, 1989.

Roman, Ernan. *Integrated Direct Marketing*. New York: McGraw-Hill Publishing Co., 1988.

Schultz, Marilyn Smith. *Mail Order On The Kitchen Table*. McAllen, TX: Tribute, Inc., 1988.

Settle, Robert B., and Pamela L. Alreck. *Why They Buy*. New York: John Wiley & Sons, 1986.

Simon, Julian L. *How to Start and Operate a Mail Order Business*. 4th ed. New York: McGraw-Hill Publishing Co., 1987.

Sroge, Maxwell. *How to Create Successful Catalogs*. Lincolnwood, IL: NTC Business Books, 1985.

Sroge, Maxwell. *Inside The Leading Mail Order Houses*. Lincolnwood, IL: NTC Business Books, 1987.

Stern, Edward. The Direct Marketing Market Place. Boca Raton, FL: Hilary House, Annual.

Stone, Bob, and John Wyman. *Successful Telemarketing*. Lincolnwood, IL: NTC Business Books, 1986.

Stone, Bob. *Successful Direct Marketing Methods*. 4th ed. Lincolnwood, IL: NTC Business Books, 1988.

Warsaw, Steve. *Sucessful Catalogs*. New York: Retail Reporting Corporation, 1989.

Weintz, Walter H. *The Solid Gold Mailbox*. New York: John Wiley & Sons, 1987.

Weiss, Michael J. *The Clustering of America*. New York: Harper & Row, 1988.

About the Author

Richard S. ("Dick") Hodgson started in the direct marketing field at the age of 14, when he began operating his own lettershop, The Gateway Advertising Service. Over the years, his jobs have included printer, linotype operator, salesman, photographer, radio announcer and producer, reporter, editor, U.S. Marine Corps Lieutenant Colonel, college instructor, public relations director, president of a publishing company, advertising agency account executive, advertising and sales promotion director, creative director, corporation executive and consultant.

Today Dick Hodgson is President of Sargeant House, a Westtown, Pennsylvania, company which provides direct marketing consulting and catalog development services to leading firms throughout the world. He conducts regular direct marketing and catalog seminars throughout the U.S. and Europe and is a member of the boards of directors of QVC Network, Inc., and Foster & Gallagher, Inc. He is a frequent visiting lecturer at prestigious colleges and universities throughout the country.

Before establishing his consulting business in 1975, Mr. Hodgson was vice president of The Franklin Mint in Franklin Center, Pennsylvania. He joined The Franklin Mint as creative director in 1972 and was asked to organize and launch The Franklin Mint Gallery of American Art. Its success won him the Marketing Communicator of the Year Award presented by Marketing Communications Executives International.

He has been the recipient of numerous other honors, including the prestigious Ed Mayer Award, in recognition of his outstanding contribution to direct marketing education; the Jesse H. Neale Editorial Achievement Award for outstanding business journalism; the Dartnell Gold Medal Award for excellence in business letter writing; Direct Marketer of the Year, presented by the Philadelphia Direct Marketing Association; Sales Promotion Man of the Year awarded by the Sales Promotion Executives Association; the Gold Mailbox by The Direct Marketing Association; and the Benny Award by Printing Industries of America.

Dick is widely recognized as the world's leading authority on catalogs and direct mail. He is, in fact, the most prolific author on direct marketing subjects. His monumental 1,500-page *Direct Mail & Mail Order Handbook* published by Dartnell is the most widely circulated book in the field and he has written more than a dozen other books including *The Greatest Direct Mail Sales Letters of All Time, Direct Mail in the Political Process, Direct Mail Showmanship, How to Work With Mailing Lists, How to Promote Meeting Attendance,* and *Encyclopedia of Direct Mail.* He is currently preparing *Basics of Direct Marketing,* an extensive series of teaching manuals for the Direct Marketing Educational Foundation. His column on Catalog Trends appears regularly in *Catalog Age* magazine.

Mr. Hodgson has long been active in advertising and marketing organizations. He has served as International president of the Sales Promotion Executives Association, as well as president of both the Boston and Chicago chapters, and was a member of the board of directors of both SPEA and its successor association, Marketing Communications Executives International. He also has served as president of the Mail Advertising Club of Chicago, as first vice-president of the Chicago Federated Advertising Club, and as first vice-president of the Chicago Business Papers Publishers Association. He was a four-term member of the board of directors for the Direct Marketing Association and developed the association's original public relations program. Currently he is on the board of directors of the Direct Marketing Educational Foundation.

A native of Breckenridge, Minnesota, Dick Hodgson is a graduate of the North Dakota State School of Science and attended Gustavus Adolphus College, Western Michigan college and Northwestern University. He and his wife, Lois, live on a pre-Revolutionary farm in Chester County, Pennsylvania, approximately thirty miles southwest of Philadelphia.

Index

A
Action, type of, and value of outside lists, 67–68
Action devices, use of, 226
Actives, 66
Address, in mailing list, 52
Age group, in mailing list, 53
Aldens, 1, 5
   development of RFMR profile by, 57
   use of testimonials by, 21–22
Alreck, Pamela L., 8
Ambassador International
   guarantee policy of, 26
   and product innovation, 91
   and unique product offers, 88
American Beauty roses, and product innovation, 97
American Express
   credit plan offered by, 24
   use of packets by, 356
Art directors, role of, in catalog design, 123
Art versus photography, 279–81
Audience, consideration of, in order form design, 205–6
Authority
   as factor in starting mail order catalog, 28
   perceived, as factor in catalog marketing, 20–22
Availability, perceived, as factor in catalog marketing, 19 20
Avery, Sewell, 47
A & W Wholesalers, little extra enclosure of, 316

B
Baby boomers, 7–9
Back covers, 179–83
Back end, emphasis on in catalog marketing, 49
Background tints, 131–32
Back order, handling of, 311–12
Back order notices, 294–95
Baker, Bill, 34
Baldwin-Cooke, direct mail thinking used by, 34
Banana Republic, Inc., unique art style of, 280, 281
Basic eye-flow, 138
Bauer, Eddie
   follow-up policy of, 323
   little extra enclosure of, 316, 317
   use of special signature in catalog, 20
Bean, L. L., 1, 31
   golden rule of, 342
   presentation style used by, 115
   shipping/handling charges used by, 210, 211
   unique selling position used by, 39–40, 41
Bean, Leon Leonwood, 331
Bedbug letter, 333
Beneficial sentence, in catalog copy, 144
Bergen, Candice, 97
Bids, obtaining, 282
Bill to/ship to, in business-to-business mailing list, 53
Bingo card, 85
Bishop, Eleanor, 143, 145, 147
Black Box Corporation, use of newsletters/newspapers by, 358–59
Blair
   ship letters policy of, 300–1
   use of packets by, 356
Blair, John L., 301
Breck's
   cover techniques used by, 180
   customer service enclosures used by, 314–15
   little extra enclosure of, 316
   order form of, 208, 209
   personalization techniques used by, 182–83
   pricing policy in, 23
   and product innovation, 91
   and seasonality, 353
   shipping/handling charges used by, 211
   solo mailings of, 354, 355
   and unique product offerings, 89
   unique selling position used by, 39
   use of personalized wraps by, 196–200, 228
Bright idea, as factor in starting mail order catalog, 31
Broadway-Hale stores, 115
Brooks Brothers, packaging strategy of, 298
Brookstone
   customer service enclosure policy of, 305
   little extra enclosure of, 316
   and perceived availability, 19
   use of benefits-oriented copy by, 151–52, 153

Brownstone Studio, packaging strategy of, 298–99
Burch, David, 5
Business lists
    information in data base for, 53–56
        bill to/ship to, 54
        company address, 54
        company name, 53
        company size, 54–56
        credit rating, 54
        headquarters/branch, 54
        Standard Industrial Classification, 54
Business Leaders file (McGraw-Hill), 63
Business-to-business catalogs
    order forms in, 228–29
    shipping costs, 215
Buyer, information about individual on business-to-business database, 55–56

C

CACI, 63
Camera format, choice of, 276–79
Captions, 135
Card decks, 356
Carlson, Len, 43, 98, 115
Catalog(s)
    definition of, 2
    in electronic age, 13–14
    growth of, 2–3, 4–13
    mail order, 4. *See also* Mail order catalog(s)
    number of, 2–3
    reference, 4
    retail traffic–building, 4
    selection of mailing drop date for, 178–79
    specialization in, 3–4
    types of, 2–3
    unique selling position in, 16
    worldwide, 14
  Catalog business expansion
    balancing seasonality, 353
    developing spin-off catalogs, 352
    mailing multiple catalogs, 345–49
    moving off plateau, 352–53
    special catalog editions, 349–51
    telephone marketing, 361–62
    using alternate direct mail media, 353
        card decks, 356
        mini-catalogs, 357–58
        newsletters and newspapers, 358–61
        packets, 354–56
        self-mailers, 358
        solo mailings, 354
Catalog buyers, importance of help to, 18
Catalog buying, comparison to retail buying, 82
Catalog continuity, developing, 114–17

Catalog copy
    adding personal touch in, 159–65
    basic role of, 143
    beneficial sentences in, 144
    benefits for consumer in, 150–51
    benefits in headings, 151–52
    checklist for, 173
    COIK, 169
    copywriter's packet, 169–72
        competitors' copy, 170
        customer comments, 172
        editorial reference, 171
        old copy, 170
        results from previous catalogs, 170
        sales records, 171–72
        specification sheet, 171
        vendors' data, 170–71
    descriptive sentence in, 144
    editing, 168
        committee, 169
        cross-out/write-in test, 168
        hat trick, 168
    evaluation of, 174
    features versus benefits, 147–59
    gathering the facts, 166–67
    guidelines for, 143–47
    heads in, 143–44, 151–52
    length of, 152, 154–56
    making common product unique, 157–59
    reviewing competitor's copy, 166
    reviewing old copy, 165–66
    sandwich in, 144
    starting point for, 167–68
    statistics in, 144
    white mail exposure, 166
    zinger in, 144
Catalog costs, establishing, 289–90
Catalog database
    creation of customer profile in, 56–57
    lifestyle indicators in, 59–60
    overlays in, 61–63
    RFMR profile in, 57–58
    screening codes in, 60–61
        credit code, 60
        customer service code, 60–61
Catalog design
    background tints, 131–32
    captions, 135
    color in, 130, 133
    continuous circle technique, 136–37
    reverse copy, 128–29
    role of art directors in, 123
    space as a design element, 133
    tips for more effective, 138
        basic eye-flow, 138

copy, 139–40
    grid layouts, 141–42
    illustrations, 138–39
    proximity, 140
    shapes, 140
typefaces in, 124–38
Catalog hot spots, 175
    back covers, 179–83
    center spread, 186
    front cover, 176–79
    inside back cover, 186
    other inserts, 187–88
    pages 2–5, 183
    pages facing the order form, 186–87
    special selling potential of, 175
Catalog hypnosis, 117, 188–89
Catalog marketing
    attitude in, 34
    catalog-oriented personnel and facilities, 47–48
    differences in, 15–18
    emphasis on back end, 49
    as graphics medium, 16, 18
    importance of mailing lists to, 76–77
    importance of memorability, 16
    long-range strategy in, 42
    mailing lists in, 45–46
    management involvement in, 40, 42
    open-door organization for, 46–47
    perceived authority in, 20–22
    perceived availability in, 19–20
    perceived satisfaction in, 24–27
    perceived value in, 22–24
    product selection for, 43–45
    success factors in direct marketing thinking, 34
    unique selling position in, 34–40
    willingness to gamble in, 43
Catalog of Catalog Design, 279
Catalog operations, involvement of management in, 40, 42
Catalog organization, 105–22
    catazines, 118–21
    creating eye-flow in, 109–13
    developing catalog continuity, 114–17
    developing change of pace in, 117
    indexing, 106–7, 108
    magalogs, 118–21
    number of pages in, 107, 109
    spreads in, 109
    starting points in, 113–14
    table of contents in, 106–7
Catalog photography, costs in, 274–75
Catalog production, 261–63
    art versus photography, 279–81
    getting bids, 282
    paper selection, 267–69
    production team, 263–64
    relations with suppliers, 282
    selecting color separator, 272–73
    selecting photographer, 274
        choosing camera format, 276–79
        location model shots, 275–76
        location still life shots, 276
        studio model shots, 275
        studio still lifes, 275
    selecting printer, 269–72
        backup facilities, 272
        charges, 272
        equipment, 271
        full service, 271
        representation, 271
        scheduling, 271–72
    selecting printing process, 264
        gravure, 265
        letterpress, 264
        offset, 265
        offset versus gravure, 266
    time needed for, 261–63
    typesetting, 282
Catalog projections, 287–88
    daily reports, 288
    list analysis, 289
    monthly reports, 289
    weekly reports, 288–89
Catalog prospecting, 10
Catalog response curves, 17
Catalog results evaluation
    catalog projections, 287–88
        daily reports, 288
        list analysis, 289
        monthly reports, 289
        weekly reports, 288–89
    efficiency per square inch, 283–86
    establishing catalog costs, 289–90
    flow chart analysis, 290–91
    presentation factors, 286–87
    production cost analysis, 290
Catalog seasons, 346
Catalog success strategies, 293–94
    customer service enclosures, 304
    follow-ups, 320–25
    instant response, 297–298
    little extra enclosures, 316–17
    order acknowledgments, 294–97
    package enclosures, 316–20
    personal touch, 325–28
    ship letters, 300–4
Catalog wraps, 189, 191–202
Catazines, 118
Celebrity, use of, in product offerings, 97
Center spread, 186

Chef's Catalog
   order form of, 209
   shipping/handling charges used by, 211
Circles of convenience, 78–79
Claritas Corp., 63
COIK (clear only if known), 169
Colonial Williamsburg, catazine style of, 120
Color
   functional use of, 133
   typefaces in, 130–31
Color match, 273
Color reproduction
   color match, 273
   pleasing color, 273
   swatch match, 273
Color separation, electronic, 279
Color separator, selecting, 272–73
Company address, in business-to-business mailing list, 54
Company name, in business-to-business mailing list, 53
Company size, as factor in developing business-to-business catalog mailing list, 54–56
Competitors' copy, in copywriter's packet, 170
Compiled lists, pull of, 77
Computerized mailing lists, as factor in growth of catalogs, 9–10
Consumer Electronics Show, 84
Container Corporation of America, 47
Continuity in catalog covers, 178
Continuous circle technique, 136–37
Cook, Joan, package enclosure of, 302, 320
Copy, 139–40
Copywriter's packet, 167, 169–72
   competitor's copy, 170
   customer comments, 172
   editorial reference, 171
   old copy, 170
   results from previous catalogs, 170
   sales records, 171–72
   specification sheet, 171
   vendors' data, 170–71
Country Store
   order acknowledgment by, 296
   and product innovation, 92, 94
   use of imprinted boxes by, 299
   welcoming of new customer by, 296, 297
Cover letters, on inside front cover, 184
Covers, checklist for selecting merchandise for, 203
Credit cards, as factor in growth of catalogs, 10–11
Credit clearance systems, 48
Credit code, as screening code in catalog database, 60
Credit rating, in business-to-business mailing list, 53
Cross-out/write-in test, in editing catalog copy, 168
Cullinan, George J., 57–58

Current
   package enclosure of, 319–20
   shipping/handling charges used by, 211
   use of action devices by, 226
   use of laundry list technique by, 227
   use of newsletters/newspapers by, 360
Customer
   definition of, 331
   lifetime value of, 42
   as ultimate authority in product selection, 103–4
Customer comments, in copywriter's packet, 172
Customer names, pull of, 77
Customer profile, creating, 56–57
Customer review, of order form, 229
Customers
   in product selection, 86
   welcoming new, 296, 297
Customer service code, as screening code in catalog database, 60–61
Customer service enclosures, 304–15
Customer service plan, creation of, 335–39
Customer service program
   creating customer service plan, 335–39
   guidelines for developing, 331–35
   measuring effectiveness of, 339
Customer service review of order form, 229
Customer testimonials, 21

D

Daily reports, 288
Database versus mailing list, 51–52
Demographic Research Co., 63
Demographics, 9–10
Descriptive sentence in catalog copy, 144
Desire, as factor in starting mail order catalog, 31
Devoke, shipping/handling charges used by, 214
Direct Mail List Rates and Data, 69–70
Direct marketing, feminizing of, 7
Direct Marketing Association Mail Preference Service (MPS), 53
Direct marketing thinking, 34
Direct response lists, pull of, 77
Distribution field, catalogs in, 3
Divider pages, 189
Dohme, Cheryl, 325–26
Donnelley, R. R., & Sons, 349
Donnelley, Reuben H., 73
Drawing Board
   handling of supplemental information order form, 217
   personal touch policy of, 325
   and product innovation, 95
   shipping/handling charges used by, 213
D.R.I. Industries, customer service enclosure policies of, 309

Dun & Bradstreet, 54
Duplication, eliminating, in mailing lists, 69

E

Early Winters
    catalog copy for, 157–59
    importance of unique/exclusive products, 87, 88
    product information folder of, 312–14
    and product innovation, 91
    and unique product offers, 88
Edge index, 107
Editorial reference, in copywriter's packet, 171
Edmund Scientific, and product innovation, 96
Efficiency per square inch, 283–86
Electronic color separation, 279
Electronics, catalogs in age of, 13–14
Elephants In Your Mailbox (Horchow), 99
Employee participation, in product selection, 86–87
Engineer's layout, 133
Exclusiveness
    importance of, in catalog marketing, 19–20
    importance of, in product selection, 87–90
    use of, as advantage, 20
Eye camera studies, 109, 110, 130–31, 138–40
Eye-flow, creating in catalog organization, 109–13

F

Facilities
    catalog-oriented in catalog marketing, 48
    as factor in starting mail order catalog, 29
Fact Book on Direct Marketing, 74
Feminizing, of direct marketing, 7
Fenvessy, Stanley, 332, 333, 334, 335
Fenvessy on Fulfillment-Catalog Executive's Guide (Fenvessy), 335
Fidelity Products, order form of, 209
Fingerhut, and product innovation, 94
Flag waver, 193
Flag-waver flap, 196
Flow chart analysis, 290–91
Focal point, establishing, in catalog organization, 110
Follow-ups, 320–25
Form letters, for customer service, 332
Forms & Worms, little extra enclosure of, 316
Forslund, Carl
    use of editorial supplements by, 121
    use of personal style copy by, 164–65
Foster & Gallagher
    and seasonality, 353
    and unique product offers, 88
Foster House, catazine style of, 119
Franklin, Benjamin, 25
Franklin Mint
    and product innovation, 91, 92, 96
    ship letter policy of, 302

FRAT (frequency, recency, amount of purchase and type of purchase), 59
Free sheets, 267
Free shipping and handling, 211
Frequency, in RFMR profile, 57
Front cover, 176–79
Fuller Brush
    order form of, 209
    shipping/handling charges used by, 214

G

Gamble, willingness to, in catalog marketing, 43
Garden Way Manufacturing Co., use of newsletters/newspapers by, 358
Gaze motion, in establishing eye flow, 112
Getting bids, in catalog production, 282
Gift shipment order form, 217–23
Goodwill building, 326–27
Graham, Larry, 299
Graphics medium, catalogs as, 16, 18
Gravure, 265–66
    versus offset, 266
Gravure papers, 268
Grid layouts, 141–42
Gucci, and product innovation, 91
Gump's, and product innovation, 92

H

Haband
    merchandise substitution policy of, 311
    use of packets by, 356
Habernickel, Duke, merchandise substitution policy of, 311
Half-life evaluation, 288
Hammacher Schlemmer
    order form of, 206, 208
Hanover House, spin-off catalogs by, 352
Harrods, use of magalog technique by, 121
Harry & David, and seasonality, 353
Hat trick, in editing catalog copy, 168
Haverhill's, and product innovation, 94
Head
    in catalog copy, 143–44
    typefaces for, 127
Headquarters/branch, in business-to-business mailing list, 53
Helvetica, 124
Hermes, use of magalog technique by, 121
His & Hers: — The Fantasy World of the Neiman-Marcus Catalogue (Marcus), 99
Histacount, and unique product offerings, 89
Hog Wild, and product innovation, 96
HomeOffice, exclusive product offerings by, 90
Horchow, Roger, 99–100

© COPYRIGHT 1991 DARTNELL CORPORATION

Horchow Collection
   handling of supplemental information order form, 217
   and product innovation, 95
   and product selection, 99
   shipping/handling charges used by, 212
   spin-off catalogs of, 353
   use of newsletters/newspapers by, 359–60
Hot line names, 65, 66, 78

I

Illustrations, 138–39
Imprinted boxes, 299
Impulse buying, importance of in catalog marketing, 186–87
Impulse scales, on order forms, 215–16
Inactives, 66
Indexes, in catalog organization, 106–7, 108
Industrial lists. *See* Business lists
Industrial sales call, cost of, 12
Information society, as factor in growth of catalogs, 4–5
Inmac
   catalog copy for, 147–50
   pictorial index used by, 108
Inserts, as hot spot, 187–88
Inside back cover, 186
Instant response, 297–298
International Jewelry Trade Shows, 84
Italic type, 126

J

Jackson & Perkins
   and seasonality, 353
   self-mailers of, 359
   use of self-mailers by, 358, 359
Jet-ink imaging, 179–80, 181
Johnny Appleseed, exclusive product offerings by, 90

K

Katz, Lillian, 33
Kestnbaum, Robert, 59
Kicker wrap, 189
Kimball, Miles
   order form of, 206, 207
   and product innovation, 95
   shipping/handling charges used by, 211
K Promotions, 21

L

Lands' End, 348
   catalogs of, 348
   catazine style of, 119
   cover techniques used by, 177
   customer service enclosure policy of, 305, 307–8
   guarantee policy of, 26
   merchandise substitution policy of, 311
   package enclosure of, 320
   personal approach of, 327, 328
   principles of doing business, 341
   and product innovation, 93
   ship letter policy of, 302, 303
   shipping/handling charges used by, 214
   shipping policy of, 298
   use of editorial supplements by, 121
Last transaction, in RFMR profile, 58
Laundry lists, use of, 226–27
Law of proximity, 140
Lawson Traphagen Hill, 201
L'eggs
   follow-up policy of, 322–23
   little extra enclosure of, 316
Length of time on the file, in RFMR profile, 59
Letterpress, 264
Letter shops, 74
Lewis, Herschell Gordon, 174, 186
Lifestyle indicators, 59–60
   products purchased, 59
Lifestyle Selector (NDL), 63, 73
List analysis, 289
List brokers, 70–73
List compilers, 64, 73
List consultants, 74
List managers, 74
List rental, 65
   actives, 66
   costs of, 65
   hot line names in, 65
   inactives, 66
   role of list brokers in, 70–73
List segmentation, 46
Location model shots, 275–76
Longevity of catalog customers, 270
Long-range strategy, in catalog marketing, 42

M

Magalogs, 118–21
Mailing drop date, selection of, 178–79
Mailing houses, 75
Mailing lists. *See also* Business lists; *entries beginning with List*
   basic information in, 52–53
      address, 52
      age group, 53
      mail preference, 53
      name, 52
      phone number, 52–53
      postal code, 52
      sex, 53

circles of convenience in, 78–79
computerized, 9–10
constance of change in, 76–77
"customer-get-a-customer" program, 75–76
versus database, 51–52
eliminating duplication in, 69
as factor in starting mail order catalog, 28–29
factors in building, 64–66
    compiling own, 64
    exchanging list, 64–65
    list rental, 65–66
    list compiler in, 64
importance of, to catalog marketing, 45–46, 76–77
relative value of outside, 67–68
    products/services, 67
    type of action, 67–68
    value category, 67
security of, 69–70
segmentation in, 46
service organizations, 70–75
sources of information, 69–70
usually reliable truths about, 77–78
Mail order catalogs, 1, 4
factors in evaluating potential for starting
    authority, 28
    bright idea, 31
    desire, 31
    facilities, 29
    mailing lists, 28–29
    money, 30
    products, 27–28
    staff, 29–30
Mail order guarantee, 24–27
Mail order multi-buyer, 12
Mail preference, in mailing list, 53
Mail Preference Service (MPS), 53
"Mail Smart", 68
Management, involvement of, in catalog operations, 40, 42
Manufacturers, catalog publishing by, 3
Marcus, Stanley, 6, 36, 99
Mauna Loa Macadamia Nuts
  gift shipment order form of, 219
  reply envelopes of, 224
  and seasonality, 353
Megatrends (Naisbitt), 4
Memindex, shipping/handling charges used by, 211
Memorability
  as factor in catalog success, 106
  importance of in catalog creation, 16
Merchandise, checklist for selecting, for cover, 201
Merchandise buyers, 48
Merchandise centers, as source of product, 84–85
Merchandiser, 83
Merchandise returns, acknowledging, 323

Merchandise substitution, customer service enclosure on, 310–11
Merchants, 82
Merge/purge, 69
Metromail, 73
Michaelsen, Jurgen, 22
Miller, Jack, 191
Mini-catalogs, 357–58
Mobil, 47
Mobility loyalties
  changing, 5–7
  as factor in growth of catalogs, 5–7
Monetary value, in RFMR profile, 57
Money, as factor in starting catalog, 30
Monitor order entry, of order form, 229
Monthly reports, 289
Multi-buyer lists, 12

N

Naisbitt, John, 4, 5, 11
Name, in mailing list, 52
National Bellas-Hess, 1, 5, 219
National China, Glass and Collectibles Show, 84
National Demographics & Lifestyles (NDL), 63
National Hardware Show, 84
National Housewares Show, 84
National Mail Order Merchandise Show, 84
Nature Company
  handling of supplemental information order form, 217
  shipping/handling charges used by, 211
Neckermann, use of, testimonials by, 21–22
Neiman-Marcus, 6
  follow-up policy of, 323, 325
  importance of unique/exclusive products, 87
  unique selling position used by, 36
Newsletters, 358–61
Newspapers, 358–61
Nicolai, Bill, 81, 88, 312

O

Offset, 265
  versus gravure, 266
Offset papers, 267–68
Ogilvy, David, 165–66
Omaha Steaks International, shipping/handling charges used by, 214
Open-door organization, in catalog marketing, 46–47
Options, multiple as factor in growth of catalogs, 11–12
Order acknowledgments, 294–97
Order cards, 224, 225
Order forms, 205–6
  action devices in, 226
  asking for information, 208–9

avoiding confusion in, 209
avoiding unnecessary calculating, 210
in business-to-business catalogs, 228–29
and consideration of audience, 205–6
development of, 167–68
and ease in using, 206–08
and gift shipment, 217–23
importance of, 205
and impulse selling, 215–16
including "how to order" information in, 206, 208
laundry list style, 226–27
pages facing, 186–87
and purchase requisitions, 228–29
and response envelopes, 224–26
and shipping and handling charges, 210–14
and supplemental information, 217
testing, 229
   customer review, 229
   customer service review, 229
   monitor order entry, 229
   staff review, 229
Orvis, follow-up policy of, 321, 322
Otto, use of, testimonials by, 21–22
Overlays, 61–63

P

Pace, developing change of, 117
Package enclosures, 316–20
Packaging, 298–99
Packaging material, 299–300
Packets, 354–56
Pages facing the order form, 186–87
Paper, selection of, for catalog, 267–69
"Peggy Lee" (rose), 97
Penney, J.C., 5
   order form of, 210
   and product selection, 100
   shipping/handling charges used by, 212–13
Personalization
   in catalog marketing, 52
   cost of, 183
   of product, 95
Personalized wraps, 189, 191–202
   examples of, 191–201
   reasons for using, 201–2
Personal touch
   in catalog copy, 159–65
   in direct mail, 325–28
Personnel, catalog-oriented, in catalog marketing, 47–48
Peruvian Connection, merchandise substitution policy of, 311–12
Peterman, J., Company, personal touch in catalog copy of, 159–64
Phone number, in mailing list, 52–53

Photographer, selecting, 274–75
Photography versus art, 279–81
Pictorial indexes, 107, 108
Pocket Pal, 266
Polk, R.L., 73
Population patterns, changing, as factor in growth of catalogs, 7–9
Porter's Camera Store, handling of back order notices by, 295
Postal code
   in mailing list, 52
   segmentation, 62–63
Praktikus, little extra enclosure of, 316
Premium and Incentive Shows, 84
Presentation factors, building into catalog evaluation, 286–87
Price, as factor in selecting catalog merchandise, 100–1
Price line information, ideal handling of in order form, 208
Price testing, 24
Priester's Pecans, follow-up policy of, 323, 324
Printer, selection of, for catalog, 269–72
Printer-supplied paper, advantages of using, 268–69
Printing process
   gravure, 265, 266
   letterpress, 264
   offset, 265, 266
PRIZM, 63
Product(s)
   kinds of, and value of outside lists, 67
   unique, as factor in starting mail order catalog, 27–28
Product information, customer service enclosure on, 312–14
Product innovation, 90–97
Production cost analysis, 290
Production team, 263–64
Product selection, 82–104
   buyers in, 82–83
   in catalog marketing, 43–45
   customer as ultimate authority, 103–4
   factors in, 100–3
   guides to, 98–100
   importance of exclusivity in, 87–90
   innovation in, 90–97
   merchandisers in, 83
   rebuyers in, 83
   sources of, 83–87
Products purchased, as lifestyle indicator, 59–60
Products That Think, narrative copy style of, 116, 118
Professional lists. *See* Business lists
Progressive proofs, 273
Prospecting, use of special catalogs for, 349–50
Psychographics, 10

Publishers Central Bureau, little extra enclosure of, 316
Purchase requisition, 228

Q

Quelle
   little extra enclosure of, 316
   use of, testimonials by, 21–22
   use of stopper pages by, 188
Quest For The Best (Marcus), 99
Quill
   "Customers' Bill of Rights", 298, 331, 336, 340
   customer service enclosure policy of, 308–9
   little extra enclosure of, 316
   merchandise substitution policy of, 311
   order form of, 206, 209
   personal approach of, 327
   and product innovation, 91
   sale pricing used by, 23–24
   shipping/handling charges used by, 211, 213
   unique selling position used by, 36, 38
   use of newsletters/newspapers by, 360, 361
   use of personalized wraps by, 191–93
QVC Express catalog, and gaze motion, 112

R

R+R Direct, personal touch policy of, 325
Ratio, in RFMR profile, 57–58
Reader's Digest, use of mini-catalogs, 358
Reading comprehension
   and background tints, 131–32
   and colored type, 130–31
   and ragged copy, 126
   and reverse copy, 128
   and selection of typefaces, 124–26
   and width of type measure, 127
Rebuyer, 83
Recency, in RFMR profile, 57
Reeves, Rosser, 16
Reference catalogs, 4
Regged copy, 126
Regional catalogs, creation of, 349
REI, customer service enclosures used by, 314
Reliable, and product innovation, 94
Response envelopes, 224–26
Results from previous catalogs, in copywriter's packet, 170
Retail traffic-building catalogs, 4
Return policy, customer service enclosure giving, 304–09, 310
Reverse copy, 128–29
RFM formula, (recency, frequency, monetary value), 9
RFMR (recency, frequency, monetary value, ratio) Profile, 57–58

Roman typefaces, 124
Rotogravure, 265–66
Rudin, Lou, 201

S

Sale catalog, 316, 318
Sales records, in copywriter's packet, 171–72
Sampson, Paul, 282
Samstag, Nick, 147
Sandwich, in catalog copy, 144
Sans serif type faces, 124
Satisfaction, perceived, as factor in catalog marketing, 24–27
Scotcade, business–oriented copy by, 150, 151
Screening codes, 60–61
S. D. Warren Catalog of Catalog Photography, 279
Sears, 1, 5, 46
   good, better, best product presentation used by, 22, 45
   guarantee of, 343
   order form of, 210
   product categorization, 67
   and product innovation, 97
   and product selection, 100
   satisfaction policy of, 25
   shipping/handling charges used by, 212
Sears, Richard Warren, 1
Seasonality
   balancing, 353
   in RFMR profile, 58
Security, of mailing list, 69–70
Segmentation, postal code, 62–63
Selective Software,
   shipping/handling charges used by, 214
Selectronic binding, 349
Self-mailers, 358
Selling, high cost as factor in growth of catalogs, 12–13
Service bureaus, 74
Services, kinds of, and value of outside lists, 67
Settle, Robert B., 8
Sex, in mailing list, 53
Shapes, 140
Sharper Image
   catalogs of, 348
   catazine style of, 119
   customer service enclosures of, 310
   and product innovation, 95, 96
   unique selling position used by, 35–36
Sheet-fed offset presses, 265
Sheplers
   customer service enclosures used by, 314
   unique selling position used by, 37, 38, 39
Ship letters, 300–4

Shipping and handling charges, 210
    "free," 211
    order amount, 211
    per item, 211
    per shipment, 214
    weight and distance, 212–14
Size, in catalog organization, 107, 109
Smithsonian Institution
    little extra enclosure of, 317
    unique selling position used by, 37
Solo mailing, 15–16, 354
    response curve to, 17
Sorting
    importance of, in card decks, 356
    importance of, in packet mailings, 355–56
Space, as design element, 133
Special catalog editions, 349–51
Specialization, impact of, on catalogs, 3–4
Special liquidation pieces, package enclosure of, 319–20
Specialty catalogs, 14
Spencer Gifts, catazine style of, 119
Spiegel, 1, 5
    customer service enclosure policy of, 304
    offering of credit limit by, 201
    and product innovation, 96, 97
    shipping/handling charges used by, 212, 213
    use of, testimonials by, 21–22
    use of divider pages by, 191
    use of special catalogs by, 350–51
Spin-off catalogs, developing, 352
Sporting Edge, package enclosure of, 319
Spreads, importance of in catalog organization, 109
Spring Hill
    impulse sales technique of, 215
    order form of, 208, 209
    and product innovation, 94
    and seasonality, 353
    shipping/handling charges used by, 211
    use of friend-get-a-friend technique, 74–75
    use of reply envelope insert by, 187
    use of special catalogs by, 351
Staff, as factor in starting mail order catalog, 29–30
Staff review, of order form, 229
Standard Industrial classification, in business-to-business mailing list, 53
Standard Rate & Data Service, Inc., 69
Starcrest, use of packets by, 35
Starting points, establishing in catalog organization, 113–14
Stash Tea, packaging policies used by, 300
Statistics, in catalog copy, 144
Stopper pages, 188–89
Structural motion, in establishing eye flow, 112
Studio model shots, 275

Studio still lifes, 275
Sugarman, Joe, 116, 118–19, 152
Sunset House, 43, 115
    catazine style of, 119
    presentation style of, 116
    product selection for, 98–99
Supplemental information, handling, on order form, 217
Swatch match, 273
Sweepstakes, 119

T

Table of contents, in catalog organization, 106–7
Tabletop shots, 275
Talbots
    order form of, 208
    personal approach of, 326–27
    shipping/handling charges used by, 211
Telephone, as factor in growth of catalogs, 10–11
Telephone marketing, 361–62
Telephone orders, 228
    importance of order forms by, 205
Telephone order systems, 48
Thalheimer, Richard, 33, 35
Thompson, Norm
    follow-up policy of, 320–21
    and unique product offers, 88, 89
Trade publications, as source of product, 85
Trade shows and fairs, as source of product, 83–84
Tucker, JoVon, 203, 279
Twentieth Century Plastics, follow-up policy of, 321–22
Typefaces
    color for, 130
    selection of, 124–38
Typesetting, in catalog production, 282

U

Unique selling position (USP), 16, 34–40
U.S. General Supply Corp., use of wraps by, 193–96

V

Value, perceived, as factor in catalog marketing, 22–24
Value category, and value of outside lists, 67
Variety Merchandise Show, 84
Vendors, 85
Vendors' data, in copywriter's packet, 170
Vernon, Lillian, 33
    and catalog design, 134
    exclusivity of products in, 44
    handling of supplemental information order form, 217
    merchandise substitution policy of, 311
    and product innovation, 95

© COPYRIGHT 1991 DARTNELL CORPORATION

shipping/handling charges used by, 211
use of inside front cover letter by, 184–85
use of package enclosures by, 317, 319
Vest pocket surveys, 338
Vogele, Siegfried, 138
Vogele eye camera studies, 140, 141

W

Ward, Montgomery, 1, 5, 46, 47
WATS telephone service, 11
Web-fed offset presses, 265
Web offset, 266, 267
Weekly reports, 288–89
Wheildon, Colin, 124, 138
Wheildon studies, 124–27, 128, 130, 131, 136
"Which Means" technique in catalog copy, 152
White mail, 166
Why They Buy (Settle and Alreck), 8–9
Williams, Ted, 97
Williams-Sonoma
   and effective catalog design, 128
   handling of supplemental information order form, 217
   impulse sales technique of, 215–16
   little extra enclosure of, 316
   order form of, 209
   package enclosure of, 319–20
   shipping/handling charges used by, 211
   use of personalized message, 183, 184
Women, working, as factor in growth of catalogs, 7
Wraparound, use of, as sales brochure, 319

Z

Ziegler, Mel, 280
Ziegler, Pat, 280
Zimmerman, Ron, 155, 168
Zinger, in catalog copy, 144
ZIP Code clusters, 345
ZIP Deciling, 62, 63

Sharpen Your Management Skills with These Practical Guides from Dartnell

1. Sales Manager's Handbook
No other single volume can give you comprehensive coverage, attention to detail, and practical solutions to meeting the sales manager's everyday challenges. It is the working sales manager's single-volume library, with timely case studies and practical illustrations of all aspects of the sales manager's job.
1,272 pages, Hardcover $49.95

2. Planning and Managing Sales Territories
Master the most important challenge a sales manager faces. Tackle the most difficult problems of sales territory planning and management. Operating forms and documents used by real-world managers are provided, with easy-to-read, step-by-step explanations. From defining territories to evaluating performance, you'll find the practical help you need.
240 pages, 8½ x 11, Paper $32.95

3. Successful Sales Meetings: How to Plan, Conduct, and Make Meetings Pay Off
This step-by-step, how-to sales manager's guide will help you plan, run, and evaluate results-producing sales meetings every time. From defining objectives to evaluating results, this book's many checklists and planning forms will make your job simple and productive.
247 pages, Paper $32.95

4. Dartnell's Survey of Sales Force Compensation
It's all here: how 50,000 sales reps in more than 400 companies sell $300 billion in goods and services each year; the Dartnell profile of sales professionals by age, earnings, cost to train; new findings on sales management, support, and telemarketing; plus the latest facts on sales pay by product and service, compensation method, and incentive/expense.
352 pages, Padded 3-ring binder $159.50

5. New Time Management Methods for You and Your Staff
Do more in less time. Increase the productivity of your entire team. Practical, proven time management techniques help you and your team become more efficient, effective, and profitable. More than 50 charts, checklists, and outlines give you a complete step-by-step program for putting your team on the high-productivity track of the 1990s.
Padded 3-ring binder $91.50

6. Personnel Administration Handbook
Increase the efficiency of your personnel functions with this comprehensive guide for corporate personnel and human resource executives. This practical guide provides clear, easy-to-read descriptions and analysis. Additional studies of current issues help you avoid costly mistakes and maximize the value of your company's most important assets.
Hardcover $49.95

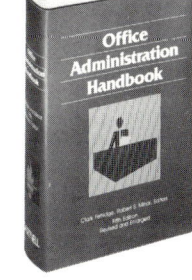

7. Office Administration Handbook
For solutions to tough problems and for dependable reference, this is the one authoritative book every administrator should have. More than 2,300 office administration problems—from cost control concerns to record keeping to employee benefits and office layout design—are covered.
Hardcover $49.95

8. How to Develop a Personnel Policy Manual
This ready-to-use working tool gives you a step-by-step organizational format, easy-to-use checklists, suggestions to guide you in developing your policies, and sample policies and statements you can use or adapt to your company's needs. Protect your company from the problems of poor policy. Manage human resources more efficiently. Build morale and a positive work environment. This do-it-yourself guide shows you how.
Padded 3-ring binder $91.50

To order: fill in and mail the attached order card.

THE DARTNELL GUARANTEE
If the product you order does not meet your satisfaction, return it within 15 days for a full refund.

1 2 3 4 5 6 7 8
9 10 11 12 13 14 15 16

Circle the numbers of the titles you wish to order. (Numbers correspond to the titles shown above.)

☐ Please send me a free catalog of all Dartnell products.

☐ Bill My Company   ☐ American Express   ☐ Master Charge   ☐ Visa

Account #   Exp. Date

Signature

Name   Title

Company Name

Address

City   State   Zip

Phone

FOR FASTER SERVICE CALL - U.S.: 1-800-621-5463
Canada: 1-800-441-7878
Fax: 312-561-3801

More Practical Management and Reference Guides from Dartnell

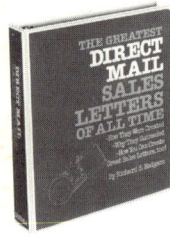

9. Greatest Direct Mail Sales Letters of All Time
What makes *some* sales letters work—again and again? Direct mail expert Richard S. Hodgson has selected and analyzed over 100 of the most successful direct mail sales letters ever written. He provides the complete text of each letter, then examines and explains in detail what made each one work. You also get special sections on how to create successful letters.
Padded 3-ring binder $91.50

10. Marketing Planning Strategies
This practical, step-by-step, cost-effective guide will help you match your programs to your resources and goals to build short- and long-term sales and avoid costly mistakes. You'll find marketing success marked with easy-to-follow explanations, examples, forms, and illustrations.
3-ring binder $91.50

11. Building a Winning Sales Force
A three-pronged approach gives you an interactive teaching and learning tool that will keep you on top and your sales force on track. Part 1 provides approaches and solutions to the sales manager's everyday problems. Part 2 is a 52-minute audiotape with situation analyses to evaluate and improve problem-solving and training skills. Part 3 gives you extra training and reinforcement material.
Boxed binder includes: 337 pages text, 12 booklets (228 pages), 52-min. audiotape $159.95

12. The Dartnell 15-Session Sales Training Kit
Get your new sales reps off on the right track. Give your veterans a no-nonsense refresher. Give them the *Dartnell 15-Session Training program*. The 15 ready-to-use sessions help you touch all the bases from planning calls and making presentations to fine-tuning sales skills and techniques to building customer satisfaction and new business.
Boxed binder includes: 15 lessons, Role play scripts, Meeting leader's guide, Wall charts, Tests and exercises $195.00

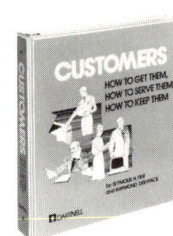

13. Customers: How to Get Them, How to Serve Them, How to Keep Them
Move ahead of the competition for good by energizing everyone in your company to give the kind of customer service that will win customers and bring them back again and again. Get practical advice on how to boost customer awareness, deal effectively with problems, win long-term customer commitment, and measure customer satisfaction. Forms, checklists, and cases give life to difficult problems and practical solutions.
3-ring binder $91.50

14. Successful Telemarketing
Increase the impact of your current marketing and sales programs with this step-by-step guide to today's most cost-effective sales technique. A comprehensive package including master planners, checklists, sample scripts, meeting formats, decision sheets, and case studies shows you how to apply basic techniques, target profitable accounts, pick market strategy, train staff, and measure results.
3-ring binder $91.50

15. Big Paybacks from Small Budget Advertising
Eliminate costly mistakes and make your advertising more cost-effective with commonsense guidelines to more responsive, more cost-conscious advertising. With this guide you'll learn how to reach your market more effectively, pick copy and art that communicate effectively, and select media for top results…a goldmine of advertising knowledge.
Padded 3-ring binder $91.50

16. Public Relations Handbook
Whatever your public relations needs, you'll turn to this comprehensive volume first for authoritative guidance. You'll get practical insights from two of the leading practitioners in the field, plus more than 40 case histories and articles. Practical information on asking the right questions, where to look for the answers, how to get the job done—it's all in one handy volume.
916 pages, 6 x 9, Hardcover $49.95

NO POSTAGE
NECESSARY
IF MAILED
IN THE
UNITED STATES

BUSINESS REPLY MAIL
FIRST CLASS   PERMIT NO. 545   CHICAGO, ILLINOIS
POSTAGE WILL BE PAID BY ADDRESSEE

DARTNELL
4660 Ravenswood Avenue,
Chicago, Ill. 60640-9981